ADOLESCENTS
AND THE
    AMERICAN
HIGH SCHOOL

ADOLESCENTS AND THE AMERICAN HIGH SCHOOL

Edited by RICHARD F. PURNELL

University of Rhode Island

Holt, Rinehart and Winston, Inc.

NEW YORK   CHICAGO   SAN FRANCISCO   ATLANTA   DALLAS
MONTREAL   TORONTO   LONDON   SYDNEY

to: Jimmy,
    Harry,
    Joan,
    Tom, and
    Betty.

PREFACE

The overriding purpose for compiling and editing this book of readings is to provide useful information about American high school students, adolescents in grades eight through twelve. If some parts of this book shift from this focus, it is done reluctantly and only to make a point that would be difficult to make otherwise. Thus, the reader will find very little direct information about college students, primitive societies' initiation rites, or cross-cultural comparisons of adolescents. These areas of the study of adolescence are certainly proper and worthwhile within other contexts but are not salient for those working with American high school students.

The organization of this book revolves around two major themes: (1) adolescence as a period of development and (2) the interactions among adolescents and between adolescents and adults. Both themes are introduced at the very beginning of the book by a look at the adolescent's high school world and the problems adults are faced with in communicating with the members of this world.

A consideration of the developmental theme is divided among the second, third, and fourth sections. These eclectically combined sections on the principal regions of human development are presented as realms of adolescent development: the physical, psychosexual, sociosexual, cognitive, and psychosocial realms. The key influences of socialization processes on adolescents are considered in the section on the psychosocial realm. Works chosen to cover the developmental theme are aimed at supplying the reader with a mosaic of the *constantly changing components* of adolescence.

What we will for the sake of convenience term the "interactional" theme encompasses knowledge about what adults bring to and what they can extract from interactions with high school students in the classroom. A second facet of this theme concerns methods for more effectively interacting with youth—especially in the classroom. The fifth section of the book reports some of the biases that bear on teacher-adolescent classroom interactions and touches on the fact that students' attitudes toward the teacher decline as the year progresses. It also shows how teachers can benefit from listening to students' views of the teacher's behavior. Section VI painstakingly presents information about a method or set of principles that has proven remarkably successful in modifying adolescent behavioral problems. The techniques reported in this section also have great value for the teacher in conducting normal classroom operations.

The last section examines the conditions and experiences of noncollege youth—who represent the vast majority of American high school adolescents and are, for the most part, seemingly forgotten. The articles in this section were chosen because they dispel some of the grosser myths and stereotypes about this group of adolescents and lay the groundwork for a restructuring of educational priorities to give them better treatment than they receive under the present system.

This book is not meant to be a complete or comprehensive text on adolescent psychology. Its touchstone for selecting works has tended to preclude the inclusion of some of the more classical formulations on adolescence, for example, Erikson's penetrating observations. However, these omissions are justified by the book's aim: to present teachers with ideas and information about adolescents that have particular relevance for teachers and are not readily available to them elsewhere.

This collection of articles, moreover, was not actively selected to represent a single, standard discipline's approach to studying adolescence —anthropological, sociological, or psychological. Instead, all orientations have been sampled for articles that meet the criterion of helping the teacher better understand and interact with the adolescent student in the classroom. If one perspective does predominate, it is that of the discipline of educational psychology.

By the same token, the articles selected have not been restricted to any one method of knowing information about adolescents. No preference is shown here for "hard-nosed," empirical studies to the exclusion of more clinical or descriptive works on adolescents. There seems no reason why a set of readings has to confine itself to one type of article— why it cannot coherently employ a mixture of methods of reporting valid information about a subject.

One further bias, already alluded to, is that this book tends to emphasize the great middle portion of American adolescents—the approximately 70 percent of youth who are not gifted, retarded, or college-bound. In a sense, it reflects more of a concern for the adolescent who either drifts through high school or presents moderate behavior problems, and it aspires to offer ideas on how to comprehend, socialize, and stimulate these youth more effectively in their quest for a meaningful and fruitful education or preparation for life.

I would like to express my sincere appreciation to the authors and contributors for their permissions to reprint their works. I am grateful to Larry Kohlberg and Bernie Horowitz for their helpful comments and suggestions. My wife deserves thanks for her help with the manuscript. Acknowledgment is given to my mentor, Cody Wilson, for having sown the seeds for this enterprise years ago.

R. F. P.

February 1970

CONTENTS

ADOLESCENTS AND THE AMERICAN HIGH SCHOOL

I. OBSERVATIONS ON AMERICAN HIGH SCHOOL STUDENTS

Introduction

Let us begin by noting that adults and adolescents are not communicating meaningfully in many important areas. This condition has come to be known as the generation gap. Beyond the label proffered to explain what it really only describes, the generation gap is a symptom of the age-grading system found in our society. Several circumstances contribute to the gap, such as the increasing rate of change in the experiences of different generations, but only minimally and as the visible handles used to pry and widen it. If this is so, then it may be helpful to observe that the inability to communicate effectively between two age-groups does not inhere in their differences. Rather, this inability is an unwanted distortion of what originally served as a means of maintaining our society's system of age-grading.

The present concern with the generation gap phenomenon is with how it affects future high school teachers and other adults who expect to deal with high school adolescents. This concern stems from the observation that people older than adolescents tend to be less and less able to communicate normally with them and grow more and more out of touch with them with increasing age. The exact nature of this relationship is not clear, but the contention here is that it need not be so.

This section points to a partial solution to adults' tendencies to block out communications from adolescents. It also begins the book with a first-hand examination of its subject. Thus, we hope to impart an orientation of attending to the concerns of adolescents and what they have to say to us about themselves and their experiences. The principle to be learned is that in order to deal effectively with youth one should train oneself to "listen" to what they have to say about themselves. We should learn how to be participant observers of adolescents. If we ignore the valuable information adolescents provide about themselves, becoming too engrossed in pat schemes for explaining adolescent behavior, we can expect to fail in our dealings with them.

The first paper is on the attitudes and opinions of adolescents on matters of mutual concern to them and to the adults who control and manipulate their lives. This represents the kind of personal interaction one should have with adolescents if one hopes to meaningfully understand them. In his dialogue with six high school juniors, the author appears to have captured the mood and value of an open, two-way exchange of personal information across generations. This approach is offered as an example of the type of exercise that should prove very useful to people who are training to work with high school students.

The second paper of this section, Borton's article on "what turns kids on," provides us with the expression of a teacher's discovery of the importance of working with and teaching to the concerns of adolescent students. His article introduces some provocative insights into the ways in which one might arrange the curriculum to serve the adolescent's concern for his "self-identity." Borton impresses on us the notion that education, through the teacher, has a fundamental commitment to attend to the student's personal concerns, and of course we learn about these concerns by being receptive to messages about them from the students.

1. DIALOGUE WITH SIX HIGH SCHOOL JUNIORS

R. F. Purnell

This dialogue with six high school juniors originated as the model for an assignment that I had given to students in my adolescent psychology course in the spring of 1968. The assignment was to tape-record a structured, open-ended interview with four to six high school adolescents, getting them to frankly present and discuss their views on some aspects of adolescence. The purpose of the assignment was to give the students an opportunity to directly and empirically examine the various "dogmas" about adolescents that they were being exposed to in the course.

Essentially, the assignment called for the students to focus on one or two topics of their own choosing about adolescents by critically developing a line of questioning based on their anticipations of the directions the interview would take. At first many of the students balked at the thought of having to secure adolescent respondents, handling a tape recorder, and constructing and conducting an interview. However, after completing their tasks and presenting their findings to the class, all were pleased with how much they had learned about adolescents from the experience. Without exception, they expressed enthusiasm for this project and what they had accomplished.

This experience accomplished several things. First, it provided feedback on the students' understandings of high school adolescents that they had acquired in the course and elsewhere. Second, this experience produced a greater appreciation for some of the problems and techniques employed in collecting empirical information about adolescents, as well as for the value of the information itself. Further, it gave the students a chance to interact with adolescents in a role other than the teacher-student or teacher-group roles before becoming committed to these roles. Perhaps this exercise of testing one's belief about adolescents against reality might be usefully performed by other prospective secondary school teachers.

The panel interview with six high school adolescents reported in this paper was conducted at a suburban high school in the greater Boston area. Ostensibly, the interview was intended to explore high school students' views on several areas about adolescents studied by interested social scientists and educators. The four areas covered in the interview were: 1) leading crowds in high schools, 2) impressions about vocational students, 3) the notion of a psychosocial moratorium for adolescents, and 4) what students strive for in high school. Erikson's untested assertion of a psychosocial moratorium was chosen because it had been discussed in the course; the other three areas were selected because they were relevant to a study the author was conducting at the time. Beyond the surface concern for high school students' impressions about others' characterizations of them, the interview also was designed to arouse the adolescents to express their "true" feelings about their experiences in high school. From all appearances, the interview succeeded on both counts.

By and large, the high school students' remarks and comments on the various issues tend to support the social scientists' and other observers' descriptions of adolescents. This is a gratifying outcome but not the exciting one, because we could not conclude anything about the social scientists' positions even if the adolescents had disagreed with them. What is exciting and valuable about the adolescents' observations about themselves is that 1) their dialogue breathes life and reality into the social scientists' "truisms" and 2) they provide the basis for insights into other areas of concern for us in high schools. Some of the more powerful remarks have been italicized by the author; the reader will undoubtedly discover others to match his own predilections.

By way of setting the scene, let us observe that three boys and three girls, all seventeen and juniors, took part in the discussion. These students were selected in response to the interviewer's request for articulate students from the various educational tracks in the school. The interview lasted approximately one hour and was recorded on videotape. No one except another student who operated the television camera was present at the interview and the respondents were promised anonymity, although they said they did not care who knew what they said. The panel was arranged with three students on each side of the interviewer in a semicircle. The students were desensitized to the videotape equipment

before the interview began. Finally, it should be noted that the interviewer was fortunate in establishing extremely good rapport with these
students, eliciting what appear to be their very sincerely expressed concerns about their experiences in and feelings about high school. But let
the reader judge that for himself as he becomes immersed in the
perspectives of these six high school juniors. The conditions that these
students express are not confined to one locale; they have been reported
by others elsewhere.

Introduction

I: Before we get started, I'd like you to give your first name and describe the program you are in. And if you have something else you'd
   like to throw into the bag, feel free to do so.
M: So, you mean, like, I say my name? Like, I'm in the technical course
   and give a description of what I consider it to be?
I: Yes. You want to start?
M: Yeah. I guess so.
I: Just use your first name.
M: OK. My name is Martin. I'm in the technical course. I feel as though
   it's designed for a student who has a desire to go on to a technical
   school and not go right out of high school into a college because the
   course wasn't designed for that. And, oh, I think it's a field where you
   have to be skillful, but yet you have to have a great amount of knowl-
   edge, too.
I: Are you in a particular technical field?
M: Well, oh, you know, that's it, I would like to specify in my field.
I: After you've finished here, then you'll be specifying one field?
M: Right.
I: (Nods to next student.)
K: My name's Kerwin and I'm in the general course. I think our prime
   objective is to graduate from high school. That's about it. I mean I
   don't want to go to another school.
I: You mean when you are finished in high school that's as much educa-
   tion as you'd like to have then?
K: No. *I had as much education as I'd like to have a few years ago.*
I: Oh, I see. Then you are just kind of like serving time now. (Laughter
   from all.)
K: Yeah.
I: Do you have any particular ambitions in terms of a certain occupa-
   tion?
K: No. Not really.

I: No? OK. How about you? (Nods to next student.)

W: My name is Wanda and I'm in the college course.

I: What does a college course mean?

W: Well, it's sort of like a factory where you turn out people to go to college.

I: I see.

W: That's about it.

I: Is there any particular interest that you have with respect to college, any particular type of college or anything like that? Or is it just college? You'd like to go to college?

W: Well, oh, I have in mind, like, oh, specific qualifications I want for a college.

I: I see. What would one or two of them be?

W: I like, oh, I want to take liberal arts. And I'd like a small one because I think you'd be a person there and there'd be more communication. And then, oh, relatively liberal, so I could study and work at my own pace.

I: I see. Thanks, Wanda. Let's go to the young lady on my left.

B: My name is Barrie and I'm in the college course. And I don't plan on going to college. I just . . . I did in the ninth grade but I don't any more.

I: You changed your mind somewhere along the way?

B: And none of the other courses (programs) or whatever they are, I mean they don't suit my needs. I want to go to art school. *So I'm just stuck in here.*

I: What was it that made you change your mind about going to college?

B: I don't know. *I lost interest in it because of too much work and everything* and, oh, that's not really what I wanted to do.

I: You were doing well in your work? It wasn't just a question of not meeting the standards?

B: That's right.

I: It was a question of what? Feeling that they were overburdening you?

B: I decided that I wanted to become a commercial artist. I think it's a big game to learn all this stuff that you can never use in college. I don't think . . .

I: What would be an example of something that you could never use in college?

B: Learning passages in *Hamlet*—32 to 35 lines long—that you could never use. And this is preparing you for college? Bull it is!

I: You don't think so?

B: NO!

I: What would you say would be better preparation for college?

B: Umm . . . in this school?

I: Just for college in general. The type of college you would like to go to.

B: Um. Well, like the free courses that they have at some colleges (names one). You can go and just sit there and do whatever you want. You can wear what you want, smoke, sit in any position. You don't have to wear dresses and people don't go around telling you your dress is too short. And, you know, *you feel that you are interested in learning the stuff—not that you are stuck in there and they shut the door and lock it on you!*

I: In other words you should be allowed to think more for yourself about how you should dress, what you should say, and how you should wear your hair? And this would provide you with a better preparation for college?

B: I think it really would.

I: And your objection to the present preparation for college was having to learn 32 passages from *Hamlet?*

B: Yeah. That's, that's about my biggest objection now. Too much to learn and it's not going to help me.

I: OK, Barrie. That's very good. Now how about the next person?

J: My name is Janice and I'm in the business course. And I feel it's preparing me to attend a two-year junior college or a business college. I'm going to be a secretary.

I: Very good. How do you feel about the preparation that you are getting?

J: It's good. I mean I couldn't take any more. . . .

I: This is something that you chose to do?

J: Yeah. I wasn't forced. I could have . . . *I changed from college course to business course.*

I: And your reasons for changing?

J: To become a secretary.

I: Thanks, Janice. And now the last person (looking at Greg).

G: My name is Greg and I'm in the college course. I'd like to go to a liberal arts college where you have a free choice in what you want to take. It will have more of a liberal attitude than a high school toward courses that you want to take. So you can think more for yourself and decide what you really want to do.

I: Do you have any particular colleges in mind?

G: No, I don't have anything in mind.

I: Next year or early next year you are going to have to start making applications. Is that a problem that you'd like to put off as much as possible?

G: I really don't know what, oh, you know everyone says I ought to go look at the colleges and talk to them before I decide, because *sometimes you get into a sort of a trap, you know. You don't really know what you're getting into.* So I am kind of wary of picking one right now and making out early applications.

On the Leading Crowd

I: The first question I'd like to get you to respond to has to do with what has been called the leading crowd. . . . A group of students who formed the nucleus of the students and who sort of controlled and manipulated what went on within and outside the school among the students. I wonder if you might take a moment to express your views on this concept . . . whether or not it is one that exists in your school and in what form.

B: I don't understand. Do you mean that they lead the school in everything or is there a class that, you know, tries to?

I: OK. Well, first, is there something that you might call a leading group in the school—leading in the sense that it sets patterns for the other students or is looked up to by the other students for setting patterns? There doesn't have to be just one leading group. But typically in a social setting we have a group of people who are more or less looked up to by everyone else, or who are in positions considered the most desirable positions. Does such a crowd exist in this school, Greg?

G: I think that the school is more or less divided and everyone has their own group—a sort of social division. I don't think . . . I think each person is basically happy with his own group and they don't try to copy the other groups. I'd say there are two or three major groups in the school—well, two anyway. There's the, oh, kids in the technical and the general programs. And then there's the kids in the lower college group, they have control of the student council and what's the big stuff like that—mixed in with others. I don't think they really lead the school in the sense that everyone looks up to them. Everyone had their own idea and they try to follow it themselves.

I: What does lower college group mean?

G: I don't mean the Honors groups.

I: Oh, I see.

G: See. They have Honors groups, too. Most of the kids are in college groups that I'm speaking about. *You know they are most of the kids who participate in the sports and they usually volunteer for dances.*

I: This is the college group?

G: They usually are pretty much interested in what goes on in the school themselves.

I: You would say, then, that there are basically three groups in this school: Honors group, college group, and what was the other?

G: The general and technical.

I: Janice, would you say that these groups have any particular names or characteristics?

J: Oh, I don't know. I think there really isn't, I mean the kids are all close, you know? And I mean it's a big school but the kids seem all close. And like everyone has their own friends and everything. But I think it's more like picking kids who have been in _____ all their life and they've gone through the _____ schools and everything. Like someone who is coming in from another town or something. . . . He automatically looks at the group that's ahead and he joins that so that he'll get to know kids. And a lot of times it isn't the right group. He'll go along with who he thinks is tops.

I: What is the major thing that is used to decide which group to join? What does a group have that would make them desirable?

J: I suppose it's what they are like, you know. The way they dress. The way they act and stuff.

I: If you were looking for a group, what would you look for?

J: These things; the way they dress. The way they acted. I mean I wouldn't pick anyone wild. I'd pick something that I like.

I: Barrie, would you give us your views on this?

B: I sure can. We have definitely two groups that are the majority of the school. *We have the Rats and the Cliques.*

I: The Rats? (B: Yeah.) And the Cliques? (B: Yeah.)

B: And there's a bunch of kids, like Greg said, in the upper or Honors course, not all in the Honors course, that can't be bothered, you know, to conform to either one of them and they really are ridiculous, you know. The Rats wear the black leather things. They are nice and all that. No offense (looking at Kerwin). And then the other ones, they wear suede jackets and all. It's really ridiculous. I, I don't know.

I: Ridiculous in what sense?

B: *That they have kind of classified themselves as a mass.* They are not identifying themselves as individuals, you know. If you go to some kid, you know, or you introduce him . . . this kid's a Rat . . . this kid's a Clique. But you never . . . like I don't think they know the kids from the other groups. Like they are the Rats and they are the Cliques.

I: Why are they called Cliques?

B: Because they are in the college group. They used to be called Colleges (pronounced collieges).

I: What brought about the change?

B: I have no idea. I got out while I was ahead.

I: What more or less influenced you to get out?

B: It was a big joke. Like, I don't know, it just wasn't for me.

I: What do you mean it was a joke? What incidents occurred?

B: Umm. No exact incidents. *It's just hanging around in one big glob, having no other friends.* Maybe your friends did not like someone you met outside of the crowd, so you couldn't hang around with that person or you'd be black-balled, you know?

I: If you are in one group, you're good and the other guys are bad, and if you are in the other group you are good and the first group is bad?

B: If you are looking at them from either point of view, like you see a Rat is all in black and so they look like a bunch of hoods, you know. Gee, that's not the kind of guy you'd like to be walking down a dark alley with, you know, he might stab you or something. The other guys, they just look like a bunch of little fairies. *There's nothing in the middle!*

I: Thanks. That's a pretty open view. Wanda, how do you feel about this—the number of groups—and what are they like?

W: I agree pretty much with Barrie, that there are two main groups, but I don't think they are as big as one might feel. They are really kind of minorities. Everybody else hangs around in smaller crowds.

I: You are saying, then, the two groups exist but they don't really constitute most of the students in the school, that they are minorities in the sense that most of the students are not in these two groups.

W: There are a lot of minorities.

I: Would you say that you are in one of these two groups?

W: No, I certainly hope not. I agree with Barrie; they are ridiculous.

I: Why are they ridiculous?

W: Everybody . . . when a certain dress style comes out, all the girls have to buy the exact same dress and they have to wear the exact same shoes and the exact same kind of stockings. And they have to read the exact same books.

I: In other words, there's a price to pay for being in the group?

W: Yeah, and when you hang around with the exact same people with the exact same taste—who at least say they do—then it's really boring because it's like a tape recorder.

I: If we say there is a price to pay for being in one of these two groups, can we also say that there are benefits to be derived from being in one of these two groups?

W: Well, I guess it depends on what you want. If you want to have a lot of friends, then, and you want to pay that price. . . .

I: Oh. By being in the group you automatically have a lot of friends. But if you are not in the group the way you can have friends is what?

W: By being yourself and making friends on your own.

I: So you would say there is a formal mechanism for getting friends and an informal way to, which is to go out and pick people who are like you and have the same tastes. The big difference being that you are not restricted to whom you can talk to or interact with if you are an individual, whereas if you are in a group you are restricted to what the group defines as being the type of people you should be around. Very good. Kerwin (nodding to him).

K: I'd like to say that I don't think there is any one leading group in the school. I agree with that. You can eliminate the several on the side. Well, I mean, oh, it might all boil down, like they say, to the Rats and the Cliques, but I mean, oh, I don't think it's that distinct. Because in earlier years, say, when you are fourteen or so, or right around that age, you find that you are classified. You are one or the other.

I: Who classifies you?

K: Oh, it's just socially. It's the way . . . like somebody says you're a Rat or a Clique. But you find as you get older that you can break away from these groups. They don't want to be classified. *As you become a little bit more mature you want to be thought of as yourself.* But as far as a leading group, I don't think there is any. Because different kids have different ideals. They have different things that they want to do. And, umm, I don't think school has that much influence over the groups. I, myself, feel that the social life has more to do with it. And what you do on the outside is reflected in here. But how much of what you do inside the school is reflected on the outside?

I: How much would you say is?

K: If you have a reputation, it's not from inside the school; it's from outside of the school. I mean something you do in the school isn't as likely to be repeated outside of the school. If somebody is going to be cautious of what's said of him, it's more likely what happens on the weekend, you know, on Friday or Saturday night.

I: You raised an interesting point. You said that when you come to the school at an earlier age you are actually typed. Someone will say you are a Rat or a Clique?

K: Well, I've always been typed as a Rat.

I: What was your reaction to being typed as a Rat?

K: I think it was a mistake. They say you are a Rat and Rats wear leather jackets. Well, I never had a leather jacket. I wouldn't wear one!

I: Would you classify yourself as a Rat now?

K: No. Because I hang around with the Rats? It's too generalized.

I: Do you run around with any Cliques?

K: Yes. They generalize too much. They say, "He's a Rat. He wears a leather jacket. He's been to court four or five times." Something like that. Sure. That might be true of certain Rats.

I: Do kids who are classified as Rats go out and do these things because it's expected of Rats (K: Oh, no) or do they become Rats . . . because they've done these things? In other words, if you happen to run around in a leather jacket, you are going to be classified as a Rat. If you happen to have gone to court four or five times, you are going to be classified as a Rat. Or is a person who is classified as a Rat someone who will try to get into court four or five times?

K: I don't think anybody would really try to get into court. I don't think they try to live up to anything. I mean you are with a certain crowd and you. do what they do because you are with them. And if you don't want to do what they do, you don't go with them. That's all there is to it. What happens while you are with them reflects on the whole group. I mean it's kind of ridiculous if they say these kids hang around the _____ and the _____ . They cause a lot of trouble smashing windows or throwing beer bottles or something. And these other kids hang around _____ and sit in their cars. *But I mean there's really no difference. Basically, everybody's the same.* You have some foul balls in each crowd.

I: What would a foul ball be like in each crowd?

K: I mean, you know, somebody that does something wrong that gives the group a bad name.

I: Like breaking a window?

K: Well, I think you'll have to agree that with the Rats you do have a worse name, you know. There are worse things done. They are the type who do worse things. They are the ones that are most often found in court.

I: For destroying property?

K: Yes, for destroying property.

I: What would be something that a Clique might do wrong?

K: Oh, I don't think, well, from what I know of them they drink. . . . I hang around with them sometimes. I know a lot of them. I find that an awful lot of them are better kids than the Rats.

I: But they don't go to court for drinking?

K: Well, some of them, like the ones that are habitual offenders, some of them I don't enjoy being with. I mean, you have to button over the top of your wallet if you want to be trusted with them. But I don't find that with the Cliques. But I think the Rats are a lot more sincere. I mean, they don't put up a front. There's too much of a front to put up with with a Clique.

I: Well, thanks a lot, Kerwin. That was very insightful. Martin, how about you on the question of leading crowds and groups, whether or not they exist, and what they are like?

M: I'd like to say that, as far as leading groups go, there are groups that have the idea that they set the school . . . they give the people, you know, well, say this kid is in a leading group and he comes in wearing a sweatshirt, and someone will look at him and say, "Gee, this person's wearing a sweatshirt! Maybe we can wear sweatshirts tomorrow." And I think that the group that you are classified in or that you fall into is due to the environment that you live in.

I: Environment outside of school?

M: Outside of school.

I: What about the environment?

M: Like he said, if you are a Rat or something . . . you'd be in the environment . . . they carry it a little too far . . . I don't know, they carry it a little too far. There's a couple of them who don't go home that often. They are pretty well on their own. They do what they want, you know.

I: Is this because of the types of occupation their fathers are in?

M: You know, people reflect a lot. They look at a child and they say, "Oh, this is from their parents. Their parents didn't give them the proper treatment that they should have had." And a lot of kids I know. . . . There are kids that are good kids and there are kids that are bad kids. And I don't feel as though it's from their parents. *At a certain age a person has to decide what he really wants to do.*

I: What would that certain age be?

M: That all depends on the individual.

I: What is it usually?

M: Oh, I don't know. I would figure, probably within their teen age.

I: Between 13 and 19?

M: Probably.

I: What would you say it was for you, to get a little personal?

M: Well, I don't really want to state an age, you know. My mother and father still have jurisdiction over what I do.

I: Well, I guess they do until you are, what? 21?

M: Yeah.

On Vocational Education

I: Let's take a moment and talk about this notion of vocational education, as one of the programs that are open to high-school students. Would you rather be in a vocational high school or do you enjoy being in this school, taking your vocational course in a regular high school?

M: Well, I enjoy these courses to an extent. And just as though I was in a vocational school I'd enjoy them. 'Cause you're not going to enjoy everything in life. You know, people say my son's going to be an engineer or my daughter's going to be such and such. But not, you know, *not everybody's made to do this thing.* And there's gotta be normal, common people that gotta do the things that are going on in life now. Everyone wants to be a doctor.

I: Things like what?

M: Well, say, working in this new school as a custodian or something. There's nothing wrong with the job, you know. It's, oh, a job that you have to work at and you make your week's pay. There's nothing dishonest about it. *I don't feel as though you should be degraded for it.*

I: Do you feel that students are degraded for aspiring to do that type of work?

M: Well, you know, we go to your first question there. These people that are classified as Rats, they are probably not in the college group. And they are looked down at as . . . (*K interrupts*).

K: Well, I think that's general. I find that a lot of the Rats are in the technical course and quite a few of them are in the college course. There's a couple of them that, people would be surprised, that have been accepted in the National Honor Society.

B: Really?

K: Yeah.

B: Why, that's wonderful!

I: Let's return to vocational education.

M: I don't think I would want to go into a vocational school completely. Because, I don't think I'd get the other half of the education *that I'm missing.* Because, right now you are at a time in life when you are . . . just . . . maybe you've made a decision on what you want to do but it's . . . the world's changing too fast, you could decide tomorrow that you might want to do something else. Because you can never tell what's gonna go on in this world. So I say now maybe I'm interested in electronics. As it stands now I'm pretty interested in it, you know, I'd like to get into the field.

I: So not only does the world change but you change, too.

M: That's right. Well, maybe five years from now I'll feel different and maybe I'll have a different concept on life.

I: Kerwin, can you make a few comments about vocational programs?

K: There isn't a vocational school in this area. And, oh, I have experience myself. My brother went to one. See, 'cause, where most of them go is_____. That's a combination, half a high school. Then they have a vocational and technical school combined. Or they go to different places like _____ Trade. And they're called "vokies" and they are looked down on. Like in _____ , you know, it's in the lower level of the school and they are called the "Cellar Rats." I think it's a complete failure in this area.

I: The Rats and the Cellar Rats?

K: They are in the cellar.

B: That's true, they are all closed up. It's a lousy surrounding.

M: I think society degrades them because if God put them in this field, this is what He wanted them to be. *And if you happen to be one of these people, you just happen to be born into this.* You're going to be in that society.

K: I don't think you are born into it. I think most of those kids were pushed into it. Because you'll find that the great percent of them would be dropouts.

M: You are what you are.

K: I think it (being born into something) has less influence in the middle class. If you were born in the very upper class, say as a Rockefeller, you are going to be upper class. But if you were born on a welfare check, the chances are pretty good that you are going to stay on welfare. *But in the middle class you have more freedom to move either way.*

I: Greg, I know you are in a college track, but how about your ideas on a vocational program?

G: I think it would, oh, I think everyone should have their own choice. If they want to go to a vocational school, I mean, the choice should be there for them to take. They shouldn't be forced into a college course if they don't want it.

I: Did you ever consider a vocational program?

G: No. It turned out that I came out of a grammar school out of _____ . And when I moved here, then they just put me in the college program. I didn't have nothing to say about it. So I was just put in it.

I: If you could have said something about it . . . ?

G: I probably would have stayed anyway. My father went to a vocational school. And he had a trade, uh, machinist, like that. And, uh, he doesn't, uh, I didn't have anyone to guide me, you know. What to do? Vocational school or college, oh.

I: Did your father have any feelings about what type of education you should get?

G: Oh, he wants me to go to college! But for himself, he said that he'd never even considered it. And right from the lower grades, you know, he knew he wanted to go to vocational school.

I: Is he satisfied with his vocational-school education? Did he miss not going to college?

G: He was satisfied himself with it.

On a Psychosocial Moratorium for Adolescents

B: I don't know. I do pretty much what I want and people, they, you know, yell at me. But I don't guess they really care. It doesn't bother me. I don't think it would wreck up my life after I graduate from

high school and go on to what I want to be. I don't think it makes
any difference. If you do what you want, all they can do is yell at
you. Unless there's something really wrong and they put you in jail
for it and that would follow you when you try to get a job or something. Other than that. . . .

I: Janice, would you say adolescence is a period during which people
are expected to be more or less responsible for what they do?

J: Well, I don't, you know, I suppose what you mean by adolescents is
teenagers?

I: I mean, yeah, we'll just talk about high-school kids.

J: Well, I feel as though, you know, they've passed the age of reason
and they know what's right and wrong.

I: The age of reason being what?

J: You know, when they are a child and in grammar school.

I: Seven is the age of reason?

J: Yeah. And they are told, you know, what to do. And I think that, I
mean, if they do something that's wrong, like really wrong, they get
in a lot of trouble.

I: Like what?

J: I don't know, like, say they go out and rob a bank. That does affect
them for the rest of their life. Something like that is put on their record. And I think just because they are an adolescent, then that
doesn't make them that they can do that and if they were at an older
age they couldn't.

I: I see. Let's use this concept in terms of more commonplace behaviors.
For example, consider an illegitimate child. Who would suffer more
for having an illegitimate child? An adolescent girl, a teenage girl, or
a full-grown or adult woman?

J: Oh, I think definitely an adult woman would suffer more for it.

I: Then you are saying that an adolescent girl is considered less responsible for her behavior?

J: I don't think she is considered less responsible, but I mean she's just
as responsible as the older woman is. But I mean she's kind of looked
on, you know, she's younger. And, I don't know, she hasn't lived as
long as the other one, I suppose. And, I don't know, she's not given a
free leg! I mean she can't go out and have an illegitimate child! They
just don't seem to get pinned for something like that as an adult
would, you know. 'Cause as soon as an adult would do something like
that they're looked on as very bad, you know. *But for an adolescent
there's always two sides to something, you know.*

K: That's the way it should be!

I: OK. So you say society should have a psychosocial moratorium? They
should be more lax with people in the high-school age group?

K: Well, adults should be more conscious of their behavior because they have had the benefit of experience and you learn from experience. They've been around longer. They should know better. But now I think a lot of kids take advantage of this. I mean, they figure he's an adult, he shouldn't do it, but as long as I'm a kid I am going to enjoy it. They won't think too badly of him if he does something.

I: Another example might be of an adolescent who decided to pick up stakes and go trotting off across the country—as opposed to a married man who is about 27. Let's not complicate it; he doesn't have any children. Suppose he just decides to pick up and leave his wife and run off across the country. The one—the 27-year-old man—is considered an adult, age-wise. The 16- or 17-year-old boy is leaving his parents, his brothers and sisters, and his community. In one case, there would be one type of reaction. In the other case, there would be another type of reaction. How do you think they'd react to the 27-year-old?

W: I think it's exactly the opposite to what Barrie said. I think that, um, kids are criticized more for doing the same thing that an adult might do. Like in that case, if an adult runs away and goes across the country, they say, well, that happens all the time. Men are always leaving their wives and things like that. But if a kid runs away they've got the police out after him and goon squads, you know. And, you know, it's a big thing because kids just *don't* run away from their parents.

I: Say both of these people are brought back to the community. How do they feel about what the man did? How do they feel about what the kid did?

W: Well, in the first place, I mean, the adult, the man doesn't have to be brought back from across the country. Because he's over 21.

I: Say they come back.

W: The kid gets murdered.

K: I don't think that particular case would have anything to do with it, because people would say, this man, he left his wife and kids. I don't think the real subject there is how old he is or how mature he is . . . because he did leave his wife and kids. But if you switch it around and that 27-year-old man is a bachelor and had nobody depending on him. . . .

I: Let's take another area. We'll talk about necking or petting in daylight down in the park. How would society react to a couple of teenagers doing it and how would they react to a couple of 42-year-old adults doing the same thing (laughter)? Greg, how do you feel?

G: Well, in that case, I'd have to say the adolescent would get away with it. It's things like that that are supposed to reflect on our moral behaviors. *Adults are supposed to be morally better than children,* 'cause adolescents have not learned that isn't morally right or something like that. Because they take it lightly, whereas adults are supposed to be examples and things like that.

I: Examples of what?

G: Examples of proper behavior (laughter).

I: Of moral behavior? (Yes.) It's not morally right to neck in the park?

G: I couldn't care less! (Laughter.) Most people would frown on it.

I: On the adults?

G: On the adults. And they probably would look at the kids and say they shouldn't be doing it. But they wouldn't think much of it. (Chatter.)

B: It depends on who's looking at it. We were at the beach one day and there was a forty-year-old couple necking out in the ocean. And we never laughed so hard in our lives, you know. Really, but, some of the people think that's disgusting. Some people could care less.

M: They've only got one life so why not let them enjoy it.

K: Well, adults are supposed to be stable.

I: And necking in the park in full daylight is not stable behavior?

M: They've recovered from that age.

I: So it's not appropriate for their age?

M: Right!

B: If they want to do it, it is!

K: I think you are only at that age (adolescence) once, and I feel I should take advantage of it. You are only going to be a teenager once!

M: How can society judge? Because, I don't know, I feel society is more or less the older people and not, I don't feel as though society is teenagers in general. Because, it's people who are at least in their twenties and possibly in their thirties and after. People look on and say, "Good God! We didn't do that when we were young!" But they don't realize what goes on in life now. How fast things change. When they were that age maybe you couldn't go on out in the car, you know, if you went out in a car with a girl that would be terrible, what people would think of you. Times just change so great.

Things To Strive for in High School

I: What are the important things for people in high school to strive for: 1) Pleasing parents, 2) getting the most out of your education, 3) living up to religious ideals, 4) being accepted and liked by people your own age?

W: Well, to me, living up to religious ideals is closest to it. *But I think it's more living up to your personal ideals.* I think by the time you reach this age you have to pretty much formulate standards by which you want to, um, develop your life. Like moral standards and religious standards and things like that. And, oh, I think the most important thing is to, ah, try to figure out what these will be and how you feel and try to live by them.

K: I think it's to take advantage of the thing you were talking about before. I don't think any one of those four points is worth anything. The way I feel, I'm going to make the most out of this time. You know, I'm only going to be a teenager once and, oh, *when you are a teenager, you can get away with more.* You can do it. So I'm going to take advantage of it and make the most out of it. And, oh, sure, I mean there might be some damage to my life later on. But I'm not worried.

I: What kind of damage could there be?

K: Well, you could oh . . . Everything's good in moderation. I mean, if you go wild and do something, you can do something that will reflect on you when you are older. *But, ah, see, that's where society goes wrong,* I mean, they limit it too young. When you're seventeen years old, you're no longer an adolescent. You're not a juvenile. You go into court. And if you go in there for drinking or assault and battery, or something like that, that's with you until the day you die. That's all there is to it. But if you are sixteen and you do it, you lose it in a few months. But, oh, you can't push anything too far.

I: Then are you saying that the most important thing for you to strive for is getting as much fun out of your teenage period as possible?

K: Definitely. It's later than you think.

I: Then these other four things would exclude having as much fun as possible?

K: I don't think it excludes them. It depends how much of an influence they put on you. My parents' philosophy is not against all those things. *But are you going to go along with everybody for your whole life? I mean there's a certain time when you are not gonna. And I think this is the best time.*

I: But then after this time, then you are going to go along with everybody?

K: Well, you have to. I mean, it's either up or down. Because *when you reach a certain age, then you are going to get older. This is supposed to be when you prepare yourself.* If you don't, I suppose in five years from now you'll be a complete failure.

I: Would you say this is a justification for not caring about the four things?

K: I don't think it allows me to do anything. I think it's just immaturity on my part. I mean, I admit it.

I: In other words, you feel you have a right to be immature?

K: *I have a right to be immature but just when you're young.* I mean, if

I want to do something, then I'll do it. And if people, you know, don't accept me because I do something like that—just to go out and have fun, you know, it might damage me, I mean there is a certain line and you can't take it too far—if people don't accept you for what you are, I mean what you really are, for your ideals and everything, I don't want to be bothered with those people.

I: So you want to be able to live up to your ideals?

K: Yeah.

I: Barrie?

B: I agree with what Kerwin said. The main reason I'm in school is just to excel in the subjects I like, which I feel now is art. And, you know, if I wanted to quit school my parents would let me. They wouldn't be too happy about it. That's my free choice. I think I'm here because I want to go to art school and I'm going to try my hardest to get in there and since I don't need any requirements, you know, the other classes, they just bore me and I sleep through most of them.

G: I think you ought to live up to your ideals. At this time in life, I don't have any structured ideals that I can write up and live up to. I think it's more important to find out what you want out of life, you know, *to a search and experiment, oh, to look for answers. Because the way things are going it's mostly confusion right now. You don't know exactly what you want to do.* Like Kerwin said, his ideals were to have fun. That's one of his ideals, you know, and in other words, if your concept of the future, or of life, or society in general is to have fun, that's one of your ideals and that's the way you are going to be! But if your ideal of society is that it's something cultural, moral, and maybe even religious, oh, based on hard work and stuff like that, these are all your own ideals. You have to search out for yourself. Find out what you want to do. And then *when you find out what you want to do, you live up to it.* To be yourself—an individualist.

I: Martin?

M: When you are a teenager you've got to make the most out of life. I guess if you feel it, you want to *get as much out of school as you can.* You are at that age where you are in that position where sometimes you want to learn and other times you don't. So you learn what you can, I guess. Because you only learn what you want to learn.

I: (Nods.)

M: I want to strive for a better life. I want to get ahead in the world. Of course, I don't want to be left behind . . . ten years from now. Maybe a college education won't get you a job that it will get you today. People say, well, what's a college education? Everybody goes to college! It'll be just like the formality of going to high school. Like twenty years before this, if you had a high-school education you got a top job. . . . I want to be prepared for the future. I don't want to have it come on me all at once. Then I'll suffer the consequences.

I: You are concerned with the future. Kerwin is concerned with the present.

2. WHAT TURNS KIDS ON? *

Terry Borton

All teachers have pets. I don't mean that all teachers encourage the "kiss-ups" who try to get good grades through flattery, but every teacher has a special interest in a few students. These pets provide the personal impetus for the vast system of American education. A teacher's conviction that he has "made a difference," even with these few students, reassures him that education is something far more complex and fundamental than training students to know the phyla, solve differential equations, or speak Spanish. Mere training, teachers admit, may soon be done better by machines than by men, but education requires an attention to the student's personal concerns which programed courses cannot give.

Yet students hate pets—and not just the "kiss-ups." Their scorn for any of those who are "in" with the teacher is notorious. But their hatred of pets is only a symptom, like their hair styles, their music, their clothes, their language, and the fact that they drop out of school in such vast numbers. These things are symbols of their alienation from an educational system which, no matter what its teachers feel, has done little to "make a difference" in the things which concern most students.

My first years of teaching were spent trying to find ways to make my classes relevant to my students' concerns—to make all students pets. In spite of administrative support and the success I sometimes had, my efforts were often frustrating. I had no way of determining what student concerns really were, no clearly defined concept of what they could become, no planned sequence of activities which would develop them, and above all, no time in the hurly-burly of public school teaching to evolve the necessary curriculum.

I did have the opportunity to help organize two summer programs to work on these problems. In each program the staff was developing cur-

* *Saturday Review*, April 15, 1967. Copyright 1967 Saturday Review, Inc.

ricula by trial and error and so it is impossible to describe here a complete curriculum of concerns, much less a plan of integrating such a curriculum with training in the basic skills. But by indicating what we taught in the limited setting of a summer school, I may be able to suggest what might be done on a larger scale and offer some speculations on the consequences.

Much of what we were trying to achieve in the two summer schools was clarified for me by a paper which I read in the middle of the second summer. Written by Gerald Weinstein and Mario Fantini of the Ford Foundation's Fund for the Advancement of Education and entitled "A Model for Developing Relevant Content for Disadvantaged Children," this paper outlined a theoretical model for developing courses around the basic concerns of students. Messrs. Weinstein and Fantini did a careful job of distinguishing between the progressive clichés about student *interests* and what they defined as *concerns,* the basic psychological and sociological drives of students. They pointed out, for instance, that a student might be *interested* in cars because he was *concerned* with his feelings of powerlessness, and that the proper approach to such a student was therefore not necessarily *Hot Rod Magazine* but some way of helping him explore his understanding of power. Weinstein and Fantini were also careful to emphasize that they did not envisage the classroom as a place for solving the emotional problems of individuals; rather they wanted to find a way to direct lessons toward the general, yet personal, concerns of an entire class.

The concepts on which Weinstein and Fantini built their model were basic to the curriculum of the summer school I will describe here, though we found that in practice their distinctions were not so easy to draw. Our first attempt at a curriculum of concerns began as a pilot project in 1965 and in 1966 developed into the Philadelphia Cooperative Schools Summer Program. This was an experimental six-week project sponsored jointly by the public, private, and parochial schools of Philadelphia and financed by the Philadelphia Board of Education and the federal government. There were two centers of sixty students each, one a high school and the other for grades five through eight. Each student body was selected to represent an ethnic, racial, social, and economic cross section of Philadelphia, and attended morning classes in heterogeneous groups of fifteen. High school classes were art, drama, urban affairs, and communications; middle school classes were drama, music, and science. The afternoons were reserved for projects of the students' own design including play production, a newspaper, psychology and sociology clubs, trips, and sports.

The Cooperative Program's statement of purpose defined the kind of student we hoped the curriculum of concerns would generate:

We want to educate students so that they become larger, more open, more independent human beings, able to function effectively in a world of rapid social and moral change. We believe that a person struggles toward these goals through a process of integrating his *thoughts*, his *concerns*, and his *actions*. Our teaching will be directed toward the development of this perspective, this sense of an integrating self.

These were idealistic goals, and they embarrassed us a little because we were not at all sure that we knew any more about how to achieve them than did the thousands of other schools which put such generalities into their statements of purpose. We had several advantages, however, that most schools do not have. First, attendance was voluntary and we had no grades whatsoever, so there was no academic pressure on our students. Second, any individual class contained some students who had received the best and most expensive preparatory school educations, and some who could barely read. We were forced then to seek what was common to all of our students no matter what their backgrounds; we were forced to teach toward generalized concerns. Third, we knew that the diversity of background, education, and belief would create tension among the students, and our previous summer's experience had taught us that this tension could be a constructive force when it brought basic student concerns to the surface.

The major concern which had arisen during the first summer was one of self-identity, and it was on this that we decided to concentrate the second year. We wanted to build a curriculum which would explore the students' own sense of the disparity between what they thought about in school, what they were concerned about in their own lives, and the way they acted. Though this dissociation of self was revealed in different forms in students of different backgrounds (e.g., the obsession with "soul," with "phonies," and with "commitment") we believed it was a concern common to all our students and one that we could build a curriculum to meet.

Our curriculum outline consisted only of a series of questions designed to move the students from a generalized concern about man's identity as man to the personal sense of identity, and finally to an examination of the actions which would express that sense of self.

1) What is human about humans? What distinguishes humans from animals? Individually? In groups?

2) What masks do humans use to hide or express what is human or personal about themselves? Is race a mask? Who am I?

3) What happens when people don't hide themselves? Do we mean that we are afraid of being what we really are when we say we don't want to make a fool of ourselves?

4) What forms will express genuine human relationships? How is personal style developed? How can we find actions to express our thoughts and feelings, and yet be accepted by others?

To explore the first of these questions, "What is human about humans?" we contrasted humans with animals and worked out a number of particular questions in each subject area. The whole unit was built around a trip to the zoo. The students were equipped with a sheet which asked a range of questions running from the factual, "What foods does this animal eat?" to the more philosophical, "Are fur and feathers the same thing as clothing?" and "Describe the 'animal' in man."

When the high school students returned from the zoo another teacher and I put on an impromptu reading of Edward Albee's *The Zoo Story* and classes the next week picked up the themes which emerged. In drama class the students tried to imitate the movement of the animals they had watched—the ponderous stumbling of the big turtles, the grace of the swans. There followed a discussion about why humans characterized so much of their action with animal metaphors. One girl who had watched a swan was eager to speak of it but, though she seemed to be an extrovert, could not bring herself to demonstrate its grace in a drama improvisation. The swan, she wrote later, was part of her personal dream, locked away in her mental "jewel box" where no one could get at it:

> I am like a crazy, complicated maze.
> I never cry, never love
> I am like egotistical egotists

> I am fear, constant fear that they might find out what I really am. I'm not really fear but fear is the blanket that protects and prohibits what I really am. I've locked it all away in a jewel box. I'm afraid that it might be hideous. I'm afraid that there won't be anything at all. I'll be disgusted if it's beautiful.

> My only request is to know it.
> When I am dying. Or dead.

During the session of improvisation in which she first spoke of her swan, she did not know what was in that jewel box. She was scared and uncertain about talking, but not disgusted and not dead. Her voice, which had been loud and tinny, became a soft contralto. She, who called herself a "project child" because she had brazened her way through so many special programs, began to take on the serenity of the swan she admired. She was not transformed—no miracle happened—but her response to that lesson convinced us that a curriculum of concerns could make a difference in students' lives.

In the urban affairs class the "zoo" curriculum was used in a different way. The students took turns sitting on the floor of a "cage" built of circling chairs while their classmates questioned them. "What district of the city do you live in? Do you feel caged in there? Do you ever hear people in your neighborhood refer to people in other parts of the city as 'animals'? Is it better to keep different animals in different cages so they won't hurt each other? What problems arise when people feel as though they're caged in? What can be done about it?" Classes in art and communications followed a similar curriculum of questions designed to lead students from their experience with animals to a better understanding of themselves as humans.

In a group discussion period that I led we got into a debate about animal and human groups. The class began by collecting a list of different kinds of animal groups (hive, herd, pack, school, etc.) and then I asked the students what animal group their own class was most like. I was unprepared for the answer I got but I was very impressed: They were like no animal group because no animal group was voluntarily composed of antagonistic animals, yet the diversity of people in the room had voluntarily come together to learn more about themselves and others. That answer struck me as extremely significant because it pointed so explicitly to the fact that man's self-consciousness allows him to utilize his own diversity for his own benefit. If a consciousness of self is one of the major differences between animals and men, then one of the most effective ways to make men more human, or more humane, would be to help them explore the significance of their own diversity. And if our curriculum of concerns was bringing students to that kind of realization perhaps we were on the track of a plan of classroom education which led to our goal of "more open, more independent human beings."

The other questions of the curriculum guide were not explored as fully as the one on "What is human about humans?" because we did not give ourselves adequate time to work out detailed curricula. As a result, the students' response to the program was not as clearcut as we would have liked. Perhaps their combination of insight and frustration is best revealed in an interview between Gerald Weinstein, who wrote the paper mentioned earlier, and some of the program's students. The interview took place in October, after the students had been back in their regular school settings. Mr. Weinstein was posing as a school official.

> *First Student:* I sat in school today and it was in geometry and I sat and I looked at everyone and I said, "Now they're really not like I am at all," because I was so angry. She was teaching geometry . . . it

was nothing. She was saying that this plane is this plane and that line runs that way and I'm feeling awful and I was looking at the people sitting there being their nice little selves . . . goody-goody girls sitting there, "Yes, teacher, you're right. I understand," and they didn't understand at all.

Mr. Weinstein: Well, what was it that made you feel bad? That they were responding that way?

First Student: No, that they weren't being themselves. They weren't feeling anything.

Mr. Weinstein: How do you know they weren't being themselves? Couldn't that have been themselves?

Second Student: That could have been her six months ago.

Mr. Weinstein: Could it? Was that you?

First Student: That was me.

Mr. Weinstein: You mean that experience you had this summer made you so different from them? And now you're unhappy?

First Student: I'm not unhappy.

Mr. Weinstein: Well, you're uncomfortable.

First Student: I'm uncomfortable but I'm not unhappy because I think I'm more of a person. And, you know, I can accept myself.

Mr. Weinstein: You're more uncomfortable but you're not more unhappy. I don't understand.

Second Student: It's not unhappy, it's just being aware of something. It makes you a little more unhappy but at least it gives you a feeling of knowing why you have this frustrating feeling of sitting there thinking, "There must be something wrong with me because I don't like this" . . . I've been going to this school since fourth grade and more and more and more, every year, I've felt there is nothing for me in this school. And yet six weeks [of the Summer Program] and I feel like I've learned something more than in all those ten years.

Formal research evaluation conducted by a team from Bryn Mawr is still under way. Attitude studies have produced ambiguous results which later followup should clarify. The results which emerged from other tests showed, interestingly enough, that the students' parents gave the program an enthusiastic rating. All but one thought there was a "change for the better" in their children and large numbers reported a substantial change for the better. Also, it was clear from research that the students formed friendships across racial and school lines to a much greater extent than occurs in regular school situations.

Whatever the final results of the program's evaluation, it would be foolhardy to generalize them into sweeping conclusions about the nature of education. Yet it would be equally foolhardy not to continue the experiment, both to benefit those students who attend and to refine the measuring tools. This will be done by the Cooperative Program planned for next year. It would also be foolhardy not to hypothesize about the implications of the past summer and to work on a theory that would help to explain such experiences. Mr. Weinstein is heading a national field group of educators who are considering the many problems involved in developing such a theory.

In the meantime the Philadelphia Board of Education is investigating several ways in which the Cooperative Program's philosophy and curriculum can be transferred to mass education: 1) by using a similar program as part of training designed to increase a teacher's ability to reach students who are unlike himself; 2) by using improvisational drama to develop awareness and self-confidence among a diverse student body; 3) by using subject matter more relevant to student concerns —by substituting an "urban affairs" class for "civics," by broadening English to "communication" which includes movies and other modern forms of expression; 4) by using a high school course in group dynamics as a way of helping students understand the concerns which motivate or block their relationships to others and their progress in school; 5) by facing conflict openly and using tension to provide an educational stimulus; and 6) by experimenting with ungraded, unmarked, noncompulsory "discovery" classes for small groups of difficult or especially talented students.

All of these activities can be conducted without changing the present orientation of the school system in any major way. They supplement, or perhaps enhance, the commitment to teach all students the skills of reading, writing, and arithmetic. But perhaps it is not too early to speculate on what changes might occur in the operation of a school if a curriculum of concerns were developed for kindergarten through twelfth grade and if it were made to serve as the basis for integrating skills training, subject matter, and the students' personal needs.

Suppose at the high school level, where one of the primary concerns of students is self-identity, the curricula were completely revised so that most subject matter was related to questions of self. Suppose the biology course stopped the yearly ritual of chopping up pickled frogs and began exploring the brain, that tantalizing source of self-identity. Suppose, instead of memorizing theorems which they will forget immediately after the exam, math students learned the mathematical concepts of computer programing and the ways that systems analysis is being used to control much of their economic and political identity. Suppose history were presented not as a series of battles and prime ministers but as the quest of man to establish his identity by religious, territorial, economic, political, and educational means.

One of the many complications of such a presentation is that the students would not graduate knowing the same facts they now know. But with the amount of knowledge doubling every ten years, selection is a necessity. If, as Jerome Bruner has suggested in *The Process of Education,* we can teach the structure of any subject to any child at any age, perhaps the structure which is directly related to a child's own concerns would stimulate a dramatic renascence in learning. At the elementary level there is evidence from programs all over the country that we have underestimated the potential of elementary children's concerns in almost every field.

If one of the major concerns of very small children is communication with the buzzing world around them, no wonder so many programs are preparing children to read at very early ages. In Philadelphia a local TV station is even running an experimental program which hopes to teach three-year-olds to read as they watch TV. Similarly, in foreign languages, the millions of bilingual four-year-old Puerto Ricans and Mexicans are making educators wonder why they teach language in high school, when after four arduous years of Spanish most of the students will not be able to speak it adequately. Perhaps if we taught children *what* they are concerned with knowing *when* they are concerned with knowing it, they would graduate knowing more and understanding more.

The curriculum of concerns suggests the vision of a new function and meaning for schools—schools that face the questions all men have experienced. I believe we can create schools that students want to attend because their education is important to them not simply as economic or social climbers, but as human beings. I believe such schools may someday educate students for a society where people are not judged by money, class, or IQ but by their understanding of others and of themselves.

II. ON THE PHYSICAL, PSYCHOSEXUAL, AND SOCIOSEXUAL REALMS OF ADOLESCENCE

Introduction

Three closely related but distinct areas of human and adolescent development are combined in this section: the physical realm, the psychosexual realm, and the sociosexual realm. Perhaps it is obvious that adults who deal with adolescents crucially need to possess at least some minimal familiarity with these realms, since they almost certainly account for a considerable portion of the behaviors and motivations of the period of adolescence.

To begin with, we note that one has little difficulty clearly understanding the grosser aspects of physical development and the vital parts they play in directly influencing adolescent behavior. We readily appreciate the effects of increases in weight, bone length, and physical strength associated with the growth spurt that initiates adolescence. Nor is it too demanding a task for us to empathize with an adolescent's feelings surrounding the onset of primary and secondary sexual characteristics. Seldom do we realize, however, the interpersonal subtleties associated with physical development or the behavioral and perceptual consequences connected with various forms of human development. These subtleties are revealed when we ponder the continuous demands for adjustment to a rapidly changing (physical) stimulus an adolescent poses for an adult. One is almost forced to wonder about the significance of the lag between what is and what was that must occur in an adult's mind. The second reading in this section presents still another set of insights into the hidden consequences of adolescent physical development: the behavioral and perceptual correlates associated with various outcomes of physical development.

Blair and Jones' paper presents a straightforward and enlightening encapsulation of the important aspects of adolescent physical development. Additionally valuable are the authors' remonstrations on the common misconceptions held by people about the physical development of adolescents. At the end of their article, they helpfully offer some special implications for education from what is known about physical development in this period of life.

Ryan and Foster, on the other hand, indulge in a study of the less obvious side of the consequences of the physical development among adolescents. (Their paper is our first encounter with an experimental study; we feel that it is captivating enough to hold your interest and hope that it will reinforce an acceptance of this approach to gaining knowledge.) Ryan and Foster's study demonstrates the relationship of some basic physical attributes to the adolescent's perceptions and preferred interactional modes with his environment. Coaches and physical education teachers would probably find this study's findings fascinating. Some of what they present has common intuitive appeal; other ideas (for example, the finding that time passes more slowly for certain types of people than for others) may tax your cognitive powers. Their basic message is clear, though: we should be at least grossly aware of the differences associated with different people's patterns of physical development in our pedagogical expectations of adolescents.

The next two articles in this section shift us to the psychosexual realm of adolescent development. One might reasonably ask, "What exactly is meant by the psychosexual realm?" In this book, it refers to the individual's store of ideas, values, attitudes, and preferences about sexual matters. The Reiss article, in dealing with this topic, presents a general overview of American teen-agers' psychosexual orientations and their consequences. Reiss adroitly reports on such absorbing topics as the significance of going steady in different social classes, permissiveness and promiscuity among adolescents, the significance of the double standard for both sexes, and the incidence of venereal disease and illegitimate birth among adolescents. Bell's paper focuses on the

generational conflict about sexual values between middle-class mothers and their teen-age daughters. He ends with a discussion of the trend of this conflict.

The last part of this section of the book is somewhat innovative and submerges us in what we will call the sociosexual realm of adolescence. This refers to a level of human motivation somewhat ignored, in our estimation, in the study of adolescence: the overriding or underlying sex-linked determinants of the individual's interactions with his or her human environment as a man or a woman.

The first article on the sociosexual realm violates our focus to make an elusive point. Chamove, Harlow, and Mitchell's study superbly makes the case for considering the sociosexual realm in adolescence and underscores examples of it with behavior from an experimental investigation that uses preadolescent Rhesus monkeys. This brief sojourn into animal psychology leads to an analysis of the sociosexual realm's behavior on the human plane from the last chapter in Douvan and Adelson's *The Adolescent Experience*. These two authors address themselves to the task of divulging the basic themes behind diverse behavior pattern differences between the sexes. Their findings regarding the issue of independence indicate that "the urge to be free, to be one's own master, is almost exclusively a masculine stirring." The evidence they cite further proposes that "the interpersonal sphere is the pivotal feature around which an adolescent girl's development focuses."

1.   PHYSICAL DEVELOPMENT *

G. M. Blair and R. S. Jones

In many respects, human development is a continuous process from conception to death, various aspects of development being closely determined by what has gone before. Moreover, many of the problems of development apply to one age of life as well as to another. However, the beginning of adolescence, known as pubescence, brings with it abrupt and psychologically significant physical changes that mark this period off from other stages of growth.

While many of these important physical changes, such as growth in height and deepening of the voice, are obvious and commonly known, others are hidden or less obvious but nonetheless significant.

Surge in Growth

Toward the end of childhood, girls at about ten or eleven and boys at about twelve or thirteen begin a period of rapid growth in height and weight (general bodily growth). This acceleration of growth is closely linked to the increased hormonal output of the pituitary gland, which serves not only as the catalyst to produce growth but also as the controller of other glands (adrenals, gonads, and thyroids) that determine both tissue growth and function. The rapid growth thus set off is maintained for a period of about three or four years, with the greatest increment in growth coming at an average age of 12.6 for girls and 14.8 for boys. During this period it is not uncommon for a child to grow as much as six to eight inches in height and to gain forty to fifty pounds in a year's time.

For a variety of reasons, physical development in this period of rapid change is characterized by asynchronies that bring concern to adoles-

* Reprinted with permission of The Macmillan Company from *Psychology of Adolescence for Teachers* by G. M. Blair and R. S. Jones. Copyright © by The Macmillan Company 1964.

cents and their parents and teachers. Skeletal and muscular development is more rapid than the learning required to make use of the new muscle mass. Motor habits that once served the child (such as gracefully falling to the floor in play) are no longer appropriate. The new body requires new learnings. Bodily proportions also undergo changes. Facial features alter, because the growth of the lower part of the face lags behind the growth of the upper part. Legs, proportionally, usually grow more rapidly than the body stem, and hands and feet anticipate by several years the total body size of their owners.

General bodily growth is paralleled by physiological changes such as cardiovascular and respiratory growth and changes in metabolism and in general movement toward the adult status. As will later be shown, these internal changes also have manifestations and initial irregularities that may become sources of concern for the young person and his parents.

Puberty and Primary and Secondary Sex Characteristics

Following closely on the heels of accelerated growth, the pituitary gland directs the adrenal cortex and the gonads into more activity. Prior to this time, virtually equal amounts of androgenic (male) and estrogenic (female) hormones are produced for both sexes by the adrenal cortex on direction of the anterior pituitary gland. Now an increased amount of hormonal production differentiates the sexes; the males producing more androgens, the females more estrogens. Moreover, the genital and sex-appropriate tissues become more sensitive to catalytic action of these sexspecific hormones. The dawn of these changes is reflected in girls by the beginning of the enlargement of breasts and in boys by an enlargement of the testes. There follows in each sex a series of physical changes whose appearance is highly predictable and whose sequence is unalterable. In girls the enlargement of breasts is followed by the pubic hair (first straight, then kinky), the menarche, and axillary hair.

In boys, after the initial enlargement of the testes, there occurs pubic hair, axillary hair, voice changes, and beard in that order.

Thus, by observing adolescents, it is fairly easy to determine the point in pubescence that they have reached. The observable secondary sex characteristics, such as development of axillary hair and voice change, while reliable clues, are as their term implies—secondary to the primary sex changes. Primary sex characteristics include reproductive organs whose maturity is signaled by the menarche in the girl and by the first ejaculation in the boy. The menarche, to which society probably attaches undue importance, does not indicate reproductive capacity, as it is usually followed by a year to two of sterility. In any case, society attaches significance to the first menstrual period, even though it is but one event in the total move toward maturity.

Just as the age at which the physical growth spurt begins varies greatly among individuals, so do the changes associated with pubescence. While the average age of menarche today is about thirteen years, the normal range is from nine to eighteen. Boys who mature about two years later show the same sort of range in the age at which they reach puberty. (The psychological significance of these normal variations, and of the difference in age at which boys and girls reach maturity, will be discussed in subsequent chapters.)

Strength, Skill, and Fitness

Physical development viewed only in terms of increases in size, body features, and secondary sex characteristics presents only the gross picture of the many physical changes that occur in adolescence. Even more significant, perhaps, are the growth patterns of strength and skill, which so clearly differentiate the adolescent from his recent childhood.

The post-pubescent boy, even though he may be the same chronological age as friends who have not yet entered pubescence, will almost certainly be stronger and will likely have greater agility, motor coordination, and bodily skills. He will, of course, rapidly overtake girls, whose strength already has increased about a year earlier and who briefly challenged him. What forces account for this development? First, it is clear that the accelerated production of male hormones (androgens) brings with it added muscular strength. Second, the nature of skeletal growth, increased shoulder breadth, larger chest cavity, and finally, the greater lung size, heart size, and increased blood pressure are all favorable conditions for physical strength. While many of these same changes are occurring among girls, their physical strength increases at a slower rate, and, of course, never equals that of males in our culture. There are two reasons for this superiority: (1) biologically, the male is favored by larger shoulder breadth, a bigger chest cavity, and better leg leverage; (2) culturally, girls receive little encouragement for the development of strength. In fact, they are encouraged in the opposite direction—to be weak and dependent, or at least to pretend that they are.

Along with increases in strength come the development of motor coordination, reaction speed, and perceptual-motor skills. For example, simple tests have been used to compare the eight-year-old, who can tap with his finger 130 times in thirty seconds, with the average eighteen-year-old, who can tap about 210 times in the same period. Reaction time, a measure of the time between a signal and a response to it, is usually reduced as much as one-third between the ages of eight and sixteen. There are, of course, great diversities among children of the same age and even of the same maturational age.

In an appraisal of physical development, one important consideration has to do with what is optimal. We speak of fat, healthy babies, but we cannot use these two adjectives together to describe any other time of life. Height-weight charts are based on the average, but may, when a large segment of youth are overweight, lead to faulty conclusions. What is average is certainly not necessarily optimal. Combining data from both growth charts and tests of physical strength and fitness clearly reveals that today many young people are overweight.

In many respects, adolescence is the healthiest time of life. The childhood diseases are past, and the degenerative disorders of adulthood are in the future. The habits of life that have to do with continued physical vigor are, however, laid down in these formative years. The young body can take enormous abuse and bounce back. Psychologically, however, the habits of abuse, once they enchain the individual, may, unless broken, assure a less-than-optimal adult life.

Common Misconceptions

Compared with some other areas of development—for example, mental development—physical development should be clearly marked and subject to little dispute. Unfortunately, this is not true. Misconceptions about physical development are shared by both adolescents and their parents.

AWKWARDNESS IS NOT UNIVERSAL

Adults expect adolescents to be clumsy, and to some extent they dismiss as adolescent awkwardness many difficulties for which a better explanation exists. Actually, even though there are asynchronies (as previously noted), and even though muscle mass tends to precede function, the adolescent can quickly and easily learn skills and controls. The grace of high school basketball players, cheer leaders, and young swimmers and divers makes "pot-bellied" parents awkward by contrast. In fact, one wonders if some of the adult criticism of adolescents is not partly due to the envy of the older generation, who see their own youth slipping away but are reluctant to accord children the place of prominence to which their youthful vigor, skill, and speed entitle them.

WARM CLIMATES DO NOT ACCELERATE MATURITY

There is evidence that occurrence of puberty is more closely allied to other conditions of life, such as diet and health, than to climate. In fact, if climate does have any effect at all, it is likely that a temperate climate promotes an earlier maturity than do either a tropical or arctic climate. It is also unlikely that ethnic factors have much bearing, although, of course, genetic factors do. Early maturity is family-related.

VIGOROUS EXERCISE DOES NOT DAMAGE THE HEART

Growing children need physical exercise just as they need food and rest. There are important cardiovascular changes in adolescence. The heart increases in size and strength, and blood pressure increases. These observations have led some to believe that in late childhood and early adolescence vigorous exercise may be harmful. There is little evidence that this is so. As a matter of fact, this author knows a boy who had an organic defect of a heart valve. He engaged in normal physical activity, including Little League baseball, upon a doctor's advice. Eventually, in his fourteenth year an operation restored the heart to normal functioning. The point is that he suffered no heart damage, even though his heart allowed for handling only a fraction of the amount of blood handled by a normal heart. (This example should *not* be construed to mean that vigorous activity is good for everyone. For some pathological conditions, exercise is not advisable.)

A STRONG BACK DOES NOT MEAN A WEAK MIND

Undoubtedly some adolescents who do poorly in academic work may compensate by developing physical strength. However, all studies relating mental ability to physical development show, if anything, a slight positive correlation between such ability and both size and strength. The exceptional cases are, of course, vivid.

ACADEMICALLY ABLE YOUTH ARE NOT MOTOR MORONS

The sedentary pursuits of the bright child may remove him from the normal game learnings that most children acquire. He may consequently appear inept. However, given an opportunity for practice, he will develop game skills as well as, or better than, his less-bright peer. The point is, of course, that he may not want to. He may never learn to dig a hole with a shovel, sweep with a broom, bat a ball, or use a screwdriver, and, if called upon to do these things, he will indeed appear awkward. Whether *all* adolescents should learn some of these more common skills is a moot question.

PHYSICAL SIZE IS NOT A GOOD MEASURE OF MATURITY

A serious error made by both parents and teachers is that physical size (height and weight) are indicators of maturity. While there is a relationship, it is so slight that little value can be placed upon it. Expecting too much of a large, immature adolescent can give him anxieties and feelings of inferiority, while treating a mature but small adolescent as a child can build resentment and aggression.

OTHER MISCONCEPTIONS

There is a host of other misconceptions related to secondary sex characteristics and appearances. The notions that excessive hairiness denotes masculinity in women, that broad hips in boys indicates feminity, and that a low forehead points to low intelligence are but a few of the nonsensical ideas that may still exist. The school should treat them as sheer nonsense, thereby relieving the anxiety of the adolescent who possesses these characteristics.

Special Implications for Education

All teachers, not just coaches and counselors, engage in exchanges with adolescents that involve both their physical and mental attributes. Especially at this period of life, physical appearance, rapid physical change, and preoccupation with the body and its processes impinge upon all adolescents' activities. Following are some of the special implications for education derived from what is known about the physical development that takes place at this period of life.

1. Asynchronies in individual growth are as inevitable as the variability in rates of growth among groups of children. Out of the differences thus produced among adolescents, and the difference between the adult model and the way they perceive themselves at the moment, arise many of the sensitive reactions of adolescents to each other and to adults. These "facts of life" cannot be changed. The teacher of adolescents can only hope to provide a better understanding of the process of growth, the changes and difficulties it may bring, and a sense of values which places greatest importance upon the less tangible elements of character and personality.

2. It should be clear that in the physical realm, just as in English or mathematics, no single schedule of activities will be suitable for all children, and remedial work in physical skills is just as appropriate as it is in reading, speech, or arithmetic.

3. Strength and motor skill, particularly among boys, is significantly correlated with popularity, feelings of adequacy, and social adjustment. The small, inept boy may have to be aided to achieve a place in the group.

4. Because of the wide range of strength and skill, even between adolescents of the same size, care must be taken to assure that unfair competition between mismatched adolescents does not develop. This author remembers vividly the instance in his own schooling when a large pre-pubescent boy was matched in boxing against a smaller post-pubescent boy. Even though the physical-education teacher finally stopped the one-sided match, a good deal of psychological damage had already been done. Naturally, such events will occur "by themselves" on the playground or in the neighborhood where pupils live. But they certainly ought to be rare at school, where teachers who know about adolescents are directing their activities.

5. Habits of diet, exercise and recreation, sleep, work, and study not only have immediate physical impact upon the adolescent, but also (and perhaps more important) may become so firmly entrenched that they continue into adult life. Schools have shown a laudable awareness of these factors upon physical development and health by requiring courses in health and hygiene and by being concerned with the carry-over value of activities learned in physical education. By and large, however, health classes may be little more than labeling parts of the body and memorizing lists of vitamins and food elements, and physical-education classes the playing of games that will never be played again after the student leaves school. What is wanted is a program in which the students are so strongly and personally involved that they will carry into their homes and their daily routines the elements of health and fitness that they learn at school. The teacher who wishes to accomplish these aims might well consider such activities as the following:

a. Have students make a distribution of heights and weights for several classes, then test groups for physical fitness.
b. Get students to conduct a dental survey.
c. Do an experiment with animals, feeding some an adequate diet and others an inadequate diet.
d. Make reports on various kinds of common physical disorders and their relations to early life.
e. Emphasize games and sports which (1) have carry-over values,

such as golf, tennis, badminton, skating, swimming, and the like, (2) do not depend for success and enjoyment on sheer physique and strength, and (3) provide the satisfaction of improving one's ability by oneself rather than by competition with others.

References

Ausubel, D. P. *Theory and problems of adolescent development.* New York: Grune & Stratton, 1954.

Knapp, C., and Jewett, A. E. (Eds.) *The growing years: Adolescence.* Washington, D. C.: Yearbook, American Association for Health, Physical Education, and Recreation, 1962.

National Society for the Study of Education. *Adolescence,* Part I, 43rd Yearbook. Chicago: University of Chicago Press, 1944. Chapters by Greulich, Jones, Stolz and Stolz.

Pressey, S. L., and Kuhlen, R. G. *Psychological development through the life span.* New York: Harper & Row, 1957, Chapter 2.

Stolz, H. R., and Stolz, L. M. *Somatic development in adolescence.* New York: Macmillan, 1951.

2. ATHLETIC PARTICIPATION AND PERCEPTUAL AUGMENTATION AND REDUCTION *

E. Dean Ryan and Robert Foster

Recently a significant relationship was found between the ability of an individual to tolerate pain and the type of athletic activity in which he chooses to participate (Ryan & Kovacic, 1966). Contact athletes (football players and wrestlers) tolerated more pain than noncontact athletes (tennis players and golfers), and the noncontact athletes in turn tolerated more pain than nonathletes. It was hypothesized that this relationship might have been due to differences in a general perceptual

* From: E. Dean Ryan and Robert Foster, "Athletic Participation and Perceptual Augmentation and Reduction," *Journal of Personality and Social Psychology, 6,* 1967, 472–476. Copyright 1967 by the American Psychological Association, and reproduced by permission.

characteristic of "augmenting" or "reducing" sensory inputs. Petrie and associates have shown that certain individuals appear to consistently reduce the intensity of their perceptions, while other individuals tend to consistently augment the intensity of perception (Petrie, 1960). Augmentation and reduction have been estimated by measuring the change in kinesthetically perceived size after stimulation. The subjects match the width of a standard bar which is felt with one hand, with an area on a tapered bar which is felt with the other hand. A large (or smaller) block is then rubbed. Thereafter, the original test bar is again equated with the tapered bar, and the difference between the two subjective estimations is measured. Those individuals who tend to consistently reduce after stimulation have been shown to be more extroverted than those who augment (Eysenck, 1957), more tolerant of pain (Petrie, Collins, & Phillips, 1960), less tolerant of sensory deprivation (Petrie et al., 1960), more mesomorphic (Wertheimer, 1955), and to judge time as passing more slowly than the augmenters (Petrie et al., 1960). In addition, significantly more reducers were found in a delinquent group and significant fewer augmenters than would be expected by chance (Petrie, McCulloch, & Kazdin, 1962). Petrie suggested that these differences are partially due to the tendency to reduce or augment the perceptual intensity of stimulation in general. Any change in the intensity of stimulation may cause subsequent stimulation to appear subjectively less intense for the "reducer" and more intense for the "augmenters."

All of the characteristics of the reducer, the tolerance of pain, intolerance of sensory deprivation, mesomorphy, extroversion, and to an extent the characteristics of the delinquent, have frequently been associated with athletic groups. It may be that the subjective reduction of sensory stimulation is associated with the choice of activities a child engages in. If indeed, the reducers suffer from lack of stimulation as suggested by Petrie et al. (1962), then they would need change, movement, speed, and possibly body contact, rather than sedentary pursuits. Conversely, it may be that the type of activity an individual engages in influences his perceptual pattern, thus encouraging augmentation or reduction.

This study was designed to investigate the relationship between a general perceptual pattern of augmentation and reduction in groups differing in athletic interests. It was hypothesized that groups participating in contact sports would possess the perceptual pattern of the reducer and thus reduce most in their estimation of kinesthetically perceived size, have faster reaction times, faster movement times, judge time as passing slower, and would tolerate most pain. Groups not interested in athletics would possess the perceptual characteristics of the augmenter, and thus reduce less in their estimation of kinesthetically perceived size,

have slower reaction times, slower movement times, judge time as passing faster, and tolerate less pain. Groups participating in noncontact
sports would tend to fall between the other two groups on all tests.

Method

SUBJECTS

A questionnaire was administered to male high school students. They
were asked their likes, dislikes, hobbies, and recreational pursuits. On
the basis of these answers three groups of subjects were selected. Group
I was composed of boys who expressed a liking for certain athletics and
were at the same time actually participating in contact sports (football
or wrestling), Group II of boys who expressed an interest in noncontact
sports and were also participating *only* in noncontact sports (golf, tennis, track), and Group III of boys who had expressed a dislike for athletics and were inactive as far as sports were concerned.

Letters were sent to parents requesting permission for sons to participate in an experiment dealing with perception. It was indicated that one
of the tests would be a measure of pain tolerance. To obtain 20 subjects
in each group it was necessary to contact 22 contact athletes, 26 noncontact athletes, and 26 nonathletes. The subjects assumed they had been
randomly selected and were unaware that athletic participation was a
factor or that the experiment was in any way related to the questionnaire administered earlier.

APPARATUS

Reaction times. The reaction-time apparatus consisted of a small base
with a 16 inch upright. On the upright were mounted in a vertical position two small neon lights and a microswitch. A second microswitch was
located in the base of the reaction timer. The upper light was amber in
color and served as the ready signal. The experimenter could vary the
ready period from ½ to 4 seconds. The onset of the lower green light,
which served as the stimulus, activated two standard electric timers.
The first timer was stopped as the subject's finger moved from the upper
microswitch, and the second timer stopped as the microswitch mounted
in the base was touched. Reaction time was read directly from the first
clock; movement time was computed by subtracting the time of the first
clock from that of the second.

Pain tolerance. And adaptation of Poser's mechanical stimulator was
used (Poser, 1962). A single plastic, aluminum-tipped football cleat was

secured to a curved fiber plate and fitted to the leg. The cleat was placed against the anterior border of the tibia, midway between the ankle and the knee. The sleeve of a standard clinical sphygmomanometer was used to secure the cleat firmly in place. Cleat pressure against the tibia was induced by inflating the armlet at a slow constant rate (approximately 5 millimeters of mercury per second) until the subject indicated verbally that he was no longer willing to endure the pain. Pressure was immediately released by deflating the cuff. The data were recorded in millimeters of mercury.

Augmentation and reduction. The apparatus used to measure augmentation and reduction was an adaptation of the kinesthetic aftereffect apparatus, originally described by Koehler and Dinnerstein (1947). The variable consisted of a wedge-shaped piece of hardwood, 30 inches long, 1 inch thick, 4.0 inches at the wide end, tapering to .5 inch at the narrow end. To maintain parallel alignment of the fingers, a sliding finger guide was fixed atop the wedge. Two hardwood blocks with parallel sides, 10 inches long and 2 inches thick, served as the standard bar and the stimulation bar. The standard bar was 1.5 inches wide and the stimulation bar 2.5 inches wide.

All subjects were tested individually and in a random order. The subject was told he would be given five different tests and was instructed to do as well as possible on each one. The sequence was the same for each subject, that is, reaction time, 2-minute time estimation, 20-second time estimation, pain tolerance, and the kinesthetic measures of augmentation and reduction.

At the conclusion of the reaction-time test the subject was asked to sit quietly with his hands resting in his lap. He was asked to judge a 2-minute period. When the subject thought 2 minutes had elapsed he would say, "time." This was repeated four times. No knowledge of results was given. The scores reported are the mean of the four trials.

Next, the subject was given a stopwatch and asked to duplicate the time interval demonstrated by the experimenter. The experimenter, holding the watch so the face was not visible to the subject, started his watch and let it run for 20 seconds. The subject, holding his own watch with the face down, was told to duplicate the time between the two clicks. This was done four times, each for a 20-second period, with the mean of all trials used for comparison.

At the completion of the 20-second test the subject was told his tolerance to pain would be measured, wherein he should make an effort to stand as much pain as possible. The pressure cleat was applied, and the subject was informed that pressure to the leg would be increased gradually and terminated when he could tolerate no more. The subject was unable to see the mercury column. After the first trial the experimenter commented that the score was considerably lower than the average of the group tested, and the subject was asked to take the test a second time, doing better if possible. The cleat was lowered 1 inch and a second trial was given.

Then the subject was blindfolded. He was instructed to grasp the standard bar between thumb and forefinger of the dominant hand and find the point that felt equal on the wedge-shaped comparison bar grasped identically in his other hand. Four base-line measurements were taken, alternating ascending and descending trials, that is, starting from the narrow end of the wedge on Trials 1 and 3 and from the wide end on the others. The standard bar was held in the subject's dominant hand during this testing period. The subject was then given the wider test block and instructed to rub with his preferred hand at a constant rate for 90 seconds. He then equated the perceived equivalent width of the original test block on the tapered bar. Again four measurements were taken, alternating ascending and descending trials, with the standard bar being held as in the original base-line measurements. This procedure was repeated for a second 90-second trial and finally for a 120-second trial.

Results

The results are presented in Tables 1 and 2, with all means other than movement time being in the predicted direction. To test the significance of the difference between groups on each test a simple analysis of variance was used.

AUGMENTATION AND REDUCTION

There were no differences between groups in judging the width of the test bar prior to stimulation, with the contact athletes judging the 1.5 inch comparison bar as 1.67 inches, the noncontact as 1.69 inches, and the nonathletes as 1.66 inches. After 90 seconds of stimulation all three groups subjectively reduced the size of the comparison bar, although the difference between groups was not significant (Table 2). By 180 seconds of stimulation both athletic groups had increased the amount of reduction, while the trend for the nonathletic group had reversed, that is, they judged the comparison bar as being wider than after 90 seconds of stimulation. At this stage the difference between groups approached the .05 level of significance, F $(2,57) = 3.13$, $p < 3.15$. By 300 seconds of stimulation the difference between groups was quite pronounced, the estimation of width being .258 inch less for the contact athletes than before stimulation, for noncontact athletes .213 inch less, and for the nonathletes, 0.95 inch less. This difference was significant beyond the .01 level, F (2,57) = 6.94.

REACTION TIME AND MOVEMENT TIME

Reaction times and movement times reported are the mean of all 20 trials. While the mean reaction times for the three groups were in the predicted direction, with the contact athletes fastest, noncontact athletes next, and the nonathletes slowest, the difference between the three groups was not significant, F (2,57) = 1.61 (Table 1). For movement time no trend was apparent, and mean scores were so similar that no test of significance was necessary.

TIME ESTIMATION

The differences between groups in estimation of 120 seconds was highly significant, F (2,57) = 19.19, with the contact athletes reducing the period by 16.44 seconds, the noncontact athletes underestimating by only 0.91 second, and the nonathletes enlarging by 2.26 seconds (Table 1).

TABLE 1
Time Measures for Athletic Subgroups

TEST	CONTACT ATHLETES	NONCONTACT ATHLETES	NON- ATHLETES	F
Mean RT (sec.)	.201	.208	.213	1.61
Mean MT (sec.)	.117	.123	.117	—
Mean estimates of 120 sec.				
Trial 1	96.55	111.50	114.90	
Trial 2	101.95	119.35	122.50	
Trial 3	110.85	119.90	125.00	
Trial 4	104.90	125.20	126.85	
Mean of 4 trials	103.56	119.09	122.26	19.19[a]
Mean estimates of 20 sec.				
Trial 1	18.05	21.15	21.75	
Trial 2	19.30	20.10	21.65	
Trial 3	18.50	21.15	21.20	
Trial 4	17.40	20.50	21.40	
Mean of 4 trials	18.31	20.73	21.50	12.86[a]

[a] $p < .01$.

TABLE 2
Differences in Kinesthetic Size Perception and in Pain Tolerance for Athletic Subgroups

	CONTACT ATHLETES	NONCONTACT ATHLETES	NON-ATHLETES	F
Mean change in kines- thetically perceived size after stimulation				
90-sec. stimulation	− .110 in.	− .108 in.	− .103 in.	ns
180-sec. stimulation	− .168	− .173	− .065	3.13 [a]
300-sec. stimulation	− .258	− .213	− .095	6.94 [b]
Mean pain tolerance (mm/Hg)				
Trial 1	286.75	231.00	207.50	14.27 [b]
Trial 2	298.00	251.00	230.75	13.78 [b]

[a] $p < .06$.
[b] $p < .01$.

When duplicating a 20-second period the trend was the same, with the contact athletes reducing 1.69, the noncontact athletes enlarging 0.73 second, and the nonathletes enlarging 1.50 seconds. The difference between groups was highly significant, $F (2,57) = 12.86$ (Table 1).

PAIN TOLERANCE

On Test 1 the amount of pressure the three groups were willing to tolerate was in the predicted direction; the difference between groups being highly significant, $F (2,57) = 14.27$. The group of contact athletes tolerated 285.75 millimeters of mercury, the noncontact athletic group 231.00, and the nonathletic group, 207.50. On the second trial, after being individually informed they had done poorly, all three groups improved, with the contact athletic group averaging 298.00 millimeters, the noncontact athletic group 251.00, and the nonathletic group, 230.75. The difference between groups was highly significant, $F (2,57) = 13.78$ (Table 2). It was impossible to make a meaningful comparison of the amount of change each group made from Trial 1 to Trial 2 as the mercury column on the sphygmomanometer only read to 300 millimeters. It should be noted that the mean score on Trial 2 for the contact athletes was 298 millimeters of mercury. Of the 20 contact athletes tested, 16 withstood the maximum pressure, while each of the remaining 4 subjects tolerated 290 millimeters. Of the noncontact athletes five tolerated the maximum pressure, while three nonathletes tolerated the maximum.

COMPARISON OF EXTREME AUGMENTERS AND REDUCERS

Due to the large individual differences apparent within each group, and because Petrie's work has dealt primarily with extreme augmenters and reducers, an analysis was made of the 15 subjects making the least reduction in their estimation of kinesthetically perceived size after 300 seconds of stimulation and the 15 subjects making the greatest reduction, regardless of their athletic background. The results shown in Table 3 parallel and substantiate the work of Petrie. There was no difference between groups in reaction time and movement time, but all other differences were in the predicted direction and highly significant. Of the extreme reducers, 7 were contact athletes, 6 noncontact athletes, and 2 nonathletes. Of the extreme augmenters, 11 were nonathletes, 1 noncontact athlete, and 3 contact athletes.

Discussion

The results of this study clearly support Petrie's theory of a generalized tendency for certain individuals to consistently reduce or diminish their perception of stimulation and for others to consistently augment or enlarge perceptions. The contact athletes showed the characteristics of the reducer, making the greatest subjective reduction of kinesthetically perceived size after stimulation, tolerating most pain, and consistently judging time as passing more slowly, than did groups composed of noncontact athletes or nonathletes.

TABLE 3
Comparison of Extreme Augmenters and
Reducers after 300 Seconds of Stimulation[a]

TEST	REDUCED MOST	REDUCED LEAST	t
Kinesthetic estimation	− .380	+ .018	
RT	.21 sec.	.21 sec.	0.45
MT	.12 sec.	.12 sec.	0.97
Time estimated 20 sec.	19.48 sec.	21.72 sec.	3.60 [b]
Time estimated 120 sec.	105.96 sec.	126.66 sec.	4.30 [b]
Pain tolerance 1	267.64 mm/Hg	223.98 mm/Hg	3.55 [b]
Pain tolerance 2	280.31 mm/Hg	245.31 mm/Hg	3.41 [b]

[a] $N = 15$ for both groups.
[b] $p < .01$.

While differences in pain tolerance could be explained by simply assuming athletes were more motivated to withstand pain, time estimation and estimation of kinesthetically perceived size are less amenable to changes in motivation. No amount of conscious effort should induce a naïve subject to vary time or kinesthetic sensitivity in one direction or another. One other point should be noted. During the testing period the experimenter was aware of the subject's classification. Since procedures were standardized for each test it is unlikely that the results could be attributed to experimenter bias. The point remains, however, that this must be considered as a possible source of error.

The usual response in estimating kinesthetically perceived size is for subjects to reduce the perceived size of a test block after stimulation with a larger block, and to enlarge the perceived size of a test block after stimulation by a smaller block. Petrie has suggested, however, that

> the reducer will tend to reduce even if he is stimulated for equal amounts of time with a block that is larger than the test object and a block that is smaller than the test object; that is to say, the total effect is for him to reduce [Petrie, Holland, & Wolk, 1963].

The opposite relation holds for the augmenter, who will regularly tend to enlarge his estimate of size. In this study only large block stimulation was used, thus minimizing the chances of finding augmentation. In spite of this, however, 30% of the nonathletic group augmented in the kinesthetic estimation of size. It should be noted further that the nonathletic group, or the augmenters, consistently overestimated time.

Two inconsistencies in experimental method employed by Petrie and by this study should be noted. First, studies by Petrie have employed only ascending trials on the tapered bar, that is, the subject always started from the smaller end of the bar. In the present study, alternating ascending and descending trials were used. Dinnerstein et al. (1962), studying groups that differed in pain tolerance, found no difference in figural aftereffects when using alternating ascending and descending trials, but found significant differences when only ascending trials were analyzed. Thus it would be expected that even greater differences would be found between athletic subgroups if methods used by Petrie had been followed. Second, Petrie suggests a minimum of 45 minutes' rest before the kinesthetic test is administered. "Such a resting period is essential in order to allow the wearing off of the effect of whatever the subject may have been handling prior to testing [Petrie et al., 1962]." In the present study approximately 30 minutes elapsed from the end of the reaction-time experiment to the start of the kinesthetic test. For approximately 5 minutes of this period the subject held a stopwatch in his preferred hand, pressing with his thumb four times. Whether the stimulation of the reaction-time test, followed by only 30 minutes of rest, had an effect on kinesthetic sensitivity is problematical. However, in light of the fact that there were no differences between groups in judgment of width prior to stimulation it would appear that differences due to time would be negligible.

The similarities between the perceptual characteristics of the contact athlete and the juvenile delinquent should be noted, and as Petrie points out, education of these individuals needs to make allowance for their vulnerabilities and strengths. Both groups appear to need stimulation, movement, and change instead of more sedentary activities. It would be expected that confinement and restriction of movement in the typical classroom would be less conducive to good study habits for the reducer than for the augmenter. Thus, an entirely different pedagogical approach would be desirable for the opposing perceptual types. Further, it would seem that a program of vigorous activity might provide a socially acceptable means of relieving sensory monotony and thus reduce the need for less desirable stimulation.

References

Dinnerstein, A. J., Lowenthal, M., Marion, R. B., and Olivo, J. Pain tolerance and kinesthetic after-effect. *Perceptual and Motor Skills*, 1962, *15*, 247–250.

Eysenck, H. J. *The dynamics of anxiety and hysteria*. London: Routledge & Kegan Paul, 1957.

Koehler, W., and Dinnerstein, D. Figural aftereffects in kinesthesis. In A. Michotte (Ed.), *Miscellanea Psychologica*. Paris: Libraire Philosophique, 1947. Pp. 196–220.

Petrie, A. Some psychological aspects of pain and the relief of suffering. *Annals of the New York Academy of Science*, 1960, *86*, 13–27.

Petrie, A., Collins, W., and Solomon, P. The tolerance for pain and sensory deprivation. *American Journal of Psychology*, 1960, *73*, 80–90.

Petrie, A., Holland, T., and Wolk, I. Sensory stimulation causing subdued experience: Audio-analgesia and perceptual augmentation and reduction. *Journal of Nervous and Mental Disorders*, 1963, *137*, 312–321.

Petrie, A., McCulloch, R., and Kazdin, P. The perceptual characteristics of juvenile delinquents. *Journal of Nervous and Mental Disorders*, 1962, *134*, 415–421.

Poser, E. G. A simple and reliable apparatus for the measurement of pain. *American Journal of Psychology*, 1962, *75*, 304–305.

Ryan, E. D., and Kovacic, C. R. Pain tolerance and athletic participation. *Perceptual Motor Skills*, 1966, *22*, 383–390.
Wertheimer, M. Figural aftereffect as a measure of metabolic deficiency. *Journal of Personality*, 1955, *24*, 56–73.

3. SEXUAL CODES IN TEEN-AGE CULTURE *

Ira L. Reiss

Teen-age sexual codes reflect quite clearly the bold outlines of adult sexual codes. The high degree of conformity in teen-age culture increases the observability of teen-age beliefs and adds to our understanding of adult beliefs. The teen-ager exists in a world somewhere between youthful idealism and adult realism, and his sexual codes reflect this state of being. In a very real sense, he is a marginal man with one foot in the world of the child and the other foot in the world of the adult.[1]

The teen-ager is at the stage at which it is vitally important for him to learn how to exist in society independent of his parents. For this reason, he transfers his dependence to his peers and strives to learn from them the secrets of entrance into the adult world. One would think that this vaguely defined status of "almost adult" would lead to confusion and weak statements of belief. To a large extent, this is the case, but, nevertheless, it is equally true that it leads to dogmatic statements of belief and a search for conviction through conformity. Teen-agers translate and adapt the sexual codes of adults to fit their particular circumstance and state of mind.[2]

* *Annals of the American Academy of Political and Social Science*, 1961, *338*, 53–62. Reprinted with permission of the author and the American Academy of Political and Social Science and Ira L. Reiss.

[1] Albert J. Reiss, "Sex Offenses: The Marginal Status of the Adolescent," *Law and Contemporary Problems*, Vol. 25 (Spring 1960), pp. 309–334.

[2] Of course, there is a biological basis for sexual behavior, but social scientists seem generally agreed that the specific way the sexual drive expresses itself is learned. The wide variety of sexual codes throughout the world testifies to the fact that whatever differences exist biologically between men and women can be compensated for by cultural training. The best brief source for cross-cultural information is Clellan S. Ford and Frank A. Beach, *Patterns of Sexual Behavior* (New York, 1954). For a discussion of this entire issue, see Ira L. Reiss, *Premarital Sexual Standards in America* (Glencoe, Ill., 1960), Chap. 1.

Going Steady

When unchaperoned dating gained prevalence in the early part of this century, it involved a much more rapid change of dating partners than occurs today. Nevertheless, by the time of World War II, going steady had taken root, and, today, it seems that slightly more than half of the high school students have some going-steady experience. Even among the early teen-agers, possibly one quarter go steady.[3]

Class differences are important in examining the going-steady complex. It seems that those high school people who go steady and plan to go to college are not likely to marry their high school steadies, and those who are from lower economic classes and who do not plan to go to college are much more likely to marry their high school steadies.[4] Thus, in looking at the custom of going steady, one must realize that there are different subtypes and that the consequences differ for each type.

Although a psychologist may point to the security of going steady as its chief reason for being, as a sociologist, I would point out how Western society has, for centuries, been developing an association of sexual behavior with mutual affection. This association is hard to achieve in casual dating; but, in steady dating, sex and affection can quite easily be combined, and, in this way, a potential strain in the social system is reduced. Another area of strain which is reduced by going steady is the conflict a girl may feel between her desire for sexual experience and her desire to maintain her reputation. For many, sexual behavior is made respectable by going steady.[5] In these ways, one may say that no other dating custom is quite as central to the understanding of teen-age sexual codes as going steady.

------

[3] For evidence, see Maureen Daly, *Profile of Youth* (Philadelphia, 1951), p. 30. It may be well to note here that the author has conducted a pilot study to test the hypothesis that the advent of the junior high school has spread heterosexual knowledge and behavior to younger age groups and thus encouraged earlier dating. In support of this, one may cite Dr. J. B. Connat's belief that the junior high imitates the high school in its social characteristics. In addition, the anticipatory socialization of sex games like "spin the bottle," "post office," and "flashlight" begin today prior to junior high levels and thus prepare students for dating in junior high. The author's evidence indicates a connection between junior high school and early dating patterns.

[4] Robert D. Herman, "The Going Steady Complex: A Re-Examination," *Marriage and Family Living*, Vol. 17 (February 1955), pp. 36–40.

[5] For evidence on this point, see Winston W. Ehrmann, *Premarital Dating Behavior* (New York, 1959), p. 141.

Girls' Sexual Codes

One of the most popular sexual codes among teen-age girls is petting-with-affection. This code is a modern day subtype of our formal abstinence standard. This subtype of abstinence seems extremely popular among high school couples who are going steady. Such couples feel it is proper to engage in heavy petting if they are going steady, the justification being that they are in love or at least extremely fond of each other. The petting-with-affection sex code probably grew along with the going-steady custom; they both illustrate adaptations of our dating institution to the newer unchaperoned dating circumstances.

What evidence do we have for such petting behavior among teen-agers? Though surely not perfect, the most extensive study of sexual behavior is that done by the Institute for Sex Research, formerly headed by Alfred C. Kinsey and now run by Paul H. Gebhard. It should be noted that the Kinsey studies are most valid for urban, white, northeastern, college-educated people, and, thus, great care must be taken when applying the results to other groups. The reader should keep in mind the tenuousness of any such generalizations made in this paper.

Kinsey's data show that, of the females who were twenty years old or older when interviewed, about one fifth to one fourth admitted they had petted to orgasm while still in their teens. Most of this behavior occurred between the ages of sixteen and twenty. About three-quarters of all the girls twenty years old or more admitted being aroused by some form of petting or kissing in their teens, and approximately 90 per cent stated they had at least been kissed during their teens.[6]

Those girls who marry in their teens start their petting and kissing behavior earlier than those who marry later. In general, the few years previous to marriage are by far the most sexually active for girls. Lower class females marry earlier, and, thus, they are more active in their teens and are more likely to marry their teen-age steadies.

The above rates are averages for Kinsey's entire sample of several thousand females; were we to take only the females born in more recent decades, the rates would be considerably higher. For example, of those females born before 1900, only 10 per cent ever petted to orgasm in their teens, whereas, of those girls born in the 1920's, almost 30 per cent, or three times the proportion, petted to orgasm in their teens.[7]

---

[6] Alfred C. Kinsey and Others, *Sexual Behavior in the Human Female* (Philadelphia, 1953), Chap. 7.

[7] *Ibid.*, p. 244.

It seems clear that we have developed not only new dating forms such as going steady but also, as we have seen, new sexual codes to go with them. These new codes allow females much more freedom in heavy petting, provided affection is involved. Of course, other girls, particularly in the early teens, adhere to standards which only permit kissing, and a few others adhere to standards which allow full sexual relations, but, by and large, petting-with-affection seems the increasingly popular sex code for high school girls.

The most recent evidence of the nature of teen-age sex codes also supports these contentions. This evidence comes from research which the author is engaged in at present.[8] Some preliminary reports on this study were made in the author's book *Premarital Sexual Standards in America*. The study involves 1,000 high school and college students, most of whom are teen-agers. Although final analysis of the study has not been completed, it is clear that petting-with-affection is an extremely popular code with teen-age girls, particularly with the teen-agers who are high school juniors and seniors.

Finally, one should note that, in my own study and in the Kinsey study, religion was another key factor affecting girls' sexual beliefs and behaviors. Those girls who were devout in their religion were much more conservative in their sexual behavior and belief. Religion was not as strong a factor for boys and did not control their behavior as much. As we shall see, amount of education was the key determinant for male sexual behavior.

Boys' Sexual Codes

Among the teen-age boys, we find a quite different code dominant. Abstinence is given some form of lip service, particularly among the more highly educated classes, but, by and large, it is not an operational code; it is not adhered to in the behavior of the majority of the teen-age boys. Even among the males destined for college, about half have coitus in their teens; among those who stop their education in high school, about three-quarters have coitus in their teens, and, among those whose education stops before high school, about eight-tenths have coitus in their teens. Thus, it is clear that the majority of all males, in this sample of Kinsey's, at least, experienced full sexual relations before reaching twenty years of age.[9]

---

[8] This investigation is supported by a Public Health Service research grant (M-4045) from the National Institute of Mental Health, Public Health Service.

[9] Alfred C. Kinsey, *Sexual Behavior in the Human Male* (Philadelphia, 1948), p. 550.

For teen-age girls, the rate of nonvirginity appears to be considerably lower. Kinsey reports approximately 20 per cent nonvirginity for females by age twenty. Of course, the greater liberality of the boys does not involve a single standard; that is, they are predominantly adherents of the double standard which allows boys to have coitus but condemns girls for the same thing. This is an ancient standard reaching back many thousands of years in Western culture. It is by no means a universal standard, however, for we do find many cultures where the sexes are treated equally.[10]

Although in recent generations, due to our greater equalitarianism and the evolving nature of the dating institution, the double standard seems to have been weakened sharply, it is still quite dominant among teen-age boys. The greater freedom allowed the male child in almost all areas of life constantly buttresses this standard and makes it seem obvious to teen-agers. Teen-agers are not sufficiently objective or sophisticated to be bothered by the contradictions in this or any other sexual code. For example, if all women abided fully by the double standard, then no men could, for the men would have no partners! Thus, this code operates only to the extent that someone violates it.

Some of these double standard teen-age boys will condemn a girl who accepts petting-with-affection, for they believe heavy petting is improper for girls. However, my own data indicate that most of these teen-age males will accept heavy petting in a going-steady relationship. They, of course, allow themselves to go further and may try to have coitus with a steady in order to see if she is a "good" girl. It is not unusual to find a relationship either broken up or its affectionate nature altered if a girl gives in to her double standard steady. Such condemnatory behavior on the part of double standard males keeps many girls from going as far sexually as they might want to. Thus, the double standard male eliminates many potential sex partners because of the attitude he takes toward such sex partners.

Teen-age double standard males are often stricter than their older brothers who accept coitus for a girl when she is in love and/or engaged. These teen-age males are supported in this rigidity by the conformity of their peer group. Double standard males typically view the act of coitus as a conquest, as a source of peer group prestige. Thus, they are quite prone to tell their friends all of the details of any affair. This characteristic tends further to discourage females from yielding to double standard males. Instead, the girl is encouraged to be, in part at

---

[10] For a full discussion of this standard, its historical sources and reasons for being, see Ira L. Reiss, *Premarital Sexual Standards in America* (Glencoe, Ill., 1960), Chap. 4.

least, a tease, that is, to show just enough sexual activity to keep the male interested but not enough to arouse his condemnation. Sexual behavior in this sense involves a great deal of the aspect of a game. Sex comes to be used as a power leverage to control the relationship. Under such circumstances, sexual desire is developed so sharply in the male and so differently in the female that the male wants the female to be both sexually active and sexually pure. Under such conditions, sexual behavior can only with great difficulty relate directly to feelings of affection.[11] This is particularly true for the act of coitus. In fact, one finds very often an inverse relation, in that boys prefer to have coitus with girls they do not care for, because they regard the girls they do care for as "too good" for such behavior. Girls, too, may control their sexual reactions, particularly with someone they care for, until they are sure they will not be condemned for their sexual response.

Thus, in the area of coitus among teen-agers, the double standard does seem to block the association of sex and affection. However, one should quickly add that, on the level of petting, sex and affection can more easily be combined, for this behavior is much more likely to be accepted for both sexes by both males and females.

Minor Standards

There are minor teen-age standards which are more permissive than petting-with-affection or the double standard. For the older teen-ager, the most popular minor standard is what I shall call permissiveness-with-affection.[12] This standard accepts full sexual intercourse for both boys and girls, provided they are involved in a stable, affectionate relationship. The degree of stability and affection required varies among adherents from feeling strong affection to being in love and engaged. Some teen-age couples who are going steady have coitus in accord with this standard. The situation here is quite different from that of the double standard boy and his girl friend, for, in permissiveness-with-affection, both the boy and girl accept for each other what they are doing. They combine sex with affection and use affection as one of the key justifications of the sexual act.

There is a class difference in sexual standards among boys. My evidence indicates that the lower classes are more likely to be strong sup-

---

[11] Lester Kirkendall has conducted extensive research on the nature of the interaction process in sexual relations, and his evidence to date seems to support my position here. He will soon publish a book on this topic.

[12] Ira L. Reiss, *op. cit.*, Chap. 6, for a full discussion of this standard.

porters of the double standard, while the upper classes, though still mostly double standard, contain a large proportion of boys who are not so dogmatic in their beliefs and a minority who accept permissiveness-with-affection. In general, the upper classes seem to stress equality of the sexes and the importance of affection more than the lower classes. A permissiveness-without-affection code seems more widespread at the lower levels.

Age is a crucial factor among teen-agers. Teen-agers under sixteen are much more likely to accept only kissing than are older teen-agers, who may accept petting or coitus. As noted earlier, religion does not restrict sexual behavior as much among boys as it does among girls. Education is a more important factor, with the more highly educated groups being the most conservative.

Promiscuity

The newspapers from time to time pick up stories of high school "sex clubs" and other forms of promiscuous teen-age sexual behavior.[13] The available evidence indicates that promiscuous coitus is common predominantly for double standard males and a few females. Promiscuous coitus is not common on an equalitarian basis, that is, where both male and female accept the behavior as right for each other. Our culture has stressed the association of sex-with-affection to such an extent that it is difficult, at least for many females, to violate this association in coitus. In the case of petting, one finds more likelihood of violation of this norm by both men and women, but, in the case of coitus, it is much more often violated by males. Ehrmann's study of 1,000 college students supports this difference between male and female sexual activity and attitudes.[14] Females, in addition to associating love with sexual behavior more than males, also have more nonsexual motives for sexual behavior, such as the desire to please the boy or to cement a relationship.[15]

During the teens, the sexual outlets of boys and girls differ considerably. The chief outlet for girls seems to be masturbation and petting, whereas for boys the chief outlets include coitus at the fore. In Kinsey's sample, about one third of the girls masturbated to orgasm in their

---

[13] For a book containing many of these "stories," see Shailer U. Lawton, M.D., and Jules Archer, *Sexual Conduct of the Teen-Ager* (New York, 1951).

[14] Ehrmann, *op. cit.*, pp. 263–266.

[15] Lester A. Kirkendall and A. E. Gravatt, "Teen-Agers' Sex Attitudes and Behavior," in Evelyn M. and Sylvanus M. Duvall (eds.), *Sexways in Fact and Faith* (New York, 1961), pp. 115–129.

teens, while over 90 per cent of the boys have so masturbated in their teens.[16] Despite their high rate of masturbation, males also have a high rate of coitus. The lower class boys rely less on masturbation and petting and more on coitus for their sexual outlets than do those boys who go to college.

The teen-age girl today is still typically the much more conservative partner and the guardian of sexual limits. However, she appears increasingly to be a half-willing guardian who more and more seeks her self-satisfaction and strives to achieve sexual equality.[17]

There is a general trend in American society toward more equalitarian and more permissive sexual codes in all areas.[18] This is true for teen-age sexual codes, too. The growth within abstinence of petting-with-affection is one sign of this increasing equalitarian and permissive force. Also, within the double standard, one finds increased willingness by males to accept some coitus on the part of females, especially if it occurs when the girl is in love and/or engaged. Finally, in the minor standard of permissiveness-with-affection, one sees this trend in the increased strength of this standard among teen-agers, particularly among older, college teen-agers. And these trends toward equalitarianism and permissiveness seem even stronger among older dating couples in their twenties. The teen-agers are relatively new at sexual behavior, and they, at first, grab the basic outlines of the older couples' codes. With the passage of time, they come to behave in a somewhat more equalitarian and permissive manner.

In my current research, there is evidence that the real change-over in a teen-ager's sexual code is more one of integrating attitudes and changing overt behavior than of changing basic attitudes. In short, it seems that a person holds his basic sexual attitudes in rudimentary form in his teens, but he is not fully ready to act upon them and has not fully learned how to combine these values into a coherent code of living. As he learns to do this, his behavior changes and so does his awareness of his beliefs and their unity, but his basic beliefs may well remain the same. This entire area of how our sexual beliefs are formed and how they change is in need of more careful study. My own research is aimed at probing some aspects of this problem.

---

[16] Kinsey, *Sexual Behavior . . . Female, op. cit.,* p. 173. See also William R. Reevy, "Adolescent Sexuality," in A. Ellis and A. Abarbanel, *The Encyclopedia of Sexual Behavior* (New York, 1961), pp. 52–67.

[17] For an interesting article discussing shifts in male and female attitudes, see J. P. McKee and A. C. Sherriffs, "Men's and Women's Beliefs, Ideals and Self Concepts," in Jerome M. Seidman (ed.), *The Adolescent* (New York, 1960), pp. 282–294.

[18] One of the major efforts of my book is to demonstrate the evidence for this trend. See Ira L. Reiss, *op. cit.,* Chap. 10.

Parents are prone to be most aware of what they consider excessive sexual behavior, for they are concerned about the consequences of such behavior as they may affect their children. Thus, parents complain about sexual acts of which they become aware, and they often believe teen-agers are sexually promiscuous. Actually, according to our best estimates, the real increases in teen-age sexual behavior over the last generation are not in the area of sexual intercourse but rather in the area of petting and in the public nature of some petting behavior.[19] Thus, these parents of today have probably had similar rates of coitus but perhaps lower rates of petting. In addition, one should note that the petting behavior today very often is not promiscuous but occurs in a stable affectionate relationship.

Youth Culture: Tame or Wild?

About twenty years ago, Kingsley Davis and Talcott Parsons wrote of a youth culture and of a parent-youth conflict and, in doing so, implied in part that youth culture was largely irresponsible, impulsive, and anti-adult.[20] Many people have come to share this view and to expect rather extreme sexual behavior from teen-agers. I myself formerly accepted this view of the teen-ager as valid. However, after examining the evidence in the key areas of teen-age sexual behavior, I must admit that I can no longer accept such a conception of youth culture without serious modification and qualification. I would submit that the vast majority of our approximately twenty million teen-agers are not only not extreme but are quite conservative and restrained in the area of premarital sexual codes and behavior when we compare them to their older brothers and sisters.

There is evidence to show that teen-agers are unsure of how far to go sexually, that they feel ill at ease on dates, and that they are concerned with such "tame" issues as whether one should kiss good night on a first date.[21] A recent study showed that teen-agers rate themselves lower in comparison to adults than adults rate them. Teen-agers in this study rated adults considerably higher than themselves on most all "good"

---

[19] Kinsey, *Sexual Behavior . . . Female, op. cit.,* pp. 275, 339 *passim.*

[20] Kingsley Davis, "The Sociology of Parent-Youth Conflict," *American Sociological Review,* Vol. 5 (October 1940), pp. 523–535; Talcott Parsons, "Age and Sex in the Social Structure of the United States," *American Sociological Review,* Vol. 7 (December 1942), pp. 604–616.

[21] H. H. Remmers and D. H. Radley, *The American Teen-Ager* (Indianapolis, 1957), pp. 83, 225–236.

qualities.[22] These are hardly the attitudes of an arrogant or antiadult youth. They seem more those of a group desirous of becoming like adults and striving toward that goal.

Further, when we look at the rates of female petting to orgasm in the Kinsey studies, we find considerably more of this behavior among girls in their twenties than among girls in their teens. The coitus rate for females doubles between the ages of twenty and twenty-five. Masturbation rates also increase considerably after the teens.[23] In all these ways, the teen-agers seem more conservative than those individuals who are in their twenties.

August Hollingshead's excellent study of a midwest community also gives evidence on the conservatism of youth. He found a very close correspondence between social class of parents and social class of teen-agers' dating partners. In this study, too, we are given a picture of youth culture that is very much like adult culture in its status consciousness. Hollingshead and others have also noted the fact that a large proportion of the teen-age population is virtually not involved in any dating. A good estimate for the high school age group would be that about one third of the boys and one fifth of the girls are not involved in dating.[24]

Venereal Disease and Pregnancy

Let us now examine two key indices, venereal disease and pregnancy, which should give us additional insights into the behavior of teen-agers. Teen-agers do have significant rates of venereal disease and illegitimacy. However, the press has largely exaggerated such rates. The teen-age rate of venereal disease for ages fifteen to nineteen is only about a third of the rate for the twenty to twenty-four age group and is also lower than that of the twenty-five to twenty-nine age group.[25]

There has been a slight rise in the number of teen-age venereal disease cases in recent years, and this has received much publicity. It is quite likely that the actual rates for teen-agers are not higher and that this slight increase is due to the greater number of teen-agers today.

[22] R. D. Hess and I. Goldblatt, "The Status of Adolescents in American Society," in Seidman, *op. cit.*, pp. 321–333.

[23] Kinsey, *Sexual Behavior . . . Female, op. cit.*, Chaps. 5, 7, 8.

[24] August B. Hollingshead, *Elmtown's Youth* (New York, 1949), p. 227. See also Maxine Davis, *Sex and the Adolescent* (New York, 1960), p. 136.

[25] T. Lefoy Richman, *Venereal Disease: Old Plague—New Challenge* (Public Affairs Pamphlet No. 292; New York, 1960), p. 7. For more technical data, see T. Lefoy Richman (ed.), *Today's Venereal Disease Control Problem* (New York: American Social Health Association, 1961), especially pp. 36–43.

More than 80 per cent of the venereal disease reported is from older groups of people. Finally, the rate of venereal disease among teen-agers is not evenly distributed in the teen-age group. As far as we can tell from reported cases, it is highly concentrated in the lower social classes.[26]

When one examines the national figures for unwed mothers, one finds that 40 per cent are teen-agers. Here, too, several qualifications are needed. First, most of these reported cases are Negro, and class status in general is low. The upper classes, according to Paul Gebhard's recent study, are much more willing to resort to abortion.[27] The upper classes, also, have a greater ability to stay out of public statistics and may, thus, show lower rates. According to Clark Vincent's study, when upper class females become pregnant before marriage, it is more likely to be the result of a love affair, whereas, when lower class females become pregnant, it is more likely to be a result of a casual affair.[28] Thus, there are important class differences here, too.

When we compare teen-age unwed motherhood with that for girls in their twenties, we find that the older girls have about the same proportion of the illegitimate children. We also find that the teen-age rates are not increasing as much as the rates for older groups. For example, in 1940 teen-age mothers were 46 per cent of the total; in 1957 they were 40 per cent.

Thus, from the evidence of national figures, it seems reasonable to conclude that it is a small and specific segment of the teen-age population that becomes involved with venereal disease or premarital pregnancy. Furthermore, the people in their twenties seem somewhat more likely to be involved in such circumstances. Also, these older couples are much more involved in adult culture in terms of their occupations and their nearness to marriage, and yet their sexual behavior is less conservative.

A warning must be added at this point concerning the venereal disease rates and unwed motherhood rates. They are far from perfect indices and, as mentioned, many higher class people manage to be excluded from them because they can afford more private means of coping with their problems. However, to the extent that we use these rates, we fail to find support for the charges made about teen-agers. It is no doubt true

[26] Richman, *Venereal Disease . . . , op. cit.,* pp. 6, 20.

[27] Paul H. Gebhard and Others, *Pregnancy, Birth, and Abortion* (New York, 1958), pp. 45, 160.

[28] Clark E. Vincent, "Illegitimacy in the United States," in Duvall (eds.), *op. cit.,* p. 143.

that teen-agers are irresponsible in the sense that they seek "to have a good time," but I would suggest that, in the area of sexual codes and behavior, the evidence shows more conservatism and responsibility than one might otherwise suspect. It may be well to avoid the over-all impressions given by a general use of the term "youth culture" as described by Parsons. Here, as elsewhere, qualification and specific research is a step toward better theoretical formulation and better understanding.

A Final Overview

What has occurred in teen-age sexual codes in recent generations is a working out of sexual practices acceptable to teen-agers. Many of these practices are at the level of petting. In short, as unchaperoned dating came into vogue and as adolescence became more prolonged due to our specialized industrial culture, young people worked out additional sexual codes to supplement and modify the older codes of abstinence and the double standard. There always were people who engaged in coitus; today there are more, but, for girls in their teens, it is still a minor activity. When we look at petting, we note something different, for here we see a much more continuous and current change among teen-agers—it is here in this middle ground that teen-agers have come to accept a petting-with-affection standard. The equalitarian and permissive aspects of this standard in many cases lead at later ages to acceptance of the more radical permissiveness-with-affection standard. However, during the teens, petting-with-affection is probably the major standard involved in stable affectionate relationships at middle and upper class levels.

At the present time, it is impossible to predict precise changes in sexual codes. This is especially true because, as we have seen, there are differences according to social class, religion, educational level, and so forth. But one can say that all the signs indicate a continued trend toward equalitarian and permissive codes. The trend seems to be toward that which now obtains in the Scandinavian countries, with the inclusion of sex education in the schools and with permissive attitudes on the formal as well as covert levels. This does not forebode the end of the double standard, for the double standard is still deeply rooted in our male dominant culture, but it does mean a continued weakening of the double standard and more qualifications of its mandates.

Teen-agers are a paradoxical group. They are not as wild as their parents or they themselves sometimes think. Teen-agers do want independence. But, judging by their sexual codes, they want independence from their parents, not from the total adult culture.

4. PARENT-CHILD CONFLICT IN SEXUAL VALUES *

Robert R. Bell

The old cliché that as one grows older he becomes more conservative may be true, if premarital sexual values held by parents are compared with the values they held when they were younger. In this paper, the interest is in the nature of sex value conflict between parents and their unmarried late adolescent and young adult children. Our discussion will focus on values held by parents and by their unmarried children toward premarital sexual intimacy.

Conceptually, our approach focuses upon values related to a specific area of sexual behavior held by individuals from two very different role perspectives. The perspectives differ because parents and children are always at different stages in the life cycle, and while parents are highly significant in the socialization of their children, other social forces increasingly come to influence the child as he grows older. The various social values that influence the child's sexual behavior are often complementary, but they may also be contradictory. Furthermore, various types of influences on the acceptance of a given set of values may operate on the child only during a given age period. For example, the youngster at age fifteen may be influenced by his age peers to a much greater extent than he will be at age twenty.

Given their different stages in the life cycle, parents and children will almost always show differences in how they define appropriate behavior for a given role. Values as to "proper" premarital sexual role behavior from the perspective of the parents are greatly influenced by the strong emotional involvement of the parent with his child. Youth, on the other hand, are going through a life cycle stage in which the actual behavior occurs, and they must relate the parent values to what they are doing or may do. There is a significant difference between defining appropriate role conduct for others to follow and defining proper role conduct to be followed by oneself. Even more important for actual behavior, there is often more than one significant group of role definers to which the young person can turn to as guides for his sex role behavior. Therefore,

* *Journal of Social Issues*, 1966, 22(2), 34–44. Reprinted with permission of the Society for the Psychological Study of Social Issues.

our discussion will focus more specifically on parent values related to premarital sexual intimacy, the peer group values of youth, and how these two different age groups, as role definers, influence the sexual values and behavior of unmarried youth.

Limits of Discussion. For several reasons, our discussion will center primarily on the middle class. First, this class level has been highly significant in influencing changes in general sexual values and behavior. Second, and on a more pragmatic level, what little research has been done on parent-child conflict over sexual values has been done with middle-class groups. Third, the general values of the middle class are coming to include an increasing proportion of the American population. This also suggests that the values and behavior of college youth are of increasing importance as this group continues to expand in size and influence within the middle class.

A further limit is that our main focus is on the generational conflict between mother and daughter. The history of change in sexual values in the United States has been complexly interwoven with the attainment of greater sex equality and freedom by the female (2). Also, the relationship between the mother and daughter tends to be the closest of the possible parent-child relationships in the family socializing of the child to future adult sex roles. Furthermore, whatever the value system verbalized and/or applied by the girl, she often has more to gain or lose personally than the boy by whatever premarital sexual decisions she makes.

We also believe that any analysis of conflict over premarital sex between generations should center on *value* changes rather than *behavioral* changes. On the basis of available evidence, it appears that there have been no significant changes in the *frequency* of premarital sexual petting or coitus since the 1920's. Kinsey has pointed out that "there has been little recognition that the premarital petting and coital patterns which were established then (1920's) are still with us" (15, p. 300). Therefore, it is important to recognize that the parents and even some of the grandparents of today were the youth who introduced the new patterns of premarital sexual behavior about forty years ago.

Parent Values about Premarital Sex

The transmission of sexual values by parents to their children is only a small part of all parent values passed on during the family socialization process. Most parents do a more deliberate and comprehensive job of transmitting values to their children in such areas as educational attainment, career choice, religious beliefs, and so forth than they do with reference to any aspect of sexual values. Often when parents do discuss sex with their children it may be from a "clinical, physiological" perspective with overtones of parental embarrassment and a desire to get a distasteful task over with.

But perhaps more important than the formal confrontation between the parent and child in sexual matters are the informal values transmitted by the parent. In the past girls were often taught that premarital sexual deviancy was dirty and shameful, and that nonconformity to premarital sexual chastity values would mean suffering great personal and social shame. This highly negative view of premarital sex is undoubtedly less common today, but the newer, more "positive" values may also have some negative consequences. Very often today the mother continues to place great value on the daughter's virginity, and stresses to the daughter the great virtues of maintaining her virginity until marriage. But the "romantic" view of the rewards for the girl who waits for coitus until after marriage are often highly unrealistic and may sometimes create problems by leading the girl to expectations that cannot be realistically met in marital sex. Morton Hunt writes with regard to this approach that "if the woman has been assured that she will, that she ought, and she *must* see colored lights, feel like a breaking wave, or helplessly utter inarticulate cries, she is apt to consider herself or her husband at fault when these promised wonders do not appear" (13, 114). Whether or not the "romantic" view of marital sex is presented by her mother the girl often encounters it in the "approved" reading list suggested by the adult world, which tells her about the positive delights of waiting for sex until after marriage. So, though premarital sexual control may be "positive" in that it is based on rewards for waiting, it can be "negative" if the rewards are unrealistic and unobtainable.

For many parents, a major problem as their child moves through adolescence and into early adult years centers around how much independence to allow the child. Because they often recall the child's younger dependency, it may be difficult to assess the independency of the same child who is now older. Also, over the years the growing child has increasingly become involved with reference groups outside—and sometimes competing with—the family. In other words, the self-role definitions by the child and the parents' definitions of the child's role undergo constant change as the child grows older. For example, "The daughter in her younger years has her role as daughter defined to a great degree by her mother. But as she grows older she is influenced by other definitions which she internalizes and applies to herself in her movement toward self-determination. The mother frequently continues to visualize the daughter's role as it was defined in the past and also attaches the same importance to her function as mother in defining her daughter's role. But given the rapid social change associated with family roles the definer, as well as the definitions, may no longer be institutionally appropriate" (5,388).

Parents may also be biased in their definitions of their child as less mature than they, the parents, were when they were the child's age. One can not recall experiences earlier in the life cycle free from influence by the events that have occurred since. This may result in many parents' thinking of their younger selves as being more mature than they actually were. At the same time the parents' view of their child's degree of maturity may be biased by their recall of him when he was younger and less mature. Thus, from the parents' perspective they may recall themselves as youngsters within the context of what has occurred since (more mature) and may see their offspring within the context of their earlier childhood (less mature).

There also may be some symbolic significance for parents who must define their children as having reached the age when something as "adult" as sexual behavior is of relevance. In part, viewing one's children as too young for sexual involvement may contribute to the parents' feeling young, while seeing their children as old enough to be involved in sexual activity may lead to some parents feeling forced to view themselves as aging. For example, the comment about a man seen out with a young woman that "she is young enough to be his daughter" may have implications for his self-role image if the young woman *is* his daughter. We have little research data on how the aging process of parents influences their definitions of appropriate behavior for their young adult children.

In general, it is probable that most parents assume that their children, especially their daughters, accept the traditional restrictive values about premarital sexual behavior unless they are forced to do otherwise. Also, because of the great emotional involvement of parents with their own children, there is a common parental tendency to attribute sexual "immorality" to other youngsters. For many parents to face the possibility that their children do not conform to their values is to suggest some failure on the part of the parents. Often, rather than admit failure, the parents may define their children as having been forced to reject the parent values by other social influences or that their children have willfully let them down.

Youth Views about Premarital Sex

The importance of age peer group influence on the values and behavior of young people has been shown by a number of social scientists (see: 6,

9, 10, 11, 12, 14, 19, 20, 21, 22). Because youth subcultures are to some degree self-developing, they often have conflict points in relation to some dominant adult values. However, the inconsistency and lack of effective adult definitions for adolescent behavior have also contributed to the emergence of youth subcultural values. That adults often view the adolescent with indecision as to appropriate behavior means that sometimes given adolescent behavior is treated one way at one time and in a different way at another time. Since the young person desires some decisiveness and precision in his role definitions, he often develops his own role prescriptions. Often when he creates his own role expectations, he demands a high degree of conformity by other adolescents as "proof" of the rightness of his definitions. It is ironical that the adolescent often thinks of himself as a social deviant. What he fails to realize is that his adolescent group deviates from the adult world, but that the requirements for conformity within his youth subculture are very strong (1, 369–74).

Youth subcultures have developed great influence over many aspects of premarital male-female interaction. The patterns of dating and courtship, appropriate behavior, success and failure are for the most part patterns defined by the youth group and not by the adult world. Yet, heterosexual relationships of youth are often based on adult role patterns, and they are therefore an important part of the youth world because they are seen by the youth as symbolizing adult status. To many young people, who are no longer defined by the adult world as children, but are not yet given full status as adults, their involvement in what they see as adult roles is important to them in seeking for adult status and recognition.

A part of the American youth subculture has been the development of new values related to premarital sexual intimacy. Reiss suggests that "It might well be that, since the 1920's, what has been occurring is a change in attitudes to match the change in behavior of that era" [premarital sexual behavior] (16, 233). The evidence suggests that for at least some college students new sex norms are emerging at the various stages of dating and courtship. One study found that "on the dating level necking is the norm for females and petting for males. During going steady and engagement, petting seems to be acceptable for both sexes. This would suggest that the young people both act and accept a higher level of intimacy than has generally been suggested by courtship norms" (3, 63).

In the past, emphasis was placed on the girl's virginity at the time of marriage; but today, many young people may only emphasize her being a virgin until she is in love, which may mean at the stage of going steady or engagement (8, Ch. 5 and 16, Ch. 6). If the girl is in love, some premarital sexual relations may be acceptable by peer group standards, although the dominant adult values—that love *and* marriage are basic prerequisites for coitus—continue. In the United States love as a prerequisite for sexual relations has long been a necessary condition for most middle-class females. The condition has not changed; rather, the point in the courtship-marriage process where it may be applied to sexual involvement has shifted. Hence, the major point of parent-child conflict over premarital sex centers around the parent value that one should be in love *and* married before entering coitus and the modified value system of youth that an emotional and interpersonal commitment is important, but that this may occur before marriage.

There are two recent studies that provide some evidence on the nature of generational conflict; one study is of youth and adults in general and the other study is specifically concerned with mothers and their daughters. Reiss, in his extensive study of premarital sexual permissiveness, provides data on values held by adults as contrasted with values in a sample of high school and college students. The respondents were asked to express their beliefs about different combinations of intimacy and degree of interpersonal commitment for both unmarried males and females. Respondents were asked if they believed petting to be acceptable when the male or female is engaged. In the adult sample the belief that petting during engagement was acceptable for the engaged male was the response of 61 per cent, and for the engaged female the response was 56 per cent. Of the student responses 85 per cent approved for the engaged male and 82 per cent for the engaged female (17, 190–91); thus adult attitudes about petting during engagement were more conservative than those of the student population. It may also be noted that for both the adult and student groups there was a single standard—that is, the acceptance rates were essentially the same for both males and females.

Reiss also asked his respondents if they believed full sexual relations to be acceptable if the male or female were engaged. Approval was the response given by 20 per cent of the adult group for males and 17 per cent for females. In the student group acceptance was given by 52 per cent for the male and 44 per cent for the female (17, 190–91). Here, as with petting, there are significant differences between the adult and the student samples, and once again both respondent groups suggest a single standard of acceptance or rejection for both males and females.

A study by Bell and Buerkle compared the attitudes of 217 coeds with those of their mothers. Both mothers and daughters were asked to respond to the question, "How important do you think it is that a girl be a virgin when she marries?" Of the mothers, 88 per cent answered "very important", 12 per cent "generally important", and 0 per cent "not important"; compared to 55 per cent, 34 per cent and 13 per cent of the daughters (4, 391). Both the mothers and daughters were also asked:

"Do you think sexual intercourse during engagement is: very wrong; generally wrong; right in many situations?" The percentages for each response category were 83 per cent, 15 per cent and 2 per cent for the mothers; and 35 per cent, 48 per cent, and 17 per cent for the daughters (4, 391).

Both of the above questions show sharp differences between the value responses of the mothers and daughters with reference to premarital chastity. Many mothers were undoubtedly influenced in their responses by having a daughter in the age setting where the questions had an immediate and highly emotional application. Nevertheless, the differences in mother and daughter responses indicate that the area of premarital sexual behavior is one of potentially great conflict. One means of minimizing conflict is for the daughter not to discuss her sexual values or behavior with her mother. In the Bell and Buerkle study it was found that only 37 per cent of the daughters, in contrast with 83 per cent of the mothers, felt daughters should freely answer questions from their mothers in regard to attitudes toward sexual intimacy (4, 392).

The area of sexual values appears to be highly influenced by emotion, especially for the mother with reference to her daughter. Generational conflict with regard to premarital sexual intimacy has a variety of implications. First, the conflict in values clearly suggests that the traditional morality is often not socially effective as a meaningful determinant of behavior. Social values have behavioral influence when they emerge as social norms with significant rewards and punishments. In the case of sexual norms, however, there are rarely clearly articulated rewards, or positive consequences, for the conforming individual. In almost all situations the effectiveness of sexual norms is dependent upon their negative sanctions, or punishments. For example, the traditional norm of female premarital chastity bases its behavioral influence primarily on negative consequences for the girl who fails to conform. This negative means of control is most commonly found as a part of the adult value system. In effect, the major sanctions over premarital chastity are based upon punishments for the girl and for her family if she deviates. Yet, in most cases the girl who has premarital coitus is not discovered by her parents or by the community. The real danger for the girl often centers around premarital pregnancy, because if that occurs and becomes known there can be no denying premarital coitus. Vincent has suggested that an important part of the negative sanction toward premarital pregnancy is not the pregnancy itself, but rather that it symbolizes premarital coitus *and* getting caught (23, Ch. 1).

The available studies indicate that fear of pregnancy is not the major deterrent for most girls (7, 344 and 15, 315). The personal values of the girl appear far more important in restricting her from engaging in premarital coitus. Yet, within the privacy of the youth world, there may operate for some girls certain values positive toward premarital coitus. For example, there may be a strong emotional desire and commitment to the boy and a positive feeling by the girl of wanting to engage in greater sexual intimacy.

There is a tendency by parents, as well as by many who give professional advice, to overlook the pleasurable aspects of sex at all ages, especially for the young who are experiencing sexual pleasure for the first time. Undoubtedly many girls engage in premarital sexual intimacy to "compensate" for some need and many may suffer some negative consequences. But it is foolish to state categorically that the "artificial" setting of premarital sex always makes it negative and unpleasant for the girl. We would be much more honest if we recognized that for many girls premarital coitus is enjoyable and the participants suffer no negative consequences. This was illustrated in the Kinsey research; it was found that "69 per cent of the still unmarried females in the sample who had had premarital coitus insisted they did not regret their experiences. Another 13 per cent recorded some minor regrets" (15, 316). Kinsey also found that "77 per cent of the married females, looking back from the vantage point of their more mature experience, saw no reason to regret their premarital coitus" (15, 316).

The Extent of Generational Conflict

With the evidence suggesting strong conflict between generations with regard to premarital sexual values, our final consideration is: how permanent is this generational conflict? We can provide some evidence on this question by examining the values of college-educated females of different ages. This appears justified because higher educated females are generally the most liberal in their views about sexual rights and expectations for women.

The evidence suggests that the premarital sexual liberalism of the college girl may be a temporary phenomenon. The coed's sexual liberalism must be seen as related to the interactional context of her being emotionally involved, and to a future commitment to an on-going paired relationship. The Bell and Buerkle study (4) found that the values of daughters toward the importance of premarital virginity were very similar to those of their mothers, until they had spent some time in college. However, at "around age 20 there emerge sharp differences between mothers and daughters in regard to premarital sexual attitudes. Behavioral studies indicate that it is at this point that sexual activity is greatly intensified, perhaps because it is at this age that college girls are entering engagement. A suggested pattern is that the college girl of 20 or 21 years of age, in her junior or senior year and engaged, has a strong 'liberal' pattern toward premarital sexual behavior and attitudes" (4, 392 and 18, 696).

We can get some indication of the persistence of premarital sexual liberalism by comparing the values of mothers by education. In the mothers' views as to the importance of premarital virginity it was found that the college educated mothers were actually as "conservative" as those mothers with lower levels of education (4, 392). It is quite possible that in the future the coeds will become as conservative as the college educated mothers. This may occur when the coed's attitudinal rationales are not related to herself, but as a mother to her own daughter. It is therefore possible that the "sexual emancipation" of the college girl exists only for a short period of time, centering mainly around the engagement years.

Yet, even if the girl becomes more conservative as she grows older, and especially with reference to her own daughter, her temporary "liberalism" probably is contributing to some shift in adult values about premarital sexual intimacy. Certainly, today's parental generation accepts greater sexual intimacy as a part of the premarital heterosexual relationship. Probably most parents assume that their adolescent and young adult children are engaging in necking and even some petting. Most parents, as long as they don't actually see the sexual intimacy, don't concern themselves about it. However, to suggest that parents may be more liberal (or tolerant) of premarital sexual intimacy does not necessarily suggest that parents are liberal if the intimacy reaches coitus.

It also appears that there has been some reduction in the severity of negative sanctions by parents if the daughter deviates and is caught. Among middle-class parents today it may be less common to reject the unwed daughter if she becomes pregnant than in the past, and more common for the parents to help her. This is not to suggest that today's parents offer any positive sanctions for premarital pregnancy, but that they may be able to adapt (often painfully) to it, rather than respond with high rejection and anger.

If our suggestion is correct (that parents take a less totally negative view of "discovered" premarital coitus), then this further suggests that traditional sexual values are being altered, since, as we have suggested, in the past the values of premarital chastity were primarily based on the negative consequences for those who deviated and were caught. If these negative consequences have been reduced, then the social force of the traditional values has been reduced as a means utilized by parents to control premarital sexual deviancy.

Conclusions

Based on the available evidence, there are several general speculations that may be made about future generational conflict over premarital sex. In general we would suggest that conflict between parents and their adolescent-young adult children with regard to premarital sexual intimacy may decrease in the future, because of several trends.

1. The trend in the United States is toward a more liberal view of sexual behavior in general. This is reflected in the generally accepted professional opinion that the woman has a right to sexual satisfaction, and that sexual satisfaction is a desirable end in itself. The trend toward a belief in a single sexual standard for both men and women, even though within the setting of marriage, is bound to influence the beliefs and behavior of the unmarried. For the unmarried, there may be an increasing tendency to attach less importance to the marriage act as the arbitrary dividing line between socially approved and socially disapproved sexual intimacy.

2. Since the evidence suggests that over the past three or four generations the rates of female premarital coital experience have not changed, and since the younger generation has developed some value frameworks for its behavior, modification of traditional values and behavior may increasingly influence the values of parents to be more liberal. That is, it may become increasingly difficult for many parents to hold their children to a set of conservative values which they, the parents, did not hold to when they were younger.

3. Parents seem increasingly unwilling to strongly punish their daughters who sexually deviate and are caught. This parental reduction of punishment may be influenced by the increasing public attention directed at such social problems as illegal abortion. For example, many parents may be more willing to accept and help an unmarried pregnant daughter than take the risk of her seeking out an illegal abortion. The possible negative consequences of abortion may appear more undesirable than the premarital pregnancy.

4. Less generational conflict will occur if parents know less about the sexual activities of their children. A great part of the social activity of young people is carried out in the privacy of their age peer setting; what they do in the way of sexual intimacy is increasingly less apt to be noted by their parents. With the development and marketing of oral contraceptives, the risks of premarital pregnancy will be greatly reduced. In the future the rates of premarital coitus may remain the same, but with the chances of pregnancy reduced parents may be less aware of their children's premarital coitus.

Over time, then, the values of parents and the adult community in general may become more liberal and the conflict between generations reduced. (There seems little possibility that the opposite will occur, i.e., the younger generation's reducing the conflict by becoming more conservative.) But in the meantime, and certainly in the near future, it appears that parents and their children will continue to live with somewhat different value systems with regard to premarital sexual values. Parents will probably continue to hold to traditional values, and assume that *their* child is conforming to those values unless his actions force them to see otherwise. The youth generation will probably continue to develop their own modified value systems and keep those values to themselves, and implicitly allow their parents to believe they are behaving according to the traditional values of premarital sexual morality. For many parents and their children, the conflict about premarital sex will continue to be characterized by the parent's playing ostrich and burying his head in the sand, and the youth's efforts to keep the sand from blowing away.

References

1. Bell, Robert R. *Marriage and family interaction.* Homewood, Ill.: The Dorsey Press, 1963.
2. Bell, Robert R. *Premarital sex in a changing society.* Englewood Cliffs, N.J.: Prentice-Hall (in press).
3. Bell, Robert R., and Blumberg, Leonard. Courtship stages and intimacy attitudes. *Family Life Coordinator,* 1960, 8, 60–63.
4. Bell, Robert R., and Buerkle, Jack V. Mother and Daughter Attitudes to Premarital Sexual Behavior. *Marriage and Family Living,* 1961, 23, 390–392.
5. Bell, Robert R., and Buerkle, Jack V. Mother-daughter conflict during the "launching stage." *Marriage and Family Living,* 1962, 24, 384–388.
6. Bernard, Jessie (Ed.). Teen-age culture. *Annals of the American Academy of Political and Social Science,* November 1961, 338.
7. Burgess, Ernest, and Wallin, Paul. *Engagement and marriage.* Chicago: Lippincott, 1953.
8. Ehrmann, Winston. *Premarital dating behavior.* New York: Holt, Rinehart and Winston, 1959.
9. Ginsberg, Eli. *Values and ideals of American youth.* New York: Columbia University Press, 1962.
10. Gottlieb, David, and Ramsey, Charles. *The American adolescent.* Homewood, Ill.: The Dorsey Press, 1964.

11. Grinder, Robert. *Studies in adolescence.* New York: Macmillan, 1963.
12. Hechinger, Grace and Fred. *Teen-age tyranny.* New York: Crest, 1962.
13. Hunt, Norton M. *The natural history of love.* New York: Knopf, 1959.
14. Kelley, Earl C. *In defense of youth.* Englewood Cliffs, N.J.: Prentice-Hall, 1962.
15. Kinsey, Alfred C., Pomeroy, Wardell B., Martin, Clyde E., and Gebhard, Paul H. *Sexual behavior in the human female.* Philadelphia: Saunders, 1953.
16. Reiss, Ira L. *Premarital sexual standards in America.* Glencoe, Ill.: Free Press, 1960.
17. Reiss, Ira L. The scaling of premarital sexual permissiveness. *Journal of Marriage and the Family,* 1964, *26,* 188–198.
18. Reiss, Ira L. Premarital sexual permissiveness among Negroes and whites. *American Sociological Review,* 1964, *29,* 688–698.
19. Remmers, H. H., and Radler, D. H. *The American teenager.* New York: Charter, 1957.
20. Seidman, Jerome. *The adolescent.* New York: Holt, Rinehart and Winston, 1960.
21. Smith, Ernest A. *American youth culture.* New York: Free Press, 1963.
22. Symonds, P. M. *From adolescent to adult.* New York: Columbia University Press, 1961.
23. Vincent, Clark. *Unmarried mothers.* Glencoe, Ill.: Free Press, 1961.

5. SEX DIFFERENCES IN THE INFANT-DIRECTED BEHAVIOR OF PREADOLESCENT RHESUS MONKEYS *

A. Chamove, H. F. Harlow, and G. Mitchell

From the reports of field studies, there is evidence that infant-directed behavior differs between the sexes both in adult and preadolescent primates (for the baboon, DeVore, 1963; for the macaque, Itani, 1959; for

* *Child Development,* 1967, *38,* 329–335. Copyright 1967, by the Society for Research in Child Development, Inc. This research was supported by USPHS grants MH-11894

the langur, Jay, 1963; and for the gorilla, Schaller, 1963). The greater interest of immature females than immature males in the newborn infant is evident at an age of 6 months or less in the chacma baboon (Bolwig, 1959). That these sex differences are not invariant is illustrated by reports of paternal behavior in the adult macaque (Itani, 1959).

Sex differences have been reported in preadolescent monkeys in the laboratory with respect to peer interaction (see Harlow & Harlow, 1965 [based on data by Hansen, 1962; Rosenblum, 1961]). However, there have been no comparisons of male and female juveniles with regard to infant-directed behavior in the laboratory. The present study was designed to measure sex differences in preadolescent-infant interactions. It was suspected that sex differences in infant-directed behavior would be present before the advent of the hormonal changes of puberty.

Method

SUBJECTS

One female infant rhesus monkey between the age of 20 and 40 days was used as a stimulus animal, and 30 preadolescent rhesus monkeys were used as Ss in this study. The 30 Ss were 15 male-female pairs (18–30 months). The pairs were matched for age, type of social rearing, and tester (E). All of the preadolescent pairs had prolonged social experience from birth. The type of social experience varied between, but not within, the matched pairs. Of the 15 pairs, 7 experienced only peer interaction; 4 received primarily maternal experience with little peer interaction; and 4 other pairs had both maternal and peer experience.

APPARATUS

The Ss were individually tested with the stimulus infant in a playpen apparatus modified from one described by Seay (1966) and illustrated in Figure 1. A center area, the combined playpen units of the original apparatus (see Harlow & Harlow, 1965, p. 297), for infant adaptation measured $60 \times 60 \times 60$ inches. The four living cages ($36 \times 36 \times 36$ inches) for the preadolescents housed two sets of adjacent pairs on opposite sides of the center area. The walls, floor, and roof of the center area and living cages were made of 0.120-inch steel wire mesh with 1-inch openings in

and FR-0167 from the National Institutes of Health to the University of Wisconsin Primate Laboratory and Regional Primate Research Center, respectively. Author Harlow's address: University of Wisconsin Primate Laboratory and Regional Primate Research Center, 1223 Capitol Court, Madison, Wisconsin 53706.

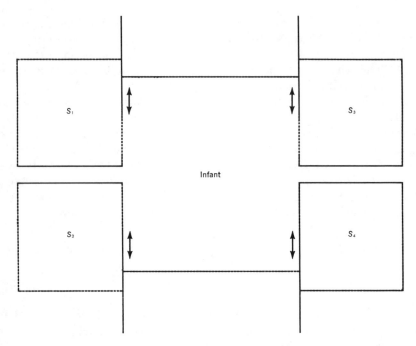

FIGURE 1   Test and adaptation apparatus.

the sides and tops and ¾-inch openings in the floors. A 36 × 36 inch sheet of Masonite prevented adjacent pairs of preadolescents from viewing one another and directed their attention toward the infant in the center during adaptation. Another 36 × 36 inch Masonite sheet was inserted between each preadolescent's living cage and the center area during individual testing.

PROCEDURE

The infant was housed in the center area throughout the experiment. The two monkeys of a matched pair were placed in adjacent living cages and allowed to see the infant for a 24-hour adaptation period. After adaptation, the second Masonite panel was inserted, and testing was begun. Two pairs of preadolescents were adapted and tested each day.

Before testing, the infant was transferred by hand to one of the living cages. As soon as the door was shut (a matter of 10–15 seconds), the E sat down, turned on a session timer and began recording behavior. Each session lasted 15 minutes. There were two Es, and both members of the same matched pair were tested by the same E; E_1 tested seven pairs and E_2 tested eight pairs.

The recording apparatus was a bank of nine clocks. Nine micro-switches activated these clocks each time they were depressed by the E. The clocks recorded durations of nine behaviors. One category measured infant-initiated contact; the other eight categories were infant-directed behaviors by the preadolescent and included: (a) ventral contact and/or embrace, (b) sexual behavior, (c) grooming and lipsmacking (maternal-related behaviors), (d) visual orientation, (e) fear or disturbance, (f) play, (g) hostility, and (h) all other physical contact with the infant. In addition, categories (a), (b), (c), (f), and (h) were combined to provide a measure of the total positive social behavior directed toward the infant.

The Wilcoxon matched-pairs, signed-ranks test (Siegel, 1956, p. 75) was applied to the matched-groups comparisons. A two-tailed test was used, and differences occurring with a probability of less than .05 were accepted as statistically significant. A Mann-Whitney U tested the E differences and a Kruskal-Wallis test examined differences between the three types of rearing.

Results

QUANTITATIVE RESULTS

Hostility and total positive social behavior were the only categories which revealed statistically significant differences between males and females. As is clearly shown in Figure 2, females directed four times as much positive social behavior toward the infant as did the males ($p < .05$). Hostility toward the infant, on the other hand, appeared to be almost exclusively a male characteristic, with males exhibiting ten times more hostility than females ($p < .01$). There were no significant differences between the two Es or between rearing conditions.

QUALITATIVE RESULTS

The infant was disturbed by being placed in a preadolescent's cage only during the first 20 or 30 seconds. She actively explored and initiated contact with 24 out of the 30 Ss. There appeared to be no relationship between the amount of maternal behavior by the preadolescent and the number of contacts initiated by the infant.

There were large individual differences in the behavior of the preadolescents. Three of the 15 males and 5 of 15 females established ventral

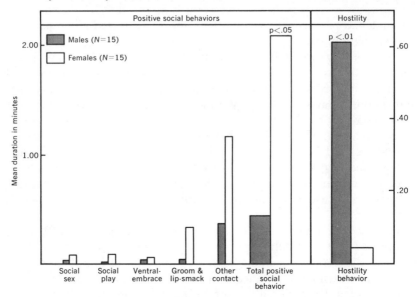

FIGURE 2   Infant-directed behavior of preadolescent monkeys.

contact with the infant, one of the females for nearly half a minute. Five of the 15 males and 10 of 15 females exhibited other maternal relevant behaviors (lipsmack and groom).

There were no sex differences in visual orientation toward the infant. Twelve of the thirty subjects directed sexual behavior toward the infant, and both male and female postures were observed in both sexes. Although the female subjects played more often with the infant than the males did, the differences were not significant. (In another study these same preadolescent males were much more playful than the females when placed with peers.) One female was extremely frightened by the infant. Although the infant made three attempts at contact, the older female withdrew each time and grimaced with fear. This same female looked at the infant only once; the rest of the time she sat huddled in a corner with her back to the infant. While 14 other preadolescents were mildly disturbed for a small fraction of the test session, none showed the extreme fear seen in this one female.

Only 4 of 15 females threatened the infant and no female aggressed, whereas 13 males threatened and/or aggressed. The male aggression was brutal only once when a male bit off one of the infant's fingertips; the session was terminated at 7½ minutes. The infant was given one week to recover from the incident and showed no disturbance upon resumption of the test session.

All of the females, with the exception of the extremely frightened one, contacted the infant, whereas only two of the males did so. Many of the preadolescents, mostly females, threatened the E, and two females retrieved and embraced the infant for several seconds as the E tried to remove it. Ironically, these last two females ignored the infant throughout most of the test session, accumulating an amount of positive social behavior which was far below the female average.

Discussion

The results indicate that there are basic sex differences in the infant-directed behaviors of immature monkeys just as there are in such peer-directed activities as mounting, sexual presenting, play, and hostility (Harlow & Harlow, 1965). Such differences were present both in monkeys that were reared with only a mother and in monkeys reared with only a peer. Early sex differences have been observed in monkeys over a wide range of social-rearing conditions at the Wisconsin Primate Laboratories, and the results suggest that while some critical amount of social experience seems necessary for the appropriate occurrence of positive social behaviors (Mitchell, Raymond, Ruppenthal, & Harlow, 1966), the experience does not have to be with infants. In the present study, the preadolescents had either no previous experience with newborn infants at all or else had such experiences only when they themselves were infants.

In humans, a biologically oriented attitude toward sex differences is usually either ignored or only briefly mentioned (Scheinfeld [1950; p. 519] is an exception). It is generally believed that sex differences are to a large extent culturally determined by a process called "sex-typing" (see Mussen, Conger, & Kagen, 1963, p. 286). No one will question that cultural variables in the human being greatly influence recognition and acceptance of sex role and sex typing, and these roles in turn affect the attitudes of human adults towards babies and infants. However, the data of the present experiment present unequivocal evidence that biological variables in monkeys also significantly influence adolescent responses directed toward infants, that is, maternal-type behaviors. To a considerable extent, cultural variables can override biological variables in the human being (Hampson & Hampson, 1961), but the relative importance of these two factors in various developmental stages remains unresolved.

The present experiment gives no direct evidence concerning the neural or hormonal mechanism producing differential attitudes in preadolescent and adolescent monkeys toward neonates or infants. It is possible that there are sex-specific neural mechanisms in monkeys and that these biological systems are primary to the characteristic behaviors of the sexes. Support for such a position is found in the early appearance of differential play, sex, dominance, and submissive patterns (Harlow & Harlow, 1965) at a time when hormonal systems specific to the two sexes either do not exist or have not yet been identified. It is possible that the preadolescent males and females in the present study may already have sex-specific hormonal systems and that these could be variables of measurable importance. If this is true, the effects reported may be produced either by sensitization of one neural mechanism which is different in the preadolescent male than it is in the female or conceivably by a differential sensitization of two different neural mechanisms which appear in both the preadolescent male and female.

The primary contribution of the present study was the identification of differential infant-directed response patterns in sexually immature male and female monkeys. The females typically exhibited maternal-like affiliative patterns towards infants, whereas the males exhibited patterns of indifference or hostility. The identification of these differential patterns provides a behavioral base for correlative neurological and hormonal investigations, even though such studies are beyond the scope of the present paper.

References

Bolwig, N. A study of the behavior of the chacma baboon, *Papio ursinus. Behaviour*, 1959, *14*, 136–163.

DeVore, I. Mother-infant relations in free-ranging baboons. In H. L. Rheingold (Ed.), *Maternal behavior in mammals.* New York: Wiley, 1963. Pp. 305–335.

Hampson, J. L., and Hampson, J. G. The ontogenesis of sexual behavior in man. In W. C. Young (Ed.), *Sex and internal secretions* (3d ed.). Vol. II. Baltimore: Williams & Wilkins, 1961. Pp. 1401–1432.

Hansen, E. W. The development of maternal and infant behavior in the rhesus monkey. Unpublished doctoral dissertation, University of Wisconsin. 1962.

Harlow, H. F., and Harlow, M. K. The affectional systems. In A. M. Schrier, H. F. Harlow, and F. Stollnitz (Eds.), *Behavior of nonhuman primates.* Vol. II. New York: Academic Press, 1965. Pp. 287–334.

Itani, J. Paternal care in the wild Japanese monkey, *Macaca fuscata. Journal of Primatology*, 1959, *2*, 61–93.

Jay, P. The Indian langur monkey (*Presbytis entellus*). In C. H. Southwick (Ed.), *Primate social behavior.* Princeton, N. J.: Van Nostrand, 1963. Pp. 114–123.

Mitchell, G. D., Raymond, E. J., Ruppenthal, G. C., and Harlow, H. F. Long-term effects of total social isolation upon behavior of rhesus monkeys. *Psychological Reports,* 1966, *18,* 567–580.

Mussen, P. H., Conger, J. J., and Kagan, J. *Child development and personality.* New York: Harper & Row, 1963.

Rosenblum, L. A. The development of social behavior in the rhesus monkey. Unpublished doctoral dissertation, University of Wisconsin, 1961.

Schaller, G. *The mountain gorilla: Ecology and behavior.* Chicago: University of Chicago Press, 1963.

Scheinfeld, A. *Your heredity and environment.* New York: Lippincott, 1950.

Seay, B. M. Maternal behavior in primiparous and multiparous rhesus monkeys. *Folia Primatologica,* 1966, *4,* 146–168.

Siegel, S. *Nonparametric statistics for the behavioral sciences.* New York: McGraw-Hill, 1956.

6. INTEGRATING THEMES *

Elizabeth Douvan and J. Adelson

There remain only the tasks of summarizing major conclusions and findings and of tying together the main threads that run through our observations of American adolescents. Most of what we have to say in this final chapter has been stated somewhere earlier in the book, or is at least implicit in the book's structure and organization. At this point we hope to draw the various themes together, to clarify and interpret some of the major findings.

The adolescent in our view is both pushed and pulled toward the future. The psychic conflicts of the period, with their regressive dangers, assemble the power of the past to urge the child to leave family and childhood. The prospect of independence and adulthood urges him to become his own man. He will move on the strength of this attraction, but if it should fail, he still has behind him the tail wind of all the childhood dangers to be escaped. We suggested at the beginning of our studies that this thrust to the future is crucial to the adolescent experience,

* *The Adolescent Experience.* New York: John Wiley & Sons, Inc., 1966. Pp. 341–354. Reprinted with permission of the publisher.

that without some such tie to adulthood, the adolescent experience has no substance, and that the child's ability to integrate a concept of his adult future would be a key solution on which a great part of his adolescent adaptation would depend.

Our studies have confirmed and strengthened this general conception. The future is by no means a remote or irrelevant prospect to American adolescents. It is crucial as it is absorbed, integrated, and expressed in current activities and attitudes. In one form or another, the future orientation appears again and again as a distinguishing feature of youngsters who are making adequate adolescent adaptations. A faulty time perspective consistently marks the groups in our studies who were isolated analytically by other measures of ego weakness or lack of personal integration.

The style and focus of future orientation differs sharply for boys and girls. The two groups focus their interest on different aspects of future identity, and they differ also in the style of expression. Boys tend to concentrate on the vocational future and their style is all business—concrete, crystallized, tied to reality, if not always realistic. They think of job preparation and channels, and of their own capabilities and tastes for particular work roles. They think of the future in an instrumental way—"This is what I think my future will be because this is what I think I am and what the job world looks like to me." It is not surprising to find that boys' vocational goals are not much colored by dreams of glory. For the most part the jobs boys choose represent modest advances over their fathers' positions, and they are jobs with which the boys have had some personal contact. Boys who have no clear vocational plans or whose job goals are deviant in some way (for example, downward-mobile or glamour-based) have less instrumental and realistic notions of steps toward their goals, and are likely to show a pattern of personal maladjustment in their current lives.

Girls focus on the interpersonal aspects of future life—on marriage and the roles of wife and mother. They are not without notions about channels and instrumental acts appropriate to their goals, but the ideas they have are less concrete than boys'. They are less concerned with real skills than boys are, and more concerned with social and interpersonal reality, as we would expect from the nature of their goals. Their reasons for choosing particular jobs reveal that girls want jobs that express feminine interests and provide a social setting for meeting prospective husbands.

Beyond this interpersonal emphasis, girls seem to bridge the present and future much more with fantasy than with reality-tied or concrete plans. The girl is less likely to say of the future, "This is what I think I will be," than she is to say, "I hope my life will be like this." The boy

checks and conditions his goals by the step-by-step instrumental procedures they imply; the girl leaps more directly in fantasy to the goal. And
this makes good sense—for her the procedures are equally ambiguous,
whether the goal is simple or grand. What she will become does not depend in any direct or simple way on her own instrumental acts, it depends rather on the man she marries.

A clear concept of her adult femininity, of feminine goals and interpersonal skills, functions for the girl like the vocational concept for the
boy. It bridges the worlds of adolescence and adulthood, brings the future concretely into current life, and allows the future to contribute
meaning and organization to adolescent activities and interests. Girls
who have relatively clear notions about and goals in adult femininity
show a high degree of personal integration. Those girls who specifically
reject a feminine future are troubled adolescents.

The different stances boys and girls assume toward the future is expressed most simply and directly in our analysis of mobility aspirations.
Mobility aspiration for the boy is no idle dream, it is rather the concrete
expression of a boy's faith in himself. The goal he chooses is realistic in
light of his talent and opportunities, but is not overblown. And it is cast
in the phrasing of reality—What is the job like? What activities and demands does it encompass, what training does it require? What are my
abilities and opportunities, do they provide me access to the field?

The girl's mobility aspirations are less formed and less fettered by
reality. She need not test her desire against her own talent and skill,
since these will not be crucial determinants of her future status. Her access to higher status will come through marriage. For most of these girls
(except those few older girls who have already experienced a lasting,
meaningful relationship with a boy) marriage itself has so little reality
that the difference between a "good" or socially advancing marriage and
any marriage at all is not significant. Since it is all a dream, in any case,
one may as well dream big. Girls' mobility plans are less careful than
boys', less cautioned by an assessment of opportunity. They are more
simply dreams.

The imminence of adulthood, the imposing need to master and incor-
porate some elements of adult identity into current life (at least in fantasy), means that the child must alter his relationship to his family in
some important ways. He must begin to detach himself from the family
and develop some measure of independence in behavior, emotions, values, and beliefs. The process of detachment has traditionally been described as high drama—the rebellious adolescent pressing for enlarged
independence and continually confronting conservative, dynastic parental control. We shall have more to say later about the detachment as it
seems to develop in American adolescents, and about the appropriate-

ness of this traditional model to the reality of American family life. At this point it is enough to say that the process as we observe it seems less dramatic and full of conflict than tradition and theory hold, and to point out again a significant difference between boys and girls.

Our findings regarding the issue of independence indicate that the urge to be free, to be one's own master, is almost exclusively a masculine stirring. Up to the age of eighteen girls show no great press for independence, certainly no need to confront authority or insist on the right to develop and distinguish independent beliefs or controls. The difference appears in our descriptive findings about adolescents' attitudes toward themselves and their family relationships. It also emerges analytically when we look at the relationship of developing independence to other areas of personal growth. In boys, the measure of independent functioning achieved relates clearly to other areas of development—to the integration of a future concept, to upward-mobility aspirations and general achievement strivings, to current adolescent adjustment. These relationships do not hold for the girls. Feminine integration does not demand a strong bid for independence during the adolescent period. Indeed we find that girls' attitudes toward parental control do not even relate very strongly to the nature or style of that control.

Close to the issue of detachment, and theoretically the central mechanism for realizing separation, is the issue of adolescent peer group ties. Here again we have the impression that the importance of the peer group has been exaggerated in theory and in much of popular complaint about adolescents. Our data again indicate that boys and girls differ both in the extent of their allegiance to the peer group and in the particular uses they make of peer ties. Boys more often hold allegiance to the group as such, conceive the group as a coherent and loyal band offering support to members and having an authority of its own. Boys recognize "the gang" as a force that could lead a boy to break rules; they think of getting into a "bad gang" as a danger to be avoided.

Girls use peer relationships differently. They are not as tied to a group as such, nor are they as sensitized to the pressure of "the gang" (except possibly in issues of taste). In general girls are more attracted to close two-person friendships. The loyalty of the best friend is the loyalty the girl depends on, needs, and seeks. In belonging to groups, the girl does not seek a band to support her as she makes a play for freedom— rather, she uses the group as a resource for finding close individual friendships. She is always on the lookout for prospective best friends. The individual friendship transcends the group (although it may exist in a group setting), and becomes the center of mutual self-exploration through shared intimacy. In their concepts about friendship and in the intimacy of their friendships, girls are more highly developed than boys.

In fact, the interpersonal seems to be the central area of growth for girls during adolescence. Our evidence indicates that the girl's development in the interpersonal sphere is the pivotal feature around which her adolescent adjustment focuses. A measure of interpersonal development was our best predictor of ego integration in girls.

We have stressed the importance of the future in adolescent adjustment, but we do not mean to underestimate the impact of the child's past on his resolution of adolescent tasks. His particular past in a particular family with its own style of interaction enters and critically affects the youngster's encounter with all of the adolescent problems. Two clear family patterns appear in our studies—the democratic family style and an autocratic or authoritarian style. In the democratic family, parents allow the adolescent a fair degree of autonomy, include the child in important decisions affecting his own behavior, and tend to use psychological and verbal discipline. Authoritarian parents set rules without consulting the children, allow little autonomy, and tend to use physical techniques for enforcing discipline. The effects of the family pattern on the adolescents are apparent, strong, and consistent. The democratic families produce adolescents who are unusually self-reliant, poised, and effective. They are free to criticize and disagree with parents, but have generally warm companionship with them. In the authoritarian families the adolescents are on the surface compliant; beneath the surface (in responses to projective measures) they are rebellious and impulsive. They tend to have an externalized morality, to define morals as what one can get away with. They are less effective and less poised in their general bearing.

The findings from our studies point to the homogenization of American adolescence across regional boundaries and, by and large, across social class lines as well. We were struck by the lack of impressive differences among these population groups. It seems that the peculiar conflicts of the age itself and the force of modern mass communications have combined to cast a universal form for the adolescent experience—a form heavily invested with middle-class values. Adolescent interests and activities, family patterns and moves toward independence, are much the same in all regions, in all social classes. Among standard background variables, only religion yielded differences that are large, consistent, and consistently interesting.

These, briefly, are the substantive findings from our studies. Beyond these conclusions supported directly by data, what can we say we have learned from the studies? We like to think that years invested bear a yield in wisdom and insight that extend beyond the relatively narrow range of empirical findings. Some broader conclusion and speculation should be part of the reward for so much demanding attention to detail.

We have two such broad comments to make, both representing insights we gained from the research, both having to do with the aptness of standard theoretical formulations of the adolescent experience. The two areas that focus these comments are first, the importance of sex differences in adolescence; and, second, the nature of the adolescent experience as it occurs in the middle range of American children.

Our initial approach to the study of adolescence, while tied theoretically to psychoanalysis, rested also on developmental descriptive notions that have dominated child psychology and particularly the study of adolescence. We hoped to go beyond the mere description of change, and to use theory to clarify sources of variation in the form and pace of adolescent change. Nonetheless, we conceived these changes, however they might vary, as organized around certain developmental tasks posed for all children in our culture somewhere near the close of childhood. The tasks we noted were the ones we have described in earlier chapters —regulating instincts; dissolving infantile dependencies, and integrating new areas of autonomy; developing stable object ties, particularly heterosexual ties; coming to terms with the superego; and exploring identity possibilities.

This conception of adolescent challenges established the outlines of our investigation, and we had at the outset some notions about the factors, including sex, that would determine different forms of the developmental crisis and its outcome. We were quite sure that achievement and occupational choice would be more crucial to the boy, that social and interpersonal issues would play a larger role in girls' preoccupations and would more surely gauge the girl's personal integration at adolescence.

What we did not anticipate was the force of the sex variable, the extent to which it defines and shades all aspects of the developmental crisis. Since all children undergo radical biological changes at puberty, and presumably also derivative instinctual changes, we assumed that the new task of regulating these instincts would also be met by all children. This would require some reworking of internal controls, some changes in self-regulation. The nature of the solutions might vary, but they would all be responses to a unifying problem and would share at least the rough outline and structure that this problem establishes.

In fact we find that the adolescent crisis for boys and girls differs in almost every regard—in the statement of developmental tasks, not just how they are phrased, but whether they arise during the era at all; in the general direction of solution alternatives available to the child, and in the individual solution expressions achieved by youngsters in our society.

One may see commonalities, of course. But our studies suggest that the observation of similarity in this case requires such a high level of ab-

straction, and such a cost to the richness of one's description and understanding of adolescent reality, that the transaction loses its relevance
and value. So, for example, we know that puberty brings basic biological changes to girls as well as boys. Mead (1955) has even pointed to
the more decisive nature of feminine puberty changes. Yet to conclude
from this that boys and girls face similar problems psychologically in
the regulation of instinctual energy seems to strain too much reality
from the situation. At some level the drives increase and must be managed in both sexes, but our findings point to the conclusion that the
drive is so successfully excluded from consciousness by the large majority of girls that they do not in any relevant psychological sense confront
an impulse problem comparable to boys' during the adolescent years.
This difference, in turn, influences the reworking of controls, the development of autonomy, and the resolution of dependencies—producing
sex-determined differences in both pace and process.

The key terms in adolescent development for the boy in our culture
are the erotic, autonomy (assertiveness, independence, achievement),
and identity. For the girl the comparable terms are the erotic, the interpersonal, and identity. Differences between the two sets of problems are
larger and more complex than a single discrepancy implies; for this discrepancy is so central that it reverberates through the entire complex.
For the girl the development of interpersonal ties—the sensitivities,
skills, ethics, and values of object ties—forms the core of identity, and it
gives expression to much of developing feminine eroticism. Feminine
sexuality, consciously inhibited from active and direct expression, seeks
more subtle, limited, and covert expression. The search for popularity,
the effort to charm, all of the many and varied interpersonal ties which
serve as setting for the girl's practice in winning and maintaining love
—these engagements filter and express a good deal of the girl's erotic
need. We have noted the greater intensity and importance of girls' like-
sexed friendships when compared to their friendships with boys or to
boys' like-sexed friendships. And we have held that the intimate friendship between girls serves a number of functions, all tied to the girl's
need to explore and understand her sexual nature as well as her individuality. It is primarily through these serial, episodic, intimate twosomes
that the girl comes to terms with her sexual nature and gradually sorts
elements of identification from aspects of individuality to form an identity. The tie to objects is both the key to her erotic realization and also
the mechanism through which she arrives at an individuated personal
identity.

For the boy, on the other hand, the integrated capacity for erotic ties
and the solution of the identity challenge demand separation and autonomy. What the girl achieves through intimate connection with others,

the boy must manage by disconnecting, by separating himself and asserting his right to be distinct. His biological sexual nature is more explicitly and individually stated than the girl's. It has less compelling interpersonal features, depends less on the existence of a fully developed
object relation and it insists on the resolution of certain authority problems in order to gain expression. The boy can know sexual gratification
outside a full or fully developed love relationship, but his sexual realization depends on severing infantile ties and asserting his independence of
them. Without autonomy, the boy's sexual realization suffers the constant hazard of crippling castration fears. To achieve full status as a sexual adult, the boy must clarify the difference between himself and his
father and assume the status of the father's independent peer. The girl's
adult sexuality, on the other hand, depends on an intricate and little understood process of consolidating a satisfactory identification with her
own mother.

The identity problem is also phrased differently for boys and girls in
our culture, and the distinction again revolves around their different requirements for object love and for autonomy. We have noted that feminine identity forms more closely about capacity and practice in the personal arts, and we have seen in our findings evidence that the girl's ego
integration co-varies with her interpersonal development. Masculine
identity, in contrast, focuses about the capacity to handle and master
nonsocial reality, to design and win for oneself an independent area of
work which fits one's individual talents and taste and permits achievement of at least some central personal goals. The boy's ego development
at adolescence already bears the mark of this formulation and reflects
his progress in mastering it. Identity is for the boy a matter of indivi-
duating internal bases for action and defending these against domination by others. For the girl it is a process of finding and defining the internal and individual through attachments to others.

The normative descriptive approach to adolescent psychology is not
the only one in which sex variation has been overlooked. When we look
at the developing literature on identity and the self-concept, we note
again the predominance of a masculine formulation. The most advanced
psychoanalytic theorists often fail to note what seems to be an imposing
distinction, at least to judge from the results of our studies and other recent research.

In Erikson's statement of the developmental tasks of adolescence and
early adulthood, the problem of individual identity is put before that of
intimacy—and there is a compelling logic to this order. For how, one
asks, can the individual form a genuine tie to another, a contact of
depth and intimacy, unless the outlines of his individual being have

been established and fortified; how can we speak of two individuals merging in intimacy unless we start with two individuals?

Yet psychic phenomena do not always follow logic in so orderly a manner. We know that in many people, the working through of identity issues continues well beyond the early adult years and that in some cases, at least, intimacy has been achieved in some degree before the individual has developed the kind of continuity and integrity of self which an identity resolution implies.

This, we would argue, is much more commonly the tone of feminine identity formation. The girl is more likely to gain a developed identity in consequence of intimacy rather than as a precursor of it. Out of her intimate connections to others, through processes of identification and projection, the woman comes to know her own individuality and to solve the question of who she is. The reasons for this arrangement lie both in the nature of feminine psychic development and in the much simpler and more obvious realm of social reality. For the fact is that in our culture at least the need to marry and find acceptance and love exert such pressure on the young girl that we can hardly imagine her having the time and energy to invest in identity-resolution until she has gained some measure of security in a stable love relationship. To do so may even involve hazards to her marriage eligibility. Too sharp a self-definition and too full an investment in a unique personal integration are not considered highly feminine; they are often thought to be unattractive in a young woman.[1]

The girl, then, is likely to arrive at an identity resolution through the interpersonal, and, then, only after she has reached some relatively satisfactory integration of intimacy and the erotic. The boy's tasks are ordered differently—his identity depends on his achieving autonomy—an acceptable integration of assertiveness and self-direction. His identity demands and forms around these qualities; beyond this, no erotic resolution except denial is available to him until he has established a degree of freedom from external control.

We have perhaps overstated the difference between boys and girls. The girl has experienced some degree of separation before she enters the intimate friendships of adolescence—after all, all social development consists of rhythmic and complementary processes of differentiation and integration, of separating from and connecting with objects. The boy, on the other hand, has been tied in more or less intimate (although imma-

---

[1] Mirra Komarovsky (1946) has reported interviews with college women in which the girls themselves reveal that they are consciously avoiding too clear and invested self-definitions because of the fear of becoming ineligible for marriage.

ture) relationships with others up to the adolescent strike for autonomy. But the tone and order of development that begins in adolescence and concludes in maturity—these, we contend, differ sharply for the two sexes. We have seen the derivative effects of the difference in our studies—the areas of achievement, autonomy, authority and control focus and express boys' major concerns and psychological growth; the object relations—friendship, dating, popularity and the understanding and management of interpersonal crisis—hold the key to adolescent growth and integration for the girl. The internalization of feminine goals also has important implications for the girl's development. Here too the goal is to form a lasting tie to another, and is not an individual achievement in the sense that the boy's vocational goal is.

We conclude, then, that there is not one adolescent crisis, but two major and clearly distinctive ones—the masculine and the feminine. If we are to think of adolescence as a relatively delimited period, we must conclude that some of the traditionally conceived problems of the period (for example, detachment from external authority, the resolution of primitive object ties) are not a part of the feminine phrasing of adolescence. If we conceive impulses to be drives that have some reasonably direct impact on conscious thought and behavior, we may even question the traditional concept of adolescence as a time of turbulent instinctual struggle as far as the girl is concerned. While we cling to the notion that somewhere beneath compliance and repression there lies a heart of fire, our impression from the study of girls is that for them adolescence is less infused with impulse and more focused on form than any traditional conception of the era could have led us to expect.

If sex differences led us to reconsider traditional conceptions of adolescence, the normative findings from our studies also made us think twice about the received version of the period. Most contemporary comment on adolescence focuses on two conspicuous but atypical enclaves of adolescents, drawn from extreme and opposing ends of the social class continuum, and representing exceptional solutions to the adolescent crisis. These are, on the one hand, the delinquent, and on the other, the sensitive, articulate, middle-class adolescent on whom the psychoanalytic view is almost exclusively based.

Now in most ways these types could not be more dissimilar. The estranged lower-class youngster relies largely on alloplastic solutions to the adolescent crisis, living out mutely, in urgent yet aimless acts of violence or bravado, a sullen resentment against the middle-class world and its values. The estranged upper-middle-class youngster is largely autoplastic in response; subject to acute intrapsychic upheavals which are expressed in neurotic symptoms, affect storms, character eccentricities, and a general value ferment. Paradoxically, these two extremes are alike, and their likeness is in being different from the normative adolescent—the adolescent of the core culture. The extremes are alike in showing an unusual degree of independence from the family; they are alike in disaffection, in acting out or thinking out a discontent with the social order; they are alike, above all, in that they adopt radical solutions to the adolescent task of ego-synthesis.

We want to suggest that one cannot generalize these processes to the adolescent population at large. The adolescent at the extremes responds to the instinctual and psychosocial upheaval of puberty by disorder, by failures of ego-synthesis, and by a tendency to abandon earlier values and object attachments. In the normative response to adolescence, however, we more commonly find an avoidance of inner and outer conflict, premature identity consolidation, ego and ideological constriction, and a general unwillingness to take psychic risks. The great advantage of the survey technique is that it allows us to study these adolescents who make up the middle majority, who evoke neither grief nor wonder, and who all too often escape our notice.

Let us begin with the question of autonomy and conflict. In the traditional view, the child at puberty is under great pressure to detach himself from the family emotionally, to find a pattern of disengagement. The instinctual revival brings with it a return of Oedipal dangers and temptations. The home is a "hothouse" and the boy at least must discover a way out, a means of escaping his dependent status in the family, and even more urgently, the dimly recognized drives and feelings toward his parents. This is the psychosexual irritation which pushes the child from home, leading him to negotiate or battle with the parents for greater freedom. The conflict of generations is joined. We add to this a psychosocial pull—the child's need to forge an individual identity—those needs which draw the child toward the future. These forces give the peer group at adolescence its critical importance. Peer group and culture supplant the family as the locus of authority and the giver of norms. Through his immersion in the peer group, through the incorporation of peer ideals and values, the youngster gains the support he needs to win autonomy from the family. And the peer group provides a haven in which the delicate task of self-exploration and self-definition can be accomplished.

This view of adolescence has a good deal to recommend it, but our reading of the interviews suggests that it needs revision in some important particulars if we are to apply it to the middle majority. This view exaggerates the degree of conflict between parent and child; it wrongly estimates the autonomy issue; and it misinterprets the role of the peer group. The normative adolescent tends to avoid overt conflict with his family. Now this is not to say that conflict is not present; but it is largely

unconscious conflict, those under-surface resentments which do not necessarily liberate or enlarge the personality, but which, paradoxically, increase the child's docility toward his parents. Even when we do find
overt conflict one senses that it has an "as if" quality to it, that it is a
kind of war game, with all the sights and sounds of battle but without
any blood being shed. More often than not the conflicts will center on
trivia, on issues of taste—clothing, grooming, and the like. One can
argue that these issues are trivial only to the adult, that they are, however, of great symbolic importance in the adolescent's quest for autonomy. True; but one can reply that parent and child play out an empty
ritual of disaffection, that they agree to disagree only on token issues, on
teen issues, and in doing so are able to sidestep any genuine encounter
of differences.

Much the same is true of autonomy. There are autonomies and autonomies. The American adolescent asks for and is freely given an unusual
degree of behavioral freedom—the right to come and go, to share in setting rules, and so on. But it is far more problematic whether he asks for
or achieves a high degree of emotional autonomy, and it is even more
doubtful that he manages much in the way of value autonomy. Indeed,
the ease with which the adolescent acquires behavioral freedom may
tend to interfere with the achievement of emotional and ideological freedom, for reasons we shall turn to in a moment. As to the peer group, its
supposed functions—as an arena for the confrontation of the self, for the
testing and trying out of identities—are present for many adolescents,
but for many more the peer group is used for the learning and display of
sociability and social skills. The peer culture is all too often a kind of
playpen, designed to keep the children out of harm's way and out of the
parents' hair. It may not work out this way; the children may begin
throwing toys at each other, or, what is worse, may begin throwing them
at the grownups in the living room. But generally it does work out just
this way. The peer group, with its artificial amusements and excite-
ments, more often acts to hinder differentiation and growth.

This is especially evident in the area of values and ideology. The traditional idea of the adolescent experience has it that the youngster becomes involved in an intense concern with ethics, political ideology,
religious belief, and so on. The moral parochialism of early childhood
was thought to be smashed by the moral fervor and incipient cosmopoli-
tanism of adolescence. The youngster's need to detach himself from the
family and its view of the moral and social order, his need to redo the
ego-superego constellation, his need to find new and more appropriate
ego ideals, his need to use ideology as a solution for instinctual
problems—all these needs came together, so it was thought, to produce
a value crisis somewhere in the course of the adolescent career. This

pattern can be found in adolescence, but it is found in a bold, sometimes stubborn, often unhappy minority. Our interviews confirm a mounting impression from other studies, that American adolescents are on the whole not deeply involved in ideology, nor are they prepared to do much individual thinking on value issues of any generality. Why is this so? We would guess this is true because to think anew and differently endangers the adolescent's connection to the community, his object attachments, and complicates the task of ego synthesis.

We can sum up in the language of personality theory. The inherent tensions of adolescence are displaced to and discharged within the matrix of peer group sociability. Intrapsychically the defenses and character positions adopted are those which curtail experience and limit the growth and differentiation of the self—repression, reaction-formation, and certain forms of ego restriction. These two modes of dealing with inner and outer experience join to produce a pseudoadaptive solution of the adolescent crisis, marked by cognitive stereotypy, value stasis, and interpersonal conformity. It is a solution which is accomplished by resisting conflict, resisting change, resisting the transformation of the self. It settles for a modest resynthesis of the ego—closely along the lines of the older organization of drives, defenses, values, and object attachments. It is characterized by an avoidance of identity-diffusion through identity-coarctation.

These rather dismal conclusions on the contemporary adolescent character are akin to those stated by Edgar Friedenberg in his brilliant book, *The Vanishing Adolescent*. Adolescence, he says, is disappearing as the period in which the individual can achieve a decisive articulation of the self. Nowadays the youngster, in his words, "merely undergoes puberty and simulates maturity." If this amiable but colorless form of adolescence is indeed a new thing in our country, then we would have to single out as one important reason the extraordinary attenuation of today's adolescence. Given the long preparation required for advanced technical training, given the uselessness of the adolescent in the labor market—parent and child settle down for a long, long period of time during which the child will, in one way or another, remain a dependent being.

Traditionally, adolescence has been the age in which the child readied himself to leave home; and when we read accounts of adolescence in the earlier part of this century we very often note between father and son a decisive encounter, a decisive testing of wills, in which the son makes a determined bid for autonomy, either by leaving home, or threatening to do so, and meaning it. The adolescent then had little of the freedom he has today; he was kept under the parental thumb, but he used his captivity well, to strengthen himself for a real departure and a real autonomy. Nowadays the adolescent and his parents are both made captive by their mutual knowledge of the adolescent's dependency. They are locked in a room with no exit, and they make the best of it by an unconscious *quid pro quo,* in which the adolescent forfeits his adolescence, and instead becomes a teenager. He keeps the peace by muting his natural rebelliousness through transforming it into structured and defined techniques for getting on people's nerves. The passions, the restlessness, the vivacity of adolescence are partly strangled, and partly drained off in the mixed childishness and false adulthood of the adolescent teen culture.

III. ON THE COGNITIVE REALM OF ADOLESCENCE

Introduction

The first paper in this section, "Sex Differences in Word Problem Solving as a Function of Age," conveniently facilitates the transition from the last section on the physical, psychosexual, and sociosexual realms of adolescent development. In his treatment of sex differences in this cognitive ability, Dougherty, a math teacher turned researcher, broadly surveys the relevant literature on word problem solving and sex differences, mustering some thought-provoking analyses that should prove especially interesting to math teachers. In the end, the author resorts to a synthesis of cognitive factors and sex-role identification in his explanation of male superiority in word problem solving ability.

The other four articles on the cognitive development of adolescents are decidedly Piagetian in flavor. In a sense, this orientation is in keeping with the epistemological bias reflected in the first section of this book: Piaget's approach to discovering knowledge about the development of thought is based on direct observations of and interactions with his subjects —in our case, adolescents. The articles are ordered so as to first explain the essentials of Piaget's paradigm and second to examine them as they are concerned with adolescence.

This is not to say that this section's articles all employ Piaget's approach to gathering data; with the possible exception of Kohlberg's paper, they do not. Rather, Yudin's article and one of Elkind's articles are probably best described as arriving at inferences about adolescent cognitive development via a formal experimental approach. It is hoped that the student will labor patiently with these articles; they are well worth the effort and do help by paraphrasing their points. This material has been gathered so that the teacher will be informed of the development and application of formal and moral thought during adolescence: it makes sense out of some otherwise annoying adolescent behaviors.

In Elkind's first article on egocentrism in adolescence, we are fortunate to have a lucid introduction to the essentials of Piaget's stages of cognitive development. This productive essay uses the study of egocentrism—seen as the negative by-product of any emergent mental system—to connect cognitive structures with the dynamics of personality. Elkind resourcefully illustrates how the cognitive structures of adolescence are related to this period's affective experiences and behavior.

In the next article, Elkind reports his study of the facility in shifting from one conceptual orientation to another in solving a concept-attainment task. The confirmation of his hypothesis that adolescents are more successful than children in shifting conceptual orientations lends itself to substantiating the Inhelder-Piaget model of conceptual development in adolescence. More than this, though, Elkind shares with us the "qualitative observations" of adolescent thinking that he encountered in this study.

Yudin's detailed study of the development of formal thought as a function of intelligence investigates the development of concept attainment among adolescents of low, middle, and high intelligence. In addition, he studies the order of difficulty in the attainment of concepts of colors, numbers, and forms. Yudin's results support a belief that many have probably nurtured for some time about the relationship of intelligence to the development of concept attainment or conceptual thinking among adolescents: that an interaction of both age and intelligence contributes toward cognitive development. This article also very meaningfully adds further confirmation to the Inhelder-Piaget assertion that adolescence is the stage when childhood's concrete operations dissolve with the development of logical operations and with the individual's lasting acquisition of the ability to reason with hypotheses.

This section closes with a crescendo by Kohlberg that partially prepares the reader for what is to come in the next section on socialization and the psychosocial realm. In view of his self-asserted Piagetian moorings and clearly conceptually based hierarchy for the development of moral thinking, it was felt that Kohlberg's paper on the moral education of adolescents belonged in this section of readings on the cognitive realm. Despite this, it would not be amiss for one to argue that his paper belongs in the next section. Kohlberg has been known to present the interactionist's viewpoint that he makes so well by asserting that his invariant developmental sequence of moral stages *is* subject to acceleration by, and ultimately depends on, socialization processes. Be that as it may, we have the benefit of Kohlberg's appreciation for the state of the "art" of morally educating adolescents and others in the schools, after which he goes on to explain his own research achievements in the area of moral development. He further provides us with a piercing analysis of the nature of justice (the ultimate virtue in his scheme of morality) and briefly makes sensible suggestions about a fundamental technique for teaching virtue.

1. SEX DIFFERENCES IN WORD PROBLEM SOLVING AS A FUNCTION OF AGE *

Knowles Dougherty

It is commonly thought in the United States that men excel women in the area of word problem solving. We shall first look at the scientific data compiled to investigate that understanding. If true, the idea that men are better at solving word problems in math warrants further investigation from two points of view. Such an investigation might bring out important considerations for those interested in improving instruction in word problem solution. In addition, it might sharpen one of the distinctions between men and women in our society.

The Data

By "word problem" we shall mean any problem stated in words, stemming from a more or less realistic situation, requiring for its solution, among other things, some mathematical calculation.

The data reported here is based on word problems ranging from something like the following, which would be read to a five or six year old,

Mary has two apples. Johnny has three apples. How many apples do Mary and Johnny have altogether?

to problems like the one below which would be presented in written form to adults:

A man has five gallons of a fuel which is thirty percent oil and seventy percent gasoline. How much pure oil must he add to have a fuel which is forty percent oil and sixty percent gasoline?

This type of problem should be familiar to anyone who has used typical American textbooks in arithmetic and mathematics or taken achievement and ability tests (like the CTMM, SAT, WISC, CAT, WAIS, and the Stanford-Binet).

In Table 1, we have listed (chronologically by average age of the subjects) all the experiments we could find in which a sex comparison was made on word problem solving ability.

I think it is fair to summarize the data in the following way. In the

TABLE 1

Experiments Bearing on the Relationship of Sex to Word Problem Solving

INVESTIGATOR AND YEAR	AGE OF SUBJECTS	SIGNIFICANT RESULT IN FAVOR OF:	TEST USED
† Miele (1958)	5–6	neither	WISC
Lesser, et al. (1964)	6	neither	word problems in add, subt, mult, and div
† Clark (1959)	8	males	CTMM
		neither	CAT
† Wozencraft (1963)	8	females	SAT
† Schiller (1934)	8, 9	males	arith reasoning
† Gainer (1962)	6–12	neither	WISC
Heilman (1933)	10	males	SAT
† Clark (1959)	10	neither	CAT and CTMM
† Wozencraft (1963)	11	neither	SAT
† Miele (1958)	7–15	males	WISC
† Clark (1959)	13	neither	CAT and CTMM
† McGuire (1961)	12–14	neither	CAT
Dougherty (see appendix)	13–15	males	word problems on algebra tests
† McNemar (1942)	11–18	males	Stanford-Binet
Milton (1958)	13–18	males	word problems
Milton (1958)	16–18	males	word problems
Maier and Burke (1967)	college	males	horse trader problem
Sweeney (1953)	college	males	reasoning problems
Milton (1957 and 1958)	college	males	word problems
Berry (1958)	college	males	word problems
Carey (1955)	college	males	word problems
† Bieri, et al. (1958)	college	males	CAT
† Miele (1958)	adult	males	WAIS
† Norman (1953)	adult	males	WAIS
† Wechsler (1958)	adult	males	WAIS

The "†" indicates that the result of the investigation appeared in Maccoby (1966, p. 339).

primary school years (ages 5 to 9) it appears that there is no (or at least no consistent) difference between boys and girls in their performance on word problems. In the intermediate grades and junior high school (ages 10 to 14) there is some spotty evidence in favor of the boys. In high school, college and adulthood (age 14 and beyond), there is overwhelming evidence that men surpass women in their ability to solve word problems.

It should also be pointed out here that in most of these studies (no matter what the age of the subjects) the variability in performance within each sex was quite high. Hence there are females who perform very well relative to the males and males who do poorly relative to females.[1]

Possible Explanations of the Data

It seems clear then that, generally, males are better than females at solving word problems. In addition the evidence shows that this male superiority does not appear consistently until about age 14. The body of this paper will be devoted to a presentation and critical analysis of the explanations which have been offered to account for these two phenomena.

1. GENERAL PHYSIOLOGICAL DEVELOPMENT

In any human development course, we learn that girls are generally ahead of boys in most respects, go well into the lead around ages 11–13, but then fall behind the boys when the latter have their growth spurt around ages 13–15. Hence it isn't until about age 14 that we see male superiority in word problem solving.

This explanation may help in accounting for the divergence of the sexes at age 14. However, there are some obvious omissions. It is difficult (if not impossible) to make the connection between physiological development and the ability to solve word problems. Indeed, even if a connection could be made, one would have to include in it reasons why it holds for word problem solution and not the host of other mental abilities in which the sexes do not diverge (Maccoby, 1966). In addition, this explanation would also have to account for why it is that girls do not perform better in the age range 11–13 when they presumably would have such a great advantage.

---

[1] One may wish to stop at this point and ask a number of questions. For a starter, see questions 1 and 2 at the end of the article.

2. GENERAL MENTAL DEVELOPMENT

Maccoby (1966) summarizes a host of studies of general intelligence by saying that girls are ahead of boys in pre-school but from then on the boys and men develop at a faster rate than the girls and women.

Again we can not completely discount this explanation since it may help to account for the divergence of the sexes at age 14. However, again there are a number of obvious omissions. As above, this general mental development explanation does not account for the fact that men do not excel women in many mental abilities. Worse yet, Sweeney (1953) found consistent sex differences in problem solving even when differences in intellectual aptitude had been controlled. Finally this explanation will not account for the fact that girls do not exceed boys in their problem solving performance at ages 5 and 6.

3. VERBAL ABILITY

It seems reasonable that since the problems are stated, after all, in words, then verbal ability could account for a good share of the ability to solve word problems. Indeed, both Berry (1959) and Milton (1957) found correlations (for men) in the range of .40 to .50 between verbal ability and problem solving performance.

Unfortunately, at any age, females score higher on tests of general verbal ability than males (Carlsmith, 1964). Hence if one were to accept this explanation for problem solving ability, one would be hard pressed to explain why men excel women and not vice versa. A possible solution to this dilemma would be an investigation of specific aspects of verbal ability and their relation to problem solving performance. There is some hope for the fruitfulness of such an investigation since the correlation (for women) between verbal ability and problem solving (Milton, 1957) is only .28 which is considerably below that reported (above) for men. It may turn out that the total verbal ability of men consists of a pattern of subabilities distinct from that of women. It is entirely possible that further literature search in this area would shed considerable light on this issue.

4. MATHEMATICAL ABILITY

Since the solution of these word problems involves some competence in mathematics, it seems reasonable to suggest that there would be a high correlation between these two abilities. Both Berry (1959) and Milton (1957) find correlations in the .70's. In addition Carlsmith (1964) reports that the literature abounds with evidence that males (especially from adolescence onward) excel females in mathematical ability.

But actually this explanation begs the question. It turns out that the sexes do not differ on the computational parts of tests of mathematical ability (Maccoby, 1966). Often the remaining part in these tests consists of word problems. Hence the high correlations reported above are simply a reflection of the fact that scores on two tests will correlate if one of them is really a significant subtest in the other.

An additional fact which this explanation would have to account for is that Milton (1957) found that there is still a significant difference between the sexes in word problem solving when the solutions involve no numerical calculations whatsoever. The fact that women are as accurate as men in arithmetic computation should lead one to believe this latter finding, but it is interesting to note that such was the case upon investigation.

5. ABSTRACT REASONING

One would have to admit that successful solution of these word problems would take some abstract analytic reasoning. Since it appears that women excel men in their ability to read, and since there appears to be no difference in the sexes in their computational skills, it would seem that the males' superiority in problem solving would have to be explained by superior reasoning ability.

As Maccoby (1966) points out, the evidence for male superiority in reasoning ability is rather weak, in spite of the fact that a few studies show it. There are other findings, supporting this explanation, which Maccoby does not report. With six year olds, Lesser (1964) found that boys did significantly better than girls on a reasoning task called "jump peg." Wesman (1949) found tenth grade boys slightly superior to the girls in abstract reasoning.

If we were able to concede male superiority in this area, we might be able to build a fairly strong case for this superiority taking effect around age 14: that is, taking an effect on problem solving. Inhelder and Piaget (1958) and Vygotsky (1962) speak of a transition in the development of conceptual thought which occurs about the age of puberty. From their observations, these men have found that it is not until adolescence that an individual is able to engage in self-directed, goal-directed conceptual thought. Although the case is weak, one might argue that successful solution of word problems requires just this kind of directed, abstract thinking. Hence, the argument would continue, boys start to solve word problems better than girls at about age 14 because they are stronger in the ability to think abstractly and always have been, but it isn't until that age that they can put the ability to use on the word problems. (It should be noted here that in the measures of problem solving ability cited here, the subject is given little opportunity to solve the problems other than by figuring it out analytically.)

Aside from the inherent weakness of the case being made here for the abstract reasoning explanation, there is some empirical evidence which leads one to give it even less credence. Maccoby (1966) concludes from her literature survey that analytic thinking is correlated with masculinity in women and femininity in men. As we shall see later in the paper, there is considerable evidence correlating masculinity (in both sexes) with problem solving performance. Thus our case for the abstract reasoning explanation is weakened: women are more feminine, feminine women are poor at analytic thinking, and women are poor at solving problems; but men are more masculine, masculine men are poor at analytic thinking, and masculine men are better at solving word problems. Hence in the case of men our case is considerably weakened, if we are to accept Milton's (1957; 1958) data on masculinity and femininity.

In addition Milton (1957), Nakamura (1958), and Sweeney (1953) have evidence that men excel women on word problem solution whether or not the problem requires restructuring. If it were the males' superiority in analytic thinking which gave him the edge in problem solving, one would predict that women would do better (relative to men) on word problems the solution to which is straightforward. According to Milton's and Nakamura's data, they don't. According to Sweeney's data they do.

Before leaving the consideration of intellectual factors as the explanation for male superiority in word problem solving, it should be pointed out that of all the intellectual factors that have been measured, males (by age 8) show the most consistent and significant superiority over females in tests of spatial ability. Due to the fact that there appears to be no connection between what apparently is required for performance on these spatial tests and what is required for performance in solving word problems, we did not look closely at the literature in this area. Honesty prevents us from overlooking the fact that our assumption, about no connection between spatial and problem solving abilities, may be dead wrong. Further research on this topic should definitely look into this possible connection to make sure that it can be disregarded. Right off the bat, however, one would be leery of the age differential: the sexes diverge at age 8 on spatial tests and at age 14 on word problem tests.

For the sake of clarity it may be advantageous to take stock, at this point, of what kind of a composite explanation we can muster from the intellectual factors considered as relevant in this paper. It appears as though some possible distinctive pattern of verbal abilities and a possible male superiority in abstract, analytic reasoning might go part way in explaining male superiority in problem solving. However, the evidence is very weak for the possibility of explaining male superiority in problem solving through intellectual factors exclusively. We are therefore also forced to look at possible non-intellectual factors for a more complete explanation of this phenomenon.

6. SEX ROLE IDENTIFICATION

Upon being presented with a summary of the data shown in Table 1, a group of thirty undergraduate women at Simmons College majoring in elementary education concentrated their explanation of the data on ideas involving sex role identification. Indeed, in the research on non-intellectual factors involved with the sex-linked differential in problem solving performance, the majority of the effort has centered around the sex-role identification factor.

Milton (1957; 1958), in an impressive and extensive series of studies, demonstrates time and again, with a fairly wide variety of high school and college-aged subjects, that regardless of sex, scores on three different masculinity-femininity measures (Terman-Miles, the relevant part of the MMPI, and a behavioral test) correlate in the .29 to .41 range with scores on a very difficult word problem test (average score around 20%). Taking the sexes separately, and using only the Terman-Miles test, the correlations are in the low .30's for men and the high .40's for women. This is to say that masculine men and women solve more word problems than their feminine counterparts.

On the theory that sex role identification does affect performance on word problem tests, Milton (1958) rewrote the word problems with a distinctly feminine flavor involving situations in which women (and not men) often find themselves. On such problems, men still outperform women, but the difference is cut in half and is no longer significant. This evidence leads one to believe that indeed sex role identification does influence performance on word problems.

To give further support to this non-intellectual explanation, Poffenberger and Norton (1963) find that high school boys report that their parents expect them to receive higher grades in math courses than the girls' parents expect them to receive. There is little doubt that the male role is associated with higher math ability in our society.

As several investigators have discovered, however, the sex role connection with problem solving is not as clear cut as it has so far been presented in this paper. Maccoby (1966) points out, if sex role identification were all there was to it, why would the difference in problem solving performance not show up in studies with elementary school students? Hartley and Klein (1957) support Maccoby's contention in that they found elementary school girls have a strikingly clear concept of sex role. If the sex role identification explanation is to account for the sex difference in word problem solving, it will be hard pressed to explain why this difference does not show itself until age 14 when sex role identification starts long before that age.

Several ideas have been brought forth to explain this inconsistency. (1) Although the sex role *concept* has been formed by the elementary school years, *identification* with the appropriate sex role may be mixed in the primary grades due to cross sex identification and may be very weak in the intermediate grades due to the psychosexual moratorium during those years. Hence the argument would be that sex role *identification* does not become strong enough to have an effect on problem solving until puberty.

(2) It is not until about age 14 that boys and girls begin to confront one another on a one-to-one basis. In order for the boy to appear more competent than the girl and to bolster his self-esteem, both the boy and girl find that it is best for the boy to arrive at the most appropriate solution to whatever problems are faced. The boy is thus encouraged to increase his problem solving ability and use it at 100% efficiency. At the same time the girl is not stimulated to build her problem solving skills nor to use those she has at full capacity. Extremely weak evidence for the above argument can be found in one of Milton's (1958) studies in which the boys and girls were given the word problems in isolation as opposed to in a mixed group. Although there were other factors involved, the girls did better in isolation than otherwise.

(3) It can be argued that it is not until puberty that boys and girls become clearly aware that the adult male's role in our society involves the ability to solve problems and that the adult female's role is more involved with other abilities. Hence it is not until age 14 or so that word problem solving is clearly defined as a masculine activity. Some fairly clear support for half of this argument comes from Poffenberger and Norton (1963). They measured high school students' attitude toward algebra in 1955 (before Sputnik and our society's increase in emphasis on math and science) and in 1960 (a few years after Sputnik). There was a significant increase in boys' positive attitude toward algebra and no increase for the girls.

As if these above three counter-arguments were not enough, those who hold to the sex role identification explanation can also take the stand that the only reason sex role identification does not effect problem solving performance before age 14 is because other factors serve to cancel the effect. Hence they could point to the argument mentioned earlier (based on Piaget's and Vygotsky's work that cognitive abilities have not developed to the point (before age 14) where real differences in problem solving become apparent). But there *are* great differences (albeit not between the sexes) in problem solving performance before age 14. Hence the sex role identification proponents would have to use other factors such as the female's early superiority in general intelligence and/or verbal ability to explain how the sex role effect is dampened before age 14.

We have mentioned that sex role identification, as the factor in explaining the sex difference in problem solving, can be criticized (the numerous counter-arguments notwithstanding) on the grounds that it does not clearly account for the fact that sex role identification begins fairly early in childhood and the sex difference in problem solving performance is not manifest until age 14. There are other grounds on which the sex role identification can be criticized.

If math is so male-appropriate, why is it that no sex difference is found at any age in computation tests? The counter-arguments are not difficult to find. (1) Word problems are often viewed as the essence of math, computation as low-level busy work. Speed and accuracy in computation is not seen as high ability in mathematics, but problem solving ability is. (2) Computational ability is seen as a result of having conformed in elementary school, while the ability to solve word problems is seen as more innate. (3) Word problems are more or less related to "real life" as compared to computation *per se*. Real life demands that males be superior in math. Hence word problem ability is more closely associated with masculinity than is the ability to compute.

All three of the above counter-arguments were brought out in discussion with the Simmons College girls. An interesting illustration of the second of the three occurred in an exchange between the instructor (of the course the girls were taking in methods of teaching math) and one of the girls in the course.

> *Instructor:* You did a nice job on that last (difficult) exam.
> *Student:* (With a shrug) Math major in high school.

It could have been that the girl was overly modest, but the instructor had the suspicion that there was something of the following in the motives behind the answer: I'm not really good in math (i.e., too masculine); it's just that I got so much training in high school.

Another argument against the sex role identification explanation is that Berry (1958, 1959), working under the same grant as Milton, found that several non-intellectual, sex-linked factors (see 8, 9, & 11 below) correlated with problem solving in groups of college students who showed the usual sex differences in problem solving performance. And, although he also measured masculinity and femininity with two different tests and the tests had high correlations with sex, they did not correlate at all with problem solving performance.

Juxtaposed with the Milton findings, Berry's results are rather disconcerting. A possible explanation for this discrepancy is that Berry's subjects (Swarthmore College and Yale University students), coming from an intellectual environment, may possess a distinct pattern of sex role attitudes. Milton's subjects came from public high schools and universities (with the exception of Stanford) in California and Colorado. Perhaps it is only particular aspects of the masculinity-femininity measure that correlate with problem solving performance. Certainly the correlations of .30 to .50 that Milton found would not preclude such a possibility. We shall speak more of this later in the paper.

In passing, we should mention a study by Minuchin, reported in Maccoby (1966), which gives some support to the above explanation of the Berry-Milton discrepancy. Minuchin gave a word problem test to the students in two schools: one judged "modern" and the other "traditional" on the grounds that at the latter, much more sex role typing was observed in the play of the students. Although the boys in both schools outperformed the girls on the test, the difference at the "modern" school was significantly *less* pronounced.

Hence the Berry data may not be so much a refutation of the Milton findings as it is a refinement of them. It seems clear that sex role identification is related to problem solving performance to such an extent that further examination of this phenomenon is warranted. The majority of the remaining non-intellectual factors to be discussed in the paper can be thought of as sub-factors which comprise part of the sex role identification factor. In other words, in discussing the remaining five factors, we will (in part at least) be trying to identify those aspects of the composite sex role identification factor which account for the significant correlations between it and problem solving performance. Obviously there are two possibilities here. The correlations may be explained by some sub-factor of sex role identification and problem solving performance. Or it may be that some factor can be identified which can account for both sex role identification and problem solving performance. Hence in addition to possible sub-factors of sex role identification, we shall also consider factors which might account for both sex role identification and problem solving performance.

7. ATTITUDES TOWARD MATHEMATICS

Studies too numerous to mention here show that in our society males have a more positive attitude toward math than females and that the differential seems to appear in the elementary school years and increases until adulthood.

Although one hesitates to throw out this factor entirely, it is obvious that it suffers from lack of specificity. We are here concerned with word problems and a sex differential that does not appear definitely until about age 14. If attitude toward math were a potent factor, it seems reasonable that female negativeness would extend to performance on computation tests. As we have seen, it doesn't appear to do so. Again, if female negativeness appears in elementary school, it ought to affect word problem solving at that age. But, as we have seen, there is no consistent male superiority in problem solving in elementary school.

It seems clear then that, if we are to consider an attitude factor, it will have to be an attitude toward something more specific than mathematics.

8. ATTITUDE TOWARD ANALYTIC THINKING

Berry (1958) found that male college students have a significantly more positive attitude toward analytic thinking than the females. In addition Berry found that, for both sexes combined, there was a .59 correlation between the scores on this Carey attitude scale and the scores on the word problem test.

The evidence in favor of this specific attitude having a great deal to do with problem solving performance is striking, especially as it relates to the sex-linked performance differential. Milton, in one of the studies he reported in 1958, found that even though women admitted (as often as men) that the best method to use in solving a particular problem was via analytic thinking, they also admitted that they would not actually use this method nearly as often as men said they would use it. The women (much more than the men) said they would actually seek help in solving the problem. Since all the tests of word problem solving being considered in this paper are conducted so that the subjects have no alternative to trying to solve the problems analytically, the fact that the women would really prefer to solve some of the problems by seeking help puts them at a decided disadvantage.

Before one puts too much credence in the importance of this attitude factor, it should be pointed out that Milton's finding above was more apparent when the problems themselves were written with the masculine bias (explained in part 6). In addition, if one uses Milton's figures on problem solving efficiency for men and women under the usual testing conditions and sets up a hypothetical situation in which subjects could solve analytically or seek help as they chose in order for the women to do as well as men, the women would have to be 100% successful in seeking accurate help and the men only 80%. Admittedly one could make a case for women being more successful than men in this area, but this would take us into more social psychology than the scope of this paper permits.

In spite of these qualifications of Milton's findings, there is additional evidence to lend credence to the importance of this factor of attitude toward analytic thinking, at least insofar as it coincides with attitude toward word problem solving. Carey (1955) gave tests in word problem solving to college students both before and after group discussions in which an attempt was made to improve the subject's attitude toward problem solving. While the performance of the male subjects was not improved by the discussions, that of the female subjects was improved significantly. Milton (1958) recorded the performance on each problem of a twenty-problem word problem test which consisted of both feminine and masculine biased problems. He found that on the first ten problems the men out-performed the women significantly, but on the last ten problems the women performed just as well as the men: that is, the women improved to the men's level of performance. Milton explains this result by conjecturing that perhaps the women's initial negative attitude toward such a test was broken down by the fact that it appeared as though the test was "sex fair".

Hence we find a good deal of evidence (with college students at least) that attitude toward analytic thinking (and word problem solving) may go a considerable way in explaining the sex difference in word problem solving. We were unable to find data on younger subjects to check this factor out as it relates to the age 14 phenomenon. This would be one area in which further literature search and/or investigation might be called for. A confounding element in this whole area of analytic thinking, sex role identification and word problem solving is the finding reported in Maccoby (1966), to which we referred earlier. Analytic ability seems to be related to femininity in males and masculinity in females. Further investigation into attitude toward analytic thinking might uncover an explanation for this and the confounding fact that masculinity (regardless of sex) seems to facilitate performance on word problems.

9. SUSCEPTIBILITY TO EXTRANEOUS INFLUENCE

In the Simmons College discussion mentioned earlier, the first explanation offered to account for the data was as follows: men seem to be able to get to the heart of the matter while women tend to dwell on the interesting extraneous elements. The other Simmons women reluctantly accepted this as true.

Witkin (1962) gives an abundance of evidence to support this contention on the part of the Simmons students. He finds males consistently more field independent than women, even though the variation within each sex is high. (This latter qualification should not concern us unduly, since there is also considerable intrasex variability in word problem solving.) Maccoby (1966) summarizes the literature on sex differences in field independence by saying that in pre-school and primary school age, children do not differ (along sex lines) in field independence. By the intermediate grades male superiority has begun to appear and it is consistent to adulthood. (There is a slight problem here with the age 14 phenomenon, but if one is devoted to a multi-factor explanation of the sex differential in word problem solving, this difficulty should not prevent us from examining this factor further.)

Guetzhow (1951) found that college men were better able than women to break set when presented first with several word problems of the same type and then given problems of a distinct nature. Carlsmith (1964) reports that Seder and Bieri found that men do better on word problems because they, as distinct from the women, disregard extraneous elements which they more clearly discriminate from the pertinent stimuli. Maier and Burke (1957) gave a horse trading problem to separate groups of subjects where each group was given a different set of alternative answers. The college men were less influenced by the responses available than were the women.

Berry (1958; 1959) found in his comprehensive study of non-intellectual factors influencing problem solving that college men are more field independent and that field independence is mildly correlated with problem solving performance *in both men and women.* Berry found these correlations (as well as those mentioned above involving attitude toward analytic thinking) to hold even after having partialed out the strong correlations between math and verbal ability and word problem solving.

Insofar as restructuring requires field independence, the findings of Milton (1957) and Nakamura (1958) suggest that this field independence factor may be weaker than the evidence above indicates. As mentioned previously, with college students given problems of two types, male superiority was consistent; they outperformed the women on both the problems involving a straightforward solution and those requiring restructuring. But even these results are not conclusive since Sweeney (1953) found that in a similar situation, male superiority was more pronounced in the problems involving restructuring.

Although the idea is intuitively appealing and there is evidence for it, before conceding that susceptibility to extraneous influence is an important factor in explaining the sex differential in problem solving performance, it would be worthwhile to investigate this connection further.

Again, all the data cited above was based on college students and shed no light whatsoever on the age 14 phenomenon. Even with the college students the connections are not impressive or clear.

10. EFFORT

On the theory that people try harder when doing activities they enjoy, and given that males (not females) have a preference for math, one can make a case that male superiority in word problem solving is simply due to the fact that men try harder. Maccoby (1966) reports that boys tend to over-achieve in high school in those subjects they prefer, whereas in grade school they tend to under-achieve in all subjects. This latter observation would not only give support for effort being a significant factor here, but also it would account for the age 14 phenomenon. When one looks at females, one is even more inclined to believe in the importance of this effort factor. Girls tend to achieve on a par with their abilities regardless of the subject. There is even evidence (Maccoby, 1966) to believe that girls tend to generally under-achieve after puberty (in high school).

Since there were no studies cited in the literature which related effort directly with sex differences in problem solving performance, it would be risky to put great importance on effort as a factor. Even if there were evidence of this type, it would simply beg the question as to why males put more effort on problem solving than females. What is worse, Maccoby (1966) points out that nursery school boys have been observed to be more apt to take on challenging tasks, thus making it more difficult to explain the age 14 phenomenon. In addition, Maccoby reports that aggressiveness tends to debilitate boys' intellectual performance and facilitate that of girls. This latter would tend to make one think that increased effort would not suffice to explain male superiority in solving word problems.

11. LACK OF TEST ANXIETY

Berry (1958) found college men to have significantly less test anxiety than the women. Maccoby (1966) reports that anxiety tends to facilitate boys' intellectual performance and debilitate that of the girls. It appears that one could argue that male superiority in problem solving performance is due to the fact that whatever slight anxiety they might have during the test helps their performance, while the unfortunate females are not only more anxious but their anxiety hurts their performance.

But this argument says nothing specific about the lack of test anxiety while taking a word problem solving test. Indeed, Berry (1959) found no correlation between test anxiety and scores on the word problem test. Hence it seems reasonable to disregard the lack of test anxiety in males as a significant factor in their superiority in solving word problems.

At this point let us take stock of what the consideration of non-intellectual factors has contributed to an explanation of the sex-linked differential in word problem solving. Of the six factors considered, it seems clear that sex-role identification has the most to offer. However, since males are naturally more masculine and females more feminine, using sex role identification as the non-intellectual factor explaining male superiority in word problem solving seems a bit like begging the question. Probing further, we found that attitude toward analytic thinking and (to a lesser extent) field independence made a little more specific the connection between masculine traits and male superiority in problem solving.

A Composite Explanation of the Data

First let us try to explain the male superiority in word problem solving as it exists in adolescence and adulthood. Superior ability in analytic reasoning and a possible distinct pattern of verbal abilities coupled with a positive attitude toward analytic thinking and field independence seem to be the factors which logically and empirically are most closely associated with the fact that males outperform females on tests of word problem solving.

Second, let us try to explain why this male superiority does not appear until about age 14. Although each of the above factors are (or could be) increasingly more prevalent in males than in females as each gets older, I believe that we must introduce the sex role identification factor in order to explain more fully the age 14 phenomenon. As we pointed out in the discussion of this latter factor, there are a number of strong logical arguments and some good empirical evidence to show that around puberty the male sex role becomes more sharply defined: to include the ability to solve word problems.

It should be quickly conceded that the above "explanation" is appallingly weak at various points, many of which were pointed out in the discussion of the various individual factors. At those points, we suggested areas in which it looked as though further investigation might be fruitful and useful, e.g., the patterns of verbal sub-abilities. There are two areas of further investigation which were not mentioned and ought to be.

(1) Practically all of the studies cited in this paper are based on measures taken at one point in the subjects' lives. It would be useful to do longitudinal studies to investigate child-rearing roots of superior ability

in solving word problems. Such investigation may uncover important differences in the ways in which boys and girls are raised in our society. It may also uncover clues for educators wishing to improve their methods of teaching the successful solution of word problems.

That such longitudinal research will not be easily done is attested by the fact that Milton (1958), in one of his studies, found no correlation between problem solving performances and any one of several questions that subjects in late adolescence answered about their personal histories. Nevertheless, Maccoby (1966) reports on data showing that nurturant mothers (for the boys) and supportive fathers (for the girls) facilitate later intellectual performance. Plank and Plank (1954) find, in the autobiographies of mathematicians, strong identification with a male figure (for the female) and the loss of a relationship with the mother (for the male mathematicians). Somewhat in contradiction to the Planks, Carlsmith (1964) reports on a great deal of literature which indicates that boys who have a close association with their fathers do well in math, and that girls who have a close association with the mothers do poorly.

Hence although previous research is sketchy and often begs the relevant question, there are some leads into possible investigation of longitudinal explanations of the male superiority in word problem solving.

(2) A second area of investigation, which has not yet been mentioned but might well be fruitful and useful, is cross-cultural research. All of the research reported in this paper was based on subjects drawn from not only U. S. society but (in most cases) a fairly restricted segment of that society, e.g., college students.

Cross-cultural research might turn up societies in which the male superiority is not present in any age. It may also locate societies which possess the male superiority but do not manifest the same age 14 phenomenon. In either case, the theories used to explain the data in the U.S. would then need to be checked against the appropriate aspects of these other societies which did not produce the same word problem solving data that we have presented in this paper.

There is great hope that such cross-cultural research might be carried out in the near future. The newspapers have recently carried articles indicating that a research project in Chicago is completing a vast survey of achievement in mathematics by school children in ten countries. This data will undoubtedly include sub-test scores dealing with performance on word problems.

1. Does the data (compiled in Table 1) seem valid? The majority of the data was collected in the 1950's and very early 1960's. If it were col-

lected today, would you expect similar results?[2] Presumably most of the data was collected on random samples of the U. S. population. Can you think of particular samples from which contradictory data might be collected? Why?

2. Can you give an explanation (before—or without—being snowed by the author's explanation) which could explain the data—given that it is (or, at least, was) valid for some population? Your explanation would have to account not only for the male superiority but also for its appearance at roughly age 14.

3. Again, assuming valid data and given some composite explanation of it (your own or the author's) if you were to teach word problem solving, how would you go about it in elementary school? in junior high? in high school?

References

Ackerman, E. I. Presentation of alternatives and its relation to set in problem solving. Ed.D. thesis, Harvard University, 1956.

Berry, Paul C. An exploration of the interrelations among some non-intellectual predictors of achievement in problem solving. Technical Reports Nos. 4 and 5, Contract Nonr 609 (20), (NR 150–166) for ONR, Yale University, New Haven, Conn., Dec. 1958 (No. 4), May 1959 (No. 5).

Carey, G. L. Reduction of sex differences in problem solving by improvement of attitude through group discussion. Technical Report No. 9, Contract Nonr 25125, 1955. (Also in *Journal of Abnormal and Social Psychology*.)

Carlsmith, Lynn. Effect of early father absence on scholastic aptitude. *Harvard Educational Review*, 1964, 34, 3–21.

Guetzkow, H. An analysis of the operation of set in problem solving behavior. *Journal of Genetic Psychology*, 1951, 45, 219–244.

Hartley, R. E., and Klein, A. Sex role concepts among elementary school-age girls. Paper read at meetings of the American Psychological Association, 1957.

Heilman, J. D. Sex differences in intellectual abilities. *Journal of Educational Psychology*, 1933, 24, 47–62.

Inhelder, B., and Piaget, J. *The growth of logical thinking from childhood to adolescence*. New York: Basic Books, 1958.

---

[2] For the first time in the history of such testing, Simmons College (female) freshmen scored higher on the math than the verbal part of the S.A.T. in Spring, 1968: culminating a trend in that direction through the 1960's.

Lesser, G. S., Fifer, G., and Clark, D. H. Mental Abilities of Children in Different Social and Cultural Groups. Cooperative Research Project No. 1635, U.S.O.E. of the Department of HEW, Hunter College, 1964.

Maccoby, Eleanor E. *The Development of Sex Differences*. Stanford, Calif.: Stanford University Press, 1966.

Maier, N. R. F., and Burke, R. J. Response availability as a factor in problem solving performance of males and females. *Journal of Personality and Social Psychology*, 1967, 5 (3), 304–310.

Milton, G. A. The effects of sex role identification upon problem solving skill. *Journal of Abnormal and Social Psychology*, 1957, 55 (2), 208–212.

Milton, G. A. Five studies of the relation between sex role identification and achievement in problem solving. Technical Report No. 3, ONR Contract Nonr 609 (20), NR 150–166, Yale University, New Haven, Conn., 1958.

Nakamura, C. Y. Conformity and problem solving. *Journal of Abnormal and Social Psychology*, 1958, 56, 315–320.

Plank, Emma H., and Plank, R. Emotional components in arithmetic learning as seen through autobiographies. In R. S. Eissler, and others (Eds.). *The psychoanalytic study of the child*, Vol. IX. New York: International Universities Press, 1954.

Poffenberger, T., and Norton, D. Sex differences in achievement motive in mathematics as related to cultural change. *Journal of Genetic Psychology*, 1963, 103, 341–350.

Polya, G. *How to solve it*. Garden City, N. Y.: Doubleday, 1957.

Sweeney, E. J. Sex differences in problem solving. Technical Report No. 1, Contract Nonr 25125, Dept. of Psychology, Stanford, 1953.

Thorndike, E. L. *The psychology of arithmetic*. New York: Macmillan, 1962.

Vygotsky, L. S. *Thought and language*. Cambridge, Mass.: M.I.T. Press, 1962.

Wesman, A. G. Separation of sex groups in test reporting. *Journal of Educational Psychology*, 40, 1949, 223–229.

Witkin, H. A., and others. *Psychological differentiation*. New York: Wiley, 1962.

Appendix

One of the studies cited in Table 1 of this paper stems from some statistics run on test scores kept from an algebra class in the year 1960–61. The school was a high school in West Virginia and the group of twenty was selected from the previous year's seventh and eighth grade classes: a group of about fifty to sixty students. I selected the six boys and six girls from the algebra group with the highest I.Q. scores. (The average I.Q. for the boys was 115.8 and for the girls, 123.5.) The reason I chose only six of each sex was because there were only six boys in the algebra class. As reported in Table 1, the ages ranged from 13 to 15.

During the academic year, I gave the class fifteen one-hour exams; they were open-book exams and covered the previous two weeks' work. For each exam, I have computed an average score for the boys and an average for the girls. Then to get the "difference score," I subtracted the girls' average from the boys'. (A large positive score means the boys' average was a great deal better than the girls'.)

Independently, I went through each of the exams and calculated the percentage of the exam which consisted of word problems. The difference scores and the percentage scores were then each ranked from 1 to 15. A rank correlation of .46 was then calculated, using the formula for the Spearman rank correlation coefficient. (Note here that no correction was made for the tied ranks. Such a correction would lessen the correlation to some extent, but certainly not to below significance.)

The Data

EXAM NO.	DIFFERENCE SCORE	RANK	PERCENTAGE OF WORD PROBLEMS	RANK
1	−4.4	12	0	13
1	−2.3	11	50	3
3	+7.3	5	100	1
4	+8.4	3	43	4
5	−13.1	15	0	13
6	−5.0	13	30	7
7	−0.6	9	40	7
8	−2.0	10	20	9.5
9	(entire exam misfired)			
10	+8.0	4	0	13
11	+0.7	8	0	13
12	+8.7	2	20	9.5
13	−11.7	14	0	13
14	+23.5	1	60	2
15	+0.8	7	30	7
16	+7.1	6	30	7

2. EGOCENTRISM IN ADOLESCENCE *

David Elkind

Within the Piagetian theory of intellectual growth, the concept of ego-centrism generally refers to a lack of differentiation in some area of subject-object interaction (Piaget, 1962). At each stage of mental development, this lack of differentiation takes a unique form and is manifested in a unique set of behaviors. The transition from one form of ego-centrism to another takes place in a dialectic fashion such that the mental structures which free the child from a lower form of egocentrism are the same structures which ensnare him in a higher form of egocentrism. From the developmental point of view, therefore, egocentrism can be regarded as a negative by-product of any emergent mental system in the sense that it corresponds to the fresh cognitive problems engendered by that system.

Although in recent years Piaget has focused his attention more on the positive than on the negative products of mental structures, egocentrism continues to be of interest because of its relation to the affective aspects of child thought and behavior. Indeed, it is possible that the study of egocentrism may provide a bridge between the study of cognitive structure, on the one hand, and the exploration of personality dynamics, on the other (Cowan, 1966; Gourevitch & Feffer, 1962). The purpose of the present paper is to describe, in greater detail than Inhelder and Piaget (1958), what seems to me to be the nature of egocentrism in adolescence and some of its behavioral and experiential correlates. Before doing that, however, it might be well to set the stage for the discussion with a brief review of the forms of egocentrism which precede this mode of thought in adolescence.

Forms of Egocentrism in Infancy and Childhood

In presenting the childhood forms of egocentrism, it is useful to treat each of Piaget's major stages as if it were primarily concerned with re-

° *Child Development*, 1967, *38*, 1025–1034. Copyright 1967, by the Society for Research in Child Development, Inc. Preparation of this paper was supported in part by grant No. 6881 from the Office of Education. Author's address: Department of Psychology, University of Rochester, Rochester, New York 14627.

solving one major cognitive task. The egocentrism of a particular stage can then be described with reference to this special problem of cognition. It must be stressed, however, that while the cognitive task characteristic of a particular stage seems to attract the major share of the child's mental energies, it is not the only cognitive problem with which the child is attempting to cope. In mental development there are major battles and minor skirmishes, and if I here ignore the lesser engagements it is for purposes of economy of presentation rather than because I assume that such engagements are insignificant.

SENSORI-MOTOR EGOCENTRISM (0–2 YEARS)

The major cognitive task of infancy might be regarded *as the conquest of the object.* In the early months of life, the infant deals with objects as if their existence were dependent upon their being present in immediate perception (Charlesworth, 1966; Piaget, 1954). The egocentrism of this stage corresponds, therefore, to a lack of differentiation between the object and the sense impressions occasioned by it. Toward the end of the first year, however, the infant begins to seek the object even when it is hidden, and thus shows that he can now differentiate between the object and the "experience of the object." This breakdown of egocentrism with respect to objects is brought about by mental representation of the absent object.[1] An internal representation of the absent object is the earliest manifestation of the symbolic function which develops gradually during the second year of life and whose activities dominate the next stage of mental growth.

PRE-OPERATIONAL EGOCENTRISM (2-6 YEARS)

During the preschool period, the child's major cognitive task can be regarded as *the conquest of the symbol.* It is during the preschool period that the symbolic function becomes fully active, as evidenced by the rapid growth in the acquisition and utilization of language, by the appearance of symbolic play, and by the first reports of dreams. Yet this new capacity for representation, which loosed the infant from his egocentrism with respect to objects, now ensnares the preschool children in a new egocentrism with regard to symbols. At the beginning of this period, the child fails to differentiate between words and their referents

---

[1] It is characteristic of the dialectic of mental growth that the capacity to represent internally the absent object also enables the infant to cognize the object as externally existent.

(Piaget, 1952b) and between his self-created play and dream symbols and reality (Kohlberg, 1966; Piaget, 1951). Children at this stage believe that the name inheres in the thing and that an object cannot have more than one name (Elkind, 1961a, 1962, 1963).

The egocentrism of this period is particularly evident in children's linguistic behavior. When explaining a piece of apparatus to another child, for example, the youngster at this stage uses many indefinite terms and leaves out important information (Piaget, 1952b). Although this observation is sometimes explained by saying that the child fails to take the other person's point of view, it can also be explained by saying that the child assumes words carry much more information than they actually do. This results from his belief that even the indefinite "thing" somehow conveys the properties of the object which it is used to represent. In short, the egocentrism of this period consists in a lack of clear differentiation between symbols and their referents.

Toward the end of the pre-operational period, the differentiation between symbols and their referents is gradually brought about by the emergence of concrete operations (internalized actions which are roughly comparable in their activity to the elementary operations of arithmetic). One consequence of concrete operational thought is that it enables the child to deal with two elements, properties, or relations at the same time. A child with concrete operations can, for example, take account of both the height and width of a glass of colored liquid and recognize that, when the liquid is poured into a differently shaped container, the changes in height and width of the liquid compensate one another so that the total quantity of liquid is conserved (Elkind, 1961b; Piaget, 1952a). This ability, to hold two dimensions in mind at the same time, also enables the child to hold both symbol and referent in mind simultaneously, and thus distinguish between them. Concrete operations are, therefore, instrumental in overcoming the egocentrism of the pre-operational stage.

CONCRETE OPERATIONAL EGOCENTRISM (7–11 YEARS)

With the emergence of concrete operations, the major cognitive task of the school-age child becomes that of *mastering classes, relations, and quantities.* While the preschool child forms global notions of classes, relations, and quantities, such notions are imprecise and cannot be combined one with the other. The child with concrete operations, on the other hand, can nest classes, seriate relations, and conserve quantities. In addition, concrete operations enable the school-age child to perform elementary syllogistic reasoning and to formulate hypotheses and explanations about concrete matters. This system of concrete operations, however, which lifts the school-age child to new heights of thought, nonetheless lowers him to new depths of egocentrism.

Operations are essentially mental tools whose products, series, class hierarchies, conservations, etc., are not directly derived from experience. At this stage, however, the child nonetheless regards these mental products as being on a par with perceptual phenomena. It is the inability to differentiate clearly between mental constructions and perceptual givens which constitutes the egocentrism of the school-age child. An example may help to clarify the form which egocentrism takes during the concrete operational stage.

In a study reported by Peel (1960), children and adolescents were read a passage about Stonehenge and then asked questions about it. One of the questions had to do with whether Stonehenge was a place for religious worship or a fort. The children (ages 7–10) answered the question with flat statements, as if they were stating a fact. When they were given evidence that contradicted their statements, they rationalized the evidence to make it conform with their initial position. Adolescents, on the other hand, phrased their replies in probabilistic terms and supported their judgments with material gleaned from the passage. Similar differences between children and adolescents have been found by Elkind (1966) and Weir (1964).

What these studies show is that, when a child constructs a hypothesis or formulates a strategy, he assumes that this product is imposed by the data rather than derived from his own mental activity. When his position is challenged, he does not change his stance but, on the contrary, reinterprets the data to fit with his assumption. This observation, however, raises a puzzling question. Why, if the child regards both his thought products and the givens of perception as coming from the environment, does he nonetheless give preference to his own mental constructions? The answer probably lies in the fact that the child's mental constructions are the product of reasoning, and hence are experienced as imbued with a (logical) necessity. This "felt" necessity is absent when the child experiences the products of perception. It is not surprising, then, that the child should give priority to what seems permanent and necessary in perception (the products of his own thought, such as conservation) rather than to what seems transitory and arbitrary in perception (products of environmental stimulation). Only in adolescence do young people differentiate between their own mental constructions and the givens of perception. For the child, there are no problems of epistemology.

Toward the end of childhood, the emergence of formal operational thought (which is analogous to propositional logic) gradually frees the child from his egocentrism with respect to his own mental constructions.

As Inhelder and Piaget (1958) have shown, formal operational thought enables the young person to deal with all of the possible combinations and permutations of elements within a given set. Provided with four differently colored pieces of plastic, for example, the adolescent can work out all the possible combinations of colors by taking the pieces one, two, three and four, and none, at a time. Children, on the other hand, cannot formulate these combinations in any systematic way. The ability to conceptualize all of the possible combinations in a system allows the adolescent to construct contrary-to-fact hypotheses and to reason about such propositions "as if" they were true. The adolescent, for example, can accept the statement, "Let's suppose coal is white," whereas the child would reply, "But coal is black." This ability to formulate contrary-to-fact hypotheses is crucial to the overcoming of the egocentrism of the concrete operational period. Through the formulation of such contrary-to-fact hypotheses, the young person discovers the arbitrariness of his own mental constructions and learns to differentiate them from perceptual reality.

Adolescent Egocentrism

From the strictly cognitive point of view (as opposed to the psychoanalytic point of view as represented by Blos [1962] and A. Freud [1946] or the ego psychological point of view as represented by Erikson [1959]), the major task of early adolescence can be regarded as having to do with *the conquest of thought*. Formal operations not only permit the young person to construct all the possibilities in a system and construct contrary-to-fact propositions (Inhelder & Piaget, 1958); they also enable him to conceptualize his own thought, to take his mental constructions as objects and reason about them. Only at about the ages of 11–12, for example, do children spontaneously introduce concepts of belief, intelligence, and faith into their definitions of their religious denomination (Elkind, 1961a; 1962; 1963). Once more, however, this new mental system which frees the young person from the egocentrism of childhood entangles him in a new form of egocentrism characteristic of adolescence.

Formal operational thought not only enables the adolescent to conceptualize his thought, it also permits him to conceptualize the thought of other people. It is this capacity to take account of other people's thought, however, which is the crux of adolescent egocentrism. This egocentrism emerges because, while the adolescent can now cognize the thoughts of others, he fails to differentiate between the objects toward which the thoughts of others are directed and those which are the focus of his own concern. Now, it is well known that the young adolescent, because of the physiological metamorphosis he is undergoing, is primarily concerned with himself. Accordingly, since he fails to differentiate between what others are thinking about and his own mental preoccupations, he assumes that other people are as obsessed with his behavior and appearance as he is himself. *It is this belief that others are preoccupied with his appearance and behavior that constitutes the egocentrism of the adolescent.*

One consequence of adolescent egocentrism is that, in actual or impending social situations, the young person anticipates the reactions of other people to himself. These anticipations, however, are based on the premise that others are as admiring or as critical of him as he is of himself. In a sense, then, the adolescent is continually constructing, or reacting to, *an imaginary audience.* It is an audience because the adolescent believes that he will be the focus of attention; and it is imaginary because, in actual social situations, this is not usually the case (unless he contrives to make it so). The construction of imaginary audiences would seem to account, in part at least, for a wide variety of typical adolescent behaviors and experiences.

The imaginary audience, for example, probably plays a role in the self-consciousness which is so characteristic of early adolescence. When the young person is feeling critical of himself, he anticipates that the audience—of which he is necessarily a part—will be critical too. And, since the audience is his own construction and privy to his own knowledge of himself, it knows just what to look for in the way of cosmetic and behavioral sensitivities. The adolescent's wish for privacy and his reluctance to reveal himself may, to some extent, be a reaction to the feeling of being under the constant critical scrutiny of other people. The notion of an imaginary audience also helps to explain the observation that the affect which most concerns adolescents is not guilt but, rather, shame, that is, the reaction to an audience (Lynd, 1961).

While the adolescent is often self-critical, he is frequently self-admiring too. At such times, the audience takes on the same affective coloration. A good deal of adolescent boorishness, loudness, and faddish dress is probably provoked, partially in any case, by a failure to differentiate between what the young person believes to be attractive and what others admire. It is for this reason that the young person frequently fails to understand why adults disapprove of the way he dresses and behaves. The same sort of egocentrism is often seen in behavior directed toward the opposite sex. The boy who stands in front of the mirror for 2 hours combing his hair is probably imagining the swooning reactions he will produce in the girls. Likewise, the girl applying her makeup is more likely than not imagining the admiring glances that will come her way. When these young people actually meet, each is more concerned with being the observed than with being the observer. Gatherings of young adolescents are unique in the sense that each young person is simultaneously an actor to himself and an audience to others.

One of the most common admiring audience constructions, in the adolescent, is the anticipation of how others will react to his own demise. A certain bittersweet pleasure is derived from anticipating the belated recognition by others of his positive qualities. As often happens with such universal fantasies, the imaginary anticipation of one's own demise has been realized in fiction. Below, for example, is the passage in *Tom Sawyer* where Tom sneaks back to his home, after having run away with Joe and Huck, to discover that he and his friends are thought to have been drowned:

> But this memory was too much for the old lady, and she broke entirely down. Tom was snuffling, now, himself—and more in pity of himself than anybody else. He could hear Mary crying and putting in a kindly word for him from time to time. He began to have a nobler opinion of himself than ever before. Still, he was sufficiently touched by his aunt's grief to long to rush out from under the bed and overwhelm her with joy—and the theatrical gorgeousness of the thing appealed strongly to his nature too—but he resisted and lay still.

Corresponding to the imaginary audience is another mental construction which is its complement. While the adolescent fails to differentiate the concerns of his own thought from those of others, he at the same time overdifferentiates his feelings. Perhaps because he believes he is of importance to so many people, the imaginary audience, he comes to regard himself, and particularly his feelings, as something special and unique. Only he can suffer with such agonized intensity, or experience such exquisite rapture. How many parents have been confronted with the typically adolescent phrase, "But you don't know how it feels. . . ." The emotional torments undergone by Goethe's young Werther and by Salinger's Holden Caulfield exemplify the adolescent's belief in the uniqueness of his own emotional experience. At a somewhat different level, this belief in personal uniqueness becomes a conviction that he will not die, that death will happen to others but not to him. This complex of beliefs in the uniqueness of his feelings and of his immortality might be called *a personal fable*, a story which he tells himself and which is not true.

Evidences of the personal fable are particularly prominent in adolescent diaries. Such diaries are often written for posterity in the conviction that the young person's experiences, crushes, and frustrations are of universal significance and importance. Another kind of evidence for the personal fable during this period is the tendency to confide in a personal

God. The search for privacy and the belief in personal uniqueness leads to the establishment of an I-Thou relationship with God as a personal confidant to whom one no longer looks for gifts but rather for guidance and support (Long, Elkind, & Spilka, 1967).

The concepts of an imaginary audience and a personal fable have proved useful, at least to the writer, in the understanding and treatment of troubled adolescents. The imaginary audience, for example, seems often to play a role in middle-class delinquency (Elkind, 1967). As a case in point, one young man took $1,000 from a golf tournament purse, hid the money, and then promptly revealed himself. It turned out that much of the motivation for this act was derived from the anticipated response of "the audience" to the guttiness of his action. In a similar vein, many young girls become pregnant because, in part at least, their personal fable convinces them that pregnancy will happen to others but never to them and so they need not take precautions. Such examples could be multiplied but will perhaps suffice to illustrate how adolescent egocentrism, as manifested in the imaginary audience and in the personal fable, can help provide a rationale for some adolescent behavior. These concepts can, moreover, be utilized in the treatment of adolescent offenders. It is often helpful to these young people if they can learn to differentiate between the real and the imaginary audience, which often boils down to a discrimination between the real and the imaginary parents.

The Passing of Adolescent Egocentrism

After the appearance of formal operational thought, no new mental systems develop and the mental structures of adolescence must serve for the rest of the life span. The egocentrism of early adolescence nonetheless tends to diminish by the age of 15 or 16, the age at which formal operations become firmly established. What appears to happen is that the imaginary audience, which is primarily an anticipatory audience, is progressively modified in the direction of the reactions of the real audience. In a way, the imaginary audience can be regarded as hypothesis —or better, as a series of hypotheses—which the young person tests against reality. As a consequence of this testing, he gradually comes to recognize the difference between his own preoccupations and the interests and concerns of others.

The personal fable, on the other hand, is probably overcome (although probably never in its entirety) by the gradual establishment of what Erikson (1959) has called "intimacy." Once the young person sees himself in a more realistic light as a function of having adjusted his imaginary audience to the real one, he can establish true rather than self-interested interpersonal relations. Once relations of mutuality are established and confidences are shared, the young person discovers that others have feelings similar to his own and have suffered and been enraptured in the same way.

Adolescent egocentrism is thus overcome by a twofold transformation. On the cognitive plane, it is overcome by the gradual differentiation between his own preoccupations and the thoughts of others; while on the plane of affectivity, it is overcome by a gradual integration of the feelings of others with his own emotions.

Summary and Conclusions

In this paper I have tried to describe the forms which egocentrism takes and the mechanisms by which it is overcome, in the course of mental development. In infancy, egocentrism corresponds to the impression that objects are identical with the perception of them, and this form of egocentrism is overcome with the appearance of representation. During the preschool period, egocentrism appears in the guise of a belief that symbols contain the same information as is provided by the objects which they represent. With the emergence of concrete operations, the child is able to discriminate between symbol and referent, and so overcome this type of egocentrism. The egocentrism of the school-age period can be characterized as the belief that one's own mental constructions correspond to a superior form of perceptual reality. With the advent of formal operations and the ability to construct contrary-to-fact hypotheses, this kind of egocentrism is dissolved because the young person can now recognize the arbitrariness of his own mental constructions. Finally, during early adolescence, egocentrism appears as the belief that the thoughts of others are directed toward the self. This variety of egocentrism is overcome as a consequence of the conflict between the reactions which the young person anticipates and those which actually occur.

Although egocentrism corresponds to a negative product of mental growth, its usefulness would seem to lie in the light which it throws upon the affective reactions characteristic of any particular stage of mental development. In this paper I have dealt primarily with the affective reactions associated with the egocentrism of adolescence. Much of the material, particularly the discussion of the *imaginary audience* and the *personal fable,* is speculative in the sense that it is based as much upon my clinical experience with young people as it is upon research data. These constructs are offered, not as the final word on adolescent egocentrism, but rather to illustrate how the cognitive structures peculiar to a particular level of development can be related to the affective experience and behavior characteristic of that stage. Although I have here only considered the correspondence between mental structure and affect in adolescence, it is possible that similar correspondences can be found at the earlier levels of development as well. A consideration of egocentrism, then, would seem to be a useful starting point for any attempt to reconcile cognitive structure and the dynamics of personality.

References

Blos, P. *On adolescence.* New York: Free Press, 1962.

Charlesworth, W. R. Development of the object concept in infancy: methodological study. *American Psychologist,* 1966, *21,* 623. (Abstract)

Cowan, P. A. Cognitive egocentrism and social interaction in children. *American Psychologist,* 1966, *21,* 623. (Abstract)

Elkind, D. The child's conception of his religious denomination, I: The Jewish child. *Journal of Genetic Psychology,* 1961, *99,* 209–225. (a)

Elkind, D. The development of quantitative thinking. *Journal of Genetic Psychology,* 1961, *98,* 37–46. (b)

Elkind, D. The child's conception of his religious denomination, II: The Catholic child. *Journal of Genetic Psychology,* 1962, *101,* 185–193.

Elkind, D. The child's conception of his religious denomination, III: The Protestant child. *Journal of Genetic Psychology,* 1963, *103,* 291–304.

Elkind, D. Conceptual orientation shifts in children and adolescents. *Child Development,* 1966, *37,* 493–498.

Elkind, D. Middle-class delinquency. *Mental Hygiene,* 1967, *51,* 80–84.

Erikson, E. H. Identity and the life cycle. *Psychological issues.* Vol. I, No. 1, New York: International Universities Press, 1959.

Freud, Anna. *The ego and the mechanisms of defense.* New York International Universities Press, 1946.

Gourevitch, Vivian, and Feffer, M. H. A study of motivational development. *Journal of Genetic Psychology,* 1962, *100,* 361–375.

Inhelder, Bärbel, and Piaget, J. *The growth of logical thinking from childhood to adolescence.* New York: Basic Books, 1958.

Kohlberg, L. Cognitive stages and preschool education. *Human Development,* 1936, *9,* 5–17.

Long, Diane, Elkind, D., and Spilka, B. The child's conception of prayer. *Journal for the Scientific Study of Religion,* 1967, *6,* 101–109.

Lynd, Helen M. *On shame and the search for identity.* New York: Science Editions, 1961.

Peel, E. A. *The pupil's thinking*. London: Oldhourne, 1960.

Piaget, J. *The child's conception of the world*. London: Routledge & Kegan Paul, 1951.

Piaget, J. *The child's conception of number*. New York: Humanities Press, 1952. (a)

Piaget, J. *The language and thought of the child*. London: Routledge & Kegan Paul, 1952. (b)

Piaget, J. *The construction of reality in the child*. New York: Basic Books, 1954.

Piaget, J. *Comments on Vygotsky's critical remarks concerning "The language and thought of the child" and "Judgment and reasoning in the child."* Cambridge, Mass.: M.I.T. Press, 1962.

Weir, M. W. Development changes in problem solving strategies. *Psychological Review*, 1964, 71, 473–490.

3. CONCEPTUAL ORIENTATION SHIFTS IN CHILDREN AND ADOLESCENTS *

David Elkind

One of the relatively unexplored aspects of conceptual growth is the development of facility in shifting from one conceptual orientation to another in the course of solving a given concept-attainment task. Within the present context, "conceptual orientations" will refer both to levels of conceptualization, such as the figurative (global, perceptual), functional, and categorical (abstract) responses described by Reichard, Schneider, and Rapaport (1944) and to such dichotomous orientations as positive and negative similarity (groupings according to the presence or absence of a given property). The exploratory study to be reported here is concerned with the facility with which children and adolescents move from a functional to a figurative orientation and from a positive- to a nega-

* *Child Development*, 1966, 37, 493–498. Copyright 1966, by the Society for Research in Child Development, Inc. This research was carried out during the writer's tenure as a National Science Foundation Senior Postdoctoral Fellow at the Centre International D'Epistémologie Génétique in Geneva. The writer is indebted to the administration and teaching staff of the International School of Geneva for their friendly cooperation. Author's address: Department of Psychology, University of Rochester, Rochester, N. Y. 14627.

tive-similarity orientation. Our hypothesis is that adolescents will be more successful than children because if adolescent thought is more logically elaborate than child thought (Inhelder & Piaget, 1958), it should also be more mobile and flexible. This, at least, would seem to be one implication of the Inhelder and Piaget position.

Method

SUBJECTS

Sixty-four children and adolescents attending the International School in Geneva were the subjects. The children were drawn from several fourth-grade classrooms and constituted, in their teacher's judgment, a sample roughly representative of the ability in the group as a whole. The adolescents were drawn from several seventh- and eighth-grade classrooms and were also chosen to represent the spectrum of abilities of the classes from which they were drawn. It should be said that the majority of the subjects came from families in which the father either filled a high-level managerial post with an overseas branch of an American firm or else held a position with the diplomatic corps or with one of the international organizations located in Geneva. It can be reasonably assumed that the subjects were above average in intelligence, although no intelligence tests are given in the school. There were equal numbers of boys and girls at each age level, and the mean age and SD for the children (in months) were 120.37 and 3.95, while for the adolescents they were 166.84 and 8.15.

MATERIALS AND PROCEDURES

Two sets of 24 cards (15 × 10½ cm.) containing outline drawings were the materials. In each set there were 12 drawings of things used for transport, six of which were wheeled (car, wagon, truck, trailer, bicycle, and bus) and 6 of which were nonwheeled (steamship, sailboat, horse, camel, skis, and ice skates). The remaining 12 drawings were of tools, six of which were wheeled (rotary saw, pulley, hand drill, grinding wheel, lawn mower, roller) and six of which were nonwheeled (screwdriver, pliers, wrench, ax, and saw).

For both the level and the similarity shift conditions, the two decks were paired as follows. In the first 12 pairs, a wheeled tool was paired with a nonwheeled transport, and a nonwheeled tool was paired with a wheeled transport. For the second 12 pairs, a nonwheeled transport was paired with a wheeled transport, and a nonwheeled tool was paired with a wheeled tool. The drawings in a given pair, the ordinal position of the pair in the series, and the right-left positions of the correct drawings were determined by reference to a table of random numbers.

The two decks were used in a standard two-stimuli discrimination-learning procedure. To introduce S to the task, a sample exercise using ordinary playing cards was given. The S was told

> I am going to show you two cards at a time, one of which will always be right and the other which will always be wrong. You will have to guess which one is right and which one is wrong. If you guess the right one, I will turn on the flashlight [a small hand light with a tiny exposed bulb] like this. And if you do not guess the right one, the flashlight will not go on. At first you will have no way of knowing which card is right and which card is wrong, and you will simply have to guess. After you have made a few guesses, however, you should be able to find a rule that will tell you which card is right every time. Now I am going to show you how the game is played with these playing cards.

Two piles of playing cards were placed before S. These were prearranged so that a red and a black card would turn up each time. Whichever card S chose first was reinforced with the flashlight, and the color of that card was reinforced on all succeeding trials. If S did not succeed in arriving at the color rule after ten trials, the cards were divided as to color and S was asked how the two piles differed and what the rule might be. After the child got the rule, he was told, "Now we are going to play the same game with different cards. Remember that you are to try to find the rule that will make the light go on every time."

For the level shift condition, the concept to be attained was "wheeled" or "round" things, and cards containing wheels were always reinforced while cards containing nonwheeled things were not. Preliminary work with the cards had shown that Ss initially adopted functional orientations since this was so strongly suggested by the tool and transport content of the drawings. The task was then to shift from this initial functional hypothesis to a figurative or perceptual one, namely, wheels or round things.

For the similarity shift condition, a choice of nonwheeled objects was always reinforced, whereas the choice of a wheeled object was never rewarded. The concept to be attained involved identifying a group of objects which were alike because of negative similarity, that is to say, which lacked the common property of being wheeled. This concept was probably a more difficult one to attain since the shift from positive to negative similarity required, in addition, a shift from functional to figurative conceptualization as a necessary requisite.

It should be said that the coupling of wheeled transport with nonwheeled transport and of wheeled tools with nonwheeled tools for the second 12 pairs was done to facilitate shifting. A S holding a transport or a tool hypothesis would face a clear-cut contradiction when confronted with two tools or two transports at the same time.

CRITERION OF CORRECT PERFORMANCE

Each S was permitted as many as 72 trials or three complete presentations of the two sets of cards. If S had a run of ten or more correct responses, he was asked to verbalize the rule upon which he was operating. If he verbalized the rule correctly, no further trials were given, and he was credited with having attained the concept. If the rule was not verbalized correctly, the trials were continued until the rule was correctly verbalized or until the maximum number of trials permitted was reached. Those Ss who did not verbalize the rule were credited as not having attained the concept.

Results

LEVEL SHIFT PROBLEM

Of the 16 subjects aged 9–10 who were subjected to the level shift condition, nine succeeded in attaining the "wheeled" concept. Of the nine who succeeded, five were boys and four were girls. All 16 of the young adolescents succeeded in attaining the concept. The exact probability (based on Fisher's exact-probability test as described by Siegel [1956, pp. 96–104]) of this age difference occurring by chance was $p = .0068$, two-tailed test.

SIMILARITY SHIFT PROBLEM

On the similarity shift problem all of the 9–10-year-old children failed to make the shift, and only five of the adolescents were successful. All of the successful adolescents were boys. The exact probability of the age difference occurring by chance was $p = .0433$, two-tailed test. Likewise, the exact probability for attaining the sex difference by chance was also $p = .0433$.

OVERALL AGE DIFFERENCE

For the age groups as a whole, without regard to the type of shift or concept to be attained, the age difference in successful solutions yielded a X^2 of 6.63 which was significant beyond the .01 level.

Discussion

The present paper reports a preliminary attempt to assess developmental differences in the facility to shift conceptual orientation in the course of resolving a concept-formation task. Results suggest that adolescents are more successful than children in this regard. Adolescents were significantly more successful than children on a task requiring a shift from a functional to a figural level of conceptualization and on a task requiring a shift from a positive- to a negative-similarity orientation. These findings suggest that the thought of the adolescent is not only more logically elaborate than that of the child, as Inhelder and Piaget (1958) maintain, but also that it is more mobile and flexible and not necessarily more rigid, as Kounin (1943) seemed to imply.

In view of the fact that the problem of conceptual orientation shifts is relatively unexplored, it is perhaps appropriate to present some qualitative observations made during the course of the investigation and to suggest some hypotheses which might serve as starting points for additional research.

The first observation has to do with the sample task in which Ss had to arrive at a color rule or concept. The writer was amazed at the difficulty children had in attaining this rule. More than half required the full ten trials and, in addition, clues and prompting from E. They used position rules, order rules, and number rules, but could not arrive at the color rule even when the right and wrong cards were made into separate piles and were fanned out in front of them. The great majority of the adolescents, on the other hand, attained the color rule in less than ten trials with no prompting from E.

A second observation helps to clarify the first. In the course of the concept-attainment task proper, many adolescents spontaneously verbalized their method and said such things as, "No, that's not right. Let's try. . . ." Such spontaneous verbalizations were rare among the children, who often seemed to drift aimlessly after a few initial, more or less systematic attempts at solution. When these children were asked to state, after the completion of the trials, what the rule was, many of them actually gave one! They said such things as "things that move." When they were shown negative instances (such as the horse in the level shift condition), they replied that they had "made a mistake." This mistake was not, however, in the rule (which they continued to maintain) but, rather, in their interpretation of the object, "I guess horses move in a different way."

It thus seemed that in contrast to the adolescent, the child did not clearly distinguish between his own thought products and reality. As we have already shown in our studies of religious development (Elkind, 1961; 1962; 1963) it is not until about the age of 11 or 12 that children begin to reflect upon their own thought processes and to introduce such terms as "belief" and "intelligence" into their definitions of their religious denomination. Piaget and Inhelder (1958) have also pointed out that the child fails to form hypotheses in the strict sense of being able to verbalize them. This seeming lack of differentiation between thought and experience may mean that for the child an implicit hypothesis has an element of empirical necessity, while the data may have an element of hypothetical arbitrariness. This would explain the child's reluctance to give up his implicit hypothesis and his readiness to reinterpret the data to fit his expectations.

In the adolescent, on the other hand, thought and experience are clearly differentiated, and the adolescent is well aware of the arbitrariness of his hypotheses and their lack of necessary connection with the facts. This would explain his readiness to give them up when they are infirmed.

The differentiation hypothesis may help explain results such as those of Weir (1964) with a simple probability-learning task. Weir found a U-shaped age curve of success with adolescents performing close to the level of nursery school children whose success was due to preservation. Weir's data, like our own, suggest that the middle-childhood youngster sticks with his initially adopted strategy, whereas the adolescent—who may have initially adopted a much more complex strategy than the child—is much more ready to shift to a simpler strategy than is his elementary school counterpart.

One last observation has to do with the similarity shift task, which admittedly is not as pure as it perhaps should have been, since it involved a level shift as well. Nonetheless, the difficulty encountered by the adolescent subjects on this task was in striking contrast to the ease with which they made the simple level shift. Many of the adolescents who did not succeed demonstrated, both by runs of wrong responses and by their verbalizations, that they had formed the "wheeled" concept even though it was not reinforced. What they apparently could not do was shift from a positive- to a negative-similarity mode of conceptualization.

How explain this difficulty? Our impression, based on conversations with the teachers and administration of the task to graduate students with whom we were familiar, was that the shift from a positive- to a negative-similarity orientation occurred among the more creative subjects and not necessarily among those who were the best students. Thus, while the level shift would seem to be primarily determined by level of conceptual (convergent thinking) development, the similarity shift may well involve divergent thinking. This hypothesis should, of course, be tested. Only such testing will reveal the significance of the obtained sex difference on the similarity shift task.

References

Elkind, D. The child's conception of his religious denomination: I. The Jewish child. *Journal of Genetic Psychology*, 1961, *99*, 209–225.

Elkind, D. The child's conception of his religious denomination: II. The Catholic child. *Journal of Genetic Psychology*, 1962, *101*, 185–193.

Elkind, D. The child's conception of his religious denomination: III. The Protestant child. *Journal of Genetic Psychology*, 1963, *103*, 291–304.

Inhelder, Bärbel, and Piaget, J. *The growth of logical thinking from childhood to adolescence.* New York: Basic Books, 1958.

Kounin, J. S. Intellectual development and rigidity. In R. G. Barker, J. S. Kounin, and H. F. Wright (Eds.), *Child behavior and development.* New York: McGraw-Hill, 1943.

Reichard, S., Schneider, M., and Rapaport, D. The development of concept formation in children. *American Journal of Orthopsychiatry*, 1944, *14*, 156–162.

Siegel, S. *Nonparametric statistics for the behavioral sciences.* New York: McGraw-Hill, 1956.

Weir, M. W. Developmental changes in problem solving strategies. *Psychological Review*, 1964, *71*, 473–490.

4. FORMAL THOUGHT IN ADOLESCENCE AS A FUNCTION OF INTELLIGENCE*

Lee William Yudin

The purpose of this research was to investigate the development of concept attainment among adolescent males of low, middle, and high intelligence and to compare and contrast the attainment of concepts of color, number, and form, respectively. According to Inhelder and Piaget

* *Child Development*, 1966, *37*, 697–708. Copyright 1966, by the Society for Research in Child Development, Inc. This study was supported in part by a U.S. Public Health Service predoctoral Research Fellowship grant #17,429 and in part by Re-

(1958), adolescence represents the stage when the concrete operations of childhood, with their emphasis on elementary logical groupings, gradually give way to the development of logical operations, and when the ability to reason by hypothesis becomes permanent. Yudin (1962; 1964) and Yudin and Kates (1963) have shown that 14- and 16-year-old males of average intelligence are in fact superior in concept-attainment efficiency and strategies to 12-year-old males of similar IQ. In addition, they found no significant differences between the former two groups. What has not been made clear is whether adolescents of dissimilar intelligence will show this same pattern of development from age 12 to age 14 to age 16, or whether the attainment of formal thought and propositional logic will vary as a function of intellectual level.

Heidbreder (1946; 1947) has demonstrated that there is a rather definite and unchanging order with which concepts are attained. Her Ss repeatedly attained concepts more easily in going from the more to the less thinglike, in going from concepts of objects to concepts of form to concepts of color and, last, to concepts of number. Kates and Yudin (1964) and Yudin (1962; 1964) have shown that concepts of number are significantly more difficult to attain than concepts of color or form, while the latter two are of equal difficulty. The present study will explore this relation between the process of attainment and the nature of the concept type in a counterbalanced design which eliminates the confounding influence of practice and previous experience in the attainment of concepts.

This present research utilizes a reception paradigm defined as a set of conditions where Ss are presented with a series of instances which vary in accordance with a given schedule of information. Under this procedure, an individual has freedom, not in the instances he encounters, but only in the hypotheses he chooses to test in determining the relevant attributes from the nonrelevant, that is, in determining the criteria for acceptance. In a reception paradigm the instances presented to Ss can be either positive or negative, and they can either confirm a previous hypothesis or infirm it. These four contingencies are independent and mutually exclusive, and they exhaust the possibilities for testing particular hypotheses. The manner in which an individual attempts to deal with the information that is presented to him offers valuable clues for determining his level of cognitive development. Those individuals who main-

search grant HD-336 from the National Institutes of Health, U.S. Public Health Service. This research is based upon a doctoral dissertation submitted to the University of Massachusetts. The author would like to express his deepest appreciation to Dr. Solis L. Kates for his guidance in the execution of this research. Author's address: Irving Schwartz Institute for Children and Youth, Ford Road and Monument Avenue, Philadelphia, Pa. 19131.

tain or alter a previous hypothesis on the basis of the information conveyed by the present instance and all previous instances can be said to be following an "ideal" strategy. In this manner a person will arrive at the correct concept on the basis of a minimum number of events encountered.

When the maintaining or changing of a hypothesis is compatible with the information conveyed by the present instance only, an individual is said to be following a "compatible" strategy and failing to assimilate fully the information presented. When a hypothesis is maintained in the face of an infirming instance or changed in the face of a confirming instance, an individual is following an "incompatible" strategy. In addition to defining the strategy or approach utilized by an individual in concept attainment, one can also note his efficiency. We would thus be interested in the presence or absence of perceptual errors (the offering of a hypothesis that is incompatible with the information presented by the present instance) as well as the amount of information required for attainment.

The following hypotheses are tested in this study.

1. Intelligence is significantly related to concept-attainment performance. The greater the intelligence of S, the fewer instances that will be required for the attainment of concepts, the greater will be the percentage of strategies followed of an ideal nature, the smaller the percentages of strategies followed of a compatible and incompatible nature, and the fewer the perceptual errors.

2. Among Ss of average intelligence, the performance of 12-year-olds is less efficient when compared with 14- and 16-year-olds. These 12-year-olds will require more instances for concept attainment, will follow more strategies defined as compatible and incompatible and fewer defined as ideal, and will make more perceptual errors. In addition, 14- and 16-year-olds of average intelligence will not differ in concept-attainment performance as measured.

3. The development of formal thought among Ss of low intelligence is different from that of Ss of average intelligence. The attainment of logical operations is delayed among low-intelligence Ss and does not appear as a primary approach until the age period 14–16. Hence, no differences in performance from age 12 to age 14 are manifest. However, these same 14-year-olds as compared with these 16-year-olds (of low intelligence) will require a greater number of instances for attainment, will follow greater percentages of compatible and incompatible strategies and fewer percentages of ideal strategies in attaining the concepts, and will make a greater number of perceptual errors.

4. Among Ss of high intelligence, age is negatively related to concept

attainment in that younger Ss will require more instances for attainment, will follow more compatible and incompatible strategies and fewer ideal strategies, and will make more perceptual errors.

5. Concepts of number are more difficult to attain than either concepts of color or concepts of form, and hence Ss require a number of instances, follow more compatible and incompatible strategies, make more perceptual errors, and follow fewer ideal strategies. In addition, performance in the attainment of concepts of color and form does not differ as measured.

Method

SUBJECTS

There were 36 boys at each of the age levels, 12, 14, and 16. All Ss were within 6 months of their birthday and were enrolled in the same public school system in a small Massachusetts community of approximately 20,000 people. All 16-year-olds were tested in the town's one high school, while the younger children were tested in different buildings of the same elementary school. There were no major social-class differences among the different school locations (almost the entire community could be designated as lower-middle class), and all Ss tested were white. Within each age group, Ss were divided into three subgroups of 12 Ss each on the basis of their intelligence test scores on the Otis Beta and their average school achievement level as measured by the California Achievement Test. The low-intelligence subgroup ranged in IQ from 80 to 95 with a mean of 88.94. The Ss in the middle-intelligence subgroup had IQ's which ranged from 96 to 110 with a mean of 102.80, while the high-intelligence subgroup had IQ's which ranged from 115 to 130 with a mean of 121.26. All the Ss in the low-intelligence subgroup were achieving one or two grade levels below the average of their age group. The Ss who were achieving at their appropriate grade level were chosen for the middle-intelligence subgroup, while Ss who were achieving one or two grade levels above the mean for their age group were chosen for the high-intelligence subgroup.

TEST MATERIALS

A series of conceptual problems were presented to Ss by means of 2 × 2-inch color slides. Each slide contained either one or two instances. Each instance was composed of a figure characterized by four attributes: form, number, color, and number of borders surrounding the form(s). Each attribute was varied in three ways: Forms in each instance were one, two, or three circles ($\bigcirc$), crosses ($+$), or squares ($\square$). These forms were shown in red (R), green (G), or black (B), surrounded by one (1b), two (2b), or three (3b) black borders. For example, one instance consisted of one red circle with three borders (1R$\bigcirc$3b); another was two green squares with one border (2G$\square$1b); and still another was three black crosses with two borders (3b+2b). The instances presented to the Ss were composed of various combinations of these attribute values. In all problems the correct concept was defined by a single attribute, such as the color, red; the type of form, circles; the number, two; the number of borders, three borders.

PROCEDURE

The 12 Ss within each of the three IQ subgroups at each age level were further subdivided into six different units of two Ss each and presented with the two instruction problems and the six experimental problems in a different order. These same six sequences were administered to each IQ subgroup within each age level.

All Ss received one instruction problem which was defined by one border and a second instruction problem defined by either red, three, or crosses. For three of the sequences, the border problem was the first instruction problem, and for three it was the second. These instruction problems and their particular order were randomly assigned to the six sequences with the one restriction that the second instruction problem deal with a different attribute from the first experimental problem. Of the six experimental problems, two were of color (green and black), two of number (one and two), and two of form (square and circles). The order in which these problems were presented was randomly chosen but with the following three restrictions: (a) that the two problems of number, color, or form not appear in the same half of the test series (the first three problems constituted the first half and the next three the second half); (b) that the two problems of number, color, and form not follow each other in the test series; and (c) that each attribute appear equally often in each position in the test series.

The concept problems were presented by means of a series of color slides, each of which was an exemplar of the correct concept. The first slide shown for each problem (the focus instance) was a single instance. Each succeeding slide contained this focus instance and an additional instance which differed in only one attribute value from the focus slide. For example, for the instruction problem "crosses," the focus slide was 2G+2b. The second slide showed this same 2G+2b but with an additional instance 2R+2b beneath it, thus indicating that color was not the correct concept (all instances have to show the *same* correct attribute and these two instances were of *different* color). A third slide showed the same focus instance and also 2G + 3b. This slide eliminated borders as the relevant attribute. The fourth slide again showed the focus instance and also 1G + 2b, thus eliminating the number of forms as the relevant attribute. Since neither the color of the forms, the number of borders, nor the number of forms was the relevant attribute, the type of forms, in this case "crosses," was the correct concept. After the focus slide, each succeeding cycle of three slides contained sufficient information to enable Ss to eliminate the nondefining attributes and to arrive at the correct concept. Ten slides were provided for each concept problem with Ss in groups of approximately six writing down their best guess about the correct concept. After recording their guess on an answer sheet, Ss were required to cover their hypotheses or guesses with a form provided by E. This form also provided Ss with a list of the abbreviations to be used in recording their guesses.

All Ss attained the two instruction problems with the assistance of E. To provide uniformity, all instructions and information concerning the nature of the test situation were transmitted by means of a tape recorder. To insure that Ss had received sufficient information and training to understand the procedure involved in the attainment of concepts, the following criteria were used as the basis for including each S. For the two instruction problems, (a) a guess had to be indicated after each instance was presented, (b) S had to offer the correct guess at that point where sufficient information had been provided to attain the concept, and (c) there had to be adequate comprehension of the nature of the single-attribute guess.

The dependent variables were the following: (a) Number of instances required for attainment. The S was considered to have attained the concept after he indicated the correct concept with no subsequent incorrect hypotheses. (b) Percentage of ideal strategies. This was calculated by dividing the number of ideal strategies followed by S until attainment of the concept by the total number of instances required for attainment. (c) Percentage of compatible strategies. This was calculated by dividing the number of compatible strategies followed by S until attainment of the concept by the total number of instances required for attainment. (d) Percentage of incompatible strategies. This was calculated by dividing the number of incompatible strategies followed by S by the total number of instances required for attainment. (e) Number of perceptual errors. This dependent variable indicated the number of times S offered a hypothesis which was not compatible with the information conveyed by the presenting instance.

All Ss solved the same six problems (but some, of course, in a different order). Each problem was introduced as a new and different problem to Ss, who were advised that *any one* of the four attributes might be the correct concept regardless of the attribute value that might have been correct for the previous problem.

Results

INTELLIGENCE (FIRST HYPOTHESIS)

The Duncan Range test (Edwards, 1960, pp. 136–140) indicated that all dependent variables significantly differentiated the concept-attainment performance of Ss as a function of intelligence, with the exception of the dependent variable perceptual error (Table 1). Thus, these Ss of higher intelligence required significantly fewer instances to attain the concepts, followed greater percentages of strategies of the ideal type, and smaller percentages of strategies of the compatible and incompatible type. In addition, Ss in the low- and middle-intelligence subgroups made signifi-

TABLE 1
Summary of the Results of Duncan Range
Tests by Intelligence and Concept Type

	NUMBER OF IN-STANCES	NUMBER OF PER-CEPTUAL ERRORS	PERCENT-AGE OF IDEAL STRATEGIES	PERCENT-AGE OF COM-PATIBLE STRATEGIES	PERCENT-AGE OF INCOM-PATIBLE STRATEGIES
	$M_1:M_2$ [a]	$M_1:M_2$	$M_1:M_2$	$M_1:M_2$	$M_1:M_2$
Intelligence:					
Low vs. middle	7.57:5.48	.746:.477	43.15:65.92	37.03:25.26	19.86:8.92
Significance	<.05	N.S.	<.05	<.05	<.05
Low vs. high	7.57:4.55	.736:.130	43.15:78.56	37.05:17.90	19.86:3.67
Significance	<.05	<.05	<.05	<.05	<.05
Middle vs. high	5.48:4.55	.477:.130	65.92:78.56	25.26:17.90	8.92:3.67
Significance	<.05	<.05	<.05	<.05	<.05
Concept type:					
Color vs.					
number	4.90:7.70	.338:.634	72.46:45.36	17.84:42.51	9.43:12.22
Significance	<.05	<.05	<.05	<.05	N.S.
Color vs. form	4.90:4.96	.338:.370	72.46:69.81	17.84:19.83	9.43:10.80
Significance	N.S.	N.S.	N.S.	N.S.	N.S.
Number vs.					
form	7.76:4.96	.634:.370	45.36:69.81	51.24:19.83	12.22:10.80
Significance	<.05	<.05	<.05	<.05	N.S.

[a] M_1 = first mean; M_2 = second mean.

cantly more perceptual errors than those in the high-intelligence sub-group. The difference between the low- and middle-intelligence sub-groups on this dependent variable was in the expected direction but failed to reach statistical significance.

AGE AND THE MIDDLE-INTELLIGENCE SUBGROUP (SECOND HYPOTHESIS)

The second hypothesis was fully confirmed. The 12-year-olds of average intelligence were significantly less efficient in concept attainment than either the 14- or 16-year-olds (Table 2). These former Ss required a significantly greater number of instances to attain the concepts, followed significantly fewer percentages of ideal strategies, followed higher per-

TABLE 2
Summary of the Results of Duncan Range Tests by Age and Intelligence

	NUMBER OF IN-STANCES	NUMBER OF PER-CEPTUAL ERRORS	PERCENT-AGE OF IDEAL STRATEGIES	PERCENT-AGE OF COM-PATIBLE STRATEGIES	PERCENT-AGE OF INCOM-PATIBLE STRATEGIES
	$M_1:M_2$ [a]	$M_1:M_2$	$M_1:M_2$	$M_1:M_2$	$M_1:M_2$
Low intelligence:					
12 vs. 14	8.11:8.00	1.403:.584	35.83:37.84	39.88:44.61	25.51:17.42
Significance	N.S.	<.05	N.S.	N.S.	N.S.
12 vs. 16	8.11:6.60	1.403:.222	35.83:55.77	39.85:26.63	25.51:16.64
Significance	<.05	<.05	<.05	<.05	N.S.
14 vs. 16	8.00:6.60	.584:222	37.84:55.77	44.61:26.63	17.42:16.64
Significance	<.05	N.S.	<.05	<.05	N.S.
Middle intelligence:					
12 vs. 14	6.71:4.81	.931:.250	49.72:71.64	33.88:22.86	16.81:5.45
Significance	<.05	<.05	<.05	<.05	<.05
12 vs. 16	6.71:4.93	.931:.250	49.72:76.40	33.88:19.03	16.81:4.50
Significance	<.05	<.05	<.05	<.05	<.05
14 vs. 16	4.81:4.93	.250:.250	71.64:76.40	22.86:19.03	5.45:4.50
Significance	N.S.	N.S.	N.S.	N.S.	N.S.
High intelligence:					
12 vs. 14	5.31:4.31	.181:.125	67.99:77.64	27.16:16.88	4.59:5.46
Significance	N.S.	N.S.	N.S.	<.05	N.S.
12 vs. 16	5.31:3.89	.181:.083	67.99:90.05	27.16:9.67	4.59:.96
Significance	<.05	N.S.	<.05	<.05	N.S.
14 vs. 16	4.31:3.89	.125:.083	77.64:90.05	16.88:9.67	5.46:.96
Significance	N.S.	N.S.	N.S.	N.S.	N.S.

[a] M_1 = first mean; M_2 = second mean.

centages of compatible and incompatible strategies, and made a significantly greater number of perceptual errors. As further hypothesized, there were no significant differences on any of the dependent variables between the 14- and 16-year-old Ss.

AGE AND THE LOW-INTELLIGENCE SUBGROUP
(THIRD HYPOTHESIS)

Duncan Range Tests indicated, as hypothesized, no significant differences in concept-attainment performance between the 12- and 14-year-old low-intelligence Ss for the number of instances or the percentages of ideal, compatible, or incompatible strategies (Table 2). Contrary to that which was expected, the 14-year-olds made significantly fewer perceptual errors than the 12-year-olds (Table 2). Unlike the adolescents of average intelligence who show no significant gains in efficiency from age 14 to 16, low-intelligence adolescents make significant gains during this period and make greater use of formal thought, employing efficient hypothesis testing in their problem solving. The 16-year-olds of low intelligence, as hypothesized, required significantly fewer instances for concept attainment, followed significantly greater percentages of ideal strategies, and significantly fewer percentages of compatible strategies (Table 2). It should be noted that their performance at age 16 was below that of the adolescents of average intelligence at the same age. The differences between these Ss for the dependent-variables percentage of incompatible strategies and number of perceptual errors was in the expected direction but failed to reach statistical significance (Table 2).

AGE AND THE HIGH-INTELLIGENCE SUBGROUP
(FOURTH HYPOTHESIS)

The fourth hypothesis was, for the most part, not supported (Table 2). The only significant developmental findings were for the dependent-variable percentage of compatible strategies, with the high-intelligence 14-year-olds following significantly fewer of these strategies than the 12-year-olds of high intelligence. However, all differences between the 12-year-olds and 14-year-olds and between the 14-year-olds and the 16-year-olds were in the expected direction except for the dependent-variable percentage of incompatible strategies. That the performance of these Ss did in fact improve is indicated by the findings that the 16-year-olds of high intelligence required significantly fewer instances for attainment, followed a significantly greater percentage of ideal strategies, and a significantly lower percentage of compatible strategies than the 12-year-olds (Table 2).

CONCEPT TYPE (FIFTH HYPOTHESIS)

The fifth hypothesis was almost fully confirmed. In attaining concepts of number as compared with concepts of color or form, Ss required a significantly greater number of instances, followed significantly lower percentages of the ideal strategy, significantly greater percentages of compatible strategies, and made a significantly greater number of perceptual errors (Table 2). Further, Ss followed more incompatible strategies in attaining the number concepts as compared with the color and form concepts, but the differences were not significant. As hypothesized, there were no significant differences for any of the dependent variables in attaining concepts of color or form (Table 2).

The first guess that is offered for each problem represents a condition where the law of probability should operate. With the sequence of problems randomized from S to S and their being told that any one of the concept types could be the relevant attribute for a given problem, it might be expected that each of the four attributes would be offered as the first hypothesis with equal frequency. When we compare by X^2 the frequency with which the four concept types were offered initially according to the ordinal position in the series, the following results are obtained. All six ordinal positions in the series are found to contain frequencies of the four concept types significantly different from that which would be expected on the basis of chance. All X^2s are significant at or beyond the .05 level (Table 3). Further, in all but the first ordinal position (the first concept problem presented to Ss), the concept of number is found to be offered significantly less frequently than would be expected, while concepts other than number are offered significantly more frequently. For the first ordinal position, the difference between guesses

TABLE 3
A X^2 Comparison of the First Hypothesis Offered by Ss
According to the Ordinal Position in the Series (OPS)

OPS	NUMBER	FORM	COLOR	BORDER	X^2	p
1	18	38	25	27	7.67	<.02
2	17	25	34	32	6.59	<.05
3	16	35	23	34	9.26	<.01
4	14	15	36	43	24.07	<.001
5	13	35	23	37	13.93	<.001
6	13	25	33	37	12.44	<.001

of the concept number and guesses other than number was not significantly different. It should be added that, as experience increases, number appears to be offered as the initial guess less frequently than concepts other than number.

Discussion

ADOLESCENT DEVELOPMENT AND INTELLIGENCE

Inhelder and Piaget's (1958) conception of adolescent development involves a reorganization of thought patterns (characterized by the presence of logical operations) beginning at about 12 years of age and reaching an equilibrium at about 14–16 years of age. That these older Ss of average intelligence are more efficient in problem solving than the younger ones is evident, but what is also highlighted is that the former individuals utilize strategies that are different from those followed by the younger Ss. A 14- or 16-year-old of average intelligence is more likely than a 12-year-old of similar intelligence to assimilate incoming information in an orderly and efficient manner. He is more capable of dealing with that information which is directly perceptible (thus making significantly fewer perpetual errors) and also of deciding when to maintain or to change a previously formulated hypothesis, being able to adequately consider both present and past information (thus following significantly greater percentages of ideal strategies and significantly lower percentages of compatible and incompatible strategies).

We have indicated above that individuals less favorably endowed intellectually (IQ range 70–89) manifest a retardation in their development and thus do not begin to fully utilize formal operations until 14–16 years of age. Whether this development will reach a point of equilibrium (from 16 to 18 years of age) comparable to that seen by the average-intelligence Ss from age 14 to 16, or whether these low-intelligence Ss will increase their performance still further and become more efficient, is a matter for further study.

The Ss of superior intelligence show an efficient use of logical operations even at age 12, indicating that development of these types of mental operations has begun for them earlier than for the low- or middle-intelligence subgroups. In addition, changes in performance from age 12 to age 14 to age 16 are more nearly linear, with a considerable (but not significant) increase with increasing age. It is exactly this quality of the mind, the ability to continue to profit from experience and to manifest continual growth, which characterizes the development of an individual of superior intelligence.

In a study of concept attainment by college students (mean age of 18), Kates and Yudin (1964) found their Ss capable of attaining concepts at a level above that reached by almost all of the Ss in the present research. This would indicate that further gains are made by the intellectually gifted from age 16 to age 18 on this type of concept task.

The most important implications of these findings are not that younger adolescents are less efficient in concept attainment than older adolescents or that low-intelligence adolescents are less efficient than brighter adolescents but, rather, that an interaction of both age and intelligence contributes towards cognitive development. The attainment of logical operations as an integral aspect of functioning is not uniform or rigid for all adolescents. All are capable of functioning in this most efficient manner, but not to the same extent. Thus, while previously we might have conceived of development as following an unchanging pattern with adolescence representing the focal point for the switch to hypothesis formation and testing, we now can understand more clearly that individuals of differing abilities not only achieve at different levels but that they follow significantly different patterns of development in their obtaining similar, more efficient approaches to problem solving. Development, whether accelerated or retarded, brings with it a shift in emphasis from concreteness to abstractness and a new way of dealing with facts and relations, but experience alone is not sufficient to bring about this shift.

CONCEPT TYPE

As Heidbreder (1946; 1947) and others (Kates & Yudin, 1964; Yudin, 1962; 1964) have indicated, the attainment of concepts takes place in a hierarchy. The present results indicate that number concepts are more difficult to attain and that they impose increasing cognitive demands upon Ss. As a result, strategies utilized in the attainment of these concepts become significantly less efficient, and the ability of Ss to perceive adequately the environment and to utilize effectively the information provided decreases. It should be noted that to attain the number concept it is necessary to go beyond the directly perceptible in order to group the forms that are presented by the instances and to assign a symbol to them. For the color or form concepts, the grouping operation described above need not be carried out. Furthermore, the properties of "thingness" have to be discarded; the constancy, the shape-boundedness, and the dynamic properties of the forms all may interfere with the salience of the grouping operation.

The present findings also indicate that the number concepts were offered as the initial hypothesis for the various concept problems with the smallest frequency of all the concept types. It thus appears that number concepts are not only more difficult to attain but that a "perception" of number as a defining attribute is not readily aroused. Bruner (1957) points out that it is the ready perceiver who is able to proceed with a minimum of stimulus inputs and is thus able to use cognitive readiness not only for perceiving what *is* before him but what is *likely* to be before him. Bruner has further indicated that "the likelihood that a sensory input will be categorized in terms of a given category is not only a matter of fit between sensory input and category specification, it depends also on the accessibility, i.e., given a sensory input with equally good fit to two nonoverlapping categories, the more accessible of the two categories would 'capture' the input" (p. 132). In the present research, the first guess for each problem provides a sensory input with equally good fit to four nonoverlapping categories, and results indicate that number is the least accessible. It is not surprising, therefore, that to attain a concept of number, Ss require significantly more stimulus input than they do for the other concepts. Their reduced efficiency is accompanied by the adoption of more primitive strategies (from a genetics standpoint), and all Ss tend to operate at a more concrete level.

References

Bruner, J. On perceptual readiness. *Psychological Review*, 1957, 64, 123–152.

Edwards, A. *Experimental design in psychological research.* New York: Holt, Rinehart and Winston, 1960.

Heidbreder, Edna. The attainment of concepts: II. The problem. *Journal of Genetic Psychology*, 1946, 35, 190–223b.

Heidbreder, Edna. The attainment of concepts: III. The process. *Journal of Psychology*, 1947, 24, 93–138.

Inhelder, Barbel, and Piaget, J. *The growth of logical thinking.* London: Routledge & Kegan Paul, 1958.

Kates, S. L., & Yudin, L. W. Concept attainment and memory. *Journal of Educational Psychology*, 1964, 55, 103–109.

Yudin, L. W. A developmental study of concept attainment. Unpublished Master's thesis, University of Massachusetts, 1962.

Yudin, L. W. Concept attainment and intelligence: a developmental study. Unpublished doctoral dissertation, University of Massachusetts, 1964.

Yudin, L. W., and Kates, S. L. Concept attainment and adolescent development. *Journal of Educational Psychology*, 1963, 55, 1–9.

5. MORAL DEVELOPMENT AND THE EDUCATION OF ADOLESCENTS

Lawrence Kohlberg

Anyone who listens to adolescents knows that they are preoccupied, in one way or another, with formulating ideals for bringing order and value to their lives. It is reasonable to claim that moral concerns lie at the core of these ideals and the study of the individual's moral development is what I have long concerned myself with. Since most of my own psychological studies of moral development have been with adolescents, I have tried to collect the findings from them for this volume as they pertain to the education of adolescents.

It is usually supposed that psychology contributes to moral education by telling us appropriate *methods* of moral teaching and learning. A Skinnerian will speak of proper schedules of reinforcement in moral learning, a Freudian will speak of the importance of the balance of parental love and firmness which will promote superego-identification and so on. When Skinnerians and Freudians speak on the topic of moral education, then, they start by answering Yes to the question "Is virtue something that can be taught?" and go on to tell us how. In *Walden Two*, Skinner not only tells us that virtue comes by practice and reinforcement, but designs an ideal center which educates all its children to be virtuous in this way.

My own response to these questions was more modest. When confronted by a group of parents who asked me, "How can we make our children virtuous?" I had to answer like Socrates, "You must think I am very fortunate to know how virtue is acquired. The fact is that far from knowing whether it can be taught, I have no idea what virtue really is." Like most psychologists, I knew that science could teach me nothing as to what virtue is. Science could speak about causal relations, about the relations of means to ends but it could not speak about ends or values themselves. If I could not define virtue or the ends of moral education, could I really offer advice as to means by which virtue should be taught? Could it really be argued that the means for teaching obedience to authority are the same as the means for teaching freedom of moral opinion, that the means for teaching altruism are the same as the means for teaching competitive striving, that the making of a good storm trooper involves the same procedures as the making of a democratic leader? My response to all this was that either we must be totally silent about moral education or else speak to the nature of virtue.

The Bag of Virtues

American educational psychology is Aristotelian in that it divides the personality up into cognitive abilities, passions or motives, and traits of character. Moral character, then, consists of a bag of virtues and vices. One of the earliest major American studies of moral character, that of Hartshorne and May (1928–30), was conducted in the late twenties. Their bag of virtues included honesty, service and self-control. A more recent major study by Havighurst and Taba (1949) added responsibility, friendliness and moral courage to the Hartshorne and May's bag. Aristotle's original bag included temperance, liberality, pride, good temper, truthfulness and justice. The Boy Scout bag is well known, a Scout should be honest, loyal, reverent, clean, brave.

Given a bag of virtues, it is evident how we build character. Children should be exhorted to practice these virtues, should be told that happiness, fortune and good repute will follow in their wake, adults around them should be living examples of these virtues, and children should be given daily opportunities to practice them. Daily chores will build responsibility, the opportunity to give to the Red Cross will build service or altruism, etc.

You will hardly be surprised if I tell you that this approach to moral education doesn't work. Hartshorne and May found that participation in character education classes of this sort, in the Boy Scouts, in Sunday school did not lead to any improvement in moral character as measured by experimental tests of honesty, service and self-control, and more recent research does not provide any more positive evidence as to the effects of character-building programs.

The objection of the psychologist to the bag of virtues is that there are no such things. Virtues and vices are labels by which people award praise or blame to others, but the ways people use praise and blame toward others are not the ways in which they think when making moral decisions themselves. You or I may not find a Hell's Angel truly honest, but he may. Hartshorne and May found this out to their dismay 40 years ago by their monumental experimental studies of children's cheating and stealing. In brief, they and others since have found:

1. You can't divide the world into honest and dishonest people. Almost everyone cheats some of the time, cheating is distributed in bell-curve fashion around a level of moderate cheating.

2. If a person cheats in one situation, it does not mean he will or will not in another. There is very little correlation between situational cheating tests. In other words it is not a character trait of dishonesty which makes a child cheat in a given situation. If it were you could predict he would cheat in a second situation if he did in the first.

3. People's verbal moral values about honesty have nothing to do with how they act. People who cheat express as much or more moral disapproval of cheating as those who don't cheat. More recently than Hartshorne and May psychologists have studied moral character using psychoanalytically inspired words like "resistance to temptation," "conscience strength," "superego strength," and "moral internalization." However, they have essentially used Hartshorne and May's tests and obtain similar results of situational specificity.

A Study of Morality

But the question still beckons: how can one study morality? Current trends in the fields of ethics, linguistics, anthropology and cognitive psychology have suggested a new approach which seems to avoid the morass of semantical confusions, value-bias and cultural relativity in which the psychoanalytic and virtue approaches to morality have foundered. New scholarship in all these fields is now focusing upon structures, forms and relationships that seem to be common to all societies and all languages rather than upon the features that make particular languages or cultures different.

For twelve years, my colleagues and I studied the same group of 75 boys, following their development at three-year intervals from early adolescence through young manhood (Kohlberg, 1958, 1963, 1968; Kohlberg and Kramer, 1969; Turiel, 1966). At the start of the study, the boys were aged 10 to 16. We have now followed them through to ages 22 to 28. In addition, I have investigated moral development in other cultures —Great Britain, Canada, Taiwan, Mexico, and Turkey.

Inspired by Jean Piaget's (1948) pioneering effort to apply a structural approach to moral development, I have gradually elaborated over the years of my study a typological scheme describing general stages of moral thought which can be defined independently of the specific content of particular moral decisions or actions. In our study of 75 American boys from early adolescence on, these youths were continually presented with hypothetical moral dilemmas, all deliberately philosophical, some of them found in medieval works of casuistry. It was on the basis of their reasoning about these dilemmas at a given age that we constructed the typology of definite and universal levels of development in moral thought.

The typology contains three distinct levels of moral thinking, and within each of these levels distinguishes two related stages. These levels and stages may be considered separate moral philosophies, distinct views of the social-moral world.

We can speak of the child as having his own morality or series of moralities. Adults seldom listen to children's moralizing. If a child throws back a few adult clichés and behaves himself, most parents—and many anthropologists and psychologists as well—think that the child has adopted or internalized the appropriate parental standards.

Actually, as soon as we talk with children about morality, we find that they have many ways of making judgments which are not "internalized" from the outside, and which do not come in any direct and obvious way from parents, teachers or even peers.

Moral Stages

The *preconventional* level is the first of three levels of moral thinking; the second level is *conventional,* and the third *postconventional* or autonomous. While the preconventional child is often "well-behaved" and is responsive to cultural labels of good and bad, he interprets these labels in terms of their physical consequences (punishment, reward, exchange of favors) or in terms of the physical power of those who enunciate the rules and labels of good and bad.

This level is usually occupied by children aged four to ten, a fact well known to sensitive observers of children. The capacity of "properly behaved" children of this age to engage in cruel behavior when there are holes in the power structure is sometimes noted as tragic (*Lord of the Flies, High Wind in Jamaica*), sometimes as comic (Lucy in *Peanuts*).

The second or *conventional* level also can be described as conformist, but that is perhaps too smug a term. Maintaining the expectations and rules of the individual's family, group or nation is perceived as valuable in its own right. There is a concern not only with *conforming* to the individual's social order but in *maintaining,* supporting and justifying this order.

The *postconventional* level is characterized by a major thrust toward autonomous moral principles which have validity and application apart from authority of the groups or persons who hold them and apart from the individual's identification with those persons or groups.

Within each of these three levels there are two discernible stages. Table 1 contains the dual moral stages of each level just described.

To understand what these stages mean concretely, let us look at them with regard to two of 25 basic moral concepts or aspects used to form the dilemmas. One such aspect, for instance, is "Motive Given for Rule Obedience or Moral Action." In this instance, the six stages look like this:

1. Obey rules to avoid punishment.
2. Conform to obtain rewards, have favors returned, and so on.
3. Conform to avoid disapproval, dislike by others.
4. Conform to avoid censure by legitimate authorities and resultant guilt.
5. Conform to maintain the respect of the impartial spectator judging in terms of community welfare.
6. Conform to avoid self-condemnation.

TABLE 1
Definition of Moral Stages

I. PRECONVENTIONAL LEVEL

At this level the child is responsive to cultural rules and labels of good and bad, right or wrong, but interprets these labels in terms of either the physical or the hedonistic consequences of action (punishment, reward, exchange of favors) or in terms of the physical power of those who enunciate the rules and labels. The level is divided into the following two stages:

Stage 1: *The punishment and obedience orientation.* The physical consequences of action determine its goodness or badness regardless of the human meaning or value of these consequences. Avoidance of punishment and unquestioning deference to power are valued in their own right, not in terms of respect for an underlying moral order supported by punishment and authority (the latter being Stage 4).

Stage 2: *The instrumental relativist orientation.* Right action consists of that which instrumentally satisfies one's own needs and occasionally the needs of others. Human relations are viewed in terms like those of the market place. Elements of fairness, of reciprocity and equal sharing are present, but they are always interpreted in a physical pragmatic way. Reciprocity is a matter of "you scratch my back and I'll scratch yours," not of loyalty, gratitude or justice.

II. CONVENTIONAL LEVEL

At this level, maintaining the expectations of the individual's family, group, or nation is perceived as valuable in its own right, regardless of immediate and obvious consequences. The attitude is not only one of *conformity* to personal expectations and social order, but of loyalty to it, of actively *maintaining*, supporting, and justifying the order and of identifying with the persons or group involved in it. At this level, there are the following two stages:

Stage 3: *The interpersonal concordance or "good boy—nice girl" orientation.* Good behavior is that which pleases or helps others and is approved by them. There is much conformity to stereotypical images of what is majority or "natural" behavior. Behavior is frequently judged by intention—"he means well" becomes important for the first time. One earns approval by being "nice."

Stage 4: *The "law and order" orientation.* There is orientation toward authority, fixed rules, and the maintenance of the social order. Right behavior consists of doing one's duty, showing respect for authority and maintaining the given social order for its own sake.

III. POST-CONVENTIONAL, AUTONOMOUS, OR PRINCIPLED LEVEL

At this level, there is a clear effort to define moral values and principles which have validity and application apart from the authority of the groups or persons holding these principles and apart from the individual's own identification with these groups. This level again has two stages:

Stage 5: *The social-contract legalistic orientation.* Generally has utilitarian overtones. Right action tends to be defined in terms of general individual rights and in terms of standards which have been critically examined and agreed upon by the whole society. There is a clear awareness of the relativism of personal values and opinions and a corresponding emphasis upon procedural rules for reaching consensus. Aside from what is constitutionally and democratically agreed upon, the right is a matter of personal "values" and "opinion." The result is an emphasis upon the "legal point of view," but with an emphasis upon the possibility of changing law in terms of rational considerations of social utility (rather than freezing it in terms of Stage-4 "law and order"). Outside the legal realm, free agreement, and contract is the binding element of obligation. This is the "official" morality of the American government and Constitution.

Stage 6: *The universal ethical principle orientation.* Right is defined by the decision of conscience in accord with self-chosen *ethical principles* appealing to logical comprehensiveness, universality, and consistency. These principles are abstract and ethical (the Golden Rule, the categorical imperative); they are not concrete moral rules like the Ten Commandments. At heart, these are universal principles of *justice,* of the *reciprocity* and *equality* of the human *rights* and of respect for the dignity of human beings as *individual persons.*

In another of these 25 moral aspects, the value of human life, the six stages can be defined thus:

1. The value of human life is confused with the value of physical objects and is based on the social status or physical attributes of the possessor.

2. The value of human life is seen as instrumental to the satisfaction of the needs of its possessor or of other persons.

3. The value of human life is based on the empathy and affection of family members and others toward its possessor.

4. Life is conceived as sacred in terms of its place in a categorical moral or religious order of rights and duties.

5. Life is valued both in terms of its relation to community welfare and in terms of life being a universal human right.

6. Belief in sacredness of human life as representing a universal human value of respect for the individual.

I have called this scheme a typology. This is because about 50 per cent of most people's thinking will be at a single stage, regardless of the moral dilemma involved. We call our types *stages* because they seem to represent an *invariant developmental sequence.* "True" stages come one at a time and always in the same order.

All movement is forward in sequence, and does not skip steps. Children may move through these stages at varying speeds, of course, and may be found half in and half out of a particular stage. An individual may stop at any given stage and at any age, but if he continues to move, he must move in accord with these steps. Moral reasoning of the conventional or Stage 3–4 kind never occurs before the preconventional Stage-1 and Stage-2 thought has taken place. No adult in Stage 4 has gone through Stage 6, but all Stage-6 adults have gone at least through 4.

While the evidence is not complete, my study strongly suggests that moral change fits the stage pattern just described.

As a single example of our findings of stage-sequence, take the progress of two boys on the aspect "The Value of Human Life." The first boy, Tommy, is asked, "Is it better to save the life of one important person or a lot of unimportant people?" At age 10, he answers, "All the people that aren't important because one man just has one house, maybe a lot of furniture, but a whole bunch of people have an awful lot of furniture and some of these poor people might have a lot of money and it doesn't look it."

Clearly Tommy is Stage 1: he *confuses* the value of a human being with the value of the property he possesses. Three years later (age 13) Tommy's conceptions of life's values are most clearly elicited by the question, "Should the doctor 'mercy kill' a fatally ill woman requesting death because of her pain?" He answers, "Maybe it would be good to put her out of her pain, she'd be better off that way. But the husband wouldn't want it, it's not like an animal. If a pet dies you can get along without it—it isn't something you really need. Well, you can get a new wife, but it's not really the same."

Here his answer is Stage 2: the value of the woman's life is partly contingent on its hedonistic value to the wife herself but even more contingent on its *instrumental* value to her husband, who can't replace her as easily as he can a pet.

Three years later still (age 16) Tommy's conception of life's value is elicited by the same question, to which he replies: "It might be best for her, but her husband—it's a human life—not like an animal; it just doesn't have the same relationship that a human being does to a family. You can become attached to a dog, but nothing like a human you know."

Now Tommy has moved from a Stage-2 instrumental view of the woman's value to a Stage-3 view based on the husband's distinctively human *empathy* and love for someone in his family. Equally clearly, it lacks any basis for a universal human value of the woman's life, which would hold if she had no husband or if her husband didn't love her. Tommy, then, has moved step by step through three stages during the age 10–16. Tommy, though bright (I.Q. 120), is a slow developer in moral judgment. Let us take another boy, Richard, to show us sequential movement through the remaining three steps.

At age 13, Richard said about the mercy-killing, "If she requests it, it's really up to her. She is in such terrible pain, just the same as people are always putting animals out of their pain," and in general showed a mixture of Stage-2 and Stage-3 responses concerning the value of life. At 16, he said, "I don't know. In one way, it's murder, it's not a right or privilege of man to decide who shall live and who should die. God put life into everybody on earth and you're taking away something from that person that came directly from God, and you're destroying something that is very sacred, it's in a way part of God and it's almost destroying a part of God when you kill a person. There's something of God in everyone."

Here Richard clearly displays a Stage-4 concept of life as sacred in terms of its place in a categorical moral or religious order. The value of human life is universal, it is true for all humans. It is still, however, dependent on something else, upon respect for God and God's authority; it is not an autonomous human value. Presumably if God told Richard to murder, as God commanded Abraham to murder Isaac, he would do so.

At age 20, Richard said to the same question: "There are more and more people in the medical profession who think it is a hardship on everyone, the person, the family, when you know they are going to die. When a person is kept alive by an artificial lung or kidney it's more like being a vegetable than being a human. If it's her own choice, I think there are certain rights and privileges that go along with being a human being. I am a human being and I have certain desires for life and I think everybody else does too. You have a world of which you are the center, and everybody else does too and in that sense we're all equal."

Richard's response is clearly Stage 5, in that the value of life is defined in terms of equal and universal human rights in a context of relativity ("You have a world of which you are the center and in that sense we're all equal"), and of concern for utility or welfare consequences.

At 24, Richard says: "A human life takes precedence over any other moral or legal value, whoever it is. A human life has inherent value whether or not it is valued by a particular individual. The worth of the individual human being is central where the principles of justice and love are normative for all human relationships."

This young man is at Stage 6 in seeing the value of human life as absolute in representing a universal and equal respect for the human as an individual. He has moved step by step through a sequence culminating in a definition of human life as centrally valuable rather than derived from or dependent on social or divine authority.

In a genuine and culturally universal sense, these steps lead toward an increased *morality* of value judgment, where morality is considered as a form of judging, as it has been in a philosophic tradition running from the analyses of Kant to those of the modern analytic or "ordinary language" philosophers. The person at Stage 6 has disentangled his judgments of—or language about—human life from status and property values (Stage 1), from its uses to others (Stage 2), from interpersonal affection (Stage 3), and so on; he has a means of moral judgment that is universal and impersonal. The Stage-6 person's answers use moral words like "duty" or "morally right," and he uses them in a way implying universality, ideals, impersonality: He thinks and speaks in phrases like "regardless of who it was," or ". . . I would do it in spite of punishment."

Cultural Universality

When I first decided to explore moral development in other cultures, I was told by anthropologist friends that I would have to throw away my culture-bound moral concepts and stories and start from scratch learning a whole new set of values for each new culture. My first try consisted of a brace of villages, one Atayal (Malaysian aboriginal) and the other Taiwanese.

My guide was a young Chinese ethnographer who had written an account of the moral and religious patterns of the Atayal and Taiwanese villages. Taiwanese boys in the 10–13 age group were asked about a story involving theft of food. A man's wife is starving to death but the store owner won't give the man any food unless he can pay, which he can't. Should he break in and steal some food? Why? Many of the boys said, "He should steal the food for his wife because if she dies he'll have to pay for her funeral and that costs a lot."

My guide was amused by these responses, but I was relieved: they were of course "classic" Stage-2 responses. In the Atayal village, funerals weren't such a big thing, so the Stage-2 boys would say, "He should steal the food because he needs his wife to cook for him."

This means that we have to consult our anthropologists to know what content a Stage-2 child will include in his instrumental exchange calculations, or what a Stage-4 adult will identify as the proper social order. But one certainly doesn't have to start from scratch. What made my guide laugh was the difference in form between the children's Stage-2 thought and his own, a difference definable independently of particular cultures.

Figures 1 and 2 indicate the cultural universality of the sequence of stages which we have found. Figure 1 presents the age trends for middle-class urban boys in the U.S., Taiwan and Mexico. At age 10 in each country, the order of use of each stage is the same as the order of its difficulty or maturity.

In the United States, by age 16 the order is the reverse, from the highest to the lowest, except that Stage 6 is still little-used. At age 13, the good-boy, middle-stage (Stage 3) is not used.

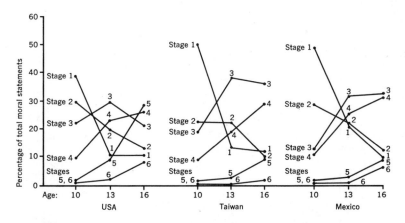

FIGURE 1   Middle-class urban boys in the U.S., Taiwan, and Mexico. At age 10, the stages are used according to difficulty. At age 13, Stage 3 is most used by all three groups. At age 16, U.S. boys have reversed the order of age 10 stages (with the exception of 6). In Taiwan and Mexico, conventional (3–4) stages prevail at age 16, with Stage 5 also little used.

The results in Mexico and Taiwan are the same, except that development is a little slower. The most conspicuous feature is that at the age of 16, Stage-5 thinking is much more salient in the United States than in Mexico or Taiwan. Nevertheless, it *is* present in the other countries, so we know that this is not purely an American democratic construct.

Figure 2 shows strikingly similar results from two isolated villages, one in Yucatán, one in Turkey. While conventional moral thought increases steadily from ages 10 to 16 it still has not achieved a clear ascendency over preconventional thought.

Trends for lower-class urban groups are intermediate in the rate of development between those for the middle-class and for the village boys. In the three divergent cultures that I studied, middle-class children were found to be more advanced in moral judgment than matched lower-class children. This was not due to the fact that the middle-class children heavily ignored some one type of thought which could be seen as corresponding to the prevailing middle-class pattern. Instead, middle-class and working-class children move through the same sequences, but the middle-class children move faster and farther.

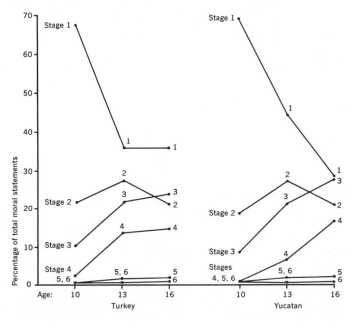

FIGURE 2   Two isolated villages, one in Turkey, the other in Yucatán, show similar patterns in moral thinking. There is no reversal of order, and preconventional (1–2) thought does not gain a clear ascendancy over conventional stages at age 16.

This sequence is not dependent upon a particular region, or any region at all in the usual sense. I found no important difference in the development of moral thinking among Catholics, Protestants, Jews, Buddhists, Moslems and atheists. Religious values seem to go through the same stages as all other values.

In summary, the nature of our sequence is not significantly affected by widely varying social, cultural or religious conditions. The only thing that is affected is the *rate* at which individuals progress through this sequence.

Implications of Universal Stages

Why should there be such a universal invariant sequence of development? In answering this question, we need first to analyze these developing social concepts in terms of their internal logical structure. At each stage, the same basic moral concept or aspect is defined, but at each higher stage this definition is more differentiated, more integrated and more general or universal. When one's concept of human life moves from Stage 1 to Stage 2 the value of life becomes more differentiated from the value of property, more integrated (the value of life enters an organizational hierarchy where it is "higher" than property so that one steals property in order to save life) and more universalized (the life of any sentient being is valuable regardless of status or property). The same advance is true at each stage in the hierarchy. Each step of development then is a better cognitive organization than the one before it, one which takes account of everything present in the previous stage, but making new distinctions and organizing them into a more comprehensive or more equilibriated structure. The fact that this is the case has been demonstrated by a series of studies indicating that children and adolescents comprehend all stages up to their own, but not more than one stage beyond their own (Rest, 1969). And importantly, *they prefer this next stage.*

We have conducted experimental moral discussion classes (Blatt and Kohlberg, 1969) which show that the child at an earlier stage of development tends to move forward when confronted by the views of a child one stage further along. In an argument between a Stage-3 and Stage-4 child, the child in the third stage tends to move toward or into Stage 4, while the Stage-4 child understands but does not accept the arguments of the Stage-3 child.

Moral thought, then, seems to behave like all other kinds of thought. Progress through the moral levels and stages is characterized by increasing differentiation and increasing integration, and hence is the same kind of progress that scientific theory represents. Like acceptable scientific theory—or like *any* theory or structure of knowledge—moral thought may be considered partially to generate its own data as it goes along, or at least to expand so as to contain in a balanced, self-consistent way a wider and wider experiential field. The raw data in the case of our ethical philosophies may be considered as conflicts between roles, or values, or as the social order in which men live.

The social worlds of all men seem to contain the same basic structures. All the societies we have studied have the same basic institutions —family, economy, law, government. In addition, however, all societies are alike because they *are* societies—systems of defined complementary roles. In order to *play* a social role in the family, school or society, the child must implicitly take the role of others toward himself and toward others in the group. These role-taking tendencies form the basis of all social institutions. They represent various patternings of shared or complementary expectations.

In the preconventional and conventional levels (Stages 1–4), moral content or value is largely accidental or culture-bound. Anything from "honesty" to "courage in battle" can be the central value. But in the higher postconventional levels, Socrates, Lincoln, Thoreau and Martin Luther King tend to speak without confusion of tongues, as it were. This is because the ideal principles of any social structure are basically alike, if only because there simply aren't that many principles which are articulate, comprehensive and integrated enough to be satisfying to the human intellect. And most of these principles have gone by the name of justice.

The Concept of Justice

Now let me point out that justice is not a character trait in the usual sense. You cannot make up behavior tests of justice, as Hartshorne and May did for honesty, service and self-control. One cannot conceive of a little set of behavior tests that would indicate that Martin Luther King or Socrates were high on the trait of justice. The reason for this is that justice is not a concrete rule of action, such as lies behind virtues like honesty. To be honest means don't cheat, don't steal, don't lie. Justice is not a rule or a set of rules, it is a moral principle. By a moral principle we mean a mode of choosing which is universal, a rule of choosing which we want all people to adopt always in all situations. We know it is all right to be dishonest and steal to save a life because it is just, because a man's right to life comes before another man's right to property. We know it is sometimes right to kill, because it is sometimes just. The

Germans who tried to kill Hitler were doing right because respect for the equal values of lives demands that we kill someone who is murdering others in order to save their lives. There are exceptions to rules, then, but no exceptions to principles. A moral obligation is an obligation to respect the right or claim of another person. A moral principle is a principle for resolving competing claims, you versus me, you versus a third person. There is only one principled basis for resolving claims, justice or equality. Treat every man's claim impartially regardless of the man. A moral principle is not only a rule of action but a reason for action. As a reason for action, justice is called respect for persons.

As another example of our Stage 6, *orientation to universal moral principles,* let me cite Martin Luther King's letter from a Birmingham jail.

> There is a type of constructive non-violent tension which is necessary for growth. Just as Socrates felt it was necessary to create a tension in the mind so that individuals could rise from the bondage of half-truths, so must we see the need for non-violent gadflies to create the kind of tension in society that will help men rise from the dark depths of prejudice and racism.
>
> One may well ask, "How can you advocate breaking some laws and obeying others?" The answer lies in the fact that there are two types of laws, just and unjust. One has not only a legal but a moral responsibility to obey just laws. One has a moral responsibility to disobey unjust laws. An unjust law is a human law that is not rooted in eternal law and natural law. Any law that uplifts human personality is just, any law that degrades human personality is unjust. An unjust law is a code that a numerical or power majority group compels a minority group to obey but does not make binding on itself. This is difference made legal.
>
> I do not advocate evading or defying the law as would the rabid segregationist. That would lead to anarchy. One who breaks an unjust law must do so openly, lovingly, and with a willingness to accept the penalty. An individual who breaks a law that conscience tells him is unjust, and willingly accepts the penalty of imprisonment in order to arouse the conscience of the community over its injustice, is in reality expressing the highest respect for the law.

King makes it clear that moral disobedience of the law must spring from the same root as moral obedience to law, out of respect for justice. We respect the law because it is based on rights, both in the sense that the law is designed to protect the rights of all and because the law is made by the principle of equal political rights. If civil disobedience is to be Stage 6, it must recognize the contractual respect for law of Stage 5, even to accepting imprisonment. That is why Stage 5 is a way of thinking about the laws which are imposed upon all while a morality of justice which claims to judge the law can never be anything but a free personal ideal. It must accept being put in jail by its enemies not of putting its enemies in jail.

Both logic and empirical study suggest there is no shortcut to autonomous morality, no Stage 6 without a previous Stage 5.

Moral Judgment and Moral Action

Our claim is that knowledge of the moral good is one. We now will try to show that virtue in action is knowledge of the good. We have already said that knowledge of the good in terms of a bag of virtues that comes from opinion or conventional belief is not virtue. An individual may believe that cheating is very bad but that does not predict that he will resist cheating in real life. Espousal of unprejudiced attitudes toward Negroes does not predict to actual action to assure civil rights in an atmosphere where others have some prejudice. However, true knowledge, knowledge of principles of justice does predict to virtuous action. With regard to cheating, the essential elements of justice are understood by both our Stage-5 and Stage-6 subjects. In cheating, the critical issue is recognition of the element of contract and agreement implicit in the situation, and the recognition that while it doesn't seem so bad if one person cheats, what holds for all must hold for one. In a recent study, 100 sixth-grade children were given experimental cheating tests and our moral judgment interview. The majority of the children were below the principled level in moral judgment, they were at our first four moral stages. Seventy-five percent of these children cheated. In contrast, only 20% of the principled subjects, that is, Stages 5 or 6, cheated. In another study conducted at the college level only 11% of the principled subjects cheated in contrast to 42% of the students at lower levels of moral judgment.

In the case of cheating, justice and the expectations of conventional authority both dictate the same behavior. What happens when they are opposed?

An experimental study by Stanley Milgram (1963) involved such an opposition. Undergraduate subjects were ordered by an experimenter to administer increasingly more severe electric shock punishment to a stooge victim in the guise of a learning experiment. In this case, the principles of justice involved in the Stage-5 social contract orientation do not clearly prescribe a decision. The victim had voluntarily agreed to participate in the experiment and the subject himself had contractually committed himself to perform the experiment. Only Stage-6 thinking clearly defined the situation as one in which the experimenter did not have the moral right to ask them to inflict pain on another person. Accordingly, 75% of the Stage-6 subjects quit or refused to shock the victim as compared to only 13% of all the subjects at lower stages.

A study of Berkeley students carries the issue into political civil disobedience. Berkeley students were faced with the decision to sit in the Administration building in the name of political freedom of communication. Haan, Smith, and Block (in press) administered moral judgment interviews to over 200 of these students. Again the situation was like the Milgram situation. A Stage-5 social contract interpretation of justice, which was held by the University administration, could take the position that a student who came to Berkeley came with foreknowledge of the rules and could go elsewhere if he didn't like them. About 50% of the Stage-5 subjects sat in. For Stage-6 students, the issue was clear-cut and 80% of them sat in. For students at the conventional levels, Stages 3 and 4, the issue was also clear-cut and only 10% of them sat in. These results will sound very heartwarming to those of us who have engaged in protest activities. Protesting is a sure sign of being at the most mature moral level. However, there was another group who was almost as disposed to sit in as the Stage-6 students. These were our Stage-2 instrumental relativists, of whom about 60% sat in. From our longitudinal studies, we know that most Stage-2 college students are in a state of confusion. In high school most were at the conventional level, and in college they kick conventional morality searching for their thing, for self-chosen values, but cannot tell an autonomous morality of justice from one of egoistic relativism, exchange and revenge. Our longitudinal studies indicate that all of our middle-class Stage-2 college students grow out of it to become principled adults.

I make the point to indicate that protest activities, like other acts, are neither virtuous nor vicious; it is only the knowledge of the good which lies behind them which gives them virtue. As an example, I would take it that a Stage-6 sense of justice would have been rather unlikely to find the Dow Chemical sit-in virtuous. The rules being disobeyed by the protesters were not unjust rules, and the sit-in was depriving individuals of rights, not trying to protect individual rights. Principled civil disobedience is not illegitimate propaganda for worthy political causes, it is the just questioning of injustice.

Having, I hope, persuaded you of one view of virtue, let us briefly consider how it may be taught. In a sense, this view implies that knowledge of the good is always within but needs to be drawn out. In a series of experimental studies (Rest, Turiel, and Kohlberg, 1969; Rest, 1969), we have found that children and adolescents prefer the highest level of thought they can comprehend. Children comprehend all lower stages than their own, and often comprehend the stage one higher than their own and occasionally two stages higher though they cannot actively express these higher stages of thought. If they comprehend the stage one higher than their own, they tend to prefer it to their own. This fact is basic to moral leadership in our society. While the majority of adults in American society are at a conventional level, Stages 3 and 4, leadership in our society has usually been expressed at the level of Stages 5 and 6, as our example of Martin Luther King suggests.

Returning to the teaching of virtue as a drawing out, the child's preference for the next level of thought shows that it is greeted as already familiar, that it is felt to be a more adequate expression of that already within, of that latent in the child's own thought. If the child were responding to fine words and external prestige he would not pick the next stage continuous with his own, but something else.

Let us now suggest a different example of the sense in which moral teaching must be a drawing out of that already within. At the age of four my son joined the pacifist and vegetarian movement and refused to eat meat, because as he said, "it's bad to kill animals." In spite of lengthy hawk argumentation by his parents about the difference between justified and unjustified killing, he remained a vegetarian for six months. Like most doves, however, his principles recognized occasions of just or legitimate killing. One night I read to him a book of Eskimo life involving a seal-killing expedition. He got angry during the story and said, "You know there is one kind of meat I would eat, Eskimo meat. It's bad to kill animals so it's all right to eat them."

For reasons I won't detail, this eye for an eye, tooth for a tooth concept of justice is Stage 1. You will recognize, however, that it is a very genuine though four-year-old sense of justice and that it contains within it the Stage-6 sense of justice in shadowy form. The problem is to draw the child's perceptions of justice from the shadows of the cave step by step toward the light of justice as an ideal form. This last example indicates a truth not indicated by our experimental example, the truth that the child initially turned from the dark images of the cave toward the light still convinced that his dark images best represent the truth. The child is initially quite confident of his moral knowledge, of the rationality and efficacy of his moral principles. The notion that the child feels ignorant and is eager to absorb the wisdom of adult authority in the moral domain is one which any teacher or parent will know is nonsense. Let me give another example. Following a developmental timetable, my son moved to an expedient Stage-2 orientation when he was six. He told me at that time, "You know the reason people don't steal is because they're afraid of the police. If there were no police around everyone would steal." Of course I told him that I and most people didn't steal because we thought it wrong, because we wouldn't want other people to take things from us and so on. My son's reply was, "I just don't see it, it's sort of crazy not to steal if there are no police."

The story indicates that, like most ordinary fathers, I have no great skill in teaching true virtue. My son, of course, has always been virtuous in the conventional sense. Even when he saw no rational reason for being honest, he received E's on his report card on the bag of virtues on obedience, responsibility, and respect for property. Unlike what we usually think, it is quite easy to teach conventionally virtuous behavior but very difficult to teach true knowledge of the good.

The first step in teaching virtue, then, is the Socratic step of creating dissatisfaction in the student about his present knowledge of the good. This we do experimentally by exposing the student to moral conflict situations for which his principles have no ready solution. Second, we expose him to disagreement and argument about these situations with his peers. Our view holds that if we inspire cognitive conflict in the student and point the way to the next step up the divided line, he will tend to see things previously invisible to him.

In practice, then, our experimental efforts at moral education have involved getting students at one level, say Stage 2, to argue with those at the next level, say Stage 3. The teacher would support and clarify the Stage-3 arguments. Then he would pit the Stage-3 students against the Stage-4 students on a new dilemma. Initial results with this method with a junior high group indicated 50% of the students moved up one stage and 10% moved up two stages. In comparison, only 10% of a control group moved up one stage in the four-month period involved (Blatt and Kohlberg, 1969).

Obviously the small procedures I have described are only a way station to genuine moral education. As my earlier comments suggested, a more complete approach means full student participation in a school in which justice is a living matter.

References

Blatt, M., and Kohlberg, L. The effects of a classroom discussion program upon the moral levels of preadolescents. *Merrill Palmer Quarterly*, 1969 (in press).

Haan, N., Smith, M. B., and Block, J. Political, family, and personality correlates of adolescent moral judgment. *Journal of Personality and Social Psychology*, 1968, *10* (3), 183–201.

Hartshorne, H., and May, M. A. *Studies in the nature of character:* Vol. 1. *Studies in deceit.* Vol. 2. *Studies in self-control.* Vol. 3. *Studies in the organization of character.* New York: Macmillan, 1928–1930.

Havighurst, R. J., and Taba, H. *Adolescent character and personality.* New York: Wiley, 1949.

Kohlberg, L. The development of modes of moral thinking and choice in the years ten to sixteen. Unpublished doctoral dissertation, University of Chicago, 1958.

Kohlberg, L. The development of children's orientations toward moral order: 1. Sequence in the development of moral thought. *Vita Humana,* 1963, *6,* 11–33.

Kohlberg, L. Stage and Sequence: the cognitive developmental approach to socialization. In D. Goslin (Ed.), *Handbook of socialization theory.* Chicago: Rand McNally, 1969.

Kohlberg, L., and Kramer, R. Continuity and discontinuity in moral development from childhood to adulthood. *Human Development,* 1969 (in press).

Milgram, S. Behavioral study of obedience. *Journal of Abnormal and Social Psychology,* 1963, *67* (4), 371–378.

Piaget, J. *The moral judgment of the child.* Glencoe, Ill.: Free Press, 1948 (originally published, 1932).

Rest, J. Hierarchies of comprehension and preference in a developmental stage model of moral thinking. Unpublished doctoral dissertation, University of Chicago, 1969.

Rest, J., Turiel, E., and Kohlberg, L. Level of moral development as a determinant of preference and comprehension of moral judgments made by others. *Journal of Personality and Social Psychology,* 1969 (in press).

Turiel, E. An experimental test of the sequentiality of developmental stages in the child's moral judgments. *Journal of Personality and Social Psychology,* 1966, *3* (6), 611–618.

IV. ON SOCIALIZATION AND THE PSYCHOSOCIAL REALM OF ADOLESCENCE

Introduction

Socialization, social learning, and the psychosocial realm are the subjects of numerous tomes in the social sciences. We shall barely sample the applications of these concepts to adolescent development. Our sample will focus on socialization processes immediately relevant to the high school experience, somewhat ignoring the multiple meanings and complex forms socialization takes among modern adolescents. This shift from the developmental areas of a more structural and functional nature dealt with in the previous two sections moves us into today's true mantle of adolescence: the social ramifications of adolescent development. Whatever turmoils and extensions adolescents face derive from these social ramifications.

Distinguishing among the concepts socialization, social learning, and psychosocial factors is not difficult if we are willing to accept the fact that they merely represent different perspectives on the same phenomenon. Socialization refers to the process by which a social group or social agent inculcates roles in the individual. Conceptually, a role is nothing more than a set of interpersonal behaviors that are associated with or expected for a given situation, although one could argue that these behaviors need not be interpersonal. Social learning is what goes on in the individual who is being socialized and we infer it in much the same way that we infer other forms of learning. The term psychosocial alludes to the personal, cognitive products an individual acquires through his own socialization experiences. Thus, to be redundant for the sake of making a point, we can speak of a high school student socially learning ambivalent psychosocial orientations toward college from the conflicting socializations he receives from his parents and his peers.

This section, then, purports to acquaint us with some of the effects of the adolescent's social milieu upon his development in high school. Our treatment of these social effects begins with two articles that introduce us to the terms and leading works in this area. Dodson's article plies the reader with definitions of basic social terminology and notions of child development. However, the reader would do well to remember that Dodson leans heavily on the sociological interpretation of behavior. His tendency to stress the importance of "mores" for understanding and dealing with human behavior, while playing down "synaptic connections" and obliquely referring to "tinkering with psyches," was once justifiable in trying to get educators to be multi-disciplinary. Today, however, the sociological perspective has been duly incorporated by educators and behavioral scientists, and Dodson's zeal ought to be de-emphasized in view of the prevailing multi-disciplinary approach to human development and education. Polsky provides a valuable overview of major theorists' works and ideas in what he calls the sociology of adolescence. The Kandel and others (1968) paper on the concept of adolescent subcultures provides a review of a sociological concept with a long history of controversy. This concept has enjoyed widespread currency in America as a socialization model of adolescent behavior. The authors trace its origin and development and then go on to analyze its alleged influences on adolescents. The student will be impressed at once with the vast number of investigators who have worked with this concept, as well as with the uncertainty with which it has been maintained over the decades and the many forms it has assumed. Kandel and her colleagues offer us a context within which to place other investigators' allusions to the notion of an adolescent subculture. Perhaps the only conclusion one can come to is that this concept is destined to the same fate as Freud's concept of identification—having been used widely to mean many things it is no longer of any particular use.

In the fourth paper, Simpson presents an analysis to illustrate what he considers the basic sociological function the adolescent peer group performs for the social system as well as for the adoles-

cent. Simpson's theme is that the extended period of adolescence in modern America functions primarily because of the central statuses provided the adolescent by his peer group. In other words, the peer group is what gives meaning to the adolescent's life.

Brittain helps remove us from the horns of a dilemma encountered by students of adolescence about the preferences adolescents show for parents and peers in conflict situations. He hypothesizes that adolescents are inclined to be swayed by parents when making certain choices, whereas in other instances they tend to follow peers. His findings support his expectations and also show the respective areas in which parents and peers are followed.

In their study of peer influences on adolescent educational aspirations and attainments, Alexander and Campbell deal with the effects of friends on the high school senior's goals to go to college. Their findings show that a senior's friends' attitudes and choices about college have important consequences for his own attitudes and choices about college—and other areas for that matter. In addition to their results, the model they use to analyze dyadic friendships deserves reading.

The next two papers move away from the influences of parents and peers per se and look at the socializing effects of the high schools on students. Boyle reviews the germane literature on the effects of high schools on student aspirations and then presents his own data on the subject. Boyle summarizes his findings with the overall observation that the population composition of a high school has important consequences for the student's aspirations, somewhat more important in large-city schools than in small-city schools. In addition, Boyle is critical of survey data and yields useful insights into the inherent weaknesses of seemingly acceptable investigations that the student should be aware of for future reference.

Willems' study is concerned with the relationships among school size, student performance, and a student's sense of obligation or responsibility to school activities. This study shows that high schools of different sizes have differential expectations about their "good" and "poor" students' feelings for participation in school activities.

The Rosen article on the effects of conflicting group membership adds at least two components to our consideration of socialization among adolescents. In the first place, it presents us with an understanding and a realistic application of the concept of reference groups—a useful notion for studying adolescents' behaviors and attitudes. The other contribution Rosen makes is an examination of the reactions of adolescents in a particular religious group to peer and parental pressures concerning a religious behavior. Rosen introduces us to the socializing influences of others on Jewish high school age boys and girls attitudes toward the ritual practice of the use of Kosher meat. We have here a miniature window on the process through which a particular minority group fails or succeeds to include a particular behavior in its young.

The final selection on the socialization process and adolescent development gives a very cursory but poignant view of the psychosocial realizations of black adolescents in America. In these two excerpts from Grier and Cobbs' *Black Rage*, the reader is thrust into the human realities of two psychiatrists' findings on the consequences of the conditions and experiences of Negro youth in America. The intent here is to present the very stark socialization effects pressed on members of a minority group—American society socializes black adolescents to feel inferior and to be satisfied with inferior statuses.

The importance of keeping track of the societal context in which adolescents must place themselves cannot be overstressed for those who would work with adolescents. In a sense, we have pointed to one way for the adult to keep abreast of society's impact on youth by demonstrating the usefulness of communicating directly with adolescents about their views of what's happening to them. A supplement to and stimulant for this source of information is available from the so-called experts who attend to the trends of society's building blocks. For one comprehensive treatment of the nature of the American society in which adolescents find themselves, the student is referred to "The Changing American People: Are We Deteriorating or Improving?" *Annals of American Academy of Political and Social Sciences,* 378 (July 1968).

1. SOCIAL ASPECTS OF CHILD DEVELOPMENT *

Dan W. Dodson

What would happen if some Passover in reverse should kill all human beings, except the infants? You would say, "They too would die." You would be right, for the existence of the infant depends upon some way of caring for him. Let us suppose, however, that there were some miraculous way through which the babies who were spared could be nurtured to maturity without coming in contact with older people who could teach them the ways of the group. What would it mean?

It would mean that we would begin anew the tortuous process of acquiring a culture. Few, if any, of the things which have meaning for us would be significant to them. There would be no language, other than cries and guttural sounds, hence communication would be restricted to primitive forms. None of the artifacts of our culture would have meaning for them. Buildings might be used for shelter, but such use would come only through trial and error experience.

None of the things we consider moral could, in likelihood, be found among them. They would stand in awe of, and perhaps ultimately develop rituals around powers which were beyond their understanding. They would be animistic in religion and it would perhaps take a thousand years to develop a monotheistic conception of deity. The simplest concepts of causation in the world about them would be unintelligible. They would ascribe causality to whatever happened to be near when something occurred. It would take a long time to determine the relation between cause and effect as we know it. The children of the most civilized society would fare no better than others, for the skills of

* Reprinted with permission from The Journal of Nursery Education (now YOUNG CHILDREN), Vol. 17, No. 2, March 1962. National Association for the Education of Young Children, 1629 21st Street, N.W., Washington, D.C.

responding to a highly complex culture are not biological and hence are not transmissible through inheritance.

Now! Let us look at the problem another way. Suppose by some strange accident the child of a mother of the Australian Bush could be exchanged for the child of a modern mother of today's Manhattan and the accident not discovered. It must be admitted that the biological characteristics would make it impossible for such an exchange to go unnoticed, but for the sake of argument suppose it could. It is not hard to believe that both children would acquire the skills which would make them capable of functioning purposively and worthily in the societies to which fate assigned them.

This type of speculation suggests that man has almost infinite capacity for adaptation. The raw stuff of his original nature gives him almost limitless ability to "become." What he becomes depends on what the culture of which he is a part demands of him. While some believe the next "breakthrough" in human advancement will be through eugenics [1] most would agree, perhaps, that this is a slow and uncertain road since we know so little about the upper limits of biological capacity. Recent studies, likewise, are beginning to challenge the limitations set on man's capacities by the psychologists. Man's psychological limitations were set and inherent, according to the older schools of thought. Said Burt *et al.* as late as 1934:

> By intelligence, the psychologist understands inborn, all-around, intellectual ability. It is inherited, or at least innate, not due to teaching or training; it is intellectual, not emotional or moral, and remains uninfluenced by industry or zeal; it is general, not specific, i.e., it is not limited to any particular kind of work, but enters into all we do or say or think. Of all our mental qualities, it is the most far reaching; fortunately, it can be measured with accuracy and ease. [2]

Of this school of thought Faris says:

> . . . a half century or so ago a miniature Dark Age descended over the field of human psychology and the doctrines of the mental testers convinced an impressed public with a secular variant of an infant damnation doctrine. [3]

Hunt, after examining the literature on intelligence and experience, concludes with much optimism that we can "find out how to govern the

---

[1] Murphy, Gardner, *The Human Potential.*

[2] Burt, et al., *How The Mind Works,* 1934.

[3] Faris, R. E., "Reflections On The Ability Dimensions In Human Society," *Am. Soc. Rev.,* 26:6.

encounters that children have with their environments" to increase intelligence.[4]

This latter type of thinking suggests significant advances in human ability through intentional control of social factors which call forth latent skills and abilities.

The Socialization Process

How does a culture produce an American, Protestant, Catholic or Jew, a Hottentot or a Russian, from a child with his original nature? Sociologists call this socialization. Original nature becomes cloaked with qualities we call human. Language, social graces, self-awareness and a conception of status emerge through a process in which the child and his social world interact. Both are altered by the impact. What is perhaps more important, each is different because of the other.

The following are some of the important factors in this process:

1. THE FORMATION OF HUMAN NATURE

Man is not born human. He is born with potentialities for becoming human. Original nature becomes cloaked with qualities we call human. This nature consists of abilities to identify with and relate to other people. It connotes those attributes which are perhaps shared solely among the human specie—consciousness of one's self in relation to others, senses of right and wrong formed by the standards of the group, an empathetic relationship whereby one enters imaginatively into the role of the other, sees himself as if he were in the place of the other and experiences the sentiments which he imputes to the other.

This dimension of growth and development cannot be overestimated. This writer spent an evening with the staff of a community center in a low income housing project. We tried to assess the impact upon human nature of children reared in that situation. Almost all the experiences these children had with others were on a mass basis. Except for the tenuous strands of family life, and many homes were broken, these children had been educated on a mass basis and had been involved in recreation only on a mass basis. If a child is ever to internalize feelings of regard for others so that he behaves toward them as he would behave toward himself because he can "put himself in their place," this skill must be learned at an early age and in small intimate group relationships. I do

---

[4] J. McV. Hunt, *Intelligence and Experience*, 1961.

not doubt but that many contemporary cruel crimes are perpetrated by persons who have never had this capacity developed within themselves.

To be human, one must be able to put himself imaginatively in the role of the other and experience how he would "feel" were he in the other's place. Cooley makes the point that human nature is universal because the primary groups in which it is cradled are universal.

2. CONCEPTION OF SELF

In the foregoing discussion words like self and role were used frequently. They signify that acquiring a concept of self is another dimension of socialization. In the early months of life a child probably does not distinguish self from mother. Be that as it may, the concept of self is a continuously changing one. Maturation brings changes of self concept. Each new contact delimits self-other perceptions. One becomes an object to himself only because he is in interaction with other selves. Cooley's classical illustration of the "looking glass" self illustrates what is involved:

> As we see our face, figure, and dress in the glass, and are interested in them because they are ours, and pleased or otherwise with them according as they do or do not answer to what we should like them to be; so in our imagination we perceive in another's mind some thought of our appearance, manners, aims, deeds, character, friends, and so on, and are variously affected by it.
>
> A self-idea of this sort seems to have three principal elements: the imagination of our appearance to the other person, the imagination of his judgment of that appearance, and some sort of self-feeling, such as pride or mortification.
>
> . . . We are ashamed to seem evasive in the presence of a straightforward man, cowardly in the presence of a brave one, gross in the eyes of a refined one, and so on. We always imagine, and in imagining share, the judgments of the other mind. A man will boast to one person of an action—say some sharp transaction in trade—which he would be ashamed to own to another.[5]

The significance of self-perception cannot be overestimated. One of the major roadblocks to later maturity is that the individual never worked out for himself a conception of self which gave his personality structure and form, or else the self-conception was so inadequate that the individual never had to develop his potentials in order to meet his self expectations. For some there is the problem of trauma to self-perception created by the interaction. Unless one has self-confidence he is

---

[5] Cooley, Chas. H., *Human Nature and The Social Order*.

seriously impaired in life's undertakings. The quality of the social relationships between an individual and those with whom he is in interaction goes a long way toward spelling out the sort of object he becomes
to himself.

3. ROLE BEHAVIOR

Closely related to conception of self is social role. Each of us perceives
himself in many roles. Others expect performances from us in line with
their, and our, role expectancies for us. Roles in early childhood may be
quite diffused. A child at play can be mother this instant, father the
next, then teacher or nurse. As soon as we become self-conscious this becomes more difficult. Children are frequently baffled by lack of clarity of
role for themselves in social groups. They must perforce take direction
from their elders. If one sits on a park bench on an afternoon when
mothers are out with their small children it is not hard to detect this
process. There are many proscriptions. "Don't do this." "Do do that."
"You are a naughty child." "Come back here—you must not go there."
All these are familiar terms. Many middle class mothers scold their children because they get dirty. The tendency to keep them nice and clean
is often the beginning of a rigid and inflexible perception of role. Regardless of the perception of role which emerges, the child is coming to
learn certain role relationships. He learns he can control his mother by
crying. He can please her by loving her. He soon learns that some roles
are naughty and others good.

4. STATUS

Another dimension of self is status. Here one learns how much esteem is
attached to one's self as a person. We also learn that in some roles we
rate higher than in others. One young woman is perceived as a queen
and carries herself in regal splendor. Another, equally beautiful, equally
competent, and equally healthy perceives herself as a commoner and
curtsies to the other. The reason? One has status and the other does not.

   It should also be noticed that status is accorded not only because of
"who one is," but status is also related to achievement. One is the
strongest. Another is the brightest. One is the prettiest. Another is so ugly
that only a mother could love him (in a culture which prizes good
looks). Some work out roles of status as leaders and occasionally lead
with such compelling power that they are referred to as charismatic
leaders, i.e., they have the gift of the gods.

   From a biologically functioning organism at birth, endowed with tremendous potentialities to "become," the average child moves through

the varied social processes to become a social being—conscious of himself in relation to others, playing many roles, some contradictory to one another—some complementing each other. Some give him status—others detract from his status. To meet the role expectations and acquire status the average child learns whatever the culture (his culture) demands in the way of language, skills and other culture content.

5. POWER AS A DIMENSION OF STATUS

In our pluralistic society one aspect of status is power. Every community has persons and groups who have more status than others. They are able to make decisions for the community which others are obliged to follow. Sometimes this power is oppressive. Sometimes it is liberating to the human spirit. It is here hypothesized that it is impossible for a youth who is a member of a group which is powerless, to grow to maturity without some hurt to his perception of self because of the compromised position of his group in the community. Perhaps the most dramatic and heartrending aspect of this problem is that occasioned when the minority group child comes to his parents and says "Johnny called me a 'nigger.' What is a 'nigger'?" Or as Frazier relates the case of the child who has an altercation with an older white youth, who says "I will tell my father and he will take care of you." His father, however, must "let him down" because the white youth's position in the community makes him invulnerable insofar as the Negro is concerned, irrespective of the justice of the latter's position.

Adler contended that the feeling of impotence in a youth was the dynamism of growth. He said a person who feels impotent tends to overemphasize for his weaknesses. While we see some evidence of this type of behavior in low income, minority communities, we also witness what he did not indicate—namely that overcompensation is not the only way of reacting to powerlessness. Another is resignation in apathy. The mass apathy in the slums of our cities is indicative of this trauma to selfhood for those who are outside the "pale of power." Such apathy is often taken for lack of ability. However, early childhood education leaders will testify that differences between young children of widely different social backgrounds are not so noticeable. As the self-conceptions wrought through interaction in the culture make themselves felt in personality, the differences begin to emerge.

6. SOCIAL CLASS AS STATUS

A closely related aspect of status is social class. Studies indicate that by the fifth year measurable differences in the behavior of children of different classes show up. Middle class mothers begin toilet-training much earlier than do lower class mothers. Thumb sucking is much more a middle class child behavior. Lower class children are allowed to do things "on their own" much earlier than are middle class children. In the later years of child development these middle class pressures become inexorable. The child's status becomes much more dependent upon his making grades in school, keeping clean, not being a rowdy, and "watching his manners." That these conforming pressures are emasculating to both sexes is evidenced by the much higher ratio of sexual frigidity and other types of sexual aberrations in middle class than in lower class adults, according to the Kinsey reports.

This discussion of the socialization process illustrates some of what happens as this pristine nature of children comes into interaction with the surrogates of the culture. Each develops a self, a role with status; each acquires power or is traumatized because of lack of it; each finds himself in some general structures which we call class. Original nature is forged into human nature. The quality of "humanness" depends upon many aspects of culture, and some aspects of capacity within the individual himself.

Some Issues

We come now to discuss some issues which bear upon child rearing in our culture. These could be expanded many times over, but the following are suggestive of the challenges which the sociological factors of the society present:

1. GROUPING

One of the most controversial, and at the same time fruitful, areas is grouping. At present there is a tendency toward peer grouping in our culture. We group children on age bases. We group them on ability bases. There is a tremendous movement toward grouping on a religious basis. Reisman has written tellingly of the change from "inner direction" to "outer direction" as aspects of our national character. He attributes this to the change in the age structure of the population; the change from a producers' to a consumers' economy; the change from the Protestant ethic to a secular motivation. A good case could be made that the reason for this phenomenon is none of these things. There is outer direction because there is peer group domination. One's reference groups are less and less those of the elder generation, family tradition, and that which represents a link of continuity between the generations. It is increasingly that of the peer group.

Another aspect of peer group influence is in its stifling of creativity, and its pull toward mediocrity. The higher challenges for a group are rarely the dynamisms generated within it. Nursery school education should experiment more with this dimension of personality growth and development. Too much adult domination brings pressures to identify with adult norms. This has been described tellingly by Eric Fromm. Too little challenge from adult relationships results in mediocrity. Sensitive leaders will be concerned with striking the right balance in grouping for all the children.

2. SOCIAL NORMS

A great challenge in child welfare is how to develop democratic "perimeters of authority" so youths will have the security of knowing "how far they can go," and where they must stop. A democratic society does not mean absence of norms. Neither, of course, does it mean oppressive authoritarianism. The former is anarchy. The latter is dictatorship. When a new teacher is sent into a classroom it is a rare thing that much is accomplished the first day. The children are "trying her out" to see how far they can go. When they discover the perimeters of authority they "settle down." The studies in discipline indicate that the impact of discipline on personality is not so much whether it is permissive or strict. It is traumatizing when it is ambivalent and equivocal. The problem is how to "shore up" the perimeters of authority so that the child is sure of where he stands. As he grows older he will need to keep testing these boundaries of authority against his altered maturity. It is good conditioning to tell a four-year-old never to cross the street without assistance. A twenty-four-year-old who never tested this conditioning against his altered maturity would be a hopeless cripple.

Undoubtedly much of the later problems of delinquency and other social disorganization among youth is the result of what sociologists would call anomie (absence of norms).

3. VALUES

The last portion of this paper relates to values. That they are a social product is obvious. Some seem universal in human societies. Undoubtedly others are unique to time and place. The studies of Piaget indicate that most values begin as moral conditioning in the early life of the child. Most proscriptions are the "thou shalt" and "thou shalt not" of adult direction. There are scarcely any shades of gray—things are either right or wrong. The basis of rightness or wrongness is because some authority figure said so. This is the "port of entry" into character development for the child. He has no other.

At given stages of maturation this is a necessary and universal aspect of training. Leaders of children's groups have no alternative than to inculcate the ways of life into which the children are born. This rigidity of moral structure is needed to give security and confidence to the very young. As the child grows older what has been taught must be reexamined as to its continued adequacy. Hence, much of what is learned as concepts of right and wrong, moral and immoral, must later be reinterpreted, unlearned, or mediated by conflicting and contradictory values. The absolutes are not the issues of character making choices. Such are rarely presented in later life. Choices of mature people are among the fine shades of gray in between. Few absolutes can be followed blindly in intelligent citizenship in later life because they are interwoven with equally compelling absolutes which alas are sometimes contradictory.

Hence, most children acquire moral controls in early life. As they mature they must learn to make increasingly rational decisions by taking into account conflicting and contradictory values, and increasingly develop ethical systems of behavior in which they bring to bear reason, knowledge, and an understanding of the role of their own prejudices. They must learn to make increasingly disciplined judgments. This process starts in the nursery school.

The Prospect

This brief summary of sociological concepts suggests the possibilities of the future. Biological improvement of the race is a long and uncertain undertaking. The psychological internalization of experience will always be an area of fruitful study. Both offer hopes for man's improvement. What has not always been clear is man's relation to man. In our individualistic society there has been a tendency to depreciate this part of man's nature.

Today, we realize behavior is determined much more by mores than by synaptic connections. While we may "tinker with the psyche" of those who suffer from traumas to self-hood (occasioned by their treatment in the society) the great hope resides in creating the kind of society which will have built-in therapeutic dimensions. Such a society will elicit far more creativeness than we now exhibit.

Biological evolution has brought all races to about the same stage of development. We are born with enormous potentials. Some capitalize on their original endowment. Others never have the sails of imagination stretched to see the vistas on the far horizons—beyond narrowly circumscribed selves.

In this day when democracy is on trial to demonstrate its ability to unlock potentials, we who lead youth have the task of engineering social processes so that our apathetic ones, those with limited perceptions of self, those whose lives are unfulfilled, are led to encounter social relationships which will demand of them a new nature, a new man. In this task we begin with the children.

This is where you in early childhood education can offer a most significant contribution.

2. THE SOCIOLOGY OF ADOLESCENCE: A REVIEW OF MAJOR STUDIES *

Howard W. Polsky

A plethora of articles on adolescent abnormal behavior from a clinical point of view is now flooding the presses. This is a sociological phenomenon which begs a special study in itself. It is the premise of this paper that the dynamics of adolescent behavior within the "family parlor" will take on more significant meaning if we have more explicit understanding of some of the major forces in our society which shape the family and the adolescent's role in it. Accordingly, "the first lesson of modern sociology is that the individual cannot understand his own experiences or gauge his own fate without locating himself within the trends of his epoch and the life chances of all the individuals of his social layer." [1]

Sutherland has pointed out that "theories may be classified regarding the points of interest in two principal groups; namely, individual differences and situational or cultural processes." [2] The relationship between these two groups of data must be grasped in order to understand both the peculiar contributions of sociology and psychology to social thought. Much of what is basic to a sociological orientation has been clearly outlined in Sutherland's approach to what he calls systematic criminal or delinquent behavior:

* *Journal of Human Relations*, 1959, 7(3), 251–270. Reprinted by permission of the author and the *Journal of Human Relations*.

[1] Mills, Wright C. *White Collar*, Oxford University Press, New York, 1951.

[2] Sutherland, E. H. *A Theory of Criminology*, Lippincott, Philadelphia, 1934. Reprinted by permission of the publisher, J. B. Lippincott Company.

Third, delinquency is adventitious when considered as a specific act of a specific person. No one can explain why a coin comes up "heads" on a particular toss. It is described as due to chance. Chance does not mean that no causes are operating, but that the causes are so complicated that they cannot be analyzed. Similarly, a specific criminal act may be the result of a complex of causes which cannot be analyzed. This does not mean that it is similar to the flipping of a coin with only two alternatives and those of equal likelihood. Rather it is like rolling loaded dice, with high probability but no certainty. It is not possible to explain adequately why one person commits a specific crime while another, with traits, experiences, and social situation almost identical, does not. The plot of a recent motion picture is based on a comparison of two boys engaged in a theft. When discovered, one ran more rapidly, escaped, and became a priest; the other ran less rapidly, was caught, and committed to a reformatory, and became a gangster. In other circumstances, the one who ran more rapidly might have become the gangster, and the one who ran less rapidly the priest. It is such combinations of factors which make it impossible to explain each individual act adequately, because it is never possible to include all these unique combinations in a generalization. On that account attention should be concentrated on systematic criminal behavior, either in the form of criminal careers or organized criminal practices. By this statement of the problem, it may be possible to discover the processes which are general and uniform and to arrive at an adequate theory of such behavior. If a theory can be developed that is adequate for systematic criminal behavior, it will be easier to explain specific acts in relation to this framework.[3]

It is important to note that the sociologist departs from the individualistically oriented psychologist when he "conceives of the social structure as active, as producing fresh motivations which cannot be predicted on the basis of one's knowledge of man's native drives."[4] He attempts to determine how the social and cultural structure generates pressure for varying kinds of social behavior, and assumes that despite individual-to-individual variations, important common group manifestations will appear in response to similar positions occupied in the societal structure and in reaction to similar social pressures. Allison Davis employs this same approach in his own studies of adolescent behavior: "This central characteristic of human social learning, namely, that human beings always learn their social behavior in some type of relation to other personalities, and therefore in an emotional context, is the crucial principle underlying any systematic effort to understand adolescent

---

[3] *Ibid.*

[4] Merton, Robert K. *Social Theory and Social Structure*, The Free Press of Glencoe, Illinois, 1949.

social and personal development. That is, every adolescent's social behavior bears the marks of his personal history in relation to his parents, his siblings, his play-group and his teachers, as well as the imprint of cultural controls." [5]

To be sure, important variations in behavior arise among members of the same social status. This is due (1) to different constitutions and psychic integrations and (2) to the differing experiences and "cumulative ordering of these experiences." Yet "the life plan of the individual, his philosophy of life, and his expectations and specific goals, normally fit into a large social framework, which is typical of his social position, and which limit the scope of his construction of a possible future." "To limit," however, this writer is cautious to add, "is not to determine. The structure of a man's future as he sees it is subject to marked individual modification from the life plan suggested by his social position in a particular society at a given time." [6]

Another key concept that links the social structures and institutions to the individual personality must be elaborated upon. This is the concept of "person": the variations of social roles which compose the individual, their objectives and values which steer and direct his conduct, and the individual's way of reacting to these roles. A role can be defined "as the act of prescribed behaviors expected of individuals who fill given positions in specific groups." [7] This concept was brought into prominence by George H. Mead [8] (developed simultaneously in many respects by sociologists Thomas and Cooley, [9] and the psychiatrist, Harry Stack Sullivan [10]) who traced the socialization of the child to a process of incorporating societal norms of behavior by putting himself in the place of others ("the generalized other") and gradually learning through a differentiating process what others expect of him so that these expectations become internalized. "His self, as he reflectively imagines and conceives it, is a reconstruction of the image of his self which others have communicated to him. . . . In analyzing the life history of a particular individual in his active relationships with others, we find a plurality of diverse, partly overlapping conceptions or images this individual progressively formed by various social sets in which he participates from infancy to

---

[5] Davis, Allison. "Socialization and Adolescent Personality," *43rd Yearbook, National Society for the Study of Education*, 1944, Part I, Ch. XI, p. 198.

[6] Gerth, Hans, and Mills, Wright C. *Character and Social Structure*, Harcourt Brace & Company, New York, 1953.

[7] Hartley, Eugene L. and Hartley, Ruth E. *Fundamentals of Social Psychology*, Alfred A. Knopf, New York, 1952, p. 485.

[8] Mead, G. H. *Mind, Self, and Society*, University of Chicago Press, Chicago, 1933.

[9] Cooley, C. L. *Human Nature and the Social Order*, Scribners, New York, 1902.

[10] Sullivan, H. S. *Conceptions of Modern Psychiatry*, The William Alanson White Psychiatric Foundation, Washington, D.C., 1947.

old age. Some of these images disappear, some become partly absorbed in later images. Consequently, his image of his self changes in the course of time; but it serves as a lasting nucleus, giving to the images constructed by others some degree of unity and continuity. It enables him to identify himself and helps others identify him as the same individual, however differently represented by different social sets and by himself at different periods of his life." [11]

The precise relationship of the assumption of roles to the internalization of significant others' expectations has been described by Logan and Wilson:

> In the internalization of the attitudes of others, the individual most often takes over those attitudes which define his own role in the group. In the early stages of participation in a social group, an individual's social role is external to him and exists only in the expectations of others. In order to secure the approval of the group, and to achieve his own objectives the person must inform himself as to the nature and character of these expectations. This is usually not difficult, since the other members are anxious for him to learn his role as soon as possible, and hence they informally and repeatedly depict it for him in their conversation and overt behavior. Through the process of socialization, the individual incorporates these expectations into his personality and thus establishes his role and its relation to the roles of others.[12]

It has been pointed out that whereas Freud in his analysis of the socialization process concerned himself almost exclusively with one or the other—parental authority or substitute—the more sociologically or culturally oriented psychologists consider equally significant other individuals and groups the individual comes into contact with at various periods throughout his life. Particularized others eventually form a pattern, and a hierarchy of values is established with varying meanings for the youth, and hence consequences for his conduct. In employing this approach, "motives are viewed as social justifications for one's own conduct, and as a means of persuading others to accept and to further one's conduct. Such statements of motive arise when we are faced with alternatives, with unexpected choices, or when there is opposition to one's role; for in routine conduct our motives are often not questioned." [13]

The above sociological orientation was the one basically employed by the major empirical study—Elmtown's Youth:

---

[11] Znaniecki, Florian. *Cultural Sciences*, University of Illinois Press, Urbana, Illinois, 1952, p. 147.

[12] Wilson, Logan, and Kolb, William L. (eds.) *Sociological Analysis*, Harcourt, Brace and Company, New York, 1949, pp. 208–209.

[13] Gerth and Mills. *op. cit.*, p. 129.

Eventually, the conclusion was reached that, from the viewpoint of the sociologist, adolescence is distinctly different from psychologists', physiologists', and educators' concept of it. *Sociologically, adolescence is the period in the life of a person when the society in which he functions ceases to regard him (male or female) as a child and does not accord to him full adult status, roles, and functions.* In terms of behavior, it is defined by the roles the person is expected to play, is allowed to play, is forced to play, or prohibited from playing by virtue of his status in society. It is not marked by a specific point in the time such as puberty, since its form, content, duration, and period in the life cycle are differently determined by various cultures and societies. Sociologically the important thing about the adolescent years is the way people regard the maturing individual. . . . We believe that adolescent behavior is a type of transitional behavior which is dependent upon the society, and more particularly upon the position the individual occupies in the social structure, rather than upon the bio-psychological phenomena connected with his age, such as puberty, or the assumed psycho-organic conditions variously referred to as "drives," "urges," and "tensions," in psychological, educational and lay usage. This is not to assert that anatomical, physiological, and psychological facts connected with this phase of the life cycle have no bearing on behavior during the adolescent years. They undoubtedly do, but their functional importance for the maturing individual is defined by the culture.[14]

The over-all finding of this book revealed that the behavior of the adolescents is related significantly to class in every major phase of social behavior—the school, the church, the job, recreation, the clique, dating, and sex. The youth's behavior is mediated by the home and the neighborhood, so that "the effects of differential learning in the home and the neighborhood during the childhood years are the basic conditioning factors which give rise to the highly significant differences in social behavior observed among the adolescents in the different classes. We shall conclude with the general proposition that, if an adolescent has been trained in the home and the neighborhood to act, let us say, like a class 1 person, and his clique associations are with class 1 boys or girls, that adolescent will reveal a class 1 behavior pattern in his non-family social activities. We believe that this generalization will apply to each class and to each area of social behavior."

Allison Davis has carried this class analysis of adolescent behavior a step further with his hypothesis of "adaptive or socialized anxiety." [15] The successful socialization of the middle class adolescents, according to

---

[14] Hollingshead, August B. *Elmtown's Youth,* John Wiley & Sons, New York, 1949.
[15] Davis, Allison. *op. cit.*

this hypothesis, depends on the extent of adaptive anxiety inculcated into the adolescent which enables him to strive for the prestige and rewards of his socioeconomic class. Anxiety is derived from social class position.

> In order to understand the prestige motivation of individuals of middle status, then, one must remember the severe social and biological punishments associated with low status. The anxiety which middle status people learn is effective, first because it involves the threat of loss of present status, and secondly because it leads as the individual may plainly see in "successful" persons, to the rewards of power, of social prestige, and of security for one's children.
>
> Now, it is a difficult task to socialize in the middle-class way of behavior of those great masses of low-status children who form the bulk of the schools' populations. . . . To the upper-middle-class child, who learns and climbs fast, the prestige rewards appear certain and relatively near. Our society cannot hope, therefore, to educate the great masses of lower-class people in any really effective manner until it has *real* rewards to offer them for learning the necessary anxiety.[16]

The discussion thus far has taken the concrete form of specifying crucial social determinants of adolescent behavior in America. To be sure adolescent behavior varies not only in different social-economic circumstances in the same culture but in different cultures as well. Cross-cultural comparisons give us insight into the American way of life—viewed as a *Gestalt*. By comparing the culture conditioning of our own children and youths of non-Western cultures, Ruth Benedict has pointed up socialization "discontinuities" (primarily between the roles of the father and the male-youth): in the area (1) of responsibility where the child neither (in the typical case) performs tasks congruent with his capacity nor does he make a contribution to society worthy in its own right. Praise is offered "regardless of whether the task is well done by adult standards, and the child acquires no sensible standard by which to measure its achievement"; in (2) the dominance-submission plane the child is subordinated in all of his activity to the adults: "There is a tendency in our culture to regard every situation as having in it the seeds of a dominance-submission relationship" even where dominance-submission is patently irrelevant, we read in the dichotomy, assuming that in every situation there must be one person dominating the other; in the (3) contrasted sex role which has been emphasized to such an extent in the literature that extended remarks are superfluous. The idea that sex is wicked or dangerous is strongly inculcated in our children from their

---

16 *Ibid.* pp. 213–214.

earliest years, lessons which are difficult to unlearn later.[17] Compare Sullivan's remarks:

> The lurid twilight which invests sex in our culture is primarily a function of two factors. We still try to discourage premarital sexual performances; hold that abstinence is the moral course before marriage. And we discourage early marriage; in fact progressively widen the gap between the adolescent awakening of lust and the proper circumstances for marriage. These two factors work through many cultural conventions to make us the most sex-ridden people of whom I have any knowledge.[18]

Kinsey's reports confirm the powerful sex urges of adolescents, particularly males.

Many studies of other cultures are now available that "lead us to the conclusion that the special problems of adolescence, the ease or difficulty, and the duration of youths' transition to a settled adult status, will vary with the economic and social circumstances and the values of particular cultures. ". . . The more or less stable and integrated nature of social organization and cultural norms displayed in these cultures (more so formerly than now) are important factors which reduce the perplexities and confusions that face youth in his transition to adulthood." [19] Because of the comparative culture studies of which some are listed above, Hall's original contribution back in 1904, when the adolescent was viewed largely as a physiological throwback to an early stage where physical and instinctual impulses predominate, has been radically modified.[20] Rather than discussing this transitional phase of human behavior in terms of physiological necessity—emphasis is now laid upon cultural and societal factors and pressures.

Before we delineate the basic sociological configuration that in our estimation successfully accounts for many aspects of transformed social adolescent behavior in America, the physical changes which add great impetus to the *break* in cultural continuities should be indicated.

The body undergoes rapid change during adolescence, more rapidly actually in the period just before pubescence. There is increased growth in height and weight:

---

[17] Benedict, Ruth. "Continuities and Discontinuities in Cultural Conditioning," *Psychiatry*, May, 1939, pp. 161–167.

[18] Sullivan, H. S. *op. cit.*, p. 144.

[19] Sherif, Muzafer, and Cantril, H. *The Psychology of Ego-Involvements*, John Wiley and Sons, New York, 1947.

[20] Hall, G. Stanley. *Adolescence, Its Psychology and Its Relation to Physiology, Anthropology, Sociology, Sex, Crime, Religion and Education*. D. Appleton and Company, New York, 1904, Two Volumes.

This growth is accompanied by changes in body proportions toward more typically masculine and feminine builds, changes in the size of most of the internal organs, appearance of the secondary sex characteristics (for example, growth of pubic hair; change of voice and growth of beard in boys; breast development in girls). At the same time there is maturation of the reproductive organs of each sex, ordinarily indicated by the onset of menstruation for girls and the secretion of spermatozoa for boys, together with the growth and development of the genitalia. Such changes do not occur, of course, without some changes in the general functioning of the bodily processes as indicated; for example, by measurements of basal metabolic rate.[21]

In addition to these physiological changes there is rapid maturation of the adolescents' capacities so that "the average person of fifteen has, by any accepted criterion, the capacities of an adult; he lacks only experience and training, but otherwise he is fully equipped to cope with his environment and to participate actively in the society of adults." [22] By general capacities such variables as muscular coordination, complex voluntary reactions, and intelligence, are referred to.[23-26] As far as growth is concerned it is important to note that girls on the average mature physiologically earlier (about a year) than boys. Also there is great individual variation within the same groups in the growth pattern. The early part of this growth period (11–12 and 15–16 years) has come to be known as the "awkward period" in which the adolescent highly sensitive to others' opinions about himself has at the same time to adjust to his rapid body changes which may not be in line with the norms of his peer group. Much concern and hence anxiety is associated with maintaining manly or feminine features.

Sprinkled through the literature of adolescence are attempts to define one-to-one relationships between physical maturation and social maturity. One such observer reports:

> As a boy becomes physiologically mature, his interests and attitudes undergo changes. Emotional reactions are so clearly dependent upon

---

[21] Sherif. *op. cit.*, p. 225.

[22] Dollard, John, and Miller, Neal, *et al. Frustration and Aggression*, Yale University Press, New Haven, 1939.

[23] Bellis, C. J. "Reaction Time and Chronological Age," *Proc. Soc. Exp. Biol. Med.*, New York, 1932–33, 30, 801–803.

[24] Miles, W. R. "Measures of Certain Human Abilities Throughout the Life Span," *Proc. Nat. Acad. Sci.*, Washington, 1931, 17, 627–633.

[25] Morrow, H. "Dear Mother: I'm in Jail," *Saturday Evening Post*, August 22, 1936.

[26] Thorndike, E. L. *et al. The Measurement of Intelligence*, Bureau of Publications, Teachers College, Columbia University, New York, 1937.

physical developments that the relation between the two can be measured. In one study attitudes were first determined by means of a scale
for measuring emotional age. The more hormones a boy passed in his
urine, the greater was his maturity as shown by this measure of his attitudes and interests. The relationship held in general among all boys included in the study and also for the development of the individual boys
from year to year, although the degree of correlation was higher in some
cases than in others.[27–28]

A somewhat analogous position is taken by some psychoanalysts, but
this time the point of fixation (the independent variable) is not the physical process alone but the attendant psychological reaction formation initiated at the early age, enduring, and manifesting itself in diverse forms
in adolescence so that there are very few new elements in the invading
forces:

> The physiological process which marks the attainment of physical sex-
> ual maturity is accompanied by a stimulation of the instinctual processes.
> . . . Aggressive impulses are intensified to the point of complete unruli-
> ness, hunger becomes voracity and the naughtiness of the latency period
> turns into the criminal behavior of adolescence. Oral and anal interests
> long submerged come to the surface again. Habits of cleanliness, labori-
> ously acquired during the latency period, give place to pleasure in dirt
> and disorder, and instead of modesty and sympathy we find exhibitionis-
> tic tendencies, brutality and cruelty to animals. The reaction formations,
> which seemed to be firmly established in the structure of the ego,
> threaten to fall to pieces. At the same time, old tendencies which had
> disappeared come into consciousness. The Oedipus wishes are fulfilled in
> the form of phantasies and daydreams, in which they have undergone
> but little distortion; in boys ideas of castration and in girls penis-envy
> once more become the center of interest. There are very few new ele-
> ments in the invading forces. Their onslaught merely brings once more
> to the surface the familiar content of the early infantile sexuality of little
> children.[29]

Here is a radical departure from the approach of the sociologists. For
the latter, the source of human conflict and maladjustment lies in the
contradictory nature of social life, in an unevenly institutionalized society. Freud and his followers, on the contrary, ascribe human conflict

---

[27] Cole, L. *Psychology of Adolescence*, Rinehart, New York, 1942.

[28] Sollenberger, R. T. "Some Relationships between the Urinary Secretion of Male
Hormones by Maturing Boys and Their Expressed Interests and Attitudes," *Journal
of Psychology*, 9:179–189, 1940.

[29] Freud, Anna. *The Ego and the Mechanisms of Defense*, The Hogarth Press and
the Institute of Psycho-Analysis, London, 1937.

to an eternal war between the animal nature of Man—which is antiso-
cial, and even antihuman,—and the restraining forces of society, any society, anywhere. In *Civilization and Its Discontents*, Freud asserts that
civilized society is perpetually menaced with disintegration through the
primary hostility of men toward one another. Their interest in their
common work would not hold them together; the passions of instinct are
stronger than reasoned interests. Culture has to call up every possible
reinforcement in order to erect barriers against the aggressive instincts
of men and hold their manifestations in check. The sociologist stresses
man's social relationships; the psychoanalyst his individual biological
and psychological make-up as determining his social relationships.[30]
The Freudians always go back—the past controlling by-and-large one's
present and one's future. A strained relationship of the past that occurred usually before the age of five or six is reasserting itself. Present
difficulties are the result of defense mechanisms erected during this previous relationship and actually predispose the individual to similar relationships by rediverting diverted repressed impulses from secondary sat-
isfactions to ones more directly in line with the instincts that were
originally repressed. Hence, in classical psychoanalysis the adolescent
period is viewed primarily as a re-enactment of "early infantile sexuality."

These *post hoc* explanations (of which the one just mentioned is typical) are disturbing to critics of Freud. One always knows where to look,
theoretically, for every disturbance and chances are—given all the complex and disguised mechanisms of defense—you will find it symboli-
cally, in one or another of them. In this connection Joseph Jastrow has
pointedly written: "Doubt rises whether the Freudian mechanisms are
real or only the hypothetical fictions assumed in support of one very
specific theory of origin." [31] When we turn to the "specific theory of origin," we find increasing difficulties with orthodox Freudianism. Recent
critical thinking is highlighted with a full-blown attack upon Freud's
analysis of instincts. The argument proceeds that Freud conceived of the
primeval instincts in mechanical opposition to society. Instincts emanat-
ing from the id are simply hungry for satisfaction and cause havoc until
they are satisfied. But man does not live alone. Society to preserve itself
(this is the Hobbesian element in Freud) tames these elements by making them conform outwardly to existing mores, folkways, and general

---

[30] Freud, Sigmund. *Civilization and Its Discontents,* translated by Joan Riviere,
The Hogarth Press Ltd., and the Institute of Psycho-Analysis, London, 1939.
[31] Jastrow, Joseph. "Psychology," *Encyclopedia of the Social Sciences,* Volume 12,
pp. 588–596.

rules of society. The neo-Freudians (among others) object to this dualistic interpretation. Analysts like Horney,[32] Sullivan,[33] and Fromm [34] (the latter utilizing Bernard's work), point out that man cannot be analyzed apart from his culture. Unlike lower orders of animals on the evolutionary ladder man does not have built into him stereotyped reaction patterns that take over at birth. In contrast to other species man undergoes a very long maturation development where he is dependent on older members about him. The raw instinct almost immediately undergoes a civilizing process. Precisely because of this long maturation period the totality of practices and attitudes taken toward the child is crucial, not the instinct per se. Freud selected sex or "libido" as the decisive instinct, because he reasoned other instincts must be satisfied or the individual perishes. It is the peculiar quality of the libido that it can undergo tremendous repressions and the individual can still function in society. This reduction of "motivation" to the libido principle (and later the death instinct) is consistent with Freud's mechanical opposition of instinct to society.

Today a profound transformation of Freudian concepts is occurring in which some of the mechanisms are retained, but the supporting theory flatly rejected. A cogent criticism along these lines has been made by Gerth and Mills:

> For Freud, the psychic structure ("drives") may be socially canalized, but is not itself subject to basic social modifications. The concept of "sublimation," for instance, implies that role-conditioned forms of psychic drives are epiphenomena of "the basic drives." These "real drives" are assumed somehow to lie in the psychic structure or in the constitution of the organism. The split between man's primordial biological nature and man's cultured personality is thus retained and a metaphysical accent is placed upon the biological or the psychic level. Emotions, urges, or various physiological processes, are "the real" motivating factors of conduct: the rest is sham, or at any rate distorted and ungenuine expressions of the real motives of the real individual.
>
> If we drop this metaphysical accent on the biological and the psychic and treat the person as just as "real" as, and in many ways more important than, the organism and the psychic structure, we are able to enlarge our conception of motivation.[35]

Davis' critique of Freud is pertinent here:

---

[32] Horney, Karen. *The Neurotic Personality of Our Time*, W. W. Norton & Company, New York, 1937.

[33] Sullivan. *op. cit.*

[34] Fromm, E. *Escape from Freedom*, Farrar and Rinehart, Inc., New York, 1941.

[35] Gerth and Mills. *op. cit.*

Freud's scheme suffers from a low order of generality. He mistook the specific for the general. Thus the fact of repression was interpreted by him as the ego's attempt to keep the sexual desires from offending the moral principles acquired from the society, or vice versa. But this whole process is meaningless apart from a tendency to maintain a system of subjective evaluation built around the conception of the self. Anything, not merely sexual desires, can be repressed. That which is repressed is whatever might threaten the unity of the self if it were admitted to awareness. . . . Thus the scientific analysis of the personality as a system of values, ends and attitudes, built around the individual's conception of himself and having as its first necessity the establishment and preservation of its unity, gives the maximum degree of generality. It therefore affords the best approach to understanding personality. All other approaches, in so far as they are correct in their observations, can be reinterpreted as special subsystems of the more general theory.[36]

Freud stressed too the so-called genetic approach to individual behavior; that is, he assumed that all individuals go through similar key childhood relationships. Further it is the stormy passage through early years which has a decisive bearing on one's later development. One really never knows whether he has successfully passed the oral and anal stages into the phallic one. In this connection it is worth noting a statement by Edward Sapir, the noted anthropologist: "With all the uncertainty that now prevails with regard to the relative permanence or modifiability of life patterns in the individual and in the race, it is unwise, however, to force the notion of the fixation of the personality in time." [37] The mechanical opposition of the instincts to environment stresses precisely this notion, and not the diverse (often conflicting) social elements which may have qualitative and transforming effects upon individuals. The universality of the family and Freud's focus upon this institution undoubtedly strengthened his position here. The reduction of the variegated environments within and without one people or nation to one common function, namely the repression of instincts, leads to a universally genetic explanation. Conversely, the more the environment is seen as a promoter as well as represser of tendencies within the individual, the more we become interested in the interacting dynamics of socially induced goals and blockages. And a universal genetic explanation becomes increasingly difficult to postulate. The extreme tendency in this school is reached with gestaltists like Lewin and Brown. The latter says in his critique on Freud, that everything Freud has to say applies

---

[36] Davis, K. *Human Society*, Macmillan Company, New York, 1949.
[37] Sapir, Edward. "Personality," *Encyclopedia of the Social Sciences*, Volume XII, pp. 585–587.

perfectly—in middle- and upper-class Viennese society.[38] It has been often asserted that the tendency to think of society as opposed to ungovernable instincts and the consequent focusing on early childhood via the unconscious and psychological determinism, ". . . provides no basis for determining the nonbiological conditions which induce deviations from prescribed patterns of conduct." [39] This sociologist proceeds to set up his own conceptual framework in which the discrepancy between socially induced goals and restricted institutional means for achieving these goals constitute normal reactions of normal people to abnormal situations.

This kind of criticism is effective in attacking the universality of the Freudian system by falling back on the natural behavioral or structural-functional approach. It is true that this is a different level of interpretation. The sociological approach is geared to predicting the probabilities of large numbers of people for behaving in one way or another; the psychological, to an individual. Each focus has its limitations and its advantages, so that the psychoanalyst may probe deeper into the early sex experiences of the youth while ignoring, relatively speaking, his social environment, his class and neighborhood, ethnic background and enormous influence of the gang and the clique to which he belongs. Ultimately it would appear the two approaches will conflict: Are "the regressing and growing, rebelling and maturing youths" reacting to that kernel of every neurosis, the Oedipus Complex? Or is it rather another manifestation of the increasing structural tensions within the social system? Is each approach partially true? If so, how can they be reconciled?

The accumulated studies of the anthropologists over the last one hundred years point to the tremendous variety of human practices and the marvelous plasticity of the human material. The anthropologist, in fact, raised the "cultural" factor to a principle of the first order. Whatever approach one ultimately chooses it would seem to be utter folly not to spell out in adequate detail the broad social-psychological and social-structural context within which the child enters adolescence and the adult later leaves. Society forces specific kinds of relationships upon a youth in his interaction with others, and the integration of his attitudinal structure will be related to the roles he assumes wittingly or unwittingly. The functioning of adolescents is not only a "defense" against infantile or childhood anxieties, but also a result of contradictory value-laden social positions and situations.

We will now try to point up several crucial social structural determinants that are relevant for an understanding of adolescent behavior in Western society, particularly in the United States. (One should add that

---

[38] Brown, J. F. "Freud and the Scientific Method," *Philosophy of Science,* 1, 1934.
[39] Merton. *op. cit.*

the reference point for many of the following observations has been white, male, middle-class youth.) Kingsley Davis has pointed up the connection of the social position of youth and the increasing complexity of modern society:

> Adolescence, then, is ordinarily the time when the lag of social development behind physical development first becomes pronounced. As society grows more complex the lag becomes greater, and adolescence as socially defined extends farther into physical adulthood. . . . This tendency for the adolescent to be more mature physically than socially is most pronounced in those settled societies placing a premium on age; but it is a condition that is to some extent inherent in the nature of all human society. Evolving through uncounted millennia, culture has developed a complexity of principles and a fullness of content that require a long time for the individual to master.[40]

Many writers have pointed out that adolescents are "primarily concerned with . . . who and what they are in the eyes of a wider circle of significant people as compared with what they themselves have come to feel they are; and how to connect the dreams, idiosyncrasies, roles, and skills cultivated earlier with the occupational and sexual prototypes of this day." [41] Gerth and Mills, in their accounting for this intensified need of adolescents for the approval of others (primarily their peers) have analyzed it as a sort of compensation for the diffused and dependent roles they are forced to take over—their physical, emotional and mental maturity notwithstanding:

> The roles played by the American adolescent approximate adult roles, yet the adolescent seems only to *play* them. In two key roles in particular, the boy is not yet fully adult: he is not integrated with a durable mate by marriage, and he does not fulfill a regular occupational role. Economically and emotionally he is still a dependent, and because of this he often strives all the harder to be accepted as an adult. He shaves the downy cheek, and plays the man with girls, older girls if possible, to the fullest extent of his abilities and opportunities, and for want of sexual gratification he masturbates.[42]

Erikson makes somewhat the same point:

> The danger of this stage (adolescence, H.P.) is role diffusion; as Biff puts it in *Death of a Salesman:* "I just can't take hold, Mom, I can't take hold of some kind of life." Where such a dilemma is based on a strong previous doubt as to one's ethnic and sexual identity, delinquent and

---

[40] Davis, K. *op. cit.*
[41] Erikson, E. H. *Childhood and Society,* W. W. Norton & Company, New York, 1950, p. 266.
[42] Gerth and Mills. *op. cit.*

outright psychotic incidents are not uncommon. Youth after youth, bewildered by his assumed role, a role forced on him by the inexorable standardization of American adolescence, runs away in one form or another: leaves school and jobs, stays out at night, or withdraws into bizarre and inaccessible moods. Once he is "delinquent," his greatest need and often his only salvation is the refusal on the part of older youths, of advisers, and of judiciary personnel to type him further by pat diagnoses and social judgments which ignore the special dynamic conditions of adolescence.[43]

In reaction to this situation there has arisen a secondary institution, a youth culture, which contrasts strongly to the roles of adults. Parsons defines the youth culture as "a very definitely rounded humanistic pattern (emphasis on fair play, athletic prowess, social graces, being popular and irresponsible, rebelliousness toward adults, etc.), rather than one of competence in the performance of specified (competitive) functions." [44]

This secondary institution has the double-barrel purpose of (1) acting as a safety valve for "attempting to keep youth completely in line with adult disciplines would probably greatly increase the strains of their position" and (2) "integrating the youth into the major institutional structures such as formal education where under teacher supervision many youth activities are thoroughly legitimized." Parsons on the whole considers the net effect of the youth culture to be "emotionally maturing":

> . . . the very insistence on independence from adult control accustoms the individual to take more and more responsibility on his own. In the youth culture phase he tends to substitute dependency on the peer group for that on the parents but gradually he becomes emancipated from even this dependency. Similarly in the relations of the sexes the youth culture offers opportunities and mechanisms for emotional maturation. The element of rebelliousness against the adult world helps to emancipate from more immature object attachments, while certain features of the "rating and dating" complex protect the individual during the process of this emancipation from deeper emotional involvements than he is yet able to accept. The very publicity of such relationships within the peer group serves as such a protection. Thus the youth culture is not only projective but exposes the individual passing through it to positively adjustive influences.[45]

---

[43] Erikson. *op. cit.*, p. 267.

[44] Parsons, Talcott. "Age and Sex in the Social Structure of the United States," *American Sociological Review*, 7, 1942, pp. 604–616.

[45] Parsons. *The Social System*, The Free Press, Glencoe, Illinois, 1951, pp. 305–306.

There is considerable evidence in the literature showing that adult values and interpretations of the social world play a considerably prominent role among adolescents in structuring the interpersonal experiences with members of their own groups. Instead of Parsons' neat conceptualization of the youth culture which stresses being useless gracefully, one could consider it as a wasteland, a reservoir of conflicting values and roles, with the adults trying to squeeze in on this world by structuring it after their own, by way of Junior Achievement, Boy Scouts, Campfire Girls and the Junior Optimists. A rigid control is exercised through the mass media of communication—comic books, movies, radio, and television; another is the organization and supervision of the mass leisure time activities; finally, the most important medium of control, the school system. Each of the above controls exercises a powerful influence upon adolescents in contemporary American society; the impact of these media upon the youth varies in terms of the various social classes and ethnic groups in which the particular youths experiment with the models and self-stylizations available to them. It would appear that in most cases social class exercises a most predominant influence:

> A girl of upper middle class background belonged to a group composed of others of similar status; during this period she maintained a good scholastic average as did other members of her group; however, after an incident in which she violated the group norms she was ostracized and within a few weeks after she became a member of a group of lower class girls her grades fell ten points until they were at the level of the others in her new group.[46]

Sherif has commented on the importance of groups for adolescents as reference points for orienting their behavior:

> What an adolescent, with the unstable and more or less transitory state of his ego links and his ego aspirations, is striving to achieve, is to stabilize his ego, ego-values—to amount to something or to anchor his ego securely—*in relation to his reference group, whatever this may be to him in his particular social milieu.* In order to achieve this, he has to and he wants to identify himself with the group or groups in question. He does his level best to incorporate (in his ego, which is, we repeat, a genetic formation) the norms of the group, whatever they may be in his particular social setting. He has to and he wants to conform to them in his be-

---

[46] Sultan, Florence, and Strodtbeck, Fred L. "Adolescent Peer Groups and Attitude toward Achievement: A Survey of the Literature," *Cultural Factors in Talent Development*, Yale University, sponsored by the SSRC. Unpublished.

havior. If conformity to these norms is achieved by ruthless competition and individualism, he does his level best to be competitive and individualistic to the limits of his capacity. If the norms of his group put a great premium on being co-operative, he does his best to be co-operative. . . .

Once the group is formed, the status experienced by the member is derived from his membership in it. His feelings of security are dependent to a large extent on his clique organization. His attitudes and identification are shaped or altered by the group norms and prestige idols that prevail in the clique.[47]

Although the literature on adolescents points to the values and goals of the adolescent groups being conditioned by class and ethnic background, the youths' exclusion from key adult roles and their reaction to the control efforts of adults, undoubtedly make for some autonomous development of attitudes and feelings toward themselves, their ethnic and class background and out-groups. No doubt more empirical studies of the social organization of youth, their day-to-day interaction with peers and adults and their attitudes and definitions of social phenomena, would enable social scientists to get a more precise statement of the cultural and social structural determinants of adolescent behavior.

Writers like Fromm, Horney, Reisman, and Erikson have written extensively on the stultifying effects of standardization and conformity in America. Erikson writes: "As adolescent and man, however, he finds himself confronted with superior machines, complicated, incomprehensible, and impersonally dictatorial in their power to standardize his pursuits and tastes. These machines do their powerful best to convert him into a consumer idiot, a fun egoist and an efficiency slave—and this by offering him what he seems to demand."[48] It would appear that it is precisely with adolescents that a break can be made with this unflattering depiction so often made of our youths. As Gerth and Mills have written:

In American society, adolescence is a juncture at which childhood roles are abandoned and adult ones not yet fully available or internalized. Adolescence is a major point of social reorientation and since the person is in this transition, previous integrations of person and psychic structure are likely to be loosened. Often these integrations undergo such extreme modification that it is no wonder some students view it as a social rebirth.[49]

---

[47] Sherif. *op. cit.*
[48] Erikson, E. H. *op. cit.*, p. 282.
[49] Gerth and Mills. *op. cit.*, 144.

Unfortunately, the knowledge available of the social behavior and attitudes of youth is of an extremely limited kind. The conclusions reached by the Yale group after a rather comprehensive survey of existing literature are very general:

> (1) Adolescent groups are differentiated by characteristics of social class, age, sex, race, religion and nationality; (2) adolescent groups so differentiated appear to have values with meaningful parallel corresponding segments of the parental or adult culture; and (3) the maintenance of peer group membership is a sufficiently desirable goal for most adolescents to strongly motivate them to abide by peer group norms.[50]

The sociological approach can be as deterministic as the psychoanalytic one. Man can never be a mere product of sociological or psychoanalytic forces or their sum. It is, however, this writer's belief that the present trend of limiting the analysis of adolescents to the family parlor must be considerably broadened. By extending the causal nexus of man's character to society, people are enabled to change themselves by changing society. As Miller has suggested, the adolescents' revolt need not only be against evil but for an order in life which is beautiful, just and rejuvenating:

> The hidden laws of fate lurked not only in the characters of people, but equally if not more imperiously in the world beyond the family parlor. Out there were the big gods, the ones whose disfavor could turn a proud and prosperous and dignified man into a frightened shell of a man whatever he thought of himself and whatever he decided or didn't decide to do.
> . . . The struggle for mastery—for the freedom of manhood or womanhood as opposed to the servility of childhood—is the struggle not only to overthrow authority but to reconstitute it anew. The viewpoint of the adolescent is precious because it is revolutionary and insists upon justice. But in truth the parent, powerful as he appears, is not the source of injustice but its deputy. . . . The way out, as the poet has said, is always *through*. We will not find it by huddling closer to the center of the charmed circle . . . nor by once again shocking the householders with yet other unveilings of domestic relations and their hypocrisies. . . . There is an organic aesthetic, a tracking of impulse and causation from the individual to the world and back again which must be reconstituted. . . .[51]

---

[50] Sultan and Strodtbeck. *op. cit.*

[51] Miller, Arthur. "The Shadows of the Gods," *Harper's Magazine*, August, 1958, Vol. 217, No. 1299, pp. 36 and 43.

3.   THE CONCEPT OF ADOLESCENT SUBCULTURE*

D. B. Kandel, G. S. Lesser, G. C. Roberts, and R. Weiss

For more than a generation, the concept of adolescent subculture [1] has been surrounded by controversy which continues to grow, with little hope for an adequate resolution in the near future.[2]

Historically, the concept of adolescent subculture has been traced to Waller's (1932) *The Sociology of Learning* (cf., Gordon, 1963; McDill, Meyers, and Rigsby, 1966; Turner, 1964) and to Margaret Mead's (1928) stress upon cultural influence rather than physiological maturation. Waller described the school as a social system comprised of a cohesive teacher subculture and a separate student youth culture, and depicted a strained student-teacher relationship resulting from the conflicting values and interests of these two groups. In Waller's view, the adolescent subculture, possessing its own status-assigning system, norms, values, and leading groups, has a distinctive and self-contained quality.

A decade after Waller's introduction of the concept of youth culture, Parsons (1942) posited the existence of a somewhat similar age-graded youth culture. Parsons characterized this youth culture as consisting of adolescent boys who derive a sense of achievement predominantly through athletics and adolescent girls who concentrate on social popularity through sexual attractiveness. This youth culture was described as

---

* Adolescents in two societies: peers, school, and family in the United States and Denmark. From pages 1.5–1.14 of Final Report, Project No. 2139, Contract No. OE-4-10-069, Bureau of Research, Office of Education, Department of Health, Education and Welfare, 1968. Reprinted with permission of the authors.

---

[1] This term generally has been used interchangeably with such terms as "adolescent society," "youth culture," "teen-age culture," and so forth (cf., Boocock, 1966, p. 27).

[2] For example, in the *Review of Educational Research* appraisals of the status of this concept, Hess (1960) presents the issue as "one of the minor conceptual controversies in the study of adolescence," while Smith and Kleine (1966) see it as a "debate . . . destined for a fate similar to that of the heredity and environment controversy."

irresponsible, manifesting a ". . . strong tendency to repudiate interest in adult things and feel at least a certain recalcitrance to the pressure of adult expectations and discipline." Moreover, Parsons (1942) viewed this phenomenon as being uniquely American.

Following the introduction of the concept of adolescent subculture, much research has focused on: whether or not adolescent subcultures actually exist as distinguishable entities; if adolescent subcultures do exist, what are their sources and general nature, and what extent of influence do adolescent subcultures exercise in different areas of adolescent behavior. We next discuss some evidence on these questions.

1. Existence of Adolescent Subculture

Although there is considerable agreement that an adolescent subculture exists (e.g., Boocock, 1966; Coleman, 1961; Gordon, 1957; Gottlieb and Ramsey, 1964; Gottlieb and Reeves, 1963; Smith, 1962), this view is not without opposition; Bealer and Willits (1961), Berger (1963), Elkin and Westley (1955), Epperson (1964), and Friesen (1966) typify those who dissent from this view, sometimes offering evidence contradicting it.

Still other investigators (e.g., Jahoda and Warren, 1965) label the question of the existence of an adolescent subculture as a "psuedo issue," arguing that each of two types of investigation is useful depending upon what they reveal: the characteristics the adolescent shares with his peer group as well as those he shares with the major culture. Epperson (1964) states: "We still need a conceptual scheme that takes into consideration the multiple loyalties of the teen-ager and the relation of these loyalties to specific situations." (p. 96) This position reflects the major focus of the present study: the relative influence of peers and family in several domains of adolescent behavior in two different cultures.

Thus, Smith and Kleine (1966) present a balanced summary of the present status of the question concerning the existence of adolescent subcultures:

> The present debate concerning the existence of an adolescent subsociety appears destined for a fate similar to that of the heredity and environment controversy: the emphatic but oversimplified "yes" and "no" answers give way to more subdued complex questions. Adolescents share some values uniquely with other adolescents on the national scale; some values are shared uniquely with specific reference groups; and some values are shared with a broader adult cultural fabric of which they represent bright old strands. For some research questions, phrased at varying conceptual levels (e.g., economic, sociological, or psychological), the use of the concept "sub-culture" may permit examination of certain discon-

tinuities or continuous aspects; for other questions the concept will not be of help. (p. 427)

2. Sources and General Nature of Peer-Group Influence

Newcomb (1962) argues that peer-group influence is both "determined" and "determining," thus distinguishing antecedent factors which determined the formation and behavior of the adolescent group from the consequences of adolescent-group influences. A student's desire to attend college may motivate him to seek certain peers and behave with them in certain ways. The student's college plans and his behavior to implement these plans then may be affected by his peers.

An issue related to the sources of adolescent groups—to their "determined" properties—is the question of whether adolescents form "contracultures" or, instead, establish genuinely autonomous and independent cultural systems possessing distinctive evaluative standards. Although there is considerable belief (e.g., Coleman, 1961; Davis, 1940; Parsons, 1942; Yinger, 1960) that adolescent contracultures arise to repudiate the standards and pressures of adult society, other investigators (e.g., Schwartz and Merten, 1967; Turner, 1964) claim that an adolescent subculture is not a contraculture, resting on its power to repudiate or undermine basic adult values, but is a genuinely independent culture: ". . . the social categories inherent in the adolescent status terminology provide the members of this age-grade with their own world view, life styles, and moral standards." (Schwartz and Merten, 1967, p. 453) This latter view is consistent with the position that a crucial condition for the formation of a subculture is the existence, in effective interaction with each other, of a number of actors with similar problems of adjustment (Cohen, 1955; Gottlieb Reeves, and TenHouten, 1966).

A related alternative to the contraculture view is that adolescent peer groups operate to serve only certain limited functions: to organize particular social activities and support certain limited values and preferences (for example, in matters of taste and manners such as dress and dating patterns). This view holds that in all other basic respects beyond these limited areas, adolescent peer groups do not oppose adult standards, but are integrated with them (e.g., Bandura and Walters, 1963; Douvan and Adelson, 1966; Hollingshead, 1949; Musgrove, 1966; Remmers, 1962; Remmers et al., 1966; Riley, Riley and Moore, 1962; Schwartz and Merten, 1967; Solomon, 1961; Turner, 1964). In these analyses of the adolescent subculture, those areas of adolescent life which are dictated by peer-group influence are those in which adults do not have a great stake.

Many other explanations of the sources of adolescent subculture have been offered—almost as many as writers on the subject:

a. the speed and complexity of modern social change which undermines parental control (e.g., Davis, 1940; Keniston, 1962; Mead, 1928)

b. the affluence of a society which allows it to prolong the period of formal schooling (e.g., Bernard, 1961)

c. the unresolved ambiguity and marginality of the adolescent's role in society (e.g., Linton, 1954; Mays, 1961; Sarnoff, 1962)

d. the attempt by adult society to keep adolescents in colonial subjugation by restricting them to their own societies within the high school (e.g., Friedenberg, 1965)

e. the provision of a vehicle for emancipation from the family (e.g., Ausubel, 1954; Phelps and Horrocks, 1958)

f. the need to cushion the demands from the adult world, to mediate these demands so that the adolescent can be guided to know which of these demands he must meet and which he can ignore safely (Douvan and Gold, 1966)

g. the asynchronism between biological and social maturity and the seeking of a collective solution to this asynchronism (e.g., Elkin and Westley, 1955).

Eisenstadt's (1963) view of the sources of adolescent subculture combines several antecedent conditions: nonessential adolescent labor, pluralistic religion and secular systems, economic specialization requiring technical training, a kinship structure which does not facilitate adequately the attainment of full social status by its junior members. Clearly, no single source of adolescent subcultures will explain their existence; however, the exact combination of circumstances leading to their formation has not been established empirically.

The "determining" property of the peer group is emphasized in most studies of adolescent subculture (e.g., Gordon, 1957; Coleman, 1961; McDill, Rigsby and Meyers, 1966). We turn now to the extent and nature of these determining effects upon adolescents.

3. Extent of Influence of Adolescent Subculture

There is some agreement (e.g., Campbell, 1964; Coleman, 1961; Parsons and Bales, 1955; Sherif and Sherif, 1964; Simpson, 1959) that the adolescent subculture has marked and widespread influence on the adolescents' developing attitudes, values, interests, and aspirations and that these influences often are divergent from or in conflict with the influences of adult society. This theme is advanced most explicitly by Coleman (1961).

> The adolescent is "cut off" from the rest of society, forced inward to-
> ward his own age group, made to carry out his whole social life with
> others his own age . . . Our society has within its midst a set of small
> teen-age societies which focus teen-age interests and attitudes on things
> far removed from adult responsibilities and which may develop stan-
> dards that lead away from those goals established by the larger society.
> (pp. 3, 9)

However, this assertion has been questioned widely (e.g., Bandura
and Walters, 1963; Douvan and Adelson, 1966; Hollingshead, 1949;
Musgrove, 1966; Remmers, 1962; Remmers *et al.*, 1966; Riley, Riley, and
Moore, 1961; Schwartz and Merten, 1967; Solomon, 1961; Turner, 1964).
For example, Musgrove (1966) quotes evidence from England (Morris,
1958), France (Pitts, 1960), and the United States (e.g., Lucas and Horrocks, 1958; Peck and Havighurst, 1960; Riley, Riley, and Moore, 1961)
which supports the view of the relative unimportance of the peer group
as compared with other sources of influence. Turner (1964) contends
that peer-group effects are merely superficial and ritualistic:

> The term subculture has been applied to youth behavior on the
> grounds that a widespread and distinctive pattern of behavior is trans-
> mitted and imposed within a youth society . . . on the other hand,
> youth subculture is necessarily a more segmental part of the individual's
> life than the more common types of subculture. In addition, a suspicion
> is justified that youth subculture is frequently adopted ritualistically, so
> that it does not penetrate to the private convictions of its adherents. (p.
> 169)

Both views—that the peer group is exclusive and overpowering or
trivial and superficial—need qualification: clearly, the extent of peer-
group influence varies under different conditions and for different areas
of adolescent behavior. Although the evidence is inconsistent, variations
in the extent of peer-group influence have been studied for boys and
girls, different social-class groups, different age groups, and for schools
of different and geographic location. Campbell's (1964) view that the
peer group has stronger effects for girls than for boys is endorsed by
some studies (e.g., Anastasi and Miller, 1949; Ausubel, 1954; Tuman and
Livson, 1960) and contradicted by others (e.g., Douvan and Adelson,
1966). Some studies (e.g., Ausubel, 1954; Douvan and Adelson, 1966;
Jones, 1958; Maas, 1954; Purnell, 1966; Stone and Church, 1957) claim
that middle-class adolescents are more peer-oriented than lower class
adolescents, yet other investigators (e.g., Campbell, 1964) contest this
position. Peer influence presumably increases from freshman to senior
year in high school (e.g., Douvan and Adelson, 1966; McDill and Coleman, 1965; Parsons, 1942), and presumably is greater for adolescents

whose fathers are absent from the home (Hetherington, 1966). The variations in extent of peer influence have also been investigated for high
schools of different size (e.g., Barker and Gump, 1964), and for adolescents from rural areas, small towns, and larger cities (Coleman, 1961).
Finally, the extent of peer influence varies for different areas of adolescent behavior; these studies will be discussed further in our analysis of
the relative impact of parents and peers.

4. Effects upon Intellectual Activities

Many studies indicate that peer-group influence is deleterious to the educational and intellectual goals of the school and adult society. Coleman
(1961) cites a variety of evidence to suggest that the value system of adolescents is strongly non-intellectual, if not in some respects, anti-intellectual. Tannenbaum (1962) notes that the brilliant student is an
exceptionally prominent target for teen-age pressures to conform to certain behaviors and values, forcing him to deliberately mask his talent to
relieve these pressures. Braham (1965) cites studies which show that the
adolescent's peer group provides an intellectually negative setting rather
than an intellectually nurturing one. Douvan and Gold (1966) state the
similar conclusion that the dominant peer-value system in American
high schools is anti-intellectual and that studies of high schools reveal
the low value high school students attach to the scholarly image and
the difficulty bright and competent students face in accepting the image
as their own. Smith (1962) also agrees that adolescent cliques ". . . set
up norms contrary to those of school. These are generally deterrents to
academic achievement, diverting interests into athletics and social activities." (p. 79) Boocock (1966), surveying these and other studies of
peer-group influence on student performance, concludes that the student's peer-group has a powerful influence upon his attitudes toward
and behavior in school, often working at variance with the learning-
achievement goals of the school.

Several studies (e.g., Coleman, 1961; Gordon, 1957; Remmers and
Radler, 1957; Tannenbaum, 1962) point to one consequence of the anti-
intellectual atmosphere of the adolescent subculture: the need to dissim-
ulate in order to hide or mask intellectual accomplishment. Douvan
and Gold (1966) conclude that, while adolescents will not necessarily
punish academic achievement directly, they favor a kind of application
to the job of student which is neither too diligent nor too compliant.

As has been true of almost every observation made about the operation of the adolescent subculture, once again there are dissenters to the
non-intellectual or anti-intellectual characterization of the adolescent

group (e.g., Campbell, 1964; Peck and Gallani, 1962). For example, Turner (1964) states that his findings ". . . belie an effective youth conspiracy against academic excellence." (p. 169)

5. Effects upon Educational Plans and Aspirations

It would appear that a direct transition should exist between the topics of intellectualism and educational aspirations among adolescents, with the supposition being that a strong positive relationship operates between the two. McDill and Coleman (1963) found, however, no such positive relationship, which they explained as follows:

> Whatever the association that adults see between college and intellectualism, the adolescents who are at the center of their high school social systems see the two as quite distinct entities: college containing the promise of adult status, but intellectualism carrying the connotations of acquiescence and subordination to adults.

Nonetheless, the strong effect of the peer group on intellectual activities reappears in the studies which consider educational plans and aspirations (e.g., Alexander and Campbell, 1964; Boyle, 1966; Coleman, 1961; McDill and Coleman, 1965; McDill, Meyers, and Rigsby, 1966; Michael, 1961; Simpson, 1962; Wilson, 1959). Herriott's (1963) finding is typical, that a strong independent relationship exists between level of educational aspiration and the expectation perceived from a friend of the same age.

In addition, McDill and Coleman (1965) report that from the freshman to the senior year in high school, the contribution of peer influence and status to variation in college plans increases for both sexes; however, this increase is greater for boys than for girls.

Once again, dissenting findings appear. Haller and Butterworth (1960) found no conclusive evidence that peer interaction affects level of educational and vocational aspiration. Similarly, Turner (1964) reports no clear relationships between peer-group effects and ambition.

6. Other Effects of Peer-Group Influence

The most frequent discussions of peer-group influence describe its function as a frame of reference for emancipation from the family, the achievement of independent status, and the development of a differentiated sense of identity (e.g., Ausubel, 1954; Campbell, 1964; Muus,

1962; Phelps and Horrocks, 1958; Schmuck and Lohman, 1965; Sherif and Cantril, 1947). Almost as frequent are discussions of peer-group effects upon the adolescents' self-concept (Rivlin, 1959; Rosenberg, 1965; Sherif and Sherif, 1964, 1965a, b) and the development of appropriate sex roles (e.g., Schwartz and Merten, 1967; Smith, 1962). Schmuck and Lohman (1965) review the studies which indicate that the adolescent period is especially conducive to peer influence upon personality development.

In addition the peer group also has been shown to display strong effects upon the adolescents' religious beliefs (Rosen, 1955), political ideology (e.g., Schiff, 1964; Solomon and Fishman, 1964; Wilson, 1959), and moral development (Kohlberg, in press). Since the peer-group influence upon less serious issues of taste, preferences, and manners has been documented amply, almost the entire gamut of possible behavioral effects of the peer group upon the adolescent has some empirical confirmation. Of course, this documentation exists in scattered and unrelated studies, leaving unresolved the questions of which areas of behavior or attitude are most affected by peer influence and how these effects compare with the simultaneous impacts of other socialization forces.

To summarize the results of studies of peer group influences, most investigators agree that adolescent subcultures indeed do exist, in one form or another, as distinct entities and that their effects upon adolescents are both powerful and diverse. Proposed explanations of the sources of adolescent subcultures are speculative and appear in all shapes and sizes, ranging from dynamics based upon "contraculture" to "being in the same boat." A minority of researchers believe that adolescent subcultures are a myth, and that, since they do not exist, searches for their sources and the nature and extent of their influence are meaningless.

References

Alexander, C. N., and Campbell, E. Q. Peer influences on adolescent educational aspirations and attainments. *American Sociological Review,* 1964, 29, 568–575.

Anastasi, Anne, and Miller, Shirley. Adolescent prestige in relation to scholastic and socio-economic variables. *Journal of Social Psychology,* 1949, 29, 43–50.

Ausubel, D. P. *Theory and problems of adolescent development.* New York: Grune & Stratton, 1954.

Bandura, A., and Walters, R. H. *The social learning of deviant behavior.* New York: Holt, Rinehart, and Winston, 1963.

Barker, R. G., and Gump, P. V. *Big school, small school: high school size and student behavior.* Stanford, Calif.: Stanford University Press, 1964.

Bealer, R. C., and Willits, F. K. Rural youth: a case study in the rebelliousness of adolescents. *Annual of the American Academy of Political and Social Science,* 1961, *338,* 63–69.

Berger, B. Adolescence and beyond: an essay review of three books on the problems of growing up. *Social Forces,* 1963, *10,* 394–408.

Bernard, Jessie. Teen age culture: an overview. *Annual of the American Academy of Political and Social Science,* 1961, *338,* 1–12.

Boocock, Sarane S. Toward a sociology of learning: a selective review of existing literature. *Sociology of Education,* 1966, *39,* 1–45.

Boyle, R. P. The effect of the high school on students' aspirations. *American Journal of Sociology,* 1966, *71,* 628–639.

Braham, M. Peer group deterrents to intellectual development during adolescence. *Educational Theory,* 1965, *15,* 248–258.

Campbell, J. D. Peer relations in childhood. In M. L. Hoffman and Lois W. Hoffman (Eds.), *Review of child development research.* New York: Russell Sage, 1964. Pp. 289–322.

Cohen, A. K. *Delinquent boys.* Glencoe, Ill.: Free Press, 1955.

Coleman, J. S. *The adolescent society.* New York: Free Press, 1961.

Davis, K. The sociology of parent-youth conflict. *American Sociological Review.* 1940, *5,* 523–535.

Douvan, Elizabeth, and Adelson, J. *The adolescent experience.* New York: Wiley, 1966.

Douvan, Elizabeth, and Gold, M. Modal patterns in American adolescence. In M. L. Hoffman and Lois Hoffman (Eds.), *Review of child development research: Volume II.* New York: Russell Sage, 1966. Pp. 469–528.

Eisenstadt, S. N. Archetypical patterns of youth. In E. H. Erikson (Ed.), *Youth: change and challenge.* New York: Basic Books, 1963. Pp. 24–42.

Elkin, F., and Westley, W. A. The myth of adolescent culture. *American Sociological Review,* 1955, *20,* 680–684.

Epperson, D. C. A reassessment of indices of parental influences in "The Adolescent Society." *American Sociological Review,* 1964, *29,* 93–96.

Friedenberg, E. Z. *Coming of age in America: growth and acquiescence.* New York: Random House, 1965.

Friesen, D. A study of the subculture of students in eight selected western Canadian high schools. Unpublished doctoral dissertation, University of North Dakota, 1966.

Gordon, C. W. *The social system of the high school.* Glencoe, Ill.: Free Press, 1957.

Gordon, C. W. Essay review: James Coleman on "The Adolescent Society." *School Review*, 1963, 71, 377–385.

Gottlieb, D., and Ramsey, C. *The American adolescent.* Homewood, Ill.: Dorsey, 1964.

Gottlieb, D., and Reeves, J. *Adolescent behavior in urban areas.* New York: Free Press, 1963.

Gottlieb, D., Reeves, J., and TenHouten, W. D. *The emergence of youth societies: a cross-cultural approach.* New York: Free Press, 1966.

Haller, A. O., and Butterworth, C. E. Peer influences on levels of occupational and educational aspirations. *Social Forces*, 1960, 38, 289–295.

Herriott, R. E. Some social determinants of educational aspiration. *Harvard Educational Review*, 1963, 33, 157–177.

Hess, R. D. The adolescent: his society. *Review of Educational Research*, 1960, 30, 5–12.

Hetherington, E. Mavis. Effects of parental absence on sex-typed behaviors in Negro and white preadolescent males. *Journal of Personality and Social Psychology*, 1966, 4, 87–91.

Hollingshead, A. B. *Elmtown's youth.* New York: Wiley, 1949.

Jahoda, Marie, and Warren, N. The myths of youth. *Sociology of Education*, 1965, 38, 138–149.

Jones, Mary C. A study of socialization patterns at the high school level. *Journal of Genetic Psychology*, 1958, 93, 87–111.

Keniston, K. Social change and youth in America. In E. H. Erikson (Ed.), *Youth: change and challenge.* New York: Basic Books, 1963. Pp. 161–187.

Kohlberg, L. The development of children's orientations toward a moral order: II. Social experience, social conduct, and the development of moral thought. *Human Development*, in press.

Linton, R. The cultural background of personality. New York: Appleton-Century-Crofts, 1945.

Lucas, M. C., and Horrocks, J. E. An experimental approach to the analysis of adolescent needs. *Child Development*, 1960, 31, 479–487.

Maas, H. S. The role of member in clubs of lower-class and middle-class adolescents. *Child Development*, 1954, 25, 241–251.

Mays, J. B. Teen-age culture in contemporary Britain and Europe. *Annals of the American Academy of Political and Social Science*, 1961, 338, 22–32.

McDill, E. L., and Coleman, J. S. Family and peer influence in college plans of high school students. *Sociology of Education*, 1965, 38, 112–126.

McDill, E. L., and Coleman, J. S. High school social status, college plans, and interest in academic achievement: a panel analysis. *American Sociological Review*, 1963, *28*, 905–918.

McDill, E. L., Meyers, E. D., Jr., and Rigsby, L. C. Sources of educational climates in high schools. Final Report, December 1966, The Johns Hopkins University, Contract No. OE-3-10-080, U.S. Department of Health, Education, and Welfare.

Mead, Margaret. *Coming of Age in Samoa*. New York: Morrow, 1928.

Michael, J. A. High school climates and plans for entering college. *Public Opinion Quarterly*, 1961, *25*, 585–595.

Musgrove, F. *The family, education, and society*. London: Routledge & Kegan Paul, 1966.

Muus, R. E. *Theories of adolescence*. New York: Random House, 1962.

Newcomb, T. M. Student peer-group influence. In N. Sanford (Ed.), *The American college*. New York: Wiley, 1962. Pp. 469–488.

Parsons, T. Age and sex in the social structure of the United States. *American Sociological Review*, 1942, *7*, 604–616.

Parsons, T., and Bales, R. F. *Family, socialization, and interaction process*. Glencoe, Ill.: Free Press, 1955.

Peck, R. F., and Galliani, C. Intelligence, ethnicity, and social roles in adolescent society. *Sociometry*, 1962, *25*, 64–72.

Peck, R. F., and Havighurst, R. J. *The psychology of character and development*. New York: Wiley, 1960.

Phelps, H., and Horrocks, J. E. Factors influencing informal groups of adolescents. *Child Development*, 1958, *29*, 69–86.

Purnell, R. F. Effects of social class on adolescent reference group orientation and personality. Unpublished doctoral dissertation, University of Texas, 1966.

Remmers, H. H. Cross-cultural studies of teen-agers' problems. *Journal of Educational Psychology*, 1962, *53*, 254–261.

Remmers, H. H., and Radler, D. H. *The American teenager*. Indianapolis: Bobbs Merrill, 1957.

Remmers, H. H., and others. High school students' attitudes on two controversial issues: was in Southeast Asia and the use of personality and ability tests. Lafayette, Ind.: Purdue University Measurement and Research Center, 1966, No. 77.

Riley, Mathilde W., Riley, J. W., and Moore, Mary E. Adolescent values and the Riesman Typology: an empirical analysis. In S. M. Lipset and L. Lowenthal (Eds.), *Culture and social character*. Glencoe, Ill.: Free Press, 1961. Pp. 370–386.

Rivlin, Leanne. Creativity and the self-attitudes and sociability of high school students. *Journal of Educational Psychology*, 1959, *50*, 147–152.

Rosen, B. C. Conflicting group membership: a study of parent-peer group cross-pressures. *American Sociological Review*, 1955, *20*, 155–161.

Rosenberg, M. *Society and the adolescent self-image*. Princeton, N.J.: Princeton University Press, 1965.

Sarnoff, I. F. *Personality dynamics and development*. New York: Wiley, 1962.

Schiff, L. The campus conservative movement. Unpublished doctoral dissertation, Harvard University, 1964.

Schmuck, R., and Lohman, Anita. Peer relations and personality development. Unpublished manuscript, Institute for Social Research, University of Michigan, 1965.

Schwartz, G., and Merten, D. The language of adolescence: An anthropological approach to the youth culture. *American Journal of Sociology*, 1967, 72, 453–468.

Sherif, M., and Cantril, H. *The psychology of ego-involvements*. New York: Wiley, 1947.

Sherif, M., and Sherif, Carolyn W. *Reference groups*. New York: Harper & Row, 1964.

Sherif, M., and Sherif, Carolyn W. The adolescent in his group in its setting. II. Research procedures and findings. In M. Sherif and Carolyn W. Sherif (Eds.), *Problems of youth: transition to adulthood in a changing world*. Chicago: Aldine, 1965. Pp. 295–329.

Simpson, R. L. What is the importance of peer group status at the high school level. *High School Journal*, 1959, 291–294.

Smith, E. A. *American youth culture*. Glencoe, Ill.: Free Press, 1962.

Smith, L. M., and Kleine, P. F. The adolescent and his society. *Review of Educational Research*, 1966, 36, 424–436.

Solomon, D. Adolescents' decision: a comparison of influence from parents and that from other sources. *Marriage and Family Living*, 1961, 23, 393–395.

Solomon, F., and Fishman, J. R. Youth and peace: a psychosocial study of student peace demonstrators in Washington, D. C. *Journal of Social Issues*, 1964, 20, 54–73.

Stone, L. J., and Church, J. *Childhood and adolescence*. New York: Random House, 1957.

Tannenbaum, A. J. *Adolescents' attitudes toward academic brilliance*. New York: Teachers College, Columbia University, 1962.

Tuma, E., and Livson, N. Family socio-economic status and adolescent attitudes toward authority. *Child Development*, 1960, 31, 387–399.

Turner, R. H. *The social context of ambition*. San Francisco: Chandler, 1964.

Waller, W. *The sociology of teaching*. New York: Wiley, 1932.

Wilson, A. B. Residential segregation of social classes and aspirations of high school boys. *American Sociological Review*, 1959, 24, 836–845.

Yinger, M. Contra-culture and subculture. *American Sociological Review*, 1960, 25, 625–635.

4. WHAT IS THE IMPORTANCE OF PEER GROUP STATUS AT THE HIGH SCHOOL LEVEL? *

Richard L. Simpson

In discussions of adolescent peer groups, adults are more likely to view with alarm than to point with pride. There is talk of a "teen-age problem." The prevailing image of working-class adolescents is that they travel in gangs, like carnivorous packs, committing delinquent acts against the adult community and engaging in combat with other gangs who invade their turf. The public stereotype of middle-class adolescent groups is hardly more favorable. Not only popular writers, but also social scientists have attributed to the adolescent peer group such characteristics as irresponsibility, distaste for constituted authority and established moral codes, blind conformity to group values, and a purely hedonistic approach to life.[1]

The Russian sputnik has deepened Americans' concern over adolescent behavior. Magazine and newspaper articles have portrayed American high school students harshly, and the peer group has come in for much of the blame. The American adolescent, these articles say, rocks and rolls with the peer group while his Russian counterpart learns science. Nor is evidence lacking to support this view of the peer group. A study directed by Charles E. Bowerman and Frank Miyamoto, comparing "peer-oriented" with "parent-oriented" adolescents, finds that the peer-oriented make lower grades and show less interest in education.[2]

* Richard L. Simpson, "What Is the Importance of Peer Group Status at the High School Level?" *High School Journal,* 1959 (May), 291–294. Reprinted with permission of the author and the publisher, the University of North Carolina Press.

---

[1] See, for example, Talcott Parsons, "Age and Sex in the Social Structure of the United States," *American Sociological Review,* 7: 604–616; Edward Y. Hartshorne, "Undergraduate Society and the College Culture," *American Sociological Review,* 8: 321–331; Arnold W. Green, "Young America Takes Over the Colleges," *Commentary,* 7: 524–534; and Robert J. Havighurst and Hilda Taba, *Adolescent Culture and Personality,* New York: Wiley, 1949, *passim.*

[2] These findings are reported in Donald P. Hayes, "An Application of the Reference Group Concept to a Study of Academic Motivation," unpublished M.A. thesis, University of Washington, 1955.

If we examine the adolescent peer group from another aspect, however, the picture is not so bleak. Such a re-examination seems desirable if we are to understand the social role of the high school peer group and come to terms with the fact that it is here to stay. In this paper we hope to show that the peer group performs a basic sociological function, not only for its members but for the social system as well.

The Adolescent in the American Social Structure

Americans usually regard adolescence as the "awkward age," but in many other societies this period is relatively tranquil and devoid of problems. This fact suggests that the difficulties in adjustment experienced by so many American adolescents are not biologically inevitable, but stem from peculiarities of our social structure. In many peasant societies, children assume major work responsibilities as soon as they are physically able. During adolescence, they take on increasingly adult social roles. Their work duties are clearly relevant to their future roles as adults, and the transition from childhood through adolescence to adulthood is gradual and smooth. In other societies, the transition is more abrupt, but their social role of the adolescent is clearly defined and adjusting to it poses no problems. Throughout Polynesia, for example, adolescents are sharply differentiated from children and adults. The transition from one status to the next is marked by collective ceremonies. Adolescents are formally organized into age groups, relieved of most social responsibilities, and left free to entertain themselves.[3]

In comparison with these patterns, the situation of the adolescent in the United States is anomalous. We consider adolescents a distinct category, neither children nor adults, and we keep them in the adolescent category well into the years of biological maturity. Yet unlike the Polynesians, we do not provide a clear role definition to guide adolescent behavior. The American adolescent plays diverse roles in different groups; he is a family member, a student, a peer group participant with his own and sometimes the other sex, perhaps a work group member in an after-hours job. Despite all these group affiliations—perhaps because of the very diversity of them—he has no single "core status" or dominant role whose expectations take priority in directing his behavior and forming his self-image.

---

[3] Ralph Linton, "Age and Sex Categories," *American Sociological Review*, 7: 589–603.

The Peer Group and Adolescent Social Needs

The social striving of the American adolescent centers around the need to develop a clear status and a gratifying, consistent self-image. To do this he must gain recognition from his peers, on the basis of peer group values; no longer can recognition from his family suffice. At the same time he must develop qualities which will equip him for adult life, such as initiative, responsibility, and self-reliance.

Much of the burden of adolescent socialization rests upon the school. The formal curriculum of the school does much to produce responsible work habits, but it alone cannot meet all of the adolescent's developmental needs. The values of the school—diligence in study, respect for the social etiquette and moral codes of the middle-class adult world— are not necessarily those of the adolescent, who may or may not derive great satisfaction from achievements in terms of these adult values.

The peer group is uniquely equipped to meet the very needs which the formal curriculum leaves unmet. In the peer group, the adolescent can test new social skills and gain recognition for achievements valued by his age-mates. Dating and athletics build a well defined sex role into the adolescent's self-image. He wins recognition for his sense of humor or his loyalty to friends. At a time when he must begin to break away from his family, the peer group gives him the security of group membership. How important this can be is revealed in a study of young adult schizophrenics, by N. J. Demerath. The subjects, before their schizophrenic conditions arose, had seldom participated in intimate, informal group activities. They had lacked the ability to associate with their fellow students, had felt socially rejected, and had identified with the adult norms of scholarly excellence, moral perfection, and submissiveness. Demerath concludes that the person who successfully adjusts to adult demands must first prepare himself in informal peer group life.[4]

Extracurricular Activities and Adolescent Development

It might seem that the adolescent is doomed to acquire an unintegrated set of behavior patterns, a schizoid self-image, from his high school ex-

---

[4] N. J. Demerath, "Adolescent Status Demands and the Student Experiences of 20 Schizophrenics," *American Sociological Review*, 8: 513–518.

perience; he learns one behavior pattern from his teachers but quite another from his peer group. The academic program fosters self-reliance and responsibility but cannot harness the adolescent's desire for recognition by his peers. There exists, however, a way of tying together these adolescent social needs in a single set of activities which helps to meet both needs. Through its extracurricular activities program, the school can encourage pupils to work willingly, in natural and intimate groups, toward goals which they themselves value highly, and in ways which develop such qualities as responsibility and the capacity to make vital decisions. The student council, the dance committee, even the home room clean-up squad bring adolescents together in useful or harmless projects where they exercise leadership, meet obligations, and develop friendships. In the extracurricular program, benefits of the peer group and school are combined. A balance is struck between free initiative and guidance from above, between play and work, between individual achievement and group obligation.

Extracurricular activities are not a panacea. They are no substitute for the study of books. The pupils who win extracurricular honors will usually be those who already have received recognition in other ways —through high social status in the community and through high scholastic achievement [5]—while pupils with impoverished backgrounds and low scholastic accomplishment are left out or relegated to minor roles. Extracurricular activities may have little appeal to some pupils from underprivileged neighborhoods, among whom the thought of any activity connected with the school arouses dread or contempt.

Despite all this, it seems reasonable to claim some efficacy for extracurricular activities as one way in which the adolescent can achieve a secure status among his peers and acquire responsible habits at the same time. Through them the ambitious working-class youth can learn the social graces of the middle class; without these, book learning is not enough to make an executive of a manual laborer's son. For all who participate, extracurricular activities can draw together the separate roles of "student" and "peer group member," thus helping to clarify the uncertain status of the adolescent. They may even, in some cases, help to provide something resembling a "core status" as "member of the school community." In the current clamor to tighten discipline and produce a generation of intellectuals, it is important that we not lose sight of the essential role of the peer group in the life of the adolescent.

---

[5] For evidence that high marks are correlated with popularity and extracurricular honors, see C. Wayne Gordon, *The Social System of the High School*, Glencoe, Illinois: Free Press, 1957.

5. ADOLESCENT CHOICES AND PARENT-PEER CROSS-PRESSURES *

Clay V. Brittain

As they are commonly portrayed, adolescents confronted with parent-peer cross-pressures tend to opt in favor of the peer-group. But to what extent and under what circumstances does this image square with reality? [1] Does the tendency toward peer-conformity vary as a function of the type of choice to be made by the adolescent?

The concept of reference group is useful in attacking this problem. Following Shibutani's [2] formulation that a reference group is one whose perspective constitutes the frame of reference of the actor, both peers and parents might be thought of as reference groups; i.e., as groups each provides perspectives in terms of which adolescents make choices. Does the extent to which adolescents tend to adopt these different perspectives vary systematically across situations? We hypothesized that in making certain kinds of choices, adolescents are inclined to follow peers rather than parents; in making certain other types of choices, the opposite is true.

Procedure

Situations involving conflict between parent-peer expectations were described to the subjects—girls in grades 9 through 11. Each situation was structured around an adolescent girl who was trying to choose between two alternatives, one of which was favored by her parents and the other by her friends. The following item illustrates the procedure:

* *American Sociological Review*, 1962, 28(3), 385–391. Reprinted with permission of the author and the American Sociological Association.

---

[1] There is controversy about the legitimacy of this image. For contrasting views see Frederick Elkin and William A. Westley, "The Myth of the Adolescent Peer Culture," *American Sociological Review*, 20 (December 1955), pp. 680–684; and James S. Coleman, *The Adolescent Society*, New York: The Free Press, 1961, Ch. 1.

[2] Tamotsu Shibutani, "Reference Groups as Perspectives," *American Journal of Sociology*, 60 (May, 1955), pp. 562–569.

A large glass in the front door of the high school was broken. Jim broke the glass. But both he and Bill were seen at the school the afternoon the glass was broken and both are suspected. Bill and Jim are friends and they agree to deny that they know anything about the broken glass. As a result, the principal pins the blame on both of them. Nell is the only other person who knows who broke the glass. She was working in the typing room that afternoon. She didn't actually see the glass broken, but she heard the noise and saw Jim walking away from the door a few moments later. Nell is very much undecided what to do. The three girls she goes around with most of the time don't think Nell should tell the principal. These girls hate to see an innocent person punished. But they point out to Nell that this is a matter between Jim and Bill and between Jim and his conscience. Nell talks the matter over with her mother and father. They felt that Jim is unfairly using Bill in order to lighten his own punishment. Her parents think Nell should tell the principal who broke the glass.

Can you guess what Nell did when the principal asked her if she saw who broke the glass?

————— She told him that she didn't see it broken.

————— She told him who broke the glass.[3]

Two versions of 12 items each were constructed to make up two forms (A and B) of the present instrument, which will be called the Cross-Pressures Test, or CPT. The two forms were identical in all respects except for the opinions and preferences attributed to parents and friends. These were reversed from one form to the other. The parent-favored alternatives on Form A were the peer-favored alternatives on Form B, and vice versa.[4] The instructions accompanying the CPT were:

> The following stories are about young people like your friends and the people you know. These people are in situations where they are not sure what to do. We would like to have you read each story carefully and tell us which one of the two things the person in the story is more likely to do. Do *not* tell us what the person should do, but what she is *likely* to really do. We hope you will enjoy doing this.

The CPT was administered to an experimental group and a small control group. The experimental group responded to one form and then to

---

[3] Item number 4 on the instrument used in the study.

[4] The alternate version of the item given above read as follows: "The three girls she goes around with most of the time feel that Jim is unfairly using Bill in order to lighten his own punishment. They think that Nell should tell the principal who broke the glass. Nell talks the matter over with her mother and father. They don't think Nell should tell the principal. Nell's parents hate to see an innocent person punished. But her father points out to Nell that this a matter between Jim and Bill and between Jim and his conscience." There are obviously many situations for which this type of reversal would not be plausible.

the other; the control responded twice to the same form. Both were divided into subgroups and tested as follows:

EXPERIMENTAL GROUP	FIRST TESTING	SECOND TESTING
Group AB	Form A	Form B
Group BA	Form B	Form A
CONTROL GROUP		
Group A	Form A	Form A
Group B	Form B	Form B

One to two weeks intervened between the testing dates. The subjects were not told that they were to be tested a second time.

As can be seen from the specimen item, the dilemmas described on the CPT were double-barrelled (as well as double-horned). There is the dilemma embodied in the content of the alternatives (e.g., telling who broke the glass in the door of the high school versus not telling; or going steady with a boy having certain personal qualities versus going steady with a boy having other personal qualities), and, on top of this, the dilemma posed by the cross-pressures from parents and friends. The subjects could respond to either dilemma or to both. We anticipated that they would respond to both; i.e., the tendency to choose the parent-favored or the peer-favored alternative would depend upon what the dilemma was about. Hence, there would be marked inter-item variation in the frequency of parent-conforming and peer-conforming choices.

The experimental group data were analyzed for differential preferences for the parent-favored and peer-favored alternatives. In response to each item there were three possibilities: (1) The subject, responding to the content of the dilemma, chooses the same content alternative on both forms of the CPT. (2) The peer-favored alternative is selected on both forms. (3) The parent-favored alternative is selected on both forms. In event of 2 or 3, the choice of content alternative shifts from the first testing to the second. The data, then, were analyzed for shifts in choice of content alternatives from one form of the CPT to the other.[5] The control group was used to help establish that the shifts in the experimental group were due to differences in the forms of the test and not simply to the tendency to respond randomly.

Items on which peer-conforming response shifts were more frequent and those on which parent-conforming shifts were more frequent were identified. From the content of these items inferences were drawn about

---

[5] Biases toward parent-favored or peer-favored alternatives showed up also as differences in first test responses between experimental subgroups AB and BA. A comparison of these groups, not reported here, reveals substantially the same trends as shown in the present analysis.

the bases of preferences for peer-favored and parent-favored alternatives.

Following the second testing, 42 girls in grades 9 and 10 were individually interviewed.[6] The interview data help to clarify the above analysis
of responses to the CPT.[7]

Subjects

The subjects were girls[8] from high schools in Alabama and Georgia.
The 280 girls in the experimental group came from an urban high
school, a high school in a small city, and three small rural high schools.
Analysis of the data did not reveal any rural-urban differences. The 58
control respondents were from a high school in a small town and a rural
high school.

Results

Comparison of the experimental and control groups indicates that the
findings reported below were not due to the tendency to respond randomly, but that changes in form did elicit changes in choice of content
alternatives. The data are given in Table 1. On item one, for example,
23 per cent of the control subjects, who responded twice to the same
form, shifted content alternatives from the first testing to the second as
compared to 52 per cent in the experimental group. On each of the 12
items, shifts in choice of content alternative occur more frequently in the
experimental group. On 11 of the items the experimental-control differences were significant at the .01 level or better.

An analysis of the experimental group data is given in Table 2. The
responses to each item were first broken down in terms of the following
two categories: (1) The choice of content alternatives did not shift from
one form to the other. (2) The content choice did shift; i.e., the peer-favored or parent-favored alternative was consistently chosen. (See columns NS and S.) The second category was then broken down into peer-
conforming and parent-conforming choices. (See columns P and F.) As
can be seen from this break-down, items 1, 6, and 8 tended more strongly

---

[6] Both the interviewing and the testing were done by the writer.

[7] Sociometric data were collected in one of the schools included in the study, but
only brief reference is made to them in this paper.

[8] This imposes an important qualification in generalizing the findings. If a sample
of adolescent boys were studied in similar manner, the findings would undoubtedly
diverge at some points from those presented here.

to elicit peer-conforming choices; items 3, 4, 5, 7, 9, 11, and 12 tended to elicit parent-conforming choices. All of these differences except that for item 4 are significant at the .05 level or better. Parent-conforming and peer-conforming choices were distributed equally on item 2.

Before interpreting these findings, note the following observations. They suggest the results were not dictated simply by the method.

(1) The subjects responded naively. Of the 42 girls individually interviewed soon after the second testing, only two were able to tell how the two forms of the CPT differed.

TABLE 1
Proportion of Control Group and Experimental Group Shifting Responses

ITEM	EXPERIMENTAL GROUP $N = 280$	CONTROL GROUP $N = 58$	DIFFERENCE $P_E - P_C$	CHI SQUARE[a]
1. Which course to take in school	.52	.23	.29	15.60°°
2. Which boy to go steady with	.50	.28	.22	12.71°°
3. How to get selected for a school honor	.33	.28	.05	.94
4. Whether to report boy who damaged school property	.35	.14	.21	13.57°°
5. Whether to enter beauty contest or be cheerleader	.44	.16	.28	22.52°°
6. How to dress for football game and party	.51	.19	.32	26.42°°
7. Whether to be beauty contestant or appear on TV program	.39	.14	.25	18.56°°
8. Which dress to buy	.58	.19	.39	39.39°°
9. Which one of two boys to date	.49	.16	.33	29.00°°
10. Which part-time job to take	.34	.16	.18	10.66°
11. Whether to report adult who damaged public property	.38	.19	.19	10.23°
12. How to let boy know she is willing to date him	.36	.21	.15	6.66°

[a]Chi square computed from frequencies. df = 1, °p < .01 °°p < .001.

TABLE 2
Frequency of Shifts in Choice of Content
Alternatives From One Form to the Other

ITEM	NOT SHIFTING CONTENT ALTERNATIVES (NS)	SHIFTING CONTENT ALTERNATIVES			CHI SQUARE [a]
		TOTAL (S)	ALTERNATIVE SELECTED PARENT(P)	PEER(F)	
1. Which course to take in school	135	145	48	97	16.56°°°
2. Which boy to go steady with	141	139	70	69	.01
3. How to get selected for a school honor	187	93	63	30	11.70°°°
4. Whether to report boy who damaged school property	182	98	58	40	3.30
5. Whether to enter beauty contest or be cheerleader	156	124	93	31	28.26°°°
6. How to dress for football game and party	138	142	47	95	16.22°°°
7. Whether to be beauty contestant or appear on TV program	170	110	83	27	31.00°°°
8. Which dress to buy	118	162	59	103	11.92°°°
9. Which one of two boys to date	143	137	81	56	4.56°
10. Which part-time job to take	184	96	69	27	18.37°°°
11. Whether to report adult who damaged public property	174	106	73	33	15.09°°°
12. How to let boy know she is willing to date him	180	100	64	36	(7.84)°°
Column totals	1908	1452	808	644	—

[a]Chi square for differences between columns P and F computed on the basis of 50/50 assumption. df= 1. °p<.05; °°p<.01; °°°p<.001.

(2) Responding to the CPT seemed to be accompanied by anxiety. In informal group discussions immediately following the second testing there were expressions of irritability at having to make the choices called for. This suggests that the subjects did tend to become emotionally involved in the hypothetical situations themselves.

(3) Groups of subjects differentiated on the basis of their responses to the CPT were also differentiated on the basis of sociometric data. For example, subjects who most frequently chose peer-favored alternatives tended not to be well accepted by their peers.

(4) At least some of the response trends were consistent with what informal observation of adolescent behavior would lead one to expect. For example, choices relating to dress were especially likely to be peer-conforming.

Discussion

The findings, as reported in Table 2, are consistent with the hypothesis that responses of adolescents to parent-peer cross-pressures are a function of the content of the alternatives and that peer-conformity in adolescence, rather than being diffuse, tends to vary systematically across situations. The response variation across items supports the hypothesis.

More specific interpretations of the response trends are now in order. Why were the peer-favored alternatives more commonly selected in response to some of the hypothetical situations and parent-favored alternatives in response to others? This question relates to the more general problem of understanding the processes involved in coming to terms with conflicting pressures, which, as Merton[9] has pointed out, is salient for reference group theory.

From the content of the hypothetical dilemmas, viewed against the response trends shown in Table 2, the following hypotheses are offered:

1. The responses reflect the adolescent's perception of peers and parents as competent guides in different areas of judgment.

The general social orientation of adolescents is of a dual character. Choices tend to derive meaning from either of two general reference groups, or both: the peer society in which many status and identity needs are gratified, and the larger society in which the status positions which one can aspire to as an adult are found. When choices pertain to the latter, parents are perceived as the more competent guides. In response to the hypothetical situation involving choice of part-time jobs

[9] Robert K. Merton, *Social Theory and Social Structure*. Revised and Enlarged Edition, New York: The Free Press, 1957, p. 244.

(item 10), for example, preferences commonly were for the parent-favored rather than the peer-favored alternatives.

2. The responses reflect concern to avoid being noticeably different from peers. Two of the items to which responses showed clearcut peer-conforming trends involved a choice of dress; i.e., item 6—how to dress for a football game and party, and item 8—which one of two dresses to buy.

3. The responses reflect concern about separation from friends. Peer-conforming choices were predominant in response to item 1—which one of two courses to take in school, where the consequence of a peer-defying choice would have been some degree of separation from friends.[10]

4. A fourth hypothesis overlapping but different from those above is that the choices reflect perceived similarities and differences between self and peers and self and parents. Adolescents, for example, perceiving themselves to be more like peers in regard to tastes in clothes and in regard to feelings about school, find peer-favored alternatives in these areas psychologically closer and more acceptable. But in other areas the greater perceived similarity is between self and parents. For example, with respect to values involved in the difficult choice whether to report a person who has destroyed property (items 4 and 11), the parent-favored alternatives are closer and more acceptable.[11]

The interviews referred to above provided a source for further inferences. According to one hypothesis derived from the interview data, responses to the CPT were a function of the perceived difficulty of the content choices. Parent-conformity was more prevalent in response to dilemmas posing what were perceived to be the more difficult choices. The 42 subjects interviewed soon after the second testing were asked to rank the content choices according to difficulty. The items from the CPT, with the parent-versus-peer aspect deleted, were typed on small cards; the subjects were asked to select from among them, first the situation in which the girl would have the greatest difficulty making up her mind, then the situation in which she would have the least difficulty. This was repeated until the choices were ordered from most to least difficult. Median ranks were computed. The items eliciting predominantly peer-conforming trends fell at the least difficult end of the resulting rank order. Hence, the tendency toward parent-conformity was directly related to the perceived difficulty of the choice.

A second inference was suggested by a discrepancy between the inter-

---

[10] An example identical on both forms concerned which one of two high schools to attend. Responses to it were *predominantly peer-conforming*.

[11] This hypothesis holds, in effect, that there is a close interrelationship between what Merton refers to as normative type and comparison type reference groups. Merton, *op. cit.*, p. 283.

view data and CPT responses. Interviewees were asked to select from among the content dilemmas, as presented on the cards, the two about which a girl would most likely talk to her friends rather than her parents. Neither of the two items most frequently selected had elicited predominantly peer-conforming CPT response shifts. Choices in response to one of them (item 9—which one of two boys to date) were more frequently parent-conforming; while in response to the other (item 2—which one of two boys to go steady with) parent-conforming and peer-conforming choices were equally frequent. No such discrepancy was found when the girls were asked to select the two dilemmas about which a girl was most likely to talk to her parents rather than her friends. The three items most commonly selected (i.e., 4, 10, and 11) had all elicited predominantly parent-conforming response shifts.

This divergence of interview and test data may indicate that the latter lead to an over-estimate of parent-conformity. But it also suggests a device used by adolescents in coping with parent-peer cross-pressures, namely, avoiding communication with parents. This would be likely to occur in areas in which parent-peer conflict is most acute. If this is the case, such discrepancies as those reported here could be used to identify points at which adolescents tend to be most disturbed by cross-pressures from parents and peers.

Let me note one other aspect of the data. Despite the greater overall incidence of parent-conformity, there was greater convergence relative to peer-conforming choices. As shown in Table 2, a majority of the items elicited a preponderance of parent-conforming over peer-conforming choices. On each of the items where there was a reversal of this trend (i.e., items 1, 6, and 8) there were, however, more peer-conforming choices than parent-conforming choices on any single item. This suggests the following possibility: Analogous trends in the social behavior of adolescents create the impression that peer-conformity in adolescence is more diffuse than actually is the case. Lack of parent-adolescent communication about certain types of choices contributes to this impression.

Summary and Further Applications

The study explored the hypothesis, suggested by reference-group theory, that adolescent choices in response to parent-peer cross-pressures are dependent upon the character of the content alternatives presented. Hypothetical dilemmas were described to adolescent girls. In each dilemma a girl was confronted with a complex choice where one course of action was favored by parents and another by peers. The respondents were asked in each case to indicate what the girl would probably do.

With the situations remaining otherwise unchanged, peer-favored and parent-favored alternatives were interchanged and the hypothetical dilemmas again presented to the respondents. Comparison of responses to the two forms of the test revealed that peer-conforming choices were more prevalent in response to certain of the dilemmas and parent-conforming choices in response to others. These results were taken to support the hypothesis.

The content of the items suggested additional specific hypotheses as partial explanations of the trends toward peer-conforming and parent-conforming responses: (1) The responses reflect the adolescent's perception of peer and parents as competent guides in different areas of judgment. (2) The responses reflect a concern to avoid being noticeably different from peers. (3) The responses reflect concern about separation from peers. (4) The choices reflect perceived similarities and differences between self and peers and self and parents.

Additional data were collected by interviewing a number of the respondents. From the interview data and from discrepancies between test and interview it was hypothesized that: (1) The tendency toward parent-conformity is directly related to the perceived difficulty of the choices. (2) Adolescents attempt to come to terms with parent-peer cross-pressures by simply not communicating with parents.

The present study argues the value of the approach exemplified here in exploring an important facet of adolescence. What considerations predispose adolescents toward peer-conformity in situations where they are confronted with parent-peer cross-pressures? What are the persisting cognitive schemata against which choices in such situations are made? We believe that through applications of the present method or adaptations of it, hypotheses relating to these questions could be investigated. For example:

1. Stability of social values: Adolescents are more strongly given to peer-conformity in making choices in areas in which social values are changing rapidly, than making choices in areas in which social values are relatively stable.

2. Time perspective: Adolescents are more strongly disposed toward peer-conformity in making choices where immediate consequences are anticipated than in making choices where the emphasis is on long term effects.

In addition, the present procedure might be used to assess individual differences in predispositions toward peer-versus parent-conformity. Although the study did not deal with the problem, the subjects were found to differ from one another in their tendencies to make parent-conforming or peer-conforming choices. At the extremes four groups were indentified: (1) subjects manifesting relatively strong tendencies toward parent-conformity; (2) subjects manifesting relatively strong tendencies toward peer-conformity; (3) a mixed-conformity group composed of subjects making parent-conforming choices and peer-conforming choices with relatively great and about equal frequency; and (4) subjects making very few responses of either type; i.e., subjects whose responses were mostly consistent by content. The stability of these response biases and their possible correlates remain a problem for further study.

6. PEER INFLUENCES ON ADOLESCENT EDUCATIONAL ASPIRATIONS AND ATTAINMENTS*

C. Norman Alexander, Jr. and Ernest Q. Campbell

An individual depends on communication with significant others for the consensual validation necessary to maintain stable and consistent attitudes toward social objects. Recently, there has been a widespread convergence of social psychological theories dealing with such normative reference group processes.[1] In general, these theories involve some concept of interpersonal balance, or strain-reducing tendencies toward a perceived symmetry between one's own evaluation of a cognitive object and its evaluation by an attractive other. These hypothesized tendencies toward balance direct the researcher to consider the interaction between an individual's attitude and the attitudes of those in his communication network—in short, to study his attitudes in the context of his position as the nexus of a structure of interpersonal relationships.

* American Sociological Review, 1964, 29, 568–575. Reprinted with permission of the authors and the American Sociological Association. Based on data secured during conduct of Grants M-04302 and MH-08489, National Institute of Mental Health, Ernest Q. Campbell, Principal Investigator. The Graduate Fellowship Program, National Science Foundation, freed the time of the first author for work on this paper, an assistance gratefully acknowledged. We are indebted to Josef Perry and Richard L. Simpson for critical reading of earlier drafts of the manuscript. Dick Latteri tabulated the data as a participant in the Nation Science Foundation Undergraduate Research Participation Program at the University of North Carolina.

[1] Fritz Heider, The Psychology of Interpersonal Relations, New York: Wiley, 1958. A variety of sociological and social psychological propositions are restated in terms of Heider's balance model by James A. Davis, "Structural Balance, Mechanical Solidarity, and Interpersonal Relations," American Journal of Sociology 68 (January, 1963), pp. 444–462.

To deal with consensus in collectivities of mutual attraction—as well as with intrapersonal tendencies toward perceived symmetry—Newcomb has proposed the A-B-X model.[2] Intrapersonally, the model predicts that a condition of strain is produced when a person, A, perceives a discrepancy or lack of symmetry between his own attitude toward X (an object of perceived common relevance) and his perception of B's attitude toward the same object. The magnitude of strain is a direct function of the degree of his positive attraction to B and of the importance of X. So long as X remains of importance and perceived common relevance, A's condition of strain persists. Thus, if other factors were irrelevant, and if X were of sufficient importance, we should observe either that A comes to perceive symmetry between his own and B's attitudes toward X or that he ceases to be positively attracted to B.

On the basis of such an intrapersonal system of orientation as outlined above, we predict that—given positive attraction to B and the importance and *perceived* common relevance of X—A will tend to eliminate any perceived discrepancy between his own and B's attitudes toward X. When an interpersonal system of orientation exists—when B is also attracted to A and regards X as important and of common relevance—Newcomb postulates that actual disagreement produces a condition of "imbalance." He then hypothesizes that, through mutually adjustive communication, a condition of actual, rather than merely perceived consensus tends to result.[3]

Within this general theoretical framework the present paper deals with high school seniors' educational goals and their attainment as these are influenced by peers. Previous research has shown that the perceived characteristics of an individual's attractive peers influence his aspirations independently of the effects of his socio-economic status or the influences of his parents.[4] But peer relations have not generally been examined in terms of interpersonal systems; that is, data analyses have not involved simultaneous consideration of both A's relation to B and B's relation to A.

The balance model leads us to expect, for example, that an individual's plans regarding college attendance will be similar to those of his best friend and that similarity between them will be greater if his best friend reciprocates the choice. This implies that, if his best friend plans to go to college, a student is more likely to plan to go when the choice

---

[2] Theodore M. Newcomb, *The Acquaintance Process*, New York: Holt, Rinehart and Winston, 1961.

[3] *Ibid.*, pp. 14–15.

[4] Richard L. Simpson, "Parental Influence, Anticipatory Socialization and Social Mobility," *American Sociological Review*, 27 (August, 1962), pp. 517–522.

is reciprocated than when it is not; but if his best friend *does not* plan to go, the student is more likely to expect to attend when his choice is *not* reciprocated than when it is reciprocated. Reciprocation, as an indication of more extensive communication between the individual and his choice, should increase pressures toward consensus if college attendance is a relevant and important object of communication.

Aspects of the substantive situation, however, suggest that this straightforward, balance theory expectation needs qualification. First, it seems reasonable to expect that the relevance of the issue varies according to whether or not the student's friend plans to attend college. Because college attendance is socially valued and personally rewarding, a college-bound student is likely to exert positive influence on his friend to attend. On the other hand, it seems unlikely that a student not planning college would actively discourage his friend from attending; whatever influence he exerted would be more indirect, that is, he would not contribute positively to his friend's educational aspirations. This leads us to expect that the effects of reciprocation on the chooser's college plans will be considerably stronger when his friend is college-bound than when he does not plan to attend.

Furthermore, variables associated with reciprocation itself may also complicate these relationships. Those whose choices are reciprocated are generally more popular among their peers; and popularity is positively associated with intelligence and with the likelihood of college attendance, independently of socio-economic status.[5] Thus, students whose choices are reciprocated should be more likely to plan and go to college than those whose choices are not reciprocated. This association supports the balance expectations of differences by reciprocation when the friend plans to go to college, but operates in the opposite direction when he does not. These factors are best eliminated by holding reciprocation constant and examining the differential strength of the relation between the student's and his friend's college plans. We predict, then, only that the influence of the friend's behavior will be stronger when the choice is reciprocated than when it is not.

Actual expectations of attending college are subject to a number of reality demands apart from tendencies toward consensus with attractive others and the importance attached to obtaining a higher education. But whether or not one *expects* to attend college presumably exerts a considerable influence on one's attitudes toward the desirability of attending. Thus, we shall also examine the hypotheses that the college plans and choice-reciprocation of the student's best friend will affect (1) the strength of his desire to attend college, *if he plans to go*, and (2) *even*

---

[5] *Sociometry*, 29 (March, 1966), pp. 41–51.

though he does not expect to go, how strongly he would like to attend college, given the opportunity. Again, we shall remove the direct effects of his own status. For those who plan to go to college, we shall also ask what effect his friend's plans and the realization of these plans have on the individual's actual college attendance. Finally, for those who actually entered college and whose friends also attended, we shall relate the *specific* college they attended to the particular college attended by their best friend.

The balance model leads us to expect that individuals will tend, through communication, to become more similar with regard to important behaviors, attitudes and values of common relevance. The model also predicts, however, that individuals are more likely to choose as associates others with whom they already agree. Given only our aspiration data, we are unable to estimate either the extent to which an individual initially selects as friends those who are similar to him or the extent to which friends, once selected, influence him to become more similar to them. Undoubtedly, both processes are involved; but longitudinal data are needed to determine whether peers' plans help shape adolescent aspirations or whether the adolescent tends to select friends who have similar aspirations. Our data on the actualization of college plans are of this type, and from these data we will be able to determine whether the individual's chosen friend does influence his behavior regarding actual college attendance and attendance at a particular college.

Data Analysis

In connection with a larger study,[6] questionnaires were administered to 1,410 male seniors in 30 high schools in the Eastern and Piedmont sections of North Carolina. Each respondent was asked the following question: "What students here in school *of your own sex* do you go around with most often?" A choice is considered codable if directed to another

---

[6] "Normative Controls and the Social Use of Alcohol," National Institute of Mental Health Grants M-4302 and MH-08489, under the direction of Ernest Q. Campbell. Questionnaires were administered to 5,115 seniors of both sexes in 62 high schools. The sample in this paper includes only male students in the 30 high schools that met the following criteria:

(1) More than 15 boys responded.
(2) More than 95 per cent of the boys gave their names.
(3) More than 90 per cent of the boys completed the questionnaire.
(4) More than one-third of the boys planned to go to college.

The fourth criterion eliminated only one school that would otherwise not have been eliminated. The criterion was included because certain data are available only for the adolescents who plan to attend college.

member of the high school senior class who returned a signed question-naire. The individual's first-listed, codable choice is considered to be his "best friend." If that choice chooses the chooser as one of his first three codable choices, the choice is defined as "reciprocal." [7]

The status of an individual is determined by classification into one of five levels of parental educational attainment: [8]

I. Both parents went to college

II. Only one parent attended college

III. Both parents graduated from high school, but neither attended college

IV. Only one parent graduated from high school and he did not at-tend college

V. Neither parent graduated from high school

We say that the student expects to attend college if he responds, "Yes, definitely," to the question: "Realistically, do you expect to go to college *this coming Fall?*" His chosen friend's plans are determined by that friend's response to the same question.

Our first hypothesis is that a student at a given status level is more likely to plan to go to college if his best friend does rather than does not plan to go, and that this relationship is stronger when the choice is rather than is not reciprocated. Table 1 presents relevant data in per-centages.

To evaluate the extent to which the data support expectations—in terms of both the direction and size of the differences—we computed the values of Yule's Q at each status level for the relevant comparisons; [9] then we averaged these five Q values to obtain a mean Q. An associa-tion is assigned a positive value if it is in the expected direction and a negative value if it is contrary to expectations. The higher the mean Q values, the stronger the associations in the expected direction.

We are predicting (1) that the college plans of the student's friend in-fluence his own behavior independently of the effects of reciprocation,

---

[7] An I.B.M. procedure for determining reciprocation is described in C. Norman Alexander, Jr., "A Method for Processing Sociometric Data," *Sociometry, 26* (June, 1963), pp. 268–269.

[8] When the education of only one parent was reported, the student was assigned a rank (either II, IV or V) based on that parent's educational attainment. We selected parental education as our status measure because it is a reasonable index of the edu-cational goals that parents expect their children to share; and, applied to subjects from both rural and urban areas, it is less ambiguous than occupational classification.

[9] For example, in Table 1 the Q values at personal status level I compare the pro-portions expecting to attend college by reciprocation; the frequencies of those who do and those who do not plan college in columns 3 and 4 and columns 1 and 2, re-spectively, form the 2-x-2 table from which Q values are computed.

TABLE 1

Per Cent of Students Who Definitely Expect to Go to College—by Personal Status Level, College Plans and Reciprocation of First Choice[a]

PERSONAL STATUS LEVEL	RECIPROCATES		DOES NOT RECIPROCATE	
	CHOICE PLANS TO ATTEND	CHOICE DOESN'T PLAN TO ATTEND	CHOICE PLANS TO ATTEND	CHOICE DOESN'T PLAN TO ATTEND
I (High)	96.9	64.0	81.5	62.5
	(97)	(25)	(54)	(16)
II	78.1	39.6	69.0	41.2
	(73)	(48)	(58)	(34)
III	75.9	22.2	70.6	43.2
	(54)	(45)	(34)	(37)
IV	53.3	24.3	53.1	20.4
	(60)	(74)	(49)	(54)
V (Low)	51.0	5.3	25.5	7.0
	(49)	(152)	(51)	(114)

[a] Numbers in parentheses in all tables are the base from which the percentage derives, e.g., in the upper left-hand cell, 96.9 per cent of the 97 cases of high personal status, whose best friend reciprocates the choice and is college-bound, expect to attend college.

and (2) that the association between the student's college plans and those of his friend will be stronger when the choice is reciprocated. Thus, we expect a positive average Q value under conditions of both reciprocation and non-reciprocation, but a larger value when the choice is reciprocated than when it is not. The average Q value for the association between the student's and his friend's college plans is .777 when the choice is reciprocated and .327 when it is not. The association is in the expected direction and is much stronger under conditions of reciprocation; the data thus support the hypothesis that a student and his best friend tend to be similar in college plans and that the extent of similarity is greater when the choice is reciprocated.

Since actual expectations of college attendance depend on other factors as well as the desire to attend—e.g., intelligence, income, college proximity—less "reality-bound" attitudes toward college attendance are perhaps more appropriate to the theory. When we consider less realistic wishes or desires to go to college, however, it is obvious that these are greatly influenced by the subject's plans to attend or his expectations of being able to attend. To examine further the hypothesized influences of an individual's chosen friend and of the reciprocation of his friendship choice, we shall hold constant his *expectations* of college attendance while examining other aspects of his college plans.

Among those at a given status level who expect definitely to attend

TABLE 2
Per Cent of College-Bound Students Who Strongly Desire to Attend—by Personal Status Level, College Plans and Reciprocation of First Choice

PERSONAL STATUS LEVEL	RECIPROCATES				DOES NOT RECIPROCATE			
	CHOICE PLANS TO ATTEND		CHOICE DOESN'T PLAN TO ATTEND		CHOICE PLANS TO ATTEND		CHOICE DOESN'T PLAN TO ATTEND	
I (High)	78.9		55.6		64.7		66.7	
		(95)		(18)		(51)		(12)
II	67.1		48.6		59.6		36.8	
		(70)		(35)		(57)		(19)
III	60.0		44.4		56.7		42.9	
		(45)		(18)		(30)		(21)
IV	45.2		22.9		50.0		26.3	
		(42)		(35)		(26)		(19)
V (Low)	58.3		30.4		43.5		22.2	
		(36)		(23)		(23)		(27)

college, we expect a student to be more likely to desire strongly to go to college when his best friend plans to go. This relationship should be stronger when the friendship choice is reciprocated.

Table 2 presents the percentages, among those who definitely expect to go to college, who report a very strong desire to continue their education.[10] Again, we compute average Q values for the relation between the student's desire to attend college and his friend's plans, holding reciprocation of friendship choice constant. The summary measure of association is .474 when the choice is reciprocated and .319 when it is not, indicating substantial support for the hypothesis. We conclude, then, that one's friend's college plans affect the strength of the desire to attend college, especially among those whose choice is reciprocated.

Those who said that they did not plan to go to college were asked, "If you had a chance to go on to college next year, would you *like* to go?" Those who replied, "Yes, definitely," are said to wish to attend. Since most students whose parents are both high school graduates report that they expect to go on to college, the top three status levels are combined in Table 3 to maintain adequate cell frequencies.

Our model leads us to expect that a student whose best friend is college-bound is more likely to *want* to go to college even though he does

---

[10] This refers operationally to those who replied "It would be a terrible blow if I couldn't continue," to the question, "How strong is your desire to continue your education beyond high school?"

not expect to attend and that this association increases in strength when the choice is reciprocated. The average Q value for the hypothesized association is .451 when the choice is reciprocated and .098 when it is not. Thus, the college plans of their best friends tend to make students want to attend even when they do not have the opportunity to do so.

We have shown that his best friend's expectations of college attendance and reciprocation of friendship choice are closely related to a high school senior's educational aspirations. We now inquire whether his best friend's behaviors are associated with the actual college attendance of the student who had planned to attend. And if he did enroll in some college, we want to know whether his best friend influenced his selection of that particular college. We anticipate that the student who plans to attend college is more likely to get there when his best friend also plans to attend; and that, among those whose best friend does plan to attend, the proportion actually attending is higher when the best friend actually attends. Finally, we expect that a student and his friend are more likely to attend the same college if they initially agreed on where they planned to go, and if the student's friend either follows through with his plans when they initially agreed, or does not follow through when they initially disagreed. All of these predicted relationships should be stronger when the choice is reciprocated. Examination of *specific* college plans and their realization permits a more crucial examination of the predictive utility of the balance model than is possible with more general aspirations.

An extensive effort was made to locate all students who said that they expected to attend college. There were 707 respondents who made at least one codable choice, could be classified on relevant independent variables, expected to attend a legitimate college or university (not a

TABLE 3
Per Cent of Non-College-Bound Who Wish to Attend College—by Personal Status Level, College Plans and Reciprocation of First Choice

PERSONAL STATUS LEVEL	RECIPROCATES				DOES NOT RECIPROCATE.			
	CHOICE PLANS TO ATTEND		CHOICE DOESN'T PLAN TO ATTEND		CHOICE PLANS TO ATTEND		CHOICE DOESN'T PLAN TO ATTEND	
I–III	50.0		20.5		26.7		30.3	
		(8)		(44)		(15)		(33)
IV	31.3		7.9		38.9		34.3	
		(16)		(38)		(18)		(35)
V	41.7		25.6		28.0		17.9	
		(12)		(125)		(25)		(84)

TABLE 4
Per Cent of College-Bound Students Actually Attending—by Personal Status Level, College Plans and Reciprocation of Best Friend

PERSONAL STATUS LEVEL	RECIPROCATES		DOES NOT RECIPROCATE	
	CHOICE PLANS TO ATTEND	CHOICE DOESN'T PLAN TO ATTEND	CHOICE PLANS TO ATTEND	CHOICE DOESN'T PLAN TO ATTEND
I (High)	93.8 (97)	78.9 (19)	100.0 (51)	83.3 (12)
II	91.8 (73)	69.4 (36)	91.1 (45)	61.9 (21)
III	89.1 (46)	72.2 (18)	83.3 (30)	66.7 (21)
IV	79.1 (43)	65.7 (35)	85.7 (28)	72.2 (18)
V (Low)	75.0 (36)	46.2 (26)	66.7 (24)	46.4 (28)

barber college, mortuary school, etc.), and provided information necessary to permit a follow-up attempt—name, college intended, and supplemental questionnaire. We were able to ascertain the whereabouts of 653 and to determine definitely whether they did or did not attend college. There is little to indicate that the remaining 54 did attend college, and, although we have no conclusive evidence that they did *not*, we include them in Table 4 among those who planned to go to college but failed to do so.[11]

Table 4 presents the percentage who attended college during the fall semester following graduation from high school—by parental education and the college plans and reciprocation of their first friendship choice. Our hypothesis is that a student at a given status level is more likely to attend college if his best friend expects to go and that this association is stronger when the choice is reciprocated. The average Q value is .534

---

[11] We tried to obtain information by campus visits, mail, or telephone, from parents, high school principals and guidance counsellors, college registrars and student directories, high school classmates, and the student himself. We did not establish contact with any of the parents of these 54 unclassified students; parents' information would have been accepted as definitive. In most instances, at least one report, usually from the high school principal, indicated that the student was or had been attending a specific college or university, but when we checked with college registrars, student information centers, and where possible with peers from his high school who were attending the specific college, we found no trace of him. We feel reasonably certain that a substantial majority of these 54 did not attend college, so that classifying them as non-attenders is less erroneous than classifying them as "non-respondents."

when the choice is reciprocated and .589 when it is not. Thus, while the actual attendance of the student is positively associated with the college plans of his best friend, reciprocation of the friendship choice does not increase the strength of the association as expected.

To examine actual attendance of the student in terms of his choice's attendance we must eliminate from the analysis all students whose choices did not expect to attend or did not provide sufficient information to permit a follow-up attempt. The remaining number of students whose friends do not realize their plans to attend is too small to permit analysis by reciprocation of choice. Thus, we predict simply that a student is more likely to attend college when his best friend also attends. Table 5 supports the hypothesis: at each status level, a higher proportion attend college when the friend also attends.

Finally, we wish to consider only those cases who planned to and did attend and whose best friend also planned to and did attend an institution of higher learning. We expect a student and his friend to be more likely to attend the same college when they initially agreed on where they planned to go. If they did agree, they are more likely to attend the same college when the student's friend follows through with his intentions; but if they initially disagreed, attendance at the same college is more likely when the friend does not follow through with his plans. These relationships should be stronger when the choice is reciprocated

TABLE 5
Per Cent of College-Bound Students Actually Attending—by Personal Status Level and College Attendance of Best Friend

PERSONAL STATUS LEVEL	DOES BEST FRIEND ATTEND?	
	Yes	No
I	94.7	84.6
	(151)	(13)
II	90.6	81.3
	(128)	(16)
III	86.6	55.6
	(82)	(9)
IV	81.3	66.7
	(75)	(15)
V	71.4	57.1
	(63)	(14)

than when it is not. Thus, our hypothesis is as follows: A student and his friend are more likely to attend the same college if (1) they planned to attend the same college while in high school, and (2) when their plans were the same, the friend does attend his chosen college, but (3) when their plans differed, the friend does *not* attend the chosen college, and (4) the above relationships are stronger when the friendship choice is reciprocated.

Table 6 presents the percentage of students who actually attended the same college as their best friend—by initial agreement with best friend on choice of college, best friend's realization of his college plans, and reciprocation. Attendance at the same college is more likely when the student and his friend initially agreed on college plans, and the relationship is stronger when the choice is reciprocated; the average Q value is .781 when the choice is reciprocated and .371 when it is not. When the student and his friend agree, the friend's realization of his plans is positively associated with attendance at the same college, but the relationship is somewhat weaker when the choice is reciprocated; the Q value is .905 when the choice is reciprocated and .942 when it is not. Finally, when their plans differ, the friend's realization of his plans is negatively associated with their attending the same college. Although they support the hypothesized association, the Q values of .167 when the choice is reciprocated and .698 when it is not clearly refute the expectation that reciprocation would increase the strength of the relationship. Thus, the data support the first three sub-hypotheses, but reciprocation strengthens only the first relationship. The latter two relationships are stronger when the friendship choice is not reciprocated.

Two rather surprising aspects of these data are the extent of initial disagreement between the student and his friend, regardless of recipro-

TABLE 6
Per Cent of Students and Choices Attending the Same College—by Initial Agreement, Choice's Realization of Plans and Reciprocation

INITIAL AGREEMENT OF STUDENT AND CHOICE ON SPECIFIC COLLEGE PLANS	RECIPROCATION OF FRIENDSHIP CHOICE			
	RECIPROCATED		NON-RECIPROCATED	
	DID CHOICE REALIZE PLANS?		DID CHOICE REALIZE PLANS?	
	Yes	No	Yes	No
Agree	85.1	22.2	76.9	9.1
	(47)	(27)	(26)	(11)
Disagree	5.1	7.0	2.8	14.0
	(117)	(71)	(71)	(50)

cation, and the lack of change toward greater consensus. Only 28.2 per cent of those with reciprocated choices initially agreed on where they planned to go to college, and the corresponding figure for those with non-reciprocated choices is 23.4 per cent. Since 60.4 per cent of those who initially agreed and only 6.5 per cent of those initially disagreeing actually attend the same college, the extent of similarity actually decreases. Only 21.8 per cent of those with reciprocated choices and 19.0 per cent of those with non-reciprocated choices end up at the same college. Nevertheless, initial agreement between friends does contribute to the realization of plans to attend a specific college. While the student or his friend changed plans in 62.1 per cent of the cases where they initially disagreed, the corresponding figure among those who initially agreed is only 45.9 per cent. Whether or not an individual realizes his plans to attend a specific college appears to be influenced by agreement with his friend on where they plan to go.

The precise interpretation of these results is unclear. Balance theory predicts a tendency to change toward greater consensus, given constancy of the friendship relation. The assumption of friendship constancy during this period of great transition is a rather tenuous one, however, and we have no data to indicate whether boys who are best friends during the spring of their senior year are still best friends at the time of entry into college. Also, initial consensus refers to long-range plans, while final consensus is determined by actual behaviors; and we have already indicated that the effects of efforts to achieve balance should be most pronounced when non-attitudinal reality considerations are minimized. In any case, the fact that initial agreement and friend's realization of plans do predict relatively greater similarity supports the balance expectations, but the effects of reciprocation are not entirely consistent with the hypothesis.

Summary and Conclusions

Confirming hypothesized tendencies toward balance, we have observed that a student at a given status level is more likely to *expect* to attend college, to have a strong desire to go to college when he *does* expect to go, to *want* to go when he *does not* expect to, and actually to attend, when his best friend does rather than does not plan to go to college; these relationships are stronger when the choice is reciprocated. When the student and his friend both plan to go, he is more likely to attend if his best friend does. And, finally, given the fact that they both attend a college, the likelihood that they attend the same college is increased by initial agreement on specific college plans and by the friend's realization of his plans; reciprocation, however, has relatively little effect on actual attendance at the same college. Our findings suggest that communication among male high school seniors affects both college plans and attendance.

While previous research has shown that the perceived characteristics of an individual's friends are associated with his own educational aspirations and expectations, these data support the additional hypothesis that this similarity is even greater when his friendship choice is reciprocated, that is, when an interpersonal system of orientation is formed. In addition to demonstrating the value of a relational, sociometric approach to the study of educational aspirations, the present research suggests that the balance model has predictive power in the analysis of social behavior.

7. THE EFFECT OF THE HIGH SCHOOL ON STUDENTS' ASPIRATIONS*

Richard P. Boyle

Recent research strongly suggests that the experiences that adolescents encounter in the high school have an important influence on their aspirations for further education. Studies by Wilson, Ramsøy, Coleman, and Turner have found that, when high schools are classified according to the *average* socioeconomic status of the student body, the aspirations of the *individual* students are influenced in the direction of the majority.[1]

* *American Journal of Sociology*, 1966, 7(1), 623–639. Copyright 1966, by the University of Chicago. The data reported here came from research supported by the Royal Commission on Health Services, Ottawa, Canada. I would like to thank my colleague, Stephen P. Spitzer, for insightful comments on an earlier draft of this paper, and Professor Otto N. Larsen for guidance with the Ph.D. dissertation on which this paper is based.

[1] Alan B. Wilson, "Residential Segregation of Social Classes and Aspirations of High School Boys" (hereinafter cited as "Residential Segregation"), *American Sociological Review*, XXIV (December, 1959), 836–45; Natalie Rogoff Ramsøy, "American High Schools at Mid-Century" (New York: Bureau of Applied Social Research, Columbia University, 1961); James S. Coleman, *The Adolescent Society* (New York: Free Press, 1962); Ralph H. Turner, *The Social Context of Ambition* (San Francisco: Chandler Publishing Co., 1964). As they pertain to this paper, these studies have all been concerned with differences *between* high schools. For research into differences

Working-class students attending predominantly *middle-class* high schools plan to attend college much more frequently than those attending more working-class high schools. The. reverse process is evident among middle-class students attending predominantly working-class high schools.

On this central finding there is agreement. But on the answers to more specific questions the separate studies often disagree. In particular: (1) Given that the population composition of a high school is important, *how* important is it? What, for example, is the effect of the high school relative to the effect of family background? Some studies found the high school equal in importance to the family, while other studies found it much less important. (2) *Why* should population composition show this effect? Some writers emphasize the importance of peer-group culture, while others give greater priority to pedagogical characteristics of the high school. (3) How is this effect expressed in terms of the individual student? Again, there is disagreement over whether explanation should be in terms of values and attitudes or in terms of scholastic abilities.

Each of the four studies cited above has inherent limitations which preclude final answers to these questions. However, each study provides clues which, taken together, suggest a consistent underlying pattern. This paper will examine closely the available evidence as it pertains to each question, add to this new evidence from a recently completed Canadian study, and finally attempt, as tightly as possible, to draw together these separate fragments into a consistent, unified statement about the consequences of variation in population composition among high schools.

Family and High School; Relative Importance

The sample for Alan Wilson's study consisted of boys from eight high schools in the San Francisco metropolitan area.[2] When these high schools were classified according to population composition, and individual students were classified according to their fathers' occupations, cross-classification allowed evaluation of the independent effects of fam-

---

within high schools, as these differences influence aspirations, see especially Edward L. McDill and James Coleman, "High School Social Status, College Plans, and Interest in Academic Achievement: A Panel Analysis" (hereinafter cited as "High School Social Status"), *American Sociological Review,* XXVIII (December, 1963), 905–18, and "Family and Peer Influences in College Plans of High School Students," *Sociology of Education,* XXXVIII (Winter, 1965), 112–26.

  [2] *Op. cit.*

ily and high school on the students' plan about attending college.[3] In order to have a measure of these effects, which will allow comparison with other studies, Coleman's unweighted estimate of effect for polytomous ordinal variables has been calculated and standardized to the dichotomous form.[4] In terms of this statistic, the effect of the high school in Wilson's study was 0.22, and the effect of family background was 0.19.[5] The effect of the high school, in other words, was slightly greater than the effect of the family. Closer inspection of Wilson's data also indicates that this pattern of effect was fairly consistent over all the various categories.

Comparable data from a much larger, nationwide survey of high-school students were available to Natalie Rogoff Ramsøy.[6] Applying the same statistical analysis to these data, the effect of the high school on college plans was 0.07, while the effect of family background was 0.24.[7] The population composition of the high school was thus a much less important influence on the aspirations of the students studied by Ramsøy.

Apart from slight differences in operationalization, two major differences in the studies stand out. First, Wilson studied only boys, while Ramsøy's sample included both sexes. Perhaps the effect of the high school is much stronger for boys than for girls. Second, all of Wilson's high schools were located in a single metropolitan area, while Ramsøy used a national, and hence geographically heterogeneous, sample. This could imply either that San Francisco schools are a special case or that metropolitan high schools in general have characteristics that make them distinctive. Indirect support for this last possibility is offered by a further finding of Ramsøy's, that the effect of the high school was almost entirely concentrated in the much higher aspirations of students attending the most predominantly middle-class schools.[8] Since middle-class oc-

---

[3] Wilson first classified his high schools on the basis of census data describing the neighborhoods in which the schools were located. He then examined other indexes, such as population composition of the student bodies, and concluded that the same ranked categories would result from any classification strategy. He used three categories for high schools and four for father's occupation.

[4] This statistic may be interpreted as the average difference between proportions of students planning on college within each level of father's occupation, corrected to be comparable to the proportion-difference that would obtain if high schools had been classified into two categories instead of three (see James S. Coleman, *Introduction to Mathematical Sociology* [New York: Free Press, 1964], chap. vi).

[5] Calculated from Wilson, *op. cit.*, Table 3, p. 839.

[6] Ramsøy, *op. cit.* Students were first classified according to five "family background" categories on the basis of father's occupation and education. The proportion of students in the top two of these categories was then used to classify high schools into five ranked categories.

[7] Calculated from *ibid.*, Table 8-2, p. 318.

[8] *Ibid.*

cupations comprise a much larger proportion of the total occupational structure in large cities than in smaller communities, and since residential segregation on a large enough scale to be reflected in the high school is also most likely in large cities, it seems quite probable that the predominantly middle-class high schools in Ramsøy's sample were disproportionately those located in large metropolitan areas. There is at least a hint, in other words, that controlling for community size would resolve some of the conflict between the findings of Ramsøy and Wilson.

The two remaining studies help to evaluate the possibility that sex and community size are underlying factors which could reconcile this disagreement. Ralph Turner's study was closely similar to Wilson's in that all ten of his high schools were located in the Los Angeles metropolitan area.[9] Using an "ambition index" that combined educational, occupational, and material aspirations, Turner carried out a partial correlation analysis which showed the high school to be only slightly less important than the family in determining ambition.[10] His findings thus agree more closely with Wilson's than with Ramsøy's. Furthermore, Turner carried out his analysis separately for boys and for girls and found that there were only slight differences.[11] Population composition of the high school did show a slightly higher correlation with ambition for boys than for girls, but this sex difference does not appear great enough to account for the divergence between the findings of Wilson and Ramsøy. Turner's work therefore provides further evidence that, at least in metropolitan areas, the high school is an important influence on aspiration.

James Coleman's sample for *The Adolescent Society* included ten high schools in northern Illinois, but only two of these were located in a large metropolitan area.[12] These two schools also recruited students from distinctly different family backgrounds. When father's education was controlled, students attending the more middle-class schools were much more likely to plan on college.[13] Among the *non-metropolitan*

---

[9] Turner, *op. cit.* Students were first assigned a "background-index" value on the basis of the family breadwinner's occupation, education, and independent-employee status. The mean background-index value for all students in each high school was computed and used to index high schools.

[10] The partial correlation between school and ambition with background controlled was .21 for boys and .18 for girls. The partial correlation between background and ambition with school controlled was .29 for boys and .31 for girls (*ibid.*, Table 11a, p. 58).

[11] See n. 10, above.

[12] Coleman, *op. cit.* "Executive Heights" and "Newlawn" were both located in suburbs of Chicago.

[13] *Ibid.*, Figs. 9.9 and 9.10, pp. 270–71. The remainder of this paragraph also refers to these figures.

high schools, however, differences in college planning associated with population composition were minimal. At the same time, Coleman's work indicates little difference in the effect of the high school on boys and on girls.

When these four studies are considered as a whole, their implication is therefore clear, although tentative. The effect of population composition on the aspirations of high-school students is considerable, but it varies according to the size of the community in which the high school is located. In large cities, the effect of the high school is roughly the same as the effect of the family, but in smaller communities this effect is much weaker. Finally, the influence of the high school appears to be fairly similar for both sexes, although slightly less important for girls.

Explanatory Factors

While this pattern is clearly indicated, reasons for its existence are not obvious. The various explanations that have been proposed fall into two roughly distinct categories and suggest the operation of two mechanisms which account for the differences in aspirations under consideration. First, the manifest function of the high school is to impart knowledge and develop skills. The possibility that schools vary in their success at doing this could therefore be one important explanation. Second, a latent function of the high school may be to influence the values and attitudes of the student, thus affecting his motivation to attend college or otherwise aim high in life. These two explanations will be considered in turn.

Divergent educational standards and scholastic development.—If some high schools provide their students with a better education than other high schools, this might explain the variation in the aspirations of these students. Several authors have pointed in this direction, but they have advanced different arguments. Ramsøy suggests that it is important to consider the *structural* characteristics of the formal educational system. She argues that the decentralized nature of American education, which delegates autonomy to the local school district and does not require students to compete with one another on any sort of standardized examination, allows and encourages divergence in the educational standards of individual high schools.[14]

On the other hand, later work by Wilson emphasizes the *informal social pressures* toward divergence which arise from residential segrega-

---

[14] Ramsøy, *op. cit.*, p. 126 and *passim*.

tion along social class lines.[15] He found that within a single elementary school district, teachers in predominantly working-class schools came to expect less of their students than teachers in more middle-class schools and to key their teaching to these expectations. The result was that by sixth grade the level of the subject matter taught in class varied widely between the two kinds of schools.

A hint that this process of divergence operates in high schools as well as in elementary schools is offered by Coleman's finding that, "The amount of homework done depends largely on two things: upon the amount of homework assigned by the teachers, and upon family background." [16] Students at predominantly middle-class high schools spent more time studying than those at predominantly working-class schools, even when father's education was controlled.

The major consequences of this divergence, therefore, should be found in the level of knowledge and the scholastic abilities of the students in different kinds of high schools. However, the suggested interplay of structural restraints and informal social pressures in determining divergence has some interesting implications. Residential segregation on a large enough scale to be reflected in the high school should be most frequent in metropolitan areas. Informal social pressures should therefore be strongest among these schools. At the same time, metropolitan high schools will most typically be single units in large school districts containing several high schools. Since the local school district is the functional administrative unit in American education, it might be expected that these metropolitan high schools *would* be subject to restraints against divergence, stemming from the central school-district administration. Insofar as divergence *does* occur among these schools, therefore, it seems better explained on the basis of strong *informal* social pressures. These ideas will be important when the Canadian data are presented, because in Canada administrative centralization at the *provincial* level provides formal restraints against divergence.

While no one has actually determined exactly what the different high schools were teaching in their courses, there is empirical support for the general notion that students from similar families show greater scholastic aptitude when they attend "higher status" high schools. Wilson, Ramsøy, and Turner all report this pattern. In order to really *evaluate* the importance of this pattern as an explanation for differences in aspirations, however, a direct statistical analysis is appropriate. Control scholastic ability and then see by how much the relation between high

---

[15] Alan B. Wilson, "Social Stratification and Academic Achievement," in A. Harry Passow (ed.), *Education in Depressed Areas* (New York: Bureau of Publications, Teachers College, Columbia University, 1963), pp. 217–35.

[16] *The Adolescent Society*, pp. 266–68.

school and aspiration has been reduced (with family background controlled in both cases).

This kind of analysis is reported for two of the studies. With Ramsøy's data, this control eliminated almost all of the effect attributable to the high school.[17] The only exception occurred among the most middle-class high schools, which continued to send a higher proportion of students to college than other schools. On the other hand, Turner's partial correlation analysis showed a decrease, but not a drastic one, in the correlation between high school and ambition when scholastic ability was controlled.[18] The reduction was from .21 to .16 for boys and from .18 to .12 for girls.

The disagreement between these two sets of findings might be attributable to differences in measurement and analysis. However, it appears more reasonable to call attention to the probability that Ramsøy's *middle-class* schools were typically located in metropolitan areas. In this light, the two sets of findings are consistent in suggesting that (1) differential scholastic development is an important explanation for the effect of the high school, but (2) while this may be the total explanation in smaller communities, it is only a partial explanation in metropolitan areas.

Peer-group influence and motivation.—A second, sociologically appealing explanation would hold that student bodies in high schools of different population composition develop different subcultures, which in turn affect the motivation of the student to plan on college. Obviously, if scholastic development provides only a partial explanation for the effect of metropolitan high schools, there is a need for additional explanation. There is even some indication that peer-group influence may account for the dissimilar patterns discovered for metropolitan and non-metropolitan schools. Coleman found rural and small-town youth to be more parent-conforming and less peer-conforming than students living in metropolitan areas.[19] Again, however, adequate evaluation of the explanatory power of this factor requires a more direct analysis. The only report of such an analysis is provided by Turner.

Turner collected extensive data on those values "which can be translated into goals for the individual's behavior and those which the researches of others have suggested are linked to socioeconomic status." [20] From these he constructed a "class-value index" which showed a fairly

---

[17] This analysis is reported in John A. Michael, "High School Climates and Plans for Entering College," *Public Opinion Quarterly*, XXV (Winter, 1961), 585–95. See especially his discussion on p. 593.

[18] Turner, *op. cit.*, Table 11b, p. 59.

[19] *The Adolescent Society*, pp. 138–40.

[20] Turner, *op. cit.*, p. 66.

high correlation with ambition when family background was controlled.[21] The essential point is this: If the high school is the important remaining influence on these values, then the partial correlation between values and ambition should be reduced considerably when high school is controlled. But this did not occur. When the high school was added as a second control variable, this correlation was reduced only from .25 to .22 (for boys), and from .33 to .31 (for girls).[22] Apparently a major source of these values lies in factors indexed by neither the socioeconomic status of the student's father nor by the population composition of his high school.

This finding, of course, does not prove that the peer group is not an important source of influence on the student's motivation to go to college or to achieve high social position. It indicates only that this influence is not expressed through values of a certain kind, having to do with long-range, lifetime goals. It is quite possible that the high school, through the peer group, exerts an influence on other motivational factors. A likely candidate here may be the student's perception of what college life is like, of how enjoyable the experience is likely to be. As McDill and Coleman note, "For a teenager in a generally middle-class environment, college holds promise of such activities (as) campus social life, freedom from parental control, a shift to new friends, and all other social attributes of college." [23] In a generally working-class environment, on the other hand, these values and the expectations that college will fulfil them may not become a part of the student culture. It may be that influence by the peer group is expressed in terms of *short-range* values such as these.

Summary of explanatory mechanisms.—Quite an array of ideas and findings has been examined here, but the effort has been to show that these all fit together in suggesting an underlying pattern. At the risk of over-simplification, the suggested interplay of these different factors is represented diagramatically in Figure 1. To interpret this diagram, it may be best to start at the bottom. Whether or not students plan on college is seen as an immediate consequence of two "psychological" factors: their level of scholastic ability and certain "motivational" factors, as yet unknown. While both of these general factors are probably determined in part by experiences in other social contexts, important sources lying within the high school can be identified.

Much of the variation in scholastic ability occurs because the educational standards of high schools vary. Because educational standards vary, students in some schools develop their abilities to a higher level

---

[21] *Ibid.*, p. 91.

[22] *Ibid.*, Table 17, p. 94.

[23] McDill and Coleman, "High School Social Status," *op. cit.*, p. 918.

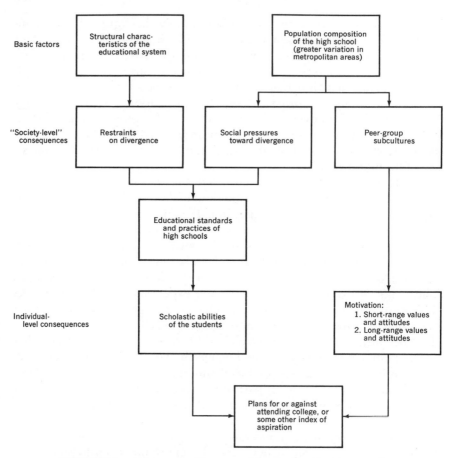

FIGURE 1   Schematic diagram of factors leading to a variation in the aspirations of students attending different high
schools.

than students in other schools. But the extent to which standards are divergent is, in turn, a consequence of the interplay of two other factors.
First, structural characteristics of the educational system (e.g., centralized or decentralized) can impose more or less severe *restraints* on this
divergence. In the United States these restraints will be strongest in
large metropolitan school districts, weak among isolated rural high
schools. Second, variation in the population composition of high schools
creates informal social pressures *toward* divergence. It is easier for
teachers to teach when the bulk of their students bring with them better
preparation for learning and greater willingness to cooperate with
school assignments. But the important point here is that those students
in generally middle-class schools who lack this background appear to be
carried along by the majority.

In more specific terms, existing research suggests that variation in scholastic development is an important explanation, that it is a *sufficient* explanation in smaller communities, but that among high schools located in large metropolitan areas it provides only a partial explanation. It is in large metropolitan areas, furthermore, that *both* structural restraints and informal social pressures should be strongest, at least in the United States.

Turning to the second explanatory mechanism, it seems likely that the adolescent subcultures which are typical of different kinds of high schools may have an important influence on the student's *motivation* to attend college. Available evidence indicates that this factor, if it operates at all, operates most strongly in metropolitan areas. There are at least two reasons why this might be so. First, since population composition should vary more widely in these areas, differences between adolescent subcultures should also be greater. Second, there is some suggestion, from Coleman, that students living in larger communities are more peer-conforming than students living in smaller communities.

However this may be, direct research into motivational factors and peer-group influences is quite limited. An attempt by Turner to locate these motivational factors with a set of values keyed to social class and long-range goals did not prove successful, but the hypothesis itself remains open.

A Study of Canadian Girls

During the late spring of 1962, questionnaires were administered to 1,701 girls in their final year at seventy high schools in western Canada.[24] Data were obtained that provided measures of family background and college aspirations.[25] In addition, high schools were classified according

---

[24] The girls were in their junior matriculation year in predominantly coeducational high schools. Completion of this year qualifies the student to enter college, although further high-school work leading to senior matriculation and college credit is possible. The year at which junior matriculation is granted varies from province to province. In Ontario and British Columbia it is granted at grade 12; in all other western provinces it is granted on completion of grade 11. The proportion of youth completing high school, and the proportion going on to college, is more similar to the United States in western Canada than in eastern Canada. For further discussion of the comparability of this sample with American students see my "Social Context and Educational Aspiration: Influence of High School and Community on College Plans" (Ph.D. dissertation, University of Washington, 1964), pp. 58–64.

[25] Father's occupation and education were used to classify students into four categories of family background, in the following way: (I) all fathers with at least some college education, whatever their occupation; (II) all other fathers with professional or managerial occupations, and all other fathers with clerical or sales occupations ex-

to population composition and the size of the community in which they were located.[26] While the Canadian educational system is quite similar to the American in most respects, there is one important difference. Administrative authority in Canadian education is much more centralized. This is particularly evident in the system of province-wide standardized examinations which determine the student's grades in all provinces except Ontario. This should result in less divergence in the standards and practices of individual high schools and a lower correlation between population composition and the scholastic abilities of the students.

The statistical procedure employed in this analysis is similar to the one used earlier to compare the findings of Wilson and Ramsøy, with one major exception. Instead of basing effect estimates on subsample proportions, the present procedure is derived in such a way as to give equal weight to each case.[27] This means that analysis is not so directly limited by the number of cases falling in each cell of the partial tables and also allows the addition of numerous control variables. As before, however, the resulting effect estimates can be interpreted as weighted averages of differences between proportions.

The effect of the high school on college aspirations, with family background controlled, is shown in Table 1. Attending a "high-status" school in comparison with one of "medium status" has a fairly strong effect on the student's aspirations (0.21), but there is almost no difference between "medium status" and "low status" schools (0.01). The effect of family background, standardized to be comparable to the dichotomous case,[28] is 0.24, or slightly more than the effect of the high school when the medium- and low-status categories are combined.

---

cept those with only grade-school educations; (III) all other clerical and sales workers, and all other blue-collar workers and farmers with at least some high-school education; (IV) all other blue-collar workers and farmers (i.e., those with only grade-school education).

[26] In each high school the percentage of girls completing questionnaires who were in the upper two family-background categories (see n. 25, above) defined three categories of high schools as follows: over 65 per cent; 33–64 per cent; less than 33 per cent. A community population of 200,000 was used to distinguish between "metropolitan" and "non-metropolitan" high schools.

[27] Coleman derives his procedure from a model of continuous time, discrete space stochastic processes. His strategy is to estimate effect parameters in such a way as to most accurately describe the observed subsample *proportions*. If, instead, one sets out to describe the distribution of individual *cases*, it turns out that effect parameters are best estimated by a weighted average of the separate proportion-differences $(p_i - p_j)$, where the weighting function is $(n_i n_j / n_i + n_j)$. For further discussion of this procedure see my "Multivariate Effect Analysis: Some Modifications and Extensions of Coleman's Work" (unpublished manuscript).

[28] See Coleman, *Introduction to Mathematical Sociology*, pp. 218–19.

TABLE 1
Proportion Planning on College by High-School Status and Family Background

FAMILY BACK-GROUND [a]	HIGH-SCHOOL STATUS [b]			EFFECT ESTIMATES	
	HIGH	MEDIUM	LOW		
High:					
I	0.71 (211)	0.45 (71)	0.48 (25)	High school: high vs. medium status	0.21
II	.47 (214)	.31 (134)	.32 (62)	Medium vs. low status	.01
III	.49 (59)	.19 (124)	.26 (184)	Family background (standardized to dichotomous form)	0.24
Low:					
IV	0.36 (42)	0.20 (143)	0.11 (227)		
Total	(526)	(472)	(498)		

[a] Measured by father's occupation and education.
[b] Proportion of students in family-background categories I and II.

This pattern of influence is somewhat different from that predicted on the basis of earlier work. The findings fit the predictions much better, however, when community size is taken into account. In Table 2 the effect of the high school is shown separately for metropolitan and non-

TABLE 2
Proportion Planning on College by High-School Status and Family Background for Metropolitan and Non-metropolitan Areas Separately

FAMILY BACK-GROUND	METROPOLITAN [a] HIGH SCHOOLS		NON-METROPOLITAN [b] HIGH SCHOOLS	
	HIGH STATUS	MEDIUM STATUS	MEDIUM STATUS	LOW STATUS
High:				
I	0.71 (211)	0.36 (28)	0.51 (43)	0.48 (25)
II	.47 (214)	.19 (31)	.35 (103)	.32 (62)
III	.49 (59)	.29 (38)	.14 (86)	.26 (184)
Low:				
IV	0.36 (42)	0.20 (25)	0.20 (118)	0.11 (227)
Total	(526)	(122)	(350)	(498)

[a] Effect estimate for high-school status, 0.25.
[b] Effect estimate for high-school status, 0.01.

metropolitan areas.[29] The relationship between community size and population composition is so pronounced that *all* of the high-status schools, but *none* of the low-status schools, were located in metropolitan areas. As a consequence, the only comparison possible among metropolitan schools is between high- and medium-status categories, while the only comparison possible among non-metropolitan schools is between medium- and low-status categories. Among the former, the effect of population composition is quite strong ($a_1 = 0.25$), while among the latter the effect is minimal ($a_1 = 0.01$). This finding is consistent with the interpretation that more centralized administration in Canada will discourage divergence among non-metropolitan high schools but that residential segregation in metropolitan areas will create even stronger pressures toward divergence.

The problem of further analysis is simplified somewhat by this finding. The only relationship that needs to be explained occurs among the metropolitan high schools. The two explanatory variables that can be investigated in this regard are scholastic ability and occupational values. Scholastic ability is defined in terms of the student's grade average, as determined by her performance on province-wide examinations.[30] As such, the present measure of ability should be more directly influenced by the educational program of the high school than the measures employed by Ramsøy and Turner. The occupational values used here represent a preference for "creativity" or "security." [31] This is very roughly similar to the "class-values" index Turner used. No measure was availa-

---

[29] For a discussion of the effects of community size evident in this table, see my "Community Influence on College Aspirations: An Empirical Evaluation of Explanatory Factors" (unpublished manuscript).

[30] There is, obviously, no universally agreed on definition of "scholastic ability." If performance in college is taken as the criterion with which to evaluate various instruments for "measuring" scholastic ability, then tests that depend strongly on scholastic achievement and prior learning have been shown to be better predictors than tests that are more "culture-free" (Lee J. Cronbach, *Essentials of Psychological Testing* [New York: Harper & Row, 1960]). The Canadian system of province-wide examinations should therefore provide a good measure of this kind of ability. In Ontario, province-wide examinations were used until recently but are no longer employed. It can only be assumed, therefore, that grade averages are still meaningful when comparing schools. Students were classified as high or low in scholastic ability, depending on whether or not their grades were 70 or above. This criterion gives roughly equal distributions in all provinces and is similar to distinguishing between A's and B's and all lower grades in the United States.

[31] The statements were "a job which will permit me to be creative and original" and "a job which will enable me to look forward to a stable, secure future." Girls choosing "creativity" more frequently planned on college. Several studies of high-school students support this finding. See, e.g., Harry Beilin, "The Pattern of Postponability and Its Relation to Social Class Mobility," *Journal of Social Psychology,*

TABLE 3
Summary of the Effect of Scholastic Ability and Values on College Plans

INDEPENDENT VARIABLE	DEPENDENT VARIABLE	CONTROL VARIABLES	EFFECT ESTIMATE
Scholastic ability	College plans	Values and family background	0.27
Values	College plans	Scholastic ability and family background	.19
Family background	College plans	Values and scholastic ability	0.26

ble of short-range values which, according to earlier discussion, are more likely to be a result of peer-group influence.

Since the partial tables on which this analysis is based are rather cumbersome, the effect estimates are summarized in Tables 3 and 4.[32] In Table 3, with family background controlled, ability and values both show fairly strong relationships with college plans. The effect of ability is about as great as the effect of background, while the effect of values is somewhat less than this. There is good reason for suspecting, in other words, that either of these "psychological" factors could provide an explanation for the higher aspirations of the students attending the high-status metropolitan schools.

With family background controlled, the high school has a pronounced effect on scholastic ability (0.30) (see Table 4). With ability *controlled,* the effect of the high school on college plans is reduced, from $a_1 = 0.22$ to $a_1 = 0.15$, a reduction of about one-third.[33] Or, in other words, the greater scholastic ability of students attending the high-status metropolitan schools is a *partial* explanation for their higher aspirations.

Whatever the explanation may be for the remaining effect of the high

XLIV (August, 1956), 33–48; Harry K. Schwarzweller, "Value-Orientations in Educational and Occupational Choices," *Rural Sociology,* XXIV (September, 1959), 246–56, and "Values and Occupational Choice," *Social Forces,* XXIX (December, 1960), 126–35.

[32] The partial tables from which these summaries are taken are similar in appearance to Tables 1 and 2. Copies of the full tables will be supplied by the author to anyone interested. Inspection of the partial tables indicates no evidence of interaction effects. At the same time, the relatively small number of girls attending the two medium-status metropolitan schools in the sample dictates caution in basing conclusions on these results. Analysis of each metropolitan school separately, however, shows consistent similarities *within* each category (high status and medium status) and consistent differences between each category. See my "Social Context and Educational Aspiration," *op. cit.,* pp. 87–89.

[33] Grade averages were not available for all girls, so the effect of high school on college plans was recalculated for this smaller sample. This figure is slightly lower than the effect estimate for the full sample.

TABLE 4
Summary of Explanatory Power of Scholastic Ability and Values
for Effect of High-School Status on College Plans
(Metropolitan High Schools Only)

INDEPENDENT VARIABLE	DEPENDENT VARIABLE	CONTROL VARIABLES	EFFECT ESTIMATE
High-school status	Scholastic ability	Family background	0.30
High-school status	College plans	Family background	.22[a]
High-school status	College plans	Family background and scholastic ability	.15
High-school status	Values	Family background	.10
High-school status	College plans	Family background	.25
High-school status	College plans	Family background and values	0.24

[a] Grade averages were not available for all girls, so the effect of high-school status on college plans was calculated separately for the full sample and for the smaller sample of girls for whom grade averages *were* available.

school, the present findings concur with Turner's in indicating that occupational values do not tap the important factors. The effect of the high school on these values is slight (0.10), and controlling for values does not appreciably reduce the effect of high-school status on college plans (the reduction is from 0.25 to 0.24).[34]

Concluding Remarks

The findings from the Canadian study accord very well with the predictions advanced on the basis of interpretation of other research. This is not altogether surprising—the framework of ideas presented here was developed after the fact, on the basis of all available information. What is not ad hoc, as a matter of fact, is the facility with which Turner's findings fit into this framework, since his work did not become known to the author until the framework presented here was fully developed. However, what is important is that the somewhat diverse findings of five independent pieces of research do fit together in a consistent pattern. The present framework thus provides an explicit target for future research.

There are serious weaknesses in the design of all the research examined here. The problems of inferring causality from survey data are especially severe with studies of social context. Where it is necessary to

[34] These estimates are for the full sample.

infer contextual characteristics on the basis of individual characteristics, it is essential that the measure of individual characteristics employed be precise and that this measure have the same meaning in different groups. In terms of the research discussed here, this means that, first, there must be enough categories of socioeconomic status to reduce intra-category variation to an effective minimum. For example, "middle class" might include both doctors and sales clerks; if the middle-class students at one school were mostly children of doctors, while at another school they were mostly children of sales clerks, the magnitude of the bias is obvious. There is some evidence that use of four categories provides satisfactory precision. Wilson carried out his analysis first with four categories of father's occupation, then with nine, then with various detailed combinations of father's and mother's education, without appreciably changing his findings.[35]

The second requirement, that the measure mean the same thing in the different groups, points to potentially more serious weaknesses. Socioeconomic status has been used in this research to "control" for family background. But there is considerable evidence that other aspects of the family, such as mobility orientation, values, and child-rearing practices, are also related to the aspirations of the children.[36] It is quite plausible to argue, for example, that working-class families living in neighborhoods where their children go to predominantly middle-class schools are not the same as other working-class families. These families may be especially concerned that their children "get ahead." At the same time, it has been shown that middle-class students attending working-class schools have *lower* aspirations than other middle-class students and that this "downward" pull is as strong as the above mentioned "upward" pull. To argue that middle-class families move to working-class neighborhoods in order to inhibit the opportunities of their children is much less plausible. The fact remains, however, that family characteristics other than socioeconomic status can and should be controlled in future research.

The best conclusion possible given the existing information, therefore,

---

[35] Wilson, "Residential Segregation," *op. cit.*, pp. 839–44.

[36] See, e.g., David J. Bordua, "Educational Aspirations and Parental Stress on College," *Social Forces*, XXXVIII (March, 1960), 262–69; Elizabeth D. Cohen, "Parental Factors in Educational Mobility" (Ph.D. dissertation, Harvard University, 1958); Glen H. Elder, Jr., *Adolescent Achievement and Mobility Aspirations* (Chapel Hill, N.C.: Institute for Research in Social Science, 1963), and "Parental Power Legitimation and Its Effect on the Adolescent," *Sociometry*, XXVI (March, 1963), 50–65; Joseph A. Kahl, "Educational and Occupational Aspirations of 'Common Man' Boys," *Harvard Educational Review*, XXIII (Summer, 1953), 186–203; Wilbur L. Layton, "Socioeconomic Status and After-High School Plans," in Ralph F. Berdie, *After High School, What?* (Minneapolis: University of Minnesota Press, 1954), pp. 178–92.

is that the framework of ideas developed in the first two sections is quite reasonable. To summarize the main findings: (1) The population composition of a high school does have an important effect on the aspirations of its students, but a much stronger effect in large cities than in smaller communities. (2) One important, but (at least in metropolitan areas) partial explanation for this effect is the differential success of high schools in developing the scholastic abilities of their students. (3) The failure of scholastic ability to explain all of the effects of metropolitan high schools points to the existence of other explanations, such as the influence of the peer group, but occupational or social-class values do not provide this explanation.

8. SENSE OF OBLIGATION TO HIGH SCHOOL ACTIVITIES AS RELATED TO SCHOOL SIZE AND MARGINALITY OF STUDENT *

Edwin P. Willems

Loyalty, commitment, individual responsibility, or what is here called "sense of obligation," all refer to a set of dispositions that parents, teachers, and group leaders commonly hope children will acquire during their developmental sequences. The concept, sense of obligation to school activities, grew out of an earlier study (Willems, 1964a) in which high school juniors were asked in personal interviews, and with reference to selected nonclass activities, "What, if any, were for you real reasons for or pulls toward attending?" Responses to this standardized query were codable into three general classes. One class, called "*own forces toward participation*" (Willems, 1964a; Willems & Willems,

* *Child Development*, 1967, *38*, 1247–1259. Copyright 1967, by the Society for Research in Child Development, Inc. Gathering of data for the 1961 phase was supported by Cooperative Research Project No. 594, Office of Education, USPHS, with Roger G. Barker and Paul V. Gump as principal investigators. The 1965 phase was supported by a Public Health Service Fellowship (5 FI MH-15, 824–03) from the National Institute of Mental Health, USPHS. Completion of data analyses and work on the paper itself were supported by a grant from the Texas Department of Mental Health and Mental Retardation and a grant in aid of research from Rice University. The author wishes to thank Don Des Jarlais, who helped with data analyses and made suggestions on the manuscript. A shorter version of this paper was presented to the biennial meeting of the Society for Research in Child Development, April 1, 1967.

1965), indicated the students' own desires, wishes, and attractions to attend the activities, for example, "I wanted to go," "I like to dance." The second class, called *"induced* forces toward participation," indicated clear and explicit external pressures to attend, or feedback from the environment encouraging attendance and discouraging nonattendance, for example, "The homeroom teacher talked me into it," "I was required to go," "We had to pay a fine if we didn't go." These two classes were of primary theoretical interest at that time. The remaining responses, less clearly specifiable, were seen as residual and uncodable, and only later did it become apparent that they indicated a ubiquitous personal disposition to attend and participate in school activities, that is, *sense of obligation* to school activities. The present paper reports the analysis of those data and a replication of the procedures 4 years later.

SENSE OF OBLIGATION

As it is used here, sense of obligation is a personal feeling of "I ought to . . ." or "I must . . ." with reference to attending, participating in, or helping with a group activity, with the stipulation that the personal feeling or disposition be reliably identifiable in a response protocol. Sense of obligation has an external social referent in the form of an activity or group, but the emphasis here is upon the subjective side, upon the person's report of his obligation or commitment, in which he feels that his attendance, participation, and help are required for the success or continued functioning of the activity or group. For example, when a student reports, "I should help with the magazine sale; the class needs money," his report reflects the social referent (the magazine sale) and his feeling that he *ought* to take part for the good of the class, that is, he feels a sense of obligation.

Emile Durkheim devoted much of his thought and writing to the emergence of "subjective sense of obligation," or simply, "sense of obligation" (see Parsons, 1949, especially pp. 376–408). For Durkheim, although it was an important concept for explaining the constraint of, and obedience to, social norms in a society, sense of obligation was implicit, subjective, and too diffuse to measure directly and empirically. Although he speculated about the conditions of sense of obligation, Durkheim did not specify just what kinds of social, environmental, or personal factors influence it. Thus, although the present studies did not derive from Durkheim's theory, they can be seen as attempts to study one set of conditions and correlates of sense of obligation that Durkheim never made clear. Further comments concerning possible relations to Durkheim's thinking will be made in the discussion.

ENVIRONMENT AND PERSONS

The more immediate theoretical context for the present studies is an amplification of Barker's (1960; 1964) theory concerning the relations between school size and the behavior and experience of students. The argument goes as follows.

For a given period of time, such as a semester, and for a given environment, such as a school, two variables can be specified: (a) the number of activities occurring, and (b) the number of students available to participate in the activities. The number of available students (S), relative to the number of activities (A), is an attribute of the institutional environment quantifiable in terms of the ratio, S/A.

The presence and participation of students are necessary conditions for the survival and continued functioning of school activities; without participants, activities will cease to function. Viewed from the level of the activities, the issue is one of maintaining harmony or fit between (a) the needs of activities, that is, tasks to be performed and obligations to be filled, and (b) the behavior of the available participants. Conceptually, the mechanism that maintains this harmony is feedback from the environment to potential participants encouraging participation and discouraging nonparticipation in the activities. The individual participant experiences this feedback in the form of external pressures, or *induced forces* (Lewin, 1951; Willems, 1964a; 1965) toward participation in activities, and these forces will increase in number as the number of potential participants, or S/A, diminishes. Willems (1964a; 1965) has reported data supporting this expectation.

The crucial step for present purposes is that, under conditions of low S/A and the impingement of many pressures or induced forces in the form of invitations, demands, exhortations, and requirements to participate, "greater functional importance" within the activity and "more responsibility" are ascribed to each participant (Barker, 1964, p. 25). The personal, subjective, dispositional accompaniment of the induced forces and ascribed functional importance and responsibility will be a heightened sense of obligation as defined above.

It is common to assume that due to differences in motives and/or abilities, which may derive from either genetic or experiential sources, some persons are better suited than others for certain tasks, responsibilities, and situations. Following Willems (1964a; 1965), in the present studies the *marginal student* is one who is relatively unsuited for school life and its activities, while the *regular student* is better suited. These labels are descriptive and represent little commitment to any particular theory of personality. If marginal students are not only relatively unsuited for school life and its activities, but are also *seen* as relatively unsuited, then (a) they will receive less feedback (fewer induced forces) toward participation, and consequently, (b) they will report a lowered sense of obligation, and (c) they will participate less frequently in responsible functions than regular students.

Finally, S/A relates differentially to the two types of students. Where S/A is low and participants are in short supply, maintenance of the activities and harmony between activity needs and individual behavior will require the participation of persons who might otherwise be seen as unsuitable or marginal. Where S/A is high and the supply of participants is large, the participation of these marginal students will not be so necessary, and (a) they will experience little, if any, feedback; (b) they will report little, if any, sense of obligation; and (c) they will participate infrequently in the responsible functions of activities. Willems (1964a; 1965) found the strong interaction between S/A and type of student in the number of induced forces reported, and Gump and Friesen (1964) and Willems (1965) found the expected interaction in the number of activities in which students had responsible functions. The main hypotheses explored in the present studies are (a) that sense of obligation, a consequence of feedback to the person, is also an interactive function of S/A and type of student; and (b) that sense of obligation, along with the feedback, mediates between S/A and participation in activities.

One further observed property of high schools is pertinent here. Barker and Barker (1964) studied 13 northeast Kansas high schools in detail, including those in the present studies. The schools ranged in size from 35 to 2,287 students, and the Barkers found that as size of school (S) increased, the number of nonclass activities (A) also increased, but at a much slower rate. The result was that as school size increased, S/A also increased, yielding a rank-difference correlation of .97 between school size and S/A. In other words, as size increased, the number of students available per activity also increased. Thus, the expectations for S/A discussed above can also be stated in terms of school size.

Method

The design of both studies was orthogonal and two-by-two, with the following variables: (a) marginal and regular students in (b) large and small schools. Data on sense of obligation were obtained from 40 students in 1961 and 80 in 1965, with equal Ns per cell in both cases. The study in 1961 included data on own forces (personal attraction), induced forces (external pressures), and sense of obligation. The study in 1965 was a replication of the earlier one, extended to include data on actual frequency, range, and depth of participation in nonclass activities.

SCHOOLS

In the 1961 phase, there was one large school with 2,287 students and four small schools ranging in size from 83 to 151 students. In 1965, there was again one large school with 2,015 students, but five small schools ranging in size from 81 to 183 students. All schools were located in the same northeast Kansas area. Students in their junior years were Ss. Table 1 summarizes the numbers of juniors and numbers of nonclass activities open to juniors during a standard semester for both studies. From the S/A column in the table it can be seen that in both cases the large school had between seven and nine times as many juniors per activity as the average of the small schools.

SUBJECTS

The procedure for preselecting marginal and regular junior students was entirely empirical, and was identical for both studies. From published research on factors that characterize students who do not complete high school (see Thomas, 1954), the following profile was selected as predictive of a tendency to drop out of school: (a) IQ below 99, (b) two grades of "D" or lower the previous semester, (c) father in a nonprofessional and nonmanagerial occupation, (d) father who did not finish grade 10, and (e) mother who did not finish grade 12. This profile was assumed to identify students who were poorly suited for school life; they were marginal students for the studies. Regular students had IQ's above 105, no grades lower than "C" the previous semester, father in a professional or managerial occupation, and father and mother who finished grades 10 and 12, respectively.

TABLE 1
Number of Juniors (S), Number of Nonclass
Activities (A), and S/A for 1961 and 1965

	N of JUNIORS	N of ACTIVITIES	S/A
Large school:			
1961	794	189	4.20
1965	702	211	3.33
Small schools (average):			
1961	22.7	48.5	.47
1965	26.4	61.2	.43

Sampling pools of marginal and regular students were identified from school records. Final sampling involved assigning serial numbers to the juniors so identified, and selecting, without replacement, equal numbers of males and females for each of the four cells in the design: small school regular, small school marginal, large school regular, and large school marginal. Equal numbers of males and females were selected because Gump and Friesen (1964) observed sex differences in rates of actual participation in activities. Forty Ss, 10 per group, were selected in 1961, and 80 Ss, 20 per group, were selected in 1965.

ACTIVITIES

Surveys were made of all the nonclass activities available to the selected juniors during the period of one semester. From these surveys, activities were chosen from each of the schools so that each activity finally chosen had as close a counterpart as possible in all the schools. The selected activities were all voluntary, that is, attendance was not required, and they had all occurred at least once during the standard semester. Table 2 shows the activities chosen for each of the schools in 1961 and 1965. Although in some cases superficial similarities break down, most of the activities across any given row of Table 2 are similar in type or variety.

GATHERING AND CODING OF DATA

One interviewer, the same throughout the period of each study, met the selected Ss in standardized individual interviews. Following introductory remarks about the ubiquity of nonclass activities, the following data were obtained.

One selected activity was mentioned at a time, and S was asked the following simple open-ended question about the activity: "What, if any, were for you real reasons for or pulls toward attending this activity?" The Ss were asked to report such "reasons or pulls" whether or not they had in fact attended. Complete, verbatim records were taken of Ss' responses, which included a wide array, for example, "Those things are fun," "My Latin teacher talked me into it," "I like to dance," "I had to; they needed girls," "It sounded interesting," "We were all expected to go."

The set of categories indicating sense of obligation, identical for both studies, was as follows:

1. Statement of felt obligation or expectation to participate in an activity. Includes the general "I should," or "I ought to . . ." for example, "We all ought to take part," "Band members were expected to go," "I felt I should."

TABLE 2
Five Activities in Each School for Which Ss Reported Sense of Obligation

SMALL SCHOOLS (1961)					LARGE SCHOOL (1961)
A	B	C	D	E	
Home basketball game	Home basketball game	Home basketball game	Home basketball game	—	Home basketball game
Post-game dance	Post-game dance	Home-coming dance	Post-game dance	—	Post-game dance
Junior play	Junior play	Junior play	Junior play	—	Talent show
Magazine sale	Magazine sale	Hat sale	Junior car wash	—	Xmas card sale
Pep club outdoor rally	Carnival & chili supper	Pep club parade	Band parade	—	Home-coming parade

SMALL SCHOOLS (1965)					LARGE SCHOOL (1965)
Home basketball game	Home basketball game	Home basketball game	Home basketball game	Home basketball game	Home basketball game
Home-coming dance	Halloween dance	Home-coming dance	Home-coming dance	Home-coming dance	Home-coming dance
Junior play	Junior play	Junior play	Junior play	Christmas program	Junior play
Magazine sale	Trash haul	Car wash	Car wash	Magazine sale	Car wash
Outdoor pep rally	Band parade	Home-coming rally	Home-coming parade	Football bonfire	Home-coming parade

2. Statement of general loyalty, commitment, or responsibility to the group or groups sponsoring the activity. Restricted to general statements (excludes specific type of support or help) for example, "It was a junior class activity, and I'm a junior," "The least we can do is support the school," "To support the class."

3. Statement of more specific obligation to support, help, or aid in maintaining the activity or the sponsoring group, for example, "The treasury needed money," "I thought it would bring the class closer together," "To uphold the name of the school," "They had so few girls already."

4. Statement of previously determined duty, job, involvement, or re-

sponsibility in the activity or group, for example, "I was in the skit," "I was in charge of it," "I was responsible for the money."

5. Statement not codable into categories 1 through 4, for example, "I like dances," "The Latin teacher talked me into it," "They have two a year."

For the study in 1961, two independent judges, neither of whom was involved in the planning or hypotheses of the study, analyzed unlabeled protocols of both large- and small-school Ss. One-fourth of the protocols were exchanged for a check of agreement, and the two judges obtained 84 per cent agreement on the placing of specific responses into specific categories. The two judges and the investigator found that most of the disagreements resulted from misunderstanding of American high school students' language on the part of one judge, a native of Turkey.

In 1965, two judges, the investigator and an assistant who had no prior knowledge of the study or its expectations, coded 25 per cent of the responses for agreement. Agreement was 92 per cent on the placing of specific responses into specific categories, including category 5, and 98 per cent on placing responses into categories 1 through 4 as against category 5. The assistant then coded all responses, unlabeled as to schools or students.

The total number of responses coded into categories 1 through 4, summed across the five activities, was an S's sense-of-obligation score. Thus, corresponding to the intuitive definition mentioned earlier, magnitude of sense of obligation was operationally defined by an external referent (a specific activity), the interview question, and coding categories delimiting a subset of the students' responses concerning the activity.

Results

Figure 1 displays the mean scores on sense of obligation for regular and marginal students in 1961 and 1965. As can be seen from Figure 1, there was strong agreement in the results of the two studies, not only in general patterns, but in terms of absolute values on the response scales. Overall, small-school students reported more sense of obligation than large-school students in both studies. In 1961 ($F = 30.32$, $p < .001$, 1 df) and 1965 ($F = 29.45$, $p < .001$, 1 df), analyses of variance yielded significant main effects for school size. However, inspection of the figure suggests that most of the school size relation was due to the differential responses of the marginal students, and the interaction statistics were significant in 1961 ($F = 4.85$, $p < .05$, 1 df) and 1965 ($F = 12.19$, $p < .001$, 1 df). In other words, as expected, the marginal students in the small schools reported as much sense of obligation as their regular

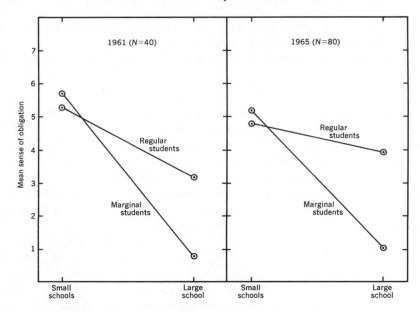

FIGURE 1   Mean numbers of responses indicating sense of
obligation in 1961 and 1965.

schoolmates, while the marginal students in the large school were a group
apart. In fact, in 1961, five of the ten marginal students in the large
school reported no codable instance of sense of obligation at all; and in
1965, eight of the twenty reported none. This strong agreement of results
from different samples of Ss, different sample sizes, 4 years apart, suggests that sense of obligation, as operationalized here, is a stable and
replicable phenomenon.

It has been observed elsewhere (Gump & Friesen, 1964; Willems,
1965) that school size and type of student produce differences in the frequency, range, and depth of participation in activities. Students in small
schools, including marginal students, have positions of leadership and
responsibility in more activities than students in large schools, especially
marginal students in large schools. Thus, it might be argued that the
small-school students in the present studies were simply describing their
frequent behavioral instances of leadership and responsibility and that
the pattern of sense of obligation can be accounted for by the differences in participation rate. If this argument were tenable, then the observed differences in sense of obligation should disappear when controlled for frequency .of participation in positions of leadership and
responsibility. Data were available to test this hypothesis.

In 1961 Gump and Friesen and in 1965 Willems obtained data on the number of activities in which each S had positions of leadership and responsibility. Examples of such positions were chairmanship of meetings; committee membership; planning of activities; performances at athletic, dramatic, and forensic events; that is, the positions that were crucial to the functioning of activities. The number of such leadership functions, called "performances," in all nonclass activities occurring during the standard semester, was used as a control, or covariate, in analyses of covariance for the data on sense of obligation from 1961 and 1965.

Figure 2 shows the mean sense-of-obligation scores adjusted for the numbers of performances. Statistically, the main effect for school size remained intact through the adjustment in 1961 ($F = 6.46$, $p < .05$, 1 df) and 1965 ($F = 11.30$, $p < .005$, 1 df). Again, as one would expect from inspection of Figure 2, the interaction effect remained intact through the adjustment in 1961 ($F = 15.30$, $p < .001$, 1 df) and 1965 ($F = 12.93$, $p < .001$, 1 df). The principal result of the adjustment in both studies was a tendency to equalize the picture for regular students in schools differing in size while leaving intact the differences between marginal students. In other words, the principal impact of school size appears to be upon marginal students.

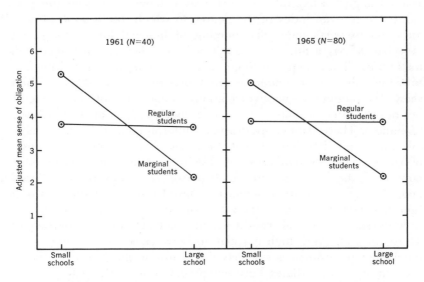

FIGURE 2   Mean numbers of responses indicating sense of obligation in 1961 and 1965, adjusted for numbers of performances.

TABLE 3
Product-Moment Correlations among Number of Responses
Indicating Sense of Obligation, Number of Own Forces,
Number of Induced Forces, and Number of Performances
(1965 Ss, N = 80)

	SENSE OF OBLIGATION	OWN FORCES	INDUCED FORCES	N OF PERFORMANCES
Sense of obligation	—	.20	.77[a]	.68[a]
Own forces	—	—	.13	.14
Induced forces	—	—	—	.58[a]

[a] $p < .01$.

Sense of obligation appears to be dependably and predictably related to school size and type of student, but data were available on several other correlates that further clarify its theoretical and empirical status. For the five activities used in the 1965 study, Willems (1965) has reported data on the number of own forces and induced forces each S reported toward participation, and the number of activities in which he had performances. The number of own forces, for example, "I just wanted to go," "I like to dance," "It was a chance to do something new," can be seen as an index of the degree to which the Ss were personally attracted to participate. The number of induced forces, for example, "We had to pay a fine if we didn't go," "The homeroom teacher talked me into it," "I was required to go," can be seen as an index of the degree to which they were under external pressure to participate. Table 3 shows the product-moment correlations among sense of obligation, number of own forces, number of induced forces, and number of actual performances. These data support several interpretations. First, the nonsignificance and low correlation between own forces and sense of obligation suggests that sense of obligation is not simply a function of how much the Ss wanted to attend personally attractive activities. Second, the high correlation between induced forces and sense of obligation, that is, the highest in the table, suggests that sense of obligation is a function of external pressures, or feedback toward participation. Third, the relatively high correlation between sense of obligation and number of performances suggests that sense of obligation is a personal disposition that mediates between pressures to participate and actual participation. This interpretation is enhanced by the fact that the correlational sequence from induced forces to sense of obligation to performances brackets higher correlations than the direct relationship between induced forces and performances.

Discussion

Two studies, 4 years apart, indicated that high school students with pre-selected and precontrolled similarities reported markedly different magnitudes of sense of obligation in different environments. Sense of obligation was defined as the personal feeling of "I ought to . . ." or "I must. . . ," that is, a personal feeling of constraint, with reference to attending, participating in, or helping with a group activity. Number of students available per activity, a close correlate of school size, had no marked effect upon regular students, especially when their reports of sense of obligation were statistically controlled for frequencies of actual participation in positions of leadership in activities. The picture was quite different for marginal students, selected for relatively poor suitability for school and its affairs. In the small schools, where there were relatively few students available for activities, these marginal students reported a sense of obligation that was similar in magnitude to their regular schoolmates. In the large school, the marginal students were a group apart and reported little, if any, sense of obligation. In fact, it would appear that the small-school marginal students were not experientially and behaviorally marginal, while their large-school counterparts were a group of relative outsiders.

Several issues remain to be discussed, the first of which is the tenability of the school size hypothesis. Each investigation involved one large school, and in each case the large school was located in an urban area, while the small schools were located in small, rural towns. It might be argued that rural-urban differences, rather than school size, account for the present findings. Two sources of information bear directly on the tenability and generality of the school size explanation. One source is a study by Campbell (1964), who asked students on questionnaires about reasons for attending activities, and focused on what he called "personal responsibility" (p. 144), a concept very similar to sense of obligation. Campbell compared the numbers of responses indicating personal responsibility reported by students (a) in a small, locally circumscribed high school; (b) in a larger consolidated high school located in a small rural town; and (c) in a larger, locally circumscribed high school. The crucial factor in Campbell's study is that all three of the schools were located in relatively small rural towns. He found reliable differences in personal responsibility between students in the small local school and both of the two other larger schools, suggesting strong support for the generality of the school size hypothesis, and weighing against rural-urban differences as an explanation.

Another source of information concerning the tenability of the size hypothesis is the growing body of literature demonstrating effects of size of social units. In laboratory problem-solving groups (Thomas & Fink, 1963; Willems, 1964b), in commercial and industrial organizations (Indik, 1963, 1965; Porter & Lawler, 1965), and in communities (Barker, 1960; Barker & Barker, 1961; Wright, 1961), there is consistent evidence that as size, that is, number of persons, of the unit increases, punctuality, attendance, identification with the group, and other indexes of participation, decrease. All of these variables can be seen as behavioral indicators of obligation.

A second issue is the present status of the concept, sense of obligation. What is available at present is a set of operations and categories that produce a stable, replicable phenomenon. Second, it appears that sense of obligation is identifiable, specifiable, and measurable, within the limits of the procedures. Third, the procedures produce a phenomenon that seems to imbed itself in a network of predictable variables. Fourth, sense of obligation as measured here appears to make a difference in what students do; it appears to predictably mediate certain relationships between the person and his environment. Thus, Barker's theory concerning the relations among S/A, type of person, and sense of obligation, with its support in the present data, explicates one set of conditions that generate what Durkheim called "subjective sense of obligation to social norms." With the specific institutional variables, group activities, and types of students as referents, the present context is much more restricted and situational than Durkheim's societal context, but such specificity enhances measurability and need not detract from possible theoretical articulation. For example, it is consistent with both Durkheim's view and the present adaptation of Barker's view to postulate that induced forces, or environmental feedback, (a) *define* the person's social obligation for him and *direct* him to it and (b) *inform* him of possible consequences of his actions in the form of sanctions and rewards. As a result of this definition, direction, and potential return, an internalized, subjective disposition, that is, sense of obligation, is shaped. If this mode of theorizing is tenable, then the possible cumulative, long-range personality and social learning effect of experiences in small and large groups becomes an important research question.

References

Barker, R. G. Ecology and motivation. In M. R. Jones (Ed.), *Nebraska symposium on motivation: 1960*. Lincoln: University of Nebraska Press, 1960. Pp. 1–49.

Barker, R. G. Ecological units. In R. G. Barker and P. V. Gump, *Big school, small school.* Stanford, Calif.: Stanford University Press, 1964. Pp. 11–28.

Barker, R. G., and Barker, Louise S. The psychological ecology of old people in Midwest, Kansas, and Yoredale, Yorkshire. *Journal of Gerontology,* 1961, *16*, 144–149.

Barker, R. G., and Barker, Louise S. Structural characteristics. In R. G. Barker and P. V. Gump, *Big school, small school.* Stanford, Calif.: Stanford University Press, 1964. Pp. 41–63.

Campbell, W. J. Some effects of high school consolidation. In R. G. Barker and P. V. Gump, *Big school, small school.* Stanford, Calif.: Stanford University Press, 1964. Pp. 139–153.

Gump, P. V., and Friesen, W. V. Participation in nonclass settings. In R. G. Barker and P. V. Gump, *Big school, small school.* Stanford, Calif.: Stanford University Press, 1964. Pp. 75–93.

Indik, B. P. Some effects of organization size on member attitudes and behavior. *Human Relations,* 1963, *16*, 369–384.

Indik, B. P. Organization size and member participation: some empirical tests of alternative explanations. *Human Relations,* 1965, *18*, 339–350.

Lewin, K. *Field theory in social science.* New York: Harper & Row, 1951.

Parsons, T. *The structure of social action.* Glencoe, Ill.: Free Press, 1949.

Porter, L. W., and Lawler, E. E. III. Properties of organization structure in relation to job attitudes and job behavior. *Psychological Bulletin,* 1965, *64*, 23–51.

Thomas, E. J., and Fink, C. F. Effects of group size. *Psychological Bulletin,* 1963, *60*, 371–384.

Thomas, R. J. An empirical study of high school drop-outs in regard to ten possibly related factors. *Journal of Educational Sociology,* 1954, *28*, 11–18.

Willems, E. P. Forces toward participation in behavior settings. In R. G. Barker and P. V. Gump, *Big school, small school.* Stanford, Calif.: Stanford University Press, 1964. Pp. 115–135. (a)

Willems, E. P. Review of research. In R. G. Barker and P. V. Gump, *Big school, small school.* Stanford, Calif.: Stanford University Press, 1964. Pp. 29–37.(b)

Willems, E. P. Participation in behavior settings in relation to three variables: size of behavior settings, marginality of persons, and sensitivity to audiences. Unpublished doctoral dissertation, University of Kansas, 1965.

Willems, E. P., and Willems, Gwendolyn, J. Comparative validity of data yielded by three methods. *Merrill-Palmer Quarterly,* 1965, *11*, 65–71.

Wright, H. F. The city-town project: a study of children in communities differing in size. Interim research report, University of Kansas, 1961.

9. CONFLICTING GROUP MEMBERSHIP: A STUDY OF PARENT-PEER GROUP CROSS-PRESSURES*

Bernard C. Rosen

Multiple group membership, particularly in heterogeneous societies, often carries with it the possibility that the individual will belong to groups with mutually conflicting normative systems.[1] Since each group seeks to transmit and enforce its own particular norms and values, the individual whose membership groups conflict is likely to be caught between the cross-pressures of contradictory group expectations and role prescriptions.

This paper is a study of the influence of two membership groups on the attitude of a group of adolescents, many of whom find themselves in a cross-pressure situation. The membership groups with which we are here concerned are among the most important to which the adolescent belongs: the *family*, his first membership group and one which plays an important role in the socialization process; and the *peer* group, the group in which the adolescent in particular finds many of his gratifications. Both groups exert pressures upon the adolescent. Frequently these pressures are mutually sustaining, but in some areas they may be in conflict, demanding from the adolescent patterns of thought and behavior which are mutually incompatible. For many adolescents one of these areas is religion.[2] In this paper we shall examine the conflicting expectations that familial and peer groups have concerning one facet of the adolescent's religious orientation. Our task is to examine the relationship between the adolescent's religious attitude and that of his membership

* *American Sociological Review*, 1955, 20, 155–161. Reprinted with permission of the author and the American Sociological Association.

---

[1] For a systematic analysis of the possibility of multiple group membership in modern societies and its consequences for the individual see T. Newcomb, *Social Psychology*, New York: Dryden, 1950, Ch. 15; and M. Sherif, *An Outline of Social Psychology*, New York: Harper, 1948, Ch. 5.

[2] It is often in adolescence that the individual first questions the religious beliefs and practices accepted unquestioningly by him in his childhood and often taught to him by his parents. See A. B. Hollingshead, *Elmtown's Youth*, New York: Wiley, 1949, Ch. 10.

groups, to determine what this relationship is when the groups are de-fined as reference groups, and to evaluate the relative influence of these groups upon the adolescent in cases where their expectations conflict.

Research Procedure

SAMPLES AND TECHNIQUES

The data for this study were collected in a small upper New York State city. The subjects are fifty adolescents—the entire universe of Jewish high school age boys and girls in the city: a fact of some importance in that it considerably facilitated charting the pressures, attractions, and structure of the adolescent's peer-clique group.

Adolescents were first questioned in unstructured interviews in order to familiarize the investigator with the formal and informal groups. Strategic adult informants, particularly youth activities leaders, and a sample of parents were also interviewed. In addition the investigator observed the adolescents at school and at play as a nonparticipant observer for about a year. At the end of the year the subjects were reinterviewed. This time a structured interview schedule was used.

INDEX OF GROUP MEMBERSHIP

Before the relative influence of the conflicting groups could be examined, it was necessary to locate the membership groups and to delineate an area in which there were conflicting norms and expectations. Information about the familial [3] group was secured from the adolescent and from a sub-sample of parents. The latter were interviewed in order to check upon the teen-agers' reports. The peer group with which we are here concerned is not the general category of the adolescent's age-mates, but only those who form his own particular sub-group or clique. In unstructured interviews adolescents were asked to describe the groupings or cliques among the Jewish adolescents of the community. A list of the names of every Jewish adolescent in town was handed to the respondent, and he was asked to tell us with whom these adolescents most frequently associated. These data were buttressed by information gained through nonparticipant observation over a period of a year. At the end

---

[3] The religious norm of the familial group is here defined as expectations of the parents, since in most families in our culture the norm is set by the parents. The terms parental group and familial group will be used here interchangeably, although it is recognized that the adolescent's membership group is the familial group (i.e. parents and siblings) and not the parental dyad.

of the year each respondent was asked to list the persons among his age-mates, both Jewish and non-Jewish, with whom he most often associated. Through combining these three sources of information we were able to locate each adolescent in a particular peer group.

The issue about which there are conflicting expectations and pressures from certain familial and peer groups is one which adolescents often report as a source of conflict between themselves and their parents. It concerns a ritual practice of traditional Judaism—the use of kosher meat.[4] As a way of establishing the position of the adolescent and that of his membership groups, the respondents were asked: "When you get married are you going to use kosher meat in your home?"; and "Is kosher meat now used in your home?" Adolescents who plan to use kosher meat, and parents who use kosher meat will be called, for purposes of this study, "observant." In cases where more than half of the members of the adolescent's peer clique-group are observant, the group will be labeled observant.[5] In terms of the attitude and presumably the expectations of their membership groups, it can be seen that adolescents fall into one of four categories: those whose parent and peer groups are both observant; those whose parent and peer groups are both non-observant; those whose parents are observant and peer group is non-observant; those whose parents are non-observant and peer group is observant. Adolescents who fall into the latter two categories are those who are likely to experience conflicting expectations and pressures.

Research Findings

PARENT-PEER GROUPS AS MEMBERSHIP GROUPS

Our first task is to examine the relationship between the attitude of the adolescent toward the use of kosher meat and the attitude of his membership groups. Unless a relationship can be shown to exist, it would be meaningless to speak of a cross-pressure situation. If the data indicate that neither group is sufficiently important on this issue to influence the adolescent to the extent of having attitudes congruent with his, it is not probable that their conflicting expectations would be perceived or experienced as a cross-pressure situation.

The data in Table 1 show that a significant relationship exists between the attitude of the adolescent and the attitude of his membership

---

[4] Traditional Judaism forbids the use of any but ritually clean (i.e. kosher) food. Only certain animals, slaughtered in a prescribed manner, may be eaten.

[5] Non-Jewish members of the clique-group are considered non-observant. This is to indicate that they are not likely to exert pressures on the Jewish adolescent to be observant, although this is a possibility.

TABLE 1
Parents and Peer Group Attitude by Adolescent's Attitude

ADOLESCENT ATTITUDE	PARENT ATTITUDE[a]		PEER GROUP ATTITUDE[b]	
	OBSERVANT	NON-OBSERVANT	OBSERVANT	NON-OBSERVANT
	Per cent	Per cent	Per cent	Per cent
Observant	60	32	80	23
Non-observant	40	68	20	77
Total per cent	100	100	100	100
Total number	25	25	20	30

[a] Chi-square: 3.9; P less than .05.
[b] Chi-square: 15.5; P less than .001.

groups. Children of observant parents are proportionately more likely to be observant than are children of non-observant parents: 60 per cent of the former state they are going to observe the kosher meat ritual in their homes after marriage, as compared with 32 per cent of the latter—a difference that is statistically significant at the .05 level. The picture is the same when we compare the attitude of adolescents and the attitude of their peer groups: 80 per cent of the respondents whose peer-clique group is observant are also observant, as compared with 23 per cent of those whose peer group is non-observant—a relationship that is significant at the .001 level. However, it may be asked whether the relationship between adolescent and peer group attitude is not in fact in the final analysis a function of parental influence, since parents sometimes determine their children's selection of friends. Parents may see to it that their children associate only with adolescents who share the parental point of view. This hypothesis is examined in Table 2, in which the parental attitude is controlled. It can be seen that if parents seek to limit their children's associates to those who share the parental attitude (we do not know that this is the case) they are successful in only a little over half the cases. Furthermore, the relationship between the attitude of the adolescent and that of his peer group observed in Table 1 is not destroyed, although the statistical significance of this relationship is reduced to the .05 level.

There is, we note further in Table 1, a tendency for adolescents to agree more closely with their peer group than with their parents: 22 per cent of the adolescents differ from their peer group, as compared with 36 per cent who differed from their parents. Also it is apparent that membership in a particular group does not explain entirely the posses-

TABLE 2
Peer Group Attitude by Adolescent's Attitude
When Parental Attitude Is Controlled [a]

ADOLESCENT ATTITUDE	OBSERVANT PARENTS		NON-OBSERVANT PARENTS	
	OBSERVANT	NON-OBSERVANT	OBSERVANT	NON-OBSERVANT
	Per cent	Per cent	Per cent	Per cent
Observant	83	38	75	12
Non-observant	17	62	25	88
Total per cent	100	100	100	100
Total number [b]	12	13	8	17

[a] Combinatorial chi-square: 8.9; P less than .05.
[b] Yates correction factor used in computation.

sion of an attitude on the part of many adolescents. In the case of this study the use of one membership group as a predictive factor would involve considerable error: in terms of the familial group this error is as high as 36 per cent.

One way of guarding against this kind of error is to relate the attitude of the adolescent to the attitude of more than one membership group. When the membership groups are found to be homogeneous in attitude on a particular issue, the probability is increased that the adolescent will possess that attitude also. Thus the relationship between the adolescent's attitude and that of his membership groups is very marked in cases where the religious orientation of the two groups is similar. The data in Table 3 show that when parent and peer group are both observant, 83 per cent of the adolescents are observant. When the membership groups are non-observant, 88 per cent of the adolescents are non-observant. In both cases the relationships between the adolescent's attitudes and those of his membership groups are statistically significant at the .001 level. The combined influence of the two groups, presumably both in terms of the examples they set and their expectations, is very effective: in all only 14 per cent of the respondents deviate from the norms of their membership groups when the groups are homogeneous in attitude.

PARENT-PEER GROUPS AS REFERENCE GROUPS

Another, and we believe more reliable method of guarding against error, is to substitute the factor reference group for that of membership group.

TABLE 3
Relationship Between Adolescents' and Membership Groups' Attitude When Membership Groups' Attitude Is Homogeneous [a]

ADOLESCENT ATTITUDE	PARENT AND PEER GROUP ARE OBSERVANT	PARENT AND PEER GROUP ARE NON-OBSERVANT
	Per cent	Per cent
Observant	83	12
Non-observant	17	88
Total per cent	100	100
Total number [b]	12	17

[a] Chi-square: 12.1; P less than .001.
[b] Yates correction factor used in computation.

Not all membership groups are necessarily significant to the individual, and those which are significant for him on one issue may not be so on another. Recently, the group which consists of significant others, persons of importance to the individual and to whom he psychologically relates himself, has been termed the reference group. A major proposition of reference group theory is that the individual's attitudes stem from and are related to those of his significant others, and that this congruence of attitudes is a function of the process of interiorization and legitimation of referent's expectations.[6]

In determining the adolescent's reference group the following criteria were used: (1) perceived importance to individual, (2) perceived model for self-evaluation, and (3) perceived bond of understanding. Respondents were asked these questions:

1. Who are the people whose good opinion of you is important to you?

---

[6] The term "reference group" seems first to have appeared in a monograph by H. Hyman, "The Psychology of Status," *Archives of Psychology*, 1942, No. 269. Hyman used the term to signify some person or social category with whom the individual compares himself in evaluating his status. M. Sherif, *op. cit.*, and T. Newcomb, *op. cit.*, stress the attitude formation functions of the reference group. R. K. Merton and A. Kitt, "Contributions to the Theory of Reference Group Behavior," in *Studies in the Scope and Method of the American Soldier*, in R. K. Merton and P. F. Lazarsfeld, editors, Glencoe: Free Press, 1950, pp. 40–105, employ the concept as a frame of reference for both self-evaluation and attitude formation.

2. How religious would you say you are? Are you comparing yourself with someone? If so, with whom are you comparing yourself?

3. Who do you think understands you better, your parents or your friends?

In answer to the first two questions adolescents were permitted to name as many persons as they felt necessary. These criteria permit the rough classification of adolescents into three categories: (1) those who named their parents more often than their peer group; (2) those who named their peers more often than their parents; (3) those who named their parents and peers with equal frequency. The group named most frequently is considered the reference group.[7] We recognize that adolescents may have other referents (e.g., teachers, or siblings) but for the purpose of this study we shall limit ourselves to only parental and peer groups as reference groups.

When the reference group rather than the membership group [8] is used as the explanatory variable, the data indicate, as in Table 4, that error (i.e. those adolescents who deviate from the norm of their designated group) is considerably reduced, particularly as compared to situations in which only one membership group is employed as the explanatory factor. No more than 14 per cent of the entire sample deviate from their reference group. The relationship between the attitude of the adolescent and the attitude of their reference group is clearly statistically significant. In this case also it can be seen that adolescents tend to conform more closely to the norm of their peers than the norm of their parents: 7 per cent deviate from their peers as compared with 19 per cent who differ from their parents.

CONFLICTING MEMBERSHIP GROUPS

The fact that relatively few adolescents deviate from the norm of their parent-peer groups considered as reference groups, but that a sizeable number differ from these groups when defined as membership groups ex-

---

[7] A somewhat different method was employed in research reported elsewhere by the writer: Bernard C. Rosen, "The Reference Group Approach to the Parental Factor in Attitude and Behavior Formation," paper read at the annual meeting of the Eastern Sociological Society, April 3, 1954. The index employed here is not a scale and admits of neither ordinal nor cardinal properties, but is a rough categorization. However, we feel that the criteria and questions with some modifications are capable of being scaled.

[8] An individual's reference group may or may not be one of his membership groups. That is, it may be a group to which he objectively belongs, believes himself to belong, or aspires to belong. In this study the reference group is also an objective membership group.

TABLE 4
Correspondence Between Attitude of Adolescent and Attitude of Reference Group

ADOLESCENT'S REFERENCE GROUP	ADOLESCENT'S ATTITUDE IS	
	LIKE HIS REFERENCE GROUP	UNLIKE HIS REFERENCE GROUP
	(Cases)	(Cases)
Parents	21	5
Parents and peers	5	1
Peers	15	1
Total number[a]	41	7

[a] Two cases designating parent and peer as reference group and corresponding to only one or the other not included.

cept in those cases where the attitude of the two groups is similar, suggests that the deviate cases may be understood in terms of the membership groups possessing different attitudes and of the adolescent interiorizing the expectations of one group rather than those of the other. When this situation obtains, the individual is likely to be placed in a cross-pressure situation in which he experiences conflicting expectations from his membership groups.

Several kinds of evidence indicate that a number of adolescents find themselves in a cross-pressure situation. Analysis of their membership groups show that 42 per cent of the adolescents belong to familial and peer groups whose attitude toward the use of kosher meat is mutually conflicting. Furthermore, these conflicting attitudes show up in the *perceived pressures* which adolescents explicitly verbalized in interviews. Usually, pressures from parents are described as contributing to the observance of rituals: many adolescents attribute their acceptance of a particular ritual to parental influence. Explanations of this acceptance were typically in terms of habituative experience in which the observance of a ritual was traced to a habit formed in the home, or in terms of constraintive experience in which case observance is more a function of parental pressure than of personal preference. The peer group on the other hand is often held responsible, both by adolescents and parents, for the adolescent's deviation from traditional norms. Respondents often ascribe their first transgression of the traditional code to the influence of their peers. This is not to say that there are not instances in which parental pressures are away from traditionalism and peer group pressures toward traditionalism, situations of this sort occur, but they are not as frequent objectively and even less frequently perceived and reported by the adolescent.

As is the case for most groups, the family and the peer groups expect conformity to their norms. Some latitude is permitted in the interpretation of these norms, but typically any radical deviation from the group pattern will be punished. In the case of the familial group the sanctions are usually verbal scoldings; in the case of the peer group deviation from the group norm may result in expulsion from the group. In one case which the writer observed a teen-age girl was isolated from her peers because of her unusually close adherence to the traditional norms of her parents, an adherence which prevented her from writing, riding, or attending sports events on the Sabbath. She is described by other adolescents as "fanatic" and "stiff-necked" and is virtually without friends among her age-mates. This is an extreme situation; usually severe sanctions are rare. Ordinarily the group achieves conformity to its norms by effectively creating a climate of opinion which gently coerces the adolescent into acceptance of the group's norms.

The data in Table 5 lend tentative support to the hypotheses that when adolescents deviate from the norm of one group they are conforming to the norm of the other group. Thus of those adolescents who differ from their parents, 78 per cent of these agree with their peer group. Conversely, of those respondents who differ from their peer group, 63 per cent agree with their parents. Here again we note that the norm of the peer group tends to have a greater appeal than that of the parents. That is, when the adolescent differs from his parents he is proportionately more likely to agree with his peer group (76 per cent of the time) than he is to agree with his parents when he differs from his peers (63

TABLE 5
Correspondence of Adolescent's Attitude With Parental Attitude by Correspondence of Adolescent's Attitude With Peer Group Attitude

ADOLESCENTS' AND PEERS' ATTITUDE ARE	ADOLESCENT'S ATTITUDE AND PARENTS' ATTITUDE ARE	
	LIKE	UNLIKE
	(Cases)	(Cases)
Like	25	14
Unlike	7	4
Total number	32	18

per cent). While this difference is not statistically significant it is in the direction of our other data. We cannot be certain from these data that adolescents who deviate from the norm of one group are doing so at the instigation of the other group. For example, adolescents who reject the norm of observant parents may do so because they feel their parents to be unnecessarily restrictive, rather than because they find the norm of the peer group more acceptable or because they are reacting to the direct promptings of their peers. However, it is probable that the group with which the adolescent agrees plays at least a supporting role, if not an active role, in alienating the adolescent from the norm of the other group. Few adolescents are in rebellion against both groups. Logically, the adolescent may agree with both groups, with one of the two, or with none. Yet in only 8 per cent of the cases does he take the last alternative, indicating perhaps a need for support of at least one of these two important groups.

We can now ask the question: when parents and peer group have conflicting attitudes, with which group does the adolescent tend to agree and is this group his reference group? The data in Table 6 show that in the cases in which parent-peer groups have conflicting attitudes, 74 per cent of the adolescents agree with their peers as compared with 26 per cent who agree with their parents. In each case the group with which he agrees is about four times as likely to be his reference group as is the group with which he does not agree. The probability that a difference as large as this could have occurred by chance is about 5 times out of a hundred.

Conclusions

The data indicate that a significant relationship exists between attitude of adolescents in this sample toward the use of kosher meat and the attitude of their familial-peer groups considered as membership groups. This relationship is even more marked when the membership groups are homogeneous in attitude or when the group is a reference group. In cases where the attitudes of the two membership groups are conflicting, the group with which adolescents agree tends to be their reference group as defined by independent criteria. The data, on the whole, point to the greater influence of the peer group. More often than not in cases where parent-peer groups have conflicting attitudes on the issue examined in this study adolescents agreed with their peers rather than their parents. The smallness of the sample, the ethnicity of the adolescents and the nature of the issue on which there is conflict make it imperative that any generalizations or conclusions drawn from these data be con-

TABLE 6
Correspondence of Adolescent's Attitude With
Membership Groups' Attitudes in Cases Where
Groups Differ by Adolescent's Reference Group[a]

	ADOLESCENT'S ATTITUDE IS	
ADOLESCENTS' REFERENCE GROUP	UNLIKE PARENTS AND LIKE PEER GROUP	UNLIKE PEER GROUP AND LIKE PARENTS
	Per cent	Per cent
Parents	21	80
Peers	79	20[b]
Total per cent	100	100
Total number[c]	14	5

[a]Chi-square: 3.6; P less than .06 but more than .05.
[b]Yates correction factor used in computation.
[c]Two cases designating parent and peer group as reference group and corresponding to one or the other not included.

sidered as highly tentative. Nonetheless, on the whole the data consistently and cumulatively indicate that for this issue and these adolescents the norm of the peer group tends to be more closely related to the attitude of the adolescent than is the norm of the parental group. Whether this relationship is a causal one and to what extent it reflects not only the pressures of the peer group but also other referents, as well as the general value system of American culture, we cannot, of course, be certain. But the data do suggest that the importance of the peer group, even in situations where parents and peer group conflict, must be taken into account in any study of adolescent attitudes.

While the necessary data to explain these findings are lacking, some tentative explanations which may lead to further research can be offered. The relationship between adolescent and parental-peer group attitudes found in this study is in keeping with a growing body of theory and empirical data which demonstrate the importance of these two groups, particularly in terms of their functions in the socialization process, in the attitude formation process. An explanation of the relative impact of these two groups on adolescents in our society may be found in the hypotheses about American character presented by Riesman.[9] His suggestion that the changing character structure of Americans is in the

---

[9] D. Riesman, *et al.*, *The Lonely Crowd*, New Haven: Yale University Press, 1950.

direction of the increasing importance of the peer group offers a potentially rewarding guide for future research. Should further research indicate that the relative number of inner-directed persons (those who internalize parental authority) is declining in our society and that the proportion of other-directed persons (those whose character is formed chiefly by the example of their peers) is growing, it would help to provide a conceptual framework in which the data in this study could be interpreted.

Whatever future research may reveal about the importance of the peer group in childhood and adulthood, it is likely to be found that at no other time is the peer group as important to the individual as it is in adolescence. In our culture the physiological changes, the lag between physical maturation and social maturity associated with adolescence create a host of problems for the adolescent. In his effort to cope with these problems the adolescent turns to his age-mates for companionship, recognition, and support. The peer group provides the teen-ager with a sense of belongingness at a time when conflicting loyalties, identifications, and values make him unsure of himself. Within the peer group the adolescent is able to acquire the status often denied him in the adult world—a status which is more predictable and based upon values and expectations he understands and can fulfill.

10.   EXCERPTS FROM *BLACK RAGE**

W. H. Grier and P. M. Cobbs

Acquiring Manhood

JIMMY

Jimmy was a twelve-year-old boy whose rapid growth had left him gawky and uncomfortable. He sat slumped in a chair, trying to conceal his ill-fitting clothes. His face was jet-black, and his expressions ranged from somber to sad. Whether relating stories of home, school, or the streets, he disguised his true feelings. At twelve he had learned one of

* Extracts from *Black Rage* by William H. Grier and Price M. Cobbs, © 1968 by William H. Grier and Price M. Cobbs, Basic Books, Inc., publishers, New York.

his first lessons—always play it cool. As much as possible, he worked to hide his inner life.

One day he stared long and hard at his fist and said: "I want to hit a white man." For once, the therapist could sense an uncensored outpouring of feelings. Then Jimmy frowned, started another sentence, and began to cry.

The anger was welcome, if unexpected, but the comment was surprising. In over three months of weekly visits, the boy had never directly mentioned white people. There had been allusions to trouble at school with boys who were not "bloods" and once he talked of his father's job at a can factory, where there were few Negroes. But Jimmy had never spoken in terms of racial feelings or problems. He had never directly felt antagonism from a white person, but when his anger spilled over, he chose that target.

He was a quiet, introverted boy who found it difficult to talk for fifty minutes. He would smile in acknowledging something pleasant, but generally he seemed to feel despair. His emotions were expressed in terms of stubbornness and obstinacy. If he felt threatened, he became passive and silent and in this manner opposed anything he did not want to do or say. This was his means of dealing with any authority, whether a teacher in school or a parent. Though he had an above-average intelligence, he was doing poorly in school. There were important things he would not do or forget to do, and his grades suffered. In talking about his life, Jimmy was vague. He had trouble seeing anything in his life as definite, with any form or shape.

One thing in his life was clear. He saw his father as weak and powerless. However much his father threatened, cajoled, or beat him, Jimmy always knew that the man was playing a role.

His father was a large man, lighter in color than his son, and grossly overweight. He dressed in rumpled suits, wrinkled shirts, and greasy ties. In some of the early family sessions, he would interrupt to complain of his various ailments. He spoke of an ulcer that was always "acting up." Mr. B. "played at" (this was Jimmy's phrase) being the minister of a storefront church, in addition to his full-time job at the factory. From an early age, Jimmy was aware that his father could never "stand up." He had heard his mother say it and he observed it himself. One of the boy's few delights was in recalling an occasion when his father cringed and sent his wife to the door to handle a bill collector. Many of Jimmy's friends did not have their fathers living at home, but he was certain that those fathers, in the same situation, would have acted the same way.

Mrs. B. was a short, dark woman with an attractive but worried face. She was neat and "fixed up" and openly compared her appearance with her husband's usually disheveled state. She did not hide her contempt for him. She constantly undermined his feeble attempts to relate to Jimmy. She was the dominant figure in the house, and she assumed this position as an unwanted burden, as something about which she had no choice. She would alternate between understanding Jimmy and dramatically washing her hands of everything.

In terms of individual psychopathology, Jimmy can be matched with thousands of teenage boys of every race and ethnic background. He is responding to his puberty with restlessness and feelings he cannot articulate directly. He is angry with his father and alternately attracted to and repelled by his mother. Every therapist has seen many Jimmys. What is different about him is that he is black and is experiencing what every black boy in this country must undergo. His personality and character structure, his emotional assets and liabilities, are being shaped as much by his blackness as by his personal environment.

Jimmy is beginning to realize that he has no power and, like his father, will not get it. At his age the concepts are misty, but he realizes that his father and the fathers of his friends are lacking something. He has had few, if any, traumatic incidents with whites. There have been no overt acts of discrimination. The family has lived in a ghetto, and all their socialization has been within that framework. But Jimmy is part of a historical legacy that spans more than three hundred years. He lives in a large city but he shares his insight with every black child in every city in this country. He must devise individual ways to meet group problems. He must find compensations, whether healthy or unhealthy. There must be a tremendous expenditure of psychic energy to cushion the shock of learning that he is denied what other men around him have. When he states his desire to attack a white man, he consciously acknowledges his wish to attack those who keep him powerless.

Both theories of personality development and clinical experience attest to the troubled path from childhood to manhood. The young man must have developed a fine expertise in making his way in a complex and ambiguous social organization. Under the most favorable signs it is a difficult task and society must turn its most benign and helping face to the young aspirant. And once the game is mastered a certain flexible readiness is required because the rules are constantly being changed.

Thus the black boy in growing up encounters some strange impediments. Schools discourage his ambitions, training for valued skills is not available to him, and when he does triumph in some youthful competition he receives compromised praise, not the glory he might expect. In time he comes to see that society has locked arms *against* him, that rather than help he can expect opposition to his development, and that he lives not in a benign community but in a society that views his growth with hostility.

For the black man in this country, it is not so much a matter of acquiring manhood as it is a struggle to feel it his own. Whereas the white man regards his manhood as an ordained right, the black man is engaged in a never-ending battle for its possession. For the black man, attaining any portion of manhood is an active process. He must penetrate barriers and overcome opposition in order to assume a masculine posture. For the inner psychological obstacles to manhood are never so formidable as the impediments woven into American society. By contrast, for a white man in this country, the rudiments of manhood are settled at birth by the possession of a penis and a white skin. This biological affirmation of masculinity and identity as master is enough to insure that, whatever his individual limitations, this society will not systematically erect obstructions to his achievement.

Throughout his life, at each critical point of development the black boy is told to hold back, to constrict, to subvert and camouflage his normal masculinity. Male assertiveness becomes a forbidden fruit, and if it is attained, it must be savored privately.

Manhood must always be defined for the setting in which it occurs. A man in a Siberian village may be very different from a man in a Chicago suburb. Biologically they share the same drives and limitations, but their societies may decree totally different roles. Manhood in this country has many meanings, but a central theme is clear. Men are very early taught that they have certain prerogatives and privileges. They are encouraged to pursue, to engage life, to attack, rather than to shrink back. They learn early that to express a certain amount of aggression and assertion is manly. Every playground, every schoolyard is filled with boys fighting and attacking, playing at being grown up. The popular heroes in this country are men who express themselves aggressively and assertively.

As boys approach adulthood, masculinity becomes more and more bound up with money making. In a capitalistic society economic wealth is inextricably interwoven with manhood. Closely allied is power—power to control and direct other men, power to influence the course of one's own and other lives. The more lives one can influence, the greater the power. The ultimate power is the freedom to understand and alter one's life. It is this power, both individually and collectively, which has been denied the black man.

Under slavery, the black man was a psychologically emasculated and totally dependent human being. Times and conditions have changed, but black men continue to exhibit the inhibitions and psychopathology that had their genesis in the slave experience. It would seem that for masculine growth and development the psychological conditions have not changed very much. Better jobs are available, housing is improving, and all the external signs of progress can be seen, but the American heritage of racism will still not allow the black man to feel himself master in his own land. Just as Jimmy is beset by forces larger than his individual experiences, so is the black man in this society, more than other men, shaped by currents more powerful than the course of his own life.

There are rules which regulate black lives far more than the lives of white men.

The simplistic view of the black family as a matriarchy is an unfortunate theme repeated too often by scholars who should know better. If a man is stripped of his authority in the home by forces outside that home, the woman naturally must assume the status of head of household. This is the safety factor inherent in a household which includes two adults and it by no means suggests that the woman prefers it that way. If a woman is widowed she may assume many masculine functions, but the household may be a patriarchy without a patriarch.

In the black household the man faces greater than usual odds in making his way. The care and rearing of children falls even more heavily on the wife; she is the culture bearer. She interprets the society to the children and takes as her task the shaping of their character to meet the world as she knows it. This is every mother's task. But the black mother has a more ominous message for her child and feels more urgently the need to get the message across. The child must know that the white world is dangerous and that if he does not understand its rules it may kill him.

When black men recall their early life, consistent themes emerge. For example, the mother is generally perceived as having been sharply contradictory. She may have been permissive in some areas and punitive and rigid in others. There are remembrances of stimulation and gratification coexisting with memories of deprivation and rejection. There is always a feeling that the behavior of the mother was purposeful and deliberate.

The black man remembers that his mother underwent frequent and rapid shifts of mood. He remembers the cruelty. The mother who sang spirituals gently at church was capable of inflicting senseless pain at home. These themes of gratification and cruelty are consistent enough to suggest that they played a critical role in preparing the boy for adulthood. It would seem that the boy had to experience the polarities of ambivalence so that he could understand his later role in a white society. He must be adequately prepared.

The black mother shares a burden with her soul sisters of three centuries ago. She must produce and shape and mold a unique type of man. She must intuitively cut off and blunt his masculine assertiveness and aggression lest these put the boy's life in jeopardy.

During slavery the danger was real. A slave boy could not show too much aggression. The feelings of anger and frustration which channeled themselves into aggression had to be thwarted. If they were not, the boy would have little or no use as a slave and would be slain. If any feelings, especially those of assertive manhood, were expressed too strongly, then that slave was a threat, not only to himself and his master but to the entire system as well. For that, he would have to be killed.

The black mother continues this heritage from slavery and simultaneously reflects the world she now knows. Even today, the black man cannot become too aggressive without hazard to himself. To do so is to challenge the delicate balance of a complex social system. Every mother, of whatever color and degree of proficiency, knows what the society in which she lives will require of her children. Her basic job is to prepare the child for this. Because of the institutionalization of barriers, the black mother knows even more surely what society requires of *her* children. What at first seemed a random pattern of mothering has gradually assumed a definite and deliberate, if unconscious, method of preparing a black boy for his subordinate place in the world.

As a result, black men develop considerable hostility toward black women as the inhibiting instruments of an oppressive system. The woman has more power, more accessibility into the system, and therefore she is more feared, while at the same time envied. And it is her lot in life to suppress masculine assertiveness in her sons.

The "Promise" of Education

A brilliant high school student was awarded a scholarship to a prestigious eastern school. Despite the enthusiastic encouragement of friends and family, he chose rather a small Negro college of modest reputation located in the South. He finally explained:
"If I go East, I can never come back."

"Back" was to home, family, friends, and a brotherhood of black people.

Black people feel bound to the concept of equality. It is a belief which allows them to live. It cannot have merely an occasional hortatory meaning for black Americans—it must be seen as a universal truth. No other conviction can sustain black people in this country. It is absorbed in childhood and built on the child's conception of fairness. Public pronouncements of every kind can find a responsive affirmation in black breasts if they only include the word "equality." The idea of all men's equality lies at the deepest level of the black man's conception of social organization. Slavery and the post-Civil War experience have made this concept dear indeed.

It extends from the broad social meanings to its implementation in everyday life. Black children are acutely sensitive to the undemocratic formation of "exclusive" groups and social bodies. This conviction finds support in the concept of brotherhood. We are not only brothers but brothers keenly aware of our equal status.

But the belief in equality produces conflict when the black child is introduced to intellectual striving, competition, and the evaluation of his innate abilities. Some youngsters are far brighter than their brethren. When their gifts allow them to soar beyond the modest accomplishments of the others, the binding requirement of equality is encountered and problems arise. One may feel that to outstrip one's brothers is a wicked thing. To announce oneself as an exception is to bring calumny down on one's head. To say that one is smarter is to say that one's brothers are dumber, and that is a difficult thing for a black student.

Those with great intellectual gifts develop the technique of denying or minimizing them. A striking example of this occurred in treatment.

A young woman revealed her intellectual gifts only gradually. She told over a period of weeks, bit by bit, that she had achieved a distinguished academic record and finally that she had been given numerous intelligence tests and on all of them had "gone off the top," which is to say she was gifted to a degree that the tests were not calibrated to measure. Her intelligence could only be estimated.

In one session this bright woman described a major Caribbean island as located in the Mediterranean. Questioned repeatedly, she stuck to her mistake. Finally the therapist suggested that she knew better and that she made the error for some other purpose. She laughed and said that her great dread during treatment was the prospect of finding that she was brighter than the therapist and that from her earliest school years she had tried to obscure her knowledge and to make herself appear less gifted than she was.

She was a vigorous champion of the cause of black people and found the idea of an intellectual aristocracy repugnant to her. Although she welcomed the challenge to match wits with white opponents and in fact rose to magnificent heights in such intellectual combat, she laid down her arms when confronted by a black antagonist.

Her situation is typical of many bright black students. Intellectual achievement is regarded as elevating oneself to a higher plane and removing oneself from the black brotherhood. The tie to blackness here is rarely perceived as the militant self-conscious pride of being black but rather as the deeper, sweeter, more profound ties to beloved figures of childhood.

Such a conflict partly explains why so many gifted black students achieve academic distinction but fail to fulfill their vocational promise. Accomplishment in school can be seen as simply carrying out the wishes of the family, whereas accomplishment in a career may represent a major move beyond the family—a move to another level of contact with those whose love is life itself.

The scholar finds himself especially torn, driven to excel academically by the ambitions of family, yet pulled to maintain an all-important equality with those same beloved ones. He yields most often to the stronger force—the leveling effect of love.

The unique quality of this conflict arises from the strength of the call for equality. All Americans feel committed to the principle of "all men, created equal," but it does not occupy a central position in their view of their place in America. It is a case of "All men are born equal, but white men are more equal than anyone else."

For black men the concept of equality functions as an ideological bulwark against the pervasive idea that Negroes are stupid. The black man clings to it as one of the nation's highest principles. By calling upon Americans to respond to a statement of national conscience and by reminding them of their declared ideals, he is defending himself against the institutionalized depreciation of black people in this country. This devotion to principles, ideals, and conscience marks all blacks with a certain idealism which seems inappropriate in so atavistic a land.

There is a separate and curious effect that American attitudes have had on the academic aspirations of black children which is related to the sexual roles adopted by boys and girls. It has often been observed that black parents push girls in the family to remain in school and in many ways encourage them and make higher education more accessible to them. On the other hand, the same family may discourage its sons, urge them to drop out of school, and make it difficult for them to obtain an education. The reasons are not immediately obvious.

> Mrs. J., who lived in the South in the 1920's, had eight children. She prodded her four daughters to obtain higher education and in spite of the family's extremely low income she made sure that the girls had some college instruction. Mrs. J. was a domestic and earned a precarious living unaided by public assistance. Her sons, she felt, "could look out for themselves," and when they were very young she told them of her need for whatever money they could earn. As a result, the oldest son quit school at fourteen and the others by the age of sixteen. All contributed to help the girls continue their education.

Here the rationale is clearer than most. Living in the South, Mrs. J. was concerned about the physical safety and protection she could offer her children. She admonished her sons to avoid conflict with white people and it would be blessing enough for her if they avoided the hostile physical encounters which could place their lives in jeopardy.

With her daughters it was a different story. Her aim was to protect them from the sexual exploitation they might suffer if they were forced to work as domestics. She knew that in the South an attractive young black girl who worked in a white household was in considerable danger of being used sexually by the men of the house. She also knew that the weapon used to bend the girl to their will was the economic threat of being fired if she refused to submit. To free the girls from this certain development, the mother sought to give them economic freedom through the education which allowed them all to become schoolteachers. As teachers, the girls would possess a dignity and an autonomy they could never have as black domestics in the South.

But even this strategy did not always succeed. The story is heard from many lips of white school administrators threatening to fire black teachers if they spurned sexual advances. If this pressure could be applied at so elevated and public a level, it must have been common indeed in the narrow secret world of the domestic servant.

For the boys, the world was quite a different place. It was exceedingly dangerous, and the first task was to develop a style of life which allowed one to survive. Avoid fights with white boys, particularly avoid gangs of white toughs, and speak with deference to white men. If one learned what situations to *avoid,* one could achieve as much safety as the South could afford a black man. Those slow to learn might not live very long in any event. The lessons were swift and cruel.

> A boy lived with his uncle, whom he adored. Their particular pleasure was spending Saturdays in town together. One such afternoon while walking along a street, they met a white man with his son, who was larger than the dark child. Without ado the white man kicked the black child and ordered his son to beat him up. The white boy beat him thoroughly while the uncle stood aside and sadly watched the proceedings.

In later life the black boy, now a man, said it took many years to forgive his uncle and even more to understand how painful it must have been for him, how wretched a life he led which required him, probably under penalty of death, to watch a child he loved being beaten and to be unable to raise a hand in protest. That boy is now a man and there are no words to convey the depth of his hatred for white men. But he carries on his daily life without a hint of rage.

If the boys learned this lesson, they learned something about the male role as well. For black men in America, in the old South and the new North, masculinity carries overtones of violence. One must either deal with and placate a violent white man or as a man defend oneself with violence against murderous threats. To position oneself, then, in relation to aggression became a vital part of masculinity. The man who fought when threatened and lived to tell the tale became a man who had dealt successfully with truly many things—a man among men, a man of violence, a man who held his manhood dear, and though his life was likely to be brief had laid hold of the essential task of men and particularly black men—survival and opposition to the foe. And although we have described earlier how they terrified the Negro community and in a sense provided a negative model for "nice families," such men (bad niggers) had profound importance for the Negro community. They provided the measure of manhood for all black men and stood in ultimate masculine opposition to the feminine counterpart who sought protection from the foe by turning to education.

Thus any man who turned from violent confrontation of the white enemy and instead followed academic pursuits would have to feel deep inside, in his heart of hearts, that he had retreated from the battle. It was his secret, this cowardice, and there was an emptiness where his manhood might have been.

This played a part in the division of roles in girls who went to school and boys who dropped out. For in one sense school was seen by black families in a very special way. Beset on all sides by a cruel enemy, school was often primarily a refuge—a place of safety for those who were to be protected—and in a sense it was a case of women and children first.

These attitudes do not complete the catalogue of black people's feelings about school and schooling but they are important. They continue to play an important part to this day because the violence to which blacks are exposed in this country is faced by no other group of people in America. If school is seen as a refuge from the white aggressor, and if the black family places its women and children within such safe confines, and if the men then turn to face the enemy—*pray show me that critic of the "weak" Negro family!*

If the critics do not understand, then one may say that such everyday heroics are not performed for the critics' sake; fortunately they are carried out for love of man for woman and both for child.

And if school is regarded as of secondary importance and as having little relevance in the heat of battle where men are called to war, pray tell us who wages war on black people? One can only feel dismay if a man lays deadly siege to your house and then criticizes you for not going about innocent daily chores.

Such are the profound influences of American racism on the black man's involvement in education. In his mind school is converted from an instrument of social mobility to a place of refuge. The roles of black boys and girls are changed from potential participants in the fullness of America to females to be protected and men to face the enemy. It is a greater source of wonder that black children choose to learn at all.

Such are the factors that make academic achievement difficult for dark students: loving but untrusting parents, discouraged teachers, institutional opposition to a learned black community, and a state of war that has both historical roots and a contemporary reality. When in spite of these barriers a student surfaces as an academician, the passage through these dark places has left its mark. He steps onstage to put his skill to work in a nation and an economy which has blocked his progress at every step and which yet offers him serious obstacles.

V. ON ADOLESCENT-TEACHER CLASSROOM INTERACTIONS

Introduction

This section starts by reiterating the central theme of the first section: that it is worthwhile listening to what adolescents can tell us about themselves and their experiences. Section five goes on to analyze the observation that high school students tend to feel increasingly negative toward their teachers as the school year progresses. Finally, it demonstrates the various ways teachers' biases work against certain adolescents in the classroom. These findings are presented in the hope that being aware of these classroom events will assist teachers in better understanding and preparing for their interactions with adolescents.

The Tuckman and Oliver article determines the relative effects of feedback from students and from supervisors on teacher classroom behavior. Their findings show that students' feedback is significantly effective compared to the absence of feedback. Moreover, supervisor feedback induces negative changes in teacher behavior, while student feedback "improves" teacher behavior. Still another important result of this study is that years of teaching experience does not significantly detract from a teacher's receptivity toward student feedback. Tuckman and Oliver also introduce the tendency for students' attitudes toward their teachers to decline as the school year progresses.

In their study, Flanders and others concentrate their efforts on the changes in student attitude toward the teacher during the school year noted by Tuckman and Oliver. Flanders and his colleagues document the negative shift in attitude on a large sample of high school students, analyze various suggested explanations for the phenomenon, and introduce Rotter's internality–externality scheme to study its connection with the shift.

The remaining papers in this section are devoted to the biases that teachers bring to the classroom and their consequences for student behavior and performance. These findings support Rosenthal's well publicized notion of the self-fulfilling prophecy, which informs us that the mental sets that teachers (and others) have about students have consequences for how the students will behave. For example, when teachers were led to believe a group of students will gain in intelligence, Rosenthal found that these students showed a greater gain in IQ than their classmates.

Gladstone's paper illustrates how teachers tend to generate moral characteristics about students for whom they have only competence information. The paper by Datta, Schaeffer, and

Davis goes beyond Gladstone's study to investigate the part played by students' sex and intelli- gence in teachers' perceptions and ratings of Negro and other seventh-grade students.

1. EFFECTIVENESS OF FEEDBACK TO TEACHERS AS A FUNCTION OF SOURCE *

Bruce W. Tuckman and Wilmot F. Oliver

The problem of modifying the behavior of teachers is one that has been submitted to close scrutiny from a variety of vantage points. Techniques such as microteaching and the use of interaction process analysis have been employed, primarily with student teachers, as a means of altering their behavior. Underscoring the entire rationale for this approach, Daw and Gage (1967) recently said:

> It is highly plausible that feedback regarding how others feel about one's behavior will affect one's behavior. Whether this maxim will hold under a given set of practical circumstances must, however, be determined empirically [p. 181].

This study was an attempt to extend this "maxim" to conditions as yet untested.

Bryan (1963) has shown that teachers will alter their behavior as the outcome of receiving feedback from their students. The purpose of this study was to replicate Bryan's basic finding, using his instrument, and then to extend this finding by determining the relative effects of feedback from students and from supervisors (i.e., administrators responsible for instruction) on teachers' behavior. Moreover, Bryan's study did not include control over the variable of amount of teaching experience of teachers whose behavior was to be changed. His experimental and control groups showed an imbalance on this variable at the conclusion of his experiment with the preponderance of less experienced teachers appearing in the experimental group. An additional purpose of the present

* From: Bruce W. Tuckman and Wilmot F. Oliver, "Effectiveness of Feedback to Teachers as a Function of Source," *Journal of Educational Psychology*, 59, 1968, 297–301. Copyright 1968 by the American Psychological Association, and reproduced by permission. This study was, in part, the doctoral dissertation of the junior author. It was supported, in part, by Grant No. 6-8327 from the United States Office of Education.

study was to systematically introduce years of teaching experience as an experimental variable so that its effects, if any, could be determined.

Finally, the present study was carried out with vocational teachers, in order to demonstrate additional generalizability for the basic finding obtained by Bryan using primarily teachers of academic subjects.

The fact that teachers change as the result of student feedback has also been demonstrated by Gage, Runkel, and Chatterjee (1960). Their study also showed that amount of change was related to the interval between pretest and posttest. Daw and Gage (1967) have shown, furthermore, that feedback from teachers can be used to alter the behavior of principals, but that the amount of change is not a function of the pretest-posttest interval.

In this study, as in previous studies in this area, the measurement of change in teacher behavior was inferential. Students were asked to rate their teacher twice, with a 12-week interval separating these ratings (during which time the treatments could take effect). Behavior change by teachers was inferred from a difference between postinterval and preinterval ratings. Remmers (1963) has shown that students, as a measuring instrument, are as reliable as the best mental and educational paper-and-pencil tests and can discriminate between aspects of teacher behavior (see also Tuckman, 1967). Thus, the dependent variable was identified as change in teachers' behavior with the recognition that this was inferential.

The expectation that years of teaching experience would be a significant variable was based on studies such as that of Ryans (1964) and Peterson (1964) who have shown that teachers' behavioral patterns change in a systematic fashion as a function of age. While age and years of teaching experience are not the same variable, they are assuredly related, with the latter being perhaps the more conceptually meaningful in an educational context.

Problem

To determine the relative effects of students and supervisors as feedback sources for teachers, four conditions were run. In the first condition student feedback alone was employed; in the second, supervisor feedback was employed alone (the supervisor being an administrator, usually a principal or vice-principal responsible for the teaching activities of teachers); in the third, both feedback sources were employed concomitantly; and in the fourth, no feedback was given. Teachers were further classified as to teaching experience and systematically assigned to conditions on that basis.

It was hypothesized that: (*a*) teachers receiving feedback would change more than teachers not receiving feedback (essentially a replication of Bryan's results); (*b*) amount of change in teachers' behavior would vary as a function of feedback source; (*c*) years of teaching experience and amount of change would be inversely related.

Method

SAMPLE

The sample consisted of 286 teachers of vocational subjects at the high school or technical institute level. Schools were selected from New Jersey and surrounding out-of-state counties and virtually all the vocational teachers in the schools used took part in the study. Participating teachers had a median class size of 15 students who were either in the tenth, eleventh, or thirteenth grade.

MEASUREMENT OF TEACHER BEHAVIOR

Teacher behavior was measured by the Student-Opinion Questionnaire (SOQ) developed by Bryan (1963). This instrument includes 10 rating scales on which teacher is judged as to his (*a*) knowledge of his subject, (*b*) ability to explain, (*c*) fairness, (*d*) ability to maintain discipline, (*e*) degree of sympathetic understanding, (*f*) ability to make you learn, (*g*) ability to be interesting, (*h*) ability to get things done efficiently, (*i*) ability to get students to think for themselves, and (*j*) general all-round teaching ability. Each scale has five points labeled: below average, average, good, very good, and the very best.

Bryan (1963) has reported reliability coefficients for the 10 items on the SOQ of from .75 to .85 for chance-half averages for 50 classes. For whole classes of 28 students on the average, coefficients of from .86 to .92 were obtained.

On the reverse side of the SOQ are four open-ended questions dealing with the course and teacher, reflecting on things that are liked about each and suggestions for the improvement of each.

FEEDBACK CONDITIONS

Students only. Students completed the SOQ, and their ratings on the 10 scales were averaged. The teacher was presented with a graph showing the average student judgment for each item. In addition, a summation of the students' responses on the open-ended questions were provided. Teachers were told that the feedback was from their students.

Supervisor only. The teacher's supervisor (either the principal, vice-principal, or assistant principal) completed the SOQ, and his ratings on each item were given to the teacher in graphical form along with a summary of his answers to the open-ended questions. The teacher was told that this rating was made by the supervisor. (In this condition, student ratings were also obtained although these were not made available to the teacher.)

Students and supervisor. The teacher's supervisor and students completed the SOQ, and feedback from each was given separately, along with identification of source in the same manner as in the first two conditions.

No feedback. Students completed the SOQ, but no feedback was provided to the teacher.

All initial testing was done in the late fall.

YEARS OF TEACHING EXPERIENCE

Based on information from a personal information form, teachers were categorized as having 1–3 years of teaching experience, 4–10 years of teaching experience, or 11 or more years of teaching experience. Teachers from each group were then randomly assigned to each condition. The overall design of the study and assignment of teachers to conditions is shown in Table 1.

TABLE 1
Design of the Experiment: Assignment of Teachers to Treatment and Experience Groups[a]

| | YEARS OF EXPERIENCE OF INSTRUCTOR | | | | | |
| | 1–3 YEARS (A_1) | | 4–10 YEARS (A_2) | | 11 OR MORE YEARS (A_3) | |
CONDITION	B_1	B_2	B_1	B_2	B_1	B_2
No student feedback (C_1)	14	18	19	18	18	13
Student feedback (C_2)	39	32	25	31	32	27

[a] Cell entries are number of observations per cell; $N = 286$; Abbreviated: B_1 = no supervisory feedback, B_2 = supervisory feedback.

MEASUREMENT OF CHANGE IN TEACHER'S BEHAVIOR

In the late spring, following a 12-week interval after the initial testing, students of each of the teachers in the study completed the SOQ. The measure of change in each condition was the sum of the differences between the preinterval judgments by the students on the 10 items and their postinterval judgments. Ratings on each item were averaged across students and the preinterval average on each item was then subtracted from the postinterval average to yield a change score on each of the 10 items. These 10-item change scores were summed to obtain a total change score. Student judgments were used throughout as a measure of change to maintain a constant measuring instrument across conditions. This was seen as justifiable since preinterval ratings by students did not differ significantly from those of supervisors in conditions where both were obtained and the latter were used as the feedback source.

All test administration was accomplished by the local vocational guidance counselor.

ANALYSIS

For purposes of analysis, the four feedback conditions (Conditions 1–4) were treated as two factors: supervisor feedback and student feedback, with two levels on each: present and absent. The four conditions were thus labeled as follows: (b_1c_1) student and supervisor feedback, (b_1c_2) supervisor feedback only, (b_2c_1) student feedback only, and (b_2c_2) no feedback (see Table 1). Years of teaching experience was the first factor and had three levels. Subsequently a $3 \times 2 \times 2$ analysis of variance using the unweighted means solution for unequal cell entries (Winer, 1962) was carried out on the total change score for each teacher. (Each teacher was used only once in the design.) In addition, direct mean comparisons were made using the Duncan multiple-range test (Duncan, 1955).[1]

---

[1] A fifth condition, called the posttest-only control group by Daw and Gage (1967), was also run with an additional 15 teachers. These teachers were rated by their students only at the end of the interval. The purpose of this condition was to determine whether the pretest or preinterval measurement had a sensitizing effect on the raters or teachers (cf. Campbell & Stanley, 1963). A comparison of the mean for this posttest-only control group to the mean on the postinterval measurement for the no-feedback group showed them to be comparable. Thus, it was concluded that test sensitization was not a source of invalidity.

Results

The results of the analysis of variance for the total change score showed that the presence of student feedback (Factor C) had a significant effect on teachers' behavior as compared to its absence ($F = 5.941$; $df = 1/274$, $p < .025$) while the presence of supervisor feedback (Factor B) produced no significant effect ($F = 1.064$; $df = 1/274$). The years-of-experience variable (Factor A) also failed to produce a significant effect ($F = 0.701$; $df = 2/274$) and none of the interactions achieved significance at the .05 level ($F < 1$ in each case).

In an effort to delineate further the feedback effects, means for the four feedback conditions were compared, as shown in Table 2. From the table it can be seen that both conditions involving student feedback showed significantly greater change than both conditions not involving student feedback.[2] Feedback from students alone and from students and supervisors combined were statistically comparable, indicating a failure for feedback from supervisors to generate any change beyond that accounted for by student feedback alone. Finally, feedback from supervisors alone produced a significantly greater negative shift (i.e., a change in the opposite direction of that recommended by the feedback) than no feedback at all.

Thus, student feedback "improved" teacher behavior as compared to no feedback. Supervisor feedback produced no additional effect when combined with student feedback, and an adverse effect when used alone.

Discussion

The first hypothesis of this study predicted that feedback (source unspecified) would yield a greater positive change than no feedback, while

---

[2] Throughout this description, results are referred to as changing "more" or "less." However, in the light of the fact that almost all of the means are negative, changing more means showing a lesser negative shift (i.e., a smaller negative change score) while changing less means showing a greater negative shift (i.e., a larger negative change score). This tendency for ratings to be less positive following the interval as compared to those preceding the interval were not attributable to a testing effect (see the preceding footnote). One must conclude that students as raters are more negatively inclined toward their teachers in the spring (after experiencing them for a year) than in the fall. Thus, the positive effect of feedback, when it occurred, was to reduce this tendency toward greater negativity of ratings (i.e., make the negative score smaller or positive).

TABLE 2
Mean Total Change Scores by Feedback Condition and
Their Comparison by Duncan Multiple-Range Test

STUDENTS ONLY	STUDENTS AND SUPERVISORS	SUPERVISORS ONLY	NO FEEDBACK
− .054	− .385	− 2.449[a]	− 1.234[a]

[a]Significantly different from all other means, $p < .01$ (with exception of difference between second and fourth means, where $p < .05$).

the second hypothesis predicted different effects for the different feedback sources. The surprising finding of this study was that teachers receiving feedback from supervisors changed more in the opposite direction from the feedback than the spontaneous shift obtained in the no-feedback condition. Thus, the first hypothesis holds true for student feedback (a replication of Bryan's findings) which led to effects in excess of the no-feedback condition. Supervisory feedback added nothing to the student feedback effect when they were combined. (If anything it reduced it, but not significantly so.) Since supervisory feedback had the opposite effect than predicted, the second hypothesis was confirmed—that is, the feedback sources did have different effects. If in the first hypothesis, it was simply predicted that feedback would produce greater changes than no feedback, it would have been confirmed. Certainly this experiment suggests that teachers react to feedback, irrespective of source, with these reactions being positive only in the case of student feedback.

The question of why teachers reacted to feedback from supervisors as they did is immediately raised. It can only be surmised that teachers are defensive toward (or even hostile to) administrators who, in the absence of much basis for judgment, attempt to tell them how to teach. Of interest, though, is the fact that within the educational milieu, the only source of feedback to teachers, typically, are their supervisors. The data collected here indicate that such feedback is doing more harm than good, with the "best" source of feedback, students, overlooked.

The third hypothesis of the present study predicted an inverse relation between years of experience and receptivity to feedback. While the obtained relationship was not sufficiently strong to prove significant, the most experienced teacher group tended to show the least receptivity to feedback from their students, as the hypothesis predicted. However, the least experienced teacher group tended to show the least receptivity (i.e., the least relatively positive shift) to feedback from their supervisor —the reverse of the hypothesis.

Finally, a last question must be raised. Why do all the change scores tend to be negative with positive change being measured in terms of the "smallness" of the negative score? The use of a group of teachers whose students made only the postinterval ratings indicated that the test-retest phenomenon was not responsible for this shift from pre- to postratings. It appeared that students are more critical of their teachers at the end of the term than at the middle. At the time when the teacher is about to evaluate and grade the student, the student perhaps replies in kind. Thus, a positive change appeared as a lessening in the "naturally" occurring negative shift. Researchers interested in using student judgments are cautioned to use the same starting and ending times for all groups to avoid the confusion of this end-of-term effect. September to January will not lead to the same effect as February to June.

References

Bryan, R. C. Reactions to teachers by students, parents, and administrators. United States Office of Education, Cooperative Research Project No. 668. Kalamazoo: Western Michigan University, 1963.

Campbell, D. T., and Stanley, J. C. Experimental and quasi-experimental designs for research on teaching. In N. L. Gage (Ed.), *Handbook of research on teaching.* Chicago: Rand McNally, 1963.

Daw, R. W., and Gage, N. L. Effect of feedback from teachers to principals. *Journal of Educational Psychology,* 1967, 58, 181–188.

Duncan, D. B. Multiple range and multiple F tests. *Biometrics,* 1955, 11, 1–42.

Gage, N. L., Runkel, P. J., and Chatterjee, B. B. Equilibrium theory and behavior change: An experiment in feedback from pupils to teachers. Report No. 6 in Studies in the generality and behavioral correlates of social perception. Urbana: Bureau of Educational Research, College of Education, University of Illinois, 1960.

Peterson, W. A. Age, teacher role, and the institutional setting. In B. J. Biddle and W. J. Ellena (Eds.), *Contemporary research on teacher effectiveness.* New York: Holt, Rinehart and Winston, 1964.

Remmers, H. H. Rating methods in research on teaching. In N. L. Gage (Ed.), *Handbook of research on teaching.* Chicago: Rand McNally, 1963.

Ryans, D. G. Characteristics of teachers. In B. J. Biddle and W. J. Ellena (Eds.), *Contemporary research on teacher effectiveness.* New York: Holt, Rinehart and Winston, 1964.

Tuckman, B. W. A *study of the effectiveness of directive versus non-*

directive vocational teachers as a function of student characteristics and course format. United States Office of Education, Project No. 6-2300, Progress Report No. 1. New Brunswick: Rutgers, The State University, 1967.

Winer, B. J. *Statistical principles in experimental design.* New York: McGraw-Hill, 1962.

2. CHANGES IN PUPIL ATTITUDES DURING THE SCHOOL YEAR*

Ned A. Flanders, Betty M. Morrison, and E. Leland Brode

Are pupils most optimistic about schoolwork as the school year begins? Does this optimism erode as the school year progresses? Are there particular patterns of teacher behavior which appear when there is less erosion of optimistic pupil attitudes? This article will attempt to answer these questions, not with complete, unequivocal answers, but with some suggestions based on two separate studies.

In a 1960–61 Minnesota study (Flanders, 1963), fairly conclusive evidence was collected indicating that over 3,000 students in two junior high schools scored highest on an attitude inventory assessing positive perceptions of their teachers and their schoolwork in October, only to have a statistically significant decrease in the scores of a January readministration of the same inventory. A follow-up administration was about the same as January, significantly lower than the October scores.

The 1960 attitude inventory consisted of 59 items roughly divided into four sub-scales on the basis of content: (*a*) teacher attractiveness, which included such items as, "I would like to have this same teacher next year," and, "This is the best teacher I ever had," (*b*) fairness of rewards and punishments, which included such items as, "This teacher punishes me for things I didn't do," and, "This teacher punishes the whole class

* From: Ned A. Flanders, Betty M. Morrison, and E. Leland Brode, "Changes in Pupil Attitudes during the School Year," *Journal of Educational Psychology*, 59, 1968, 334–338. Copyright 1968 by the American Psychological Association, and reproduced by permission. This article is based on research supported by the United States Office of Education. The first author was project director; the second author was in charge of statistical analysis; and E. Leland Brode was in charge of data collection.

when he (she) can't find out who did something," (c) teacher competence, which included such items as, "Our teacher is very good at explaining things clearly," and, "It is easy to fool this teacher," and (d) interest in schoolwork, including such items as, "This teacher makes
everything seem interesting and important," and, "Most of us get pretty
bored in this class." The response to each item was on a 5-point scale
from strongly disagree to strongly agree. All items were keyed so that a
higher score represented more positive attitudes and perceptions.

The mean score of the October administration of the attitude inventory was 217. The means of the January and May administrations were
204 and 205, respectively—both significantly lower ($p < .01$) than the
October administration. These data were collected in so-called academic
classes in Grades 7, 8, and 9, excluding such subjects as physical education, music, home economics, and shop.

The results seem quite clear. There is a significant reduction in the
average scores of positive pupil perceptions between October and January of the school year.

The Present Study

During the 1964–65 school year a Michigan Student Questionnaire
(MSQ) was administered to 101 sixth-grade classes in 15 school districts
near Ann Arbor. Thirty classes were selected for further study from the
October distribution to include the top 10, the bottom 10, and 10 near
the average of the 101 classes. The test was readministered in January
and again in May in these 30 classes, each administration involving
more than 800 pupils, and the sample can be considered representative
of over 3,000 pupils who were in the larger population.

The MSQ was essentially the same inventory used in 1960–61 except
that the items had been simplified in an effort to adjust the vocabulary
to the reading skills of sixth-grade pupils. A factor analysis of the MSQ
indicated that the most important factor was teacher attractiveness, with
additional factors of teacher competence, teacher fairness, and lack of
pupil anxiety forming a combination which was less important than the
first factor.

The means for each of the 30 classes are shown in Table 1, arranged
in terms of the top, middle, and bottom 10 classes on the October administration.

The 1964–65 results were nearly identical to the 1960–61 results.
There was a significant drop in average scores of positive pupil attitudes
during the first 4 months of the school year. The mean score for the October administration was 178.2 with a standard deviation of 26.52. The

TABLE 1
Means of 30 Classes on the 1964–65 Michigan Student Questionnaire

	ADMINISTRATION				ADMINISTRATION		
CLASS	OCT.	JAN.	MAY	CLASS	OCT.	JAN.	MAY
1	204.9	194.7	194.2	16	178.8	178.0	176.1
2	201.4	200.0	195.4	17	177.9	185.4	178.2
3	200.3	204.9	200.0	18	176.2	166.6	169.3
4	199.6	194.7	192.3	19	175.4	169.2	167.0
5	197.5	195.2	195.2	20	173.8	170.2	166.5
6	197.0	193.5	189.9	21	166.4	173.1	175.0
7	193.6	190.6	187.9	22	166.2	147.7	150.4
8	192.0	185.7	175.9	23	165.1	151.3	143.8
9	191.6	178.9	186.5	24	162.7	174.7	173.9
10	190.3	178.3	176.3	25	162.7	159.8	160.8
11	180.9	163.7	156.3	26	158.1	149.4	147.2
12	179.2	180.3	176.2	27	158.1	154.0	161.2
13	178.8	173.3	164.5	28	157.2	145.5	139.2
14	176.8	171.4	155.7	29	156.6	137.3	147.7
15	175.2	151.9	155.7	30	149.9	137.2	142.2

January administration had a mean of 172.2 and a standard deviation of 31.13; and the May administration had a mean of 170.6 and a standard deviation of 30.60.

The rest of this article will discuss the various factors that might be related to the observed change in attitude, one administration compared to the next.

FACTORS NOT ASSOCIATED WITH CHANGE IN ATTITUDE

Simple regression is not an adequate explanation of these changes. While it is true that three low classes (Classes 21, 24, and 27) showed the highest positive changes, it is also true that three other low classes (Classes 22, 23, and 28) showed large decreases. The average loss (October to May) of the bottom 10 classes was 6.2, compared to 7.6 for the total group. Furthermore, the top 10 classes do not show uniform loss but instead are symmetrically distributed about an average loss of 7.5.

The correlations between administrations, based on individual scores, were positive and fairly high: for October to January, $r = .704$; for January to May, $r = .812$; and October to May, $r = .655$. The correlation between October and May, based on 30 class averages, is higher; $r = .876$. The correlations present a picture of a fairly stable response pattern both within and between classes.

There is the possibility that change in positive pupil attitudes might be associated with the average class IQ, socioeconomic status, or the percentage of A and B letter grades assigned to the pupils by the teacher. Table 2 shows such data for the nine classes which had high change losses and the seven classes with the least amount of change. The mean IQ for the high-change group was 113.5, while it was 112.3 for the low-change group. Here the IQ scores used were those based on school records and probably involved different published tests. The median socioeconomic rating for the high-change group was 71; a median rating of 70 was obtained for the low-change group. Here a rating on the National Opinion Research Center scale (Reiss, 1961) was made of the wage earner's occupation as reported by the teacher. The mean per-

TABLE 2
Comparisons between High- and Low-Attitude Change Classes [a]

	HIGH CHANGE		
CLASS NO.	IQ	SES RATING	% OF A & B GRADES
11	121.6	81	75
23	104.2	67	33
14	111.7	71	64
15	118.5	67	52
28	109.8	74	41
8	116.8	78	57
22	110.3	67	63
13	116.0	83	80
10	112.7	70	42
	LOW CHANGE		
CLASS NO.	IQ	SES RATING	% OF A & B GRADES
3	118.1	65	91
17	114.1	78	55
25	104.1	69	48
5	113.1	70	66
16	120.7	71	81
12	100.0	63	50
27	116.1	83	62

[a] SES = socioeconomic status.

centage of A and B letter grades for the high-change group was 56.5 and for the low-change group, 64.5. While this last difference is consistent with a theory that change involving loss of positive attitudes is associated with receiving lower grades, a z test between independent proportions yielded a value of 1.66 which was not high enough to reject the null hypothesis at the .05 level of significance. All of these data suggest that changes in class attitudes are not significantly associated with average IQ, socioeconomic status, or grades given by the teacher.

TWO FACTORS ASSOCIATED WITH CHANGE IN ATTITUDE

In another study, Morrison (1966) has shown that Rotter's notion of "externality" and "internality" (Rotter, Seeman, & Liversant, 1962) can be assessed among sixth-grade pupils. By externality is meant the tendency of a pupil to believe that his successes and failures are caused by forces beyond his control. By internality is meant the tendency to believe that successes and failures are self-determined and products of one's own behavior. External children, according to Morrison's conception, would be more likely to associate the good and bad outcomes of classroom learning activities with the teacher who is a powerful source of influence. Internal children, on the other hand, would see themselves as more closely associated with the good and bad characteristics of learning outcomes.

A test of internality-externality was administered to all the pupils in the 30 classes during the January administration of tests. The test consisted of 26 items, each containing two statements, and the pupils responded by marking the statement in each item which they believed was more often true. Typical items were: (a) "If you study you will do well on a test," or (b) "People who score the highest on a test are lucky." —(a) "Most of the time children get the respect they deserve from others," or (b) "Many times a child can try hard and no one will pay attention to him."—(a) "Usually other people choose me for a friend," or (b) "Usually I choose my own friends."—(a) "Children get into trouble because their parents punish them too much," or (b) "The trouble with most children is that their parents are too easy with them."

Each item was scored 1 if the internal response was chosen and 2 if the external response was selected, giving a possible range from 26 to 52 for the total scores. The actual scores ranged from 26 to 49. Students in the lower third of the distribution (raw scores of 31 and below) were defined as internals and those in the upper third (raw scores of 36 and above) were defined as externals.

In addition to these tests each of the 30 classrooms was visited by an observer trained to code verbal communication into the 10 categories of interaction analysis developed by Flanders (1965). More than six visits were made to each class and more than 7,000 tallies were recorded by observers. The main results of interaction analysis will be reported elsewhere; the interest for the moment is in the incidence of praise and encouragement expressed by the teachers during these visits. The occurrence of this type of teacher statement varied from low of .2% to a high of 2.1% of all tallies recorded by the observer. The problems of reliability among observers and the representativeness of the interaction sampled are too complex to be discussed here. It can be said, however, that the relative objectivity of the observation data, or lack of it, would affect the data from all classes equally and cannot account for any of the differences about to be discussed.

It was hypothesized in this study that:

1. External children have a greater negative shift in attitude than do internal children.

2. The classes of low-praise teachers have a greater negative shift in attitude than do the classes of high-praise teachers.

3. The attitudes of external children are more affected by the praise and encouragement of the teacher than are the attitudes of internal children.

To test these hypotheses a two-way analysis of covariance in the case of unequal or disproportionate numbers of observations in the subclasses was performed using the third attitude inventory scores as the dependent variable and adjusting with the scores from the first administration. Table 3 includes the October means, the May means, and May means adjusted for the initial attitudes, and the change means. These are arranged in sub-groups of internal and external pupils and pupils with high-praise and low-praise teachers.

The slope of the regression line was .845, and the analysis of covariance yielded an error mean square of 520.7. The main effect for internal versus external pupils produced a mean square of 18,331 and the resulting F ratio is significant at well beyond the .01 level ($F = 35.20$, $df = 1/473$). The main effect for pupils of high-praise versus low-praise teachers produced a mean square of 7,128, also resulting in an F ratio which is significant at well beyond the .01 level ($F = 13.69$, $df = 1/473$). However, the interaction of pupil types and teacher styles resulted in a mean square of only 90, which is not significant ($F = .17$).

These results indicate that not only did external pupils have less positive attitudes than did internal pupils early in the school year, but when the May scores are adjusted by the October scores, it is apparent that external pupils experienced significantly greater declines in their attitudes than did internal pupils. Also, pupils with low-praise teachers showed greater losses in positive attitudes during the year than did pu-

TABLE 3
Initial, Final, and Adjusted Means of Attitude Scores from
Analysis of Covariance by Pupil Type and Teacher Style

| | PUPILS | | |
TEACHER STYLE	INTERNAL	EXTERNAL	ALL
High-praise			
Initial M	190.6	171.0	183.9
Final M	187.3	159.2	177.7
Adjusted M	163.7	152.1	159.7
Change M	-3.3	-11.8	-6.2
Low-praise			
Initial M	178.7	121.5	143.9
Final M	173.1	111.3	135.5
Adjusted M	159.5	146.0	151.3
Change M	-5.6	-10.2	-8.4
All			
Initial M	185.8	137.8	162.6
Final M	181.6	127.1	155.2
Adjusted M	162.0	148.0	—
Change M	-4.2	-10.7	—

pils with high-praise teachers. However, there was no evidence that the attitudes of external children were more affected by praise or lack of praise on the part of the teacher than were the attitudes of the internal children.

Discussion and Conclusions

In two separate projects the attitude inventory scores indicate that positive perceptions of pupils toward their teacher and their class activities decrease sometime during the first 4 months of the school year. In the second project these changes were shown to be unrelated to IQ, performance grades assigned by the teacher, and the socioeconomic ratings of the father's occupation. Two hypotheses about changes in attitude were supported. First, external pupils experience a greater loss of positive attitudes toward school than do internal pupils. Second, in classrooms of teachers who provide less praise and encouragement there is greater loss of positive attitudes than in classrooms of teachers who provide more praise and encouragement. The third hypothesis was not supported since the interaction effects in Table 3 are not significant.

One inference to be drawn is that the type of youngster who is more dependent on external influences seems to be more likely to suffer a loss of positive expectations than is the one who is more dependent on internal influences. In addition, pupil attitudes toward the teacher and the learning activities seem to be related to teacher behavior. Whether this difference in pupil attitudes is the result of the different teacher behaviors, or the different amounts of teacher praise and encouragement are the result of the pupils being more or less deserving of that praise, is not clear from the evidence of the present study. The absence of a significant difference between high-change and low-change classes with respect to the percentage of A and B grades given by the teacher (Table 2) would indicate that the pupils' performance was not the deciding factor. Also, previous studies (Flanders, 1963, 1965) have indicated that teacher behavior is the more dominant factor and that differences in such patterns of teacher influence tend to be greater between different teachers than between different situations for the same teacher.

In this sample, differences among the pupils had a greater effect than the presence or absence of a small amount of teacher praise and encouragement. Future studies of the erosion of positive pupil attitudes may wish to take into account other differences among pupils as well as differences in teacher behavior.

This study did not provide direct evidence concerning two opposite hypotheses about the erosion of positive pupil attitudes. One theory is that the pupils become disenchanted with the teacher during the first few months of the school year. A second theory, based on the assumption that the October scores are inflated or too high, is that as the pupils learn to trust their teacher they do not overestimate their ratings as they felt compelled to do with a strange teacher. Without going into detail, the authors tend toward the first of these two theories, primarily because the teacher's behavior is the predominant influence in the typical classroom; but much more evidence will be required before any conclusions can be reached.

Meantime, lack of loss of positive attitudes may be the mark of a good match between teaching behavior and particular attributes among pupils. Apparently, in most classrooms such a match does not exist.

References

Flanders, N. A. Helping teachers change their behavior. Terminal report, National Educational Defense Act, Title VII project, 1963.

Flanders, N. A. *Teacher influence, pupil attitudes, and achievement.*

United States Office of Education Cooperative Research Monograph No. 12. Washington, D. C.: United States Government Printing Office, 1965.

Morrison, B. M. The reactions of external and internal pupils to patterns of teacher behavior. Unpublished doctoral dissertation, University of Michigan, 1966.

Reiss, A. J., Jr. *Occupations and social status.* New York: Free Press, 1961.

Rotter, J. B., Seeman, M., and Liversant, S. Internal versus external control of reinforcements: A major variable in behavior theory. In N. F. Washburne (Ed.), *Decisions, values, and groups.* Vol. 2. London: Pergamon Press, 1962.

3. THE MORAL REPUTATION CORRELATES OF COMPETENCE REPUTATION*

Roy Gladstone

A. Problem

This experiment was designed to discover whether Ss, given socially evaluative but morally neutral information about children, would have stereotyped expectations about the moral characteristics of those children. To this end a kind of case history was developed for each of the children. The information given described two children as generally competent and two as generally incompetent. The case histories were modified into two forms varying only in the adjectives used. In one form the evaluative adjectives were varied while in the other form the adjectives "good" and "bad" were used throughout to indicate the evaluation. The latter material was designed (fruitlessly as it turned out) to discover whether the moral meaning of *good* and *bad* might not have a conditioning effect.

Both forms were followed by the same questions. The questions were of the "guess-who" form, some ascribing competency, others ascribing moral behavior. It was the latter questions, the answers to which had not been supplied, which were the critical questions. The answers to the

* *Journal of Social Psychology,* 1963, 59, 283–288. Reprinted with permission of the author and the publisher, The Journal Press.

others were ignored. All the questions were repeated twice, first as forced-choice questions, then with the inclusion of "no information given" as an alternative. The latter questions were designed to discover whether or not the Ss knew they were answering the critical questions on the basis of inference. The S could give as many answers to each question as he wished but was required to give at least one answer.

After finishing the questions the Ss were allowed to comment on the feelings they had had while dealing with the material and the questions.

B. Questionnaire

The questionnaire is largely reproduced below. Questions 4, 6, 8, 10, 12, 16, and the counterparts of those questions in the second (repeated) set of questions are the critical questions. The material was given to the Ss in reproduced form with separate answer sheets. The directions on the first and second pages were read with special emphasis upon those portions indicating that the Ss were to ask no questions after starting and to answer all the questions. It was pointed out that they could say what they thought about the material on the last page.

Directions:

Read the following information as rapidly as you can and still understand it. After finishing the material you will be asked some questions based upon it.

Fred, Jim, Ted and Jack were all the same age, they all grew up in the same small town, and then went to the same schools. They were in school before I got to know them. Fred was an excellent student and, in contrast to some students who made high grades by sheer labor, Fred had a fine head on his shoulders. Ted was a very competent mechanic. Ted's high mechanical ability enabled him to sail through his shop courses with ease.

Unfortunately, Jim and Jack were poor students. Jim's faulty arithmetic was the despair of his teacher while Jack's reading nearly drove his teachers frantic.

All four boys went out for athletics. Ted was outstanding as a half-back while Fred's expert fielding made him outstanding at baseball. Basketball was the sport chosen by Jack but persistent fumbling kept him on the sidelines. Likewise, Jim's inability to hold the ball kept him off the football team.

As might be expected, Fred and Ted liked school while Jim and Jack disliked school. Since the teachers in the school were really a decent lot, Fred and Ted's reaction pleased them and Jim and Jack's reaction really distressed them. Nevertheless, there was a general feeling that Ted and Fred would be successful while the feeling was pretty general that Jim and Jack would be unsuccessful.

One of the counselors became interested in this reaction and decided to try to discover just how valid it was. He did a study several years after the boys had graduated. He emerged with the following report:

Automobile

Jack: ancient Oldsmobile
Ted: late model Mercury
Fred: late model Buick
Jim: dilapidated Kaiser

Work and Reputation in Work

Jim: inept carpenter
Fred: good salesman
Jack: inefficient clerk
Ted: competent bank teller

Home Appearance

Jack: shabby, small
Ted: clean, fairly large, attractive
Jim: poor section of town, paint peeling
Fred: lovely, spacious

Turn this page over and go on with the next page. Read the Directions carefully.

Work rapidly in answering the following questions. Do not turn back to the information sheet. *Answer all the questions.* Some of the questions require you to make an inference from what you have read rather than being directly stated in that material. *Do not ask any questions until the papers are collected.* After that you may ask questions.

Use the answer sheet provided. There may be more than one right answer. Do not change any answers after you have put them down.

(1) Who was (were) the best student(s)?
    (a) Ted   (b) Fred   (c) Jack   (d) Jim

(2) Who was (were) liked by the teachers?
    (a) Ted   (b) Fred   (c) Jack   (d) Jim

(3) Who was (were) best in arithmetic?
    (a) Ted   (b) Fred   (c) Jack   (d) Jim

(4) Who cheated on tests?
    (a) Ted   (b) Fred   (c) Jack   (d) Jim

(5) Who was (were) best in automotive mechanics?
    (a) Ted   (b) Fred   (c) Jack   (d) Jim

(6) Who was (were) most willing to help the other children in school?
    (a) Ted   (b) Fred   (c) Jack   (d) Jim

(7) Who was (were) best in football?
   (a) Ted   (b) Fred   (c) Jack   (d) Jim
(8) Who was (were) willing to cheat in order to win on the playground?
   (a) Ted   (b) Fred   (c) Jack   (d) Jim
(9) Who was (were) best in baseball?
   (a) Ted   (b) Fred   (c) Jack   (d) Jim
(10) Who tended to pick on smaller children?
   (a) Ted   (b) Fred   (c) Jack   (d) Jim
(11) Who had most difficulty with arithmetic?
   (a) Ted   (b) Fred   (c) Jack   (d) Jim
(12) Who was outstandingly kind to the crippled mascot of the teams?
   (a) Ted   (b) Fred   (c) Jack   (d) Jim
(13) Who had most difficulty with reading?
   (a) Ted   (b) Fred   (c) Jack   (d) Jim
(14) Who failed to make the basketball team?
   (a) Ted   (b) Fred   (c) Jack   (d) Jim
(15) Whose careers seemed most desirable?
   (a) Ted   (b) Fred   (c) Jack   (d) Jim
(16) Who picked up little things on the job and brought them home for his personal use?
   (a) Ted   (b) Fred   (c) Jack   (d) Jim
(17) The teachers made predictions about the future success of the boys. Which boys were they right about?
   (a) Ted   (b) Fred   (c) Jack   (d) Jim

Go on to the next page.

On the next page the questions given above were repeated with the following alternatives: (a) No information given   (b) Ted   (c) Fred   (d) Jack   (e) Jim. This was followed by another page, mostly blank, which was headed:

While working on the preceding material most people have reactions of one sort or another which they don't have when dealing with most of the things they read and questions they answer. What reactions did you have while working on it?

C. Subjects

Forty-one Ss answered the questionnaire reproduced above while 42 answered the modified form. Four answer sheets were voided as a result of not having answers to the critical questions or of having marks on all four alternatives on all or most of those questions. The Ss were all students at the Oklahoma State University taking Introductory Psychology. There were about 60 per cent freshmen, 30 per cent sophomores, five per cent juniors and five per cent seniors. Females comprised 60 per cent of the class, males 40 per cent.

The occupations of their fathers as indicated by the Ss ranged from "farmer and laborer" to "bank director." Evaluating the occupations rather crudely with the aid of the Sims SCI Occupational Rating Scale Manual, Table 2 (1), there were about five per cent at the lower-working level, 10 per cent working, 30 per cent middle-working, 30 per cent middle, 20 per cent upper-middle, five per cent upper, and zero per cent upper-upper. The number in the upper class is probably inflated.

D. Results

When the students answered the portion of the questions on which they were allowed to answer "no information given," they showed overwhelmingly that they realized they had been given no direct information from which they might have been enabled to give answers to the critical questions. There were 448 "no information" answers to 31 answers of any other kind. The essay material gave additional evidence that the Ss were aware of the circumstances and indicated, in addition, that many Ss felt they had been confused by the information and could not remember well who had done what. Several of the Ss indicated discomfort in being forced to make an evaluation without sufficient information. Some stated rather indignantly that just because a boy is not a good student is no indication that he will cheat.

Whatever the memory faults or qualms of conscience of the Ss they were not prevented from giving overwhelming blanket disapproval to Jack and Jim, the incompetents, when forced to "guess who."

The votes were counted as follows: if S voted for Ted *or* Fred this was one vote for the team of Ted and Fred. If S voted for *both* Ted and Fred this was still counted as one vote. Some Ss voted for both teams.

On the question, "who cheated on tests?" (Question 4) the S inferred Jack and Jim (the incompetents), 78 to four. When asked who was willing to help other children (Question 6) the Ss said Ted and Fred, 78 to four. The vote on Question 8 (cheating) named Jack and Jim, 74 to five. On Question 10 (bullying) Jack and Jim were voted the culprits, 77 to three. On Question 12 (who was kind?) Ted and Fred were elected 72 to 15. On Question 16 (theft) the vote was 68 to 15 against Jack and Jim. The indignant Ss were only slightly less extreme in their indictment of Jack and Jim.

One question, "who was liked by the teachers?" was an anomaly designed to make the process of inference seem tenable. As expected, on the forced-choice question the Ss inferred that Ted and Fred would be liked, the vote being 78 to three, but the surprise came on Question 19 when the Ss were allowed to answer "no information." They answered as follows: no information, 17; Ted and Fred, 68; and Jack and Jim, three. Apparently the Ss were convinced that poor students just aren't loved by teachers. Also they were evidently confused by the switch in alternatives since many voted "no information" and "Ted" both.

There was no evidence of the conditioning effects of the words "good" and "bad." This is not to say that there was no conditioning—the overwhelming stereotyping effects gave the conditioning effects, if any, scant chance to evidence themselves. Of course it is possible to suggest that the results obtained were a partial function of the conditioning powers of all the adjectives, but the fact that many of the Ss recognized that they were answering on the basis of an incompetent-immoral stereotype militates against the conditioning hypothesis. However, only further experimentation can settle the question.

E. Conclusion

Poor Jacks and Jims.

F. Summary

Two fictitious boys were described as competent in many areas and two as incompetent in the same areas. College students, principally of the middle class, then were given forced-choice tests requiring them to decide which of the boys would be moral and kind and which immoral and not kind. Overwhelmingly the students indicated they thought the competent boys would be moral and kind and the incompetent boys would be immoral and not kind.

While verbal conditioning could be used to explain the results it seems more reasonable to assume that stereotyping is the real culprit.

Reference

1. Sims, V. M. *Sims SCI Occupational Rating Scale Manual of Directions.* New York: Harcourt, Brace & World, 1952.

4. SEX AND SCHOLASTIC APTITUDE AS VARIABLES IN TEACHER RATINGS OF THE ADJUSTMENT AND CLASSROOM BEHAVIOR OF NEGRO AND OTHER SEVENTH-GRADE STUDENTS *

Lois-ellin Datta, Earl Schaefer, and Malcolm Davis

Little is known about the associates of teachers' opinions of Negro and white pupils, although the importance of teachers' opinions and the fact that they are related to demographic variables such as sex and socioeconomic status appears to be well documented.

It has frequently been reported that teachers are more likely to describe boys than girls as maladjusted or as behavior problems (Beilin, 1959; Goldstein & Chorost, 1966; Long & Henderson, 1966; Vroegh & Handrich, 1966) and that children from well-to-do families are more likely than are lower-class children to meet with approbation and success in school (Charters, 1963). This latter finding has been interpreted as an indirect effect of social class differentials in academic preparation and opportunities (Sexton, 1961), but other studies have indicated that even among children of equal academic achievement who attend the same school, students whose parents are semi-skilled, unskilled, or unemployed are described less favorably than are students from upper- and middle-class families (Davidson & Lang, 1960).

There is considerable evidence that students who are described unfavorably by their teachers tend (*a*) to describe themselves unfavorably, (*b*) to be aware of their teachers' poor opinion of them, and (*c*) to receive lower grades than students whom the teacher describes favorably (Davidson & Lang, 1960; de Groat & Thompson, 1949; Fox, Lippitt, & Schmuck, 1964; Goldblatt & Tyson, 1962). Despite agreement that teacher attitudes toward Negro children should be highly important for

* From: Lois-ellin Datta, Earl Schaefer, and Malcolm Davis, "Sex and Scholastic Aptitude as Variables in Teachers' Ratings of the Adjustment and Classroom Behavior of Negro and Other Seventh-Grade Students," *Journal of Educational Psychology*, 59, 1968, 94–101. Copyright 1968 by the American Psychological Association, and reproduced by permission. The authors wish to thank Karen Pettigrew for statistical guidance and for computation of the tests for linearity of regression and Ann Drake for her assistance in the analysis and interpretation of results.

their classroom behavior (Clark, 1963; Coleman, 1966; Deutsch, 1960; Katz, 1964; Riessman, 1962), Katz (1967) has concluded that there has been no adequate assessment of the attitudes of white teachers toward minority-group pupils.

The present analyses were undertaken to identify for use in planning an inservice teacher education program to facilitate integration, the extent to which the variables of sex and scholastic ability are associated with teachers' descriptions of Negro and Other-than-Negro students.

Method

SUBJECTS

The subjects (Ss) were selected from seventh-grade classes in a northern Virginia suburban community which had integrated its schools in the year of the study. Ethnic group membership was inferred from attendance at segregated schools during the prior year. By this criterion, 9.8% (199) of all seventh-grade students were Negro and 90.2% (1931) were Other-than-Negro. (These students will hereafter be referred to as Others.[1]) The small total population of Negro students precluded selecting proportional random samples of Negro and Other Ss. In order to include as many Negro Ss as possible within the practical limits of teacher contact, the junior high schools with the largest numbers of Negro students were identified. Eighty-nine percent of the Negro students attended three of the system's six junior high schools. It was not possible to estimate social-class membership directly for each student; however, two of the schools were in neighborhoods judged as lower class (mixed residential and commercial buildings, low-cost housing, poor upkeep of buildings) and one, by the same criteria, was judged to be lower middle class. As these schools draw students from neighborhoods surrounding them, the social class of the student group may be at least generally inferred. In the two schools judged to draw lower-class students, 24.5% and 27.7% of the seventh-grade students were Negro. In the third school, which was judged to draw lower middle-class students, 9.8% of the seventh-grade students were Negro. A sample of 100 Negro and 100 Other Ss was chosen by a table of random numbers from the total of 177 Negro and 805 Other students attending these three schools. The students were not selected with consideration as to sex.

---

[1] The community, while predominantly white, includes a variety of ethnic groups. No direct information on family background can be obtained for the Ss. The students who had not attended a Negro school are therefore described as "Others" and the variable will be referred to as ethnic group rather than race.

PROCEDURE

One teacher was selected at random from each S's schedule card. Both to conserve teacher time and to avoid, insofar as possible, biasing the data with respect to individual differences among raters, no teacher was asked to evaluate more than five students. In the "lower middle-class" school, all 17 seventh-grade teachers were included in the survey; in the other two schools, 76.7% (23 out of 34) of the seventh-grade teachers participated. Twenty of these 40 teachers taught general education courses, five taught mathematics, and the remaining 15 taught subjects such as physical education, language, music, and art. Thirty-six of the teachers were white and 30 were women. Class assignment in the system, and therefore selection for inclusion in the sample, was random with respect to pupil and teacher ethnic group and sex.

The teachers were contacted by mail. The covering letter stated that the intention of the study was to standardize the instruments and requested the teacher's cooperation in describing the adjustment and classroom behavior of the five students selected for him or her.

The questionnaires were distributed in November 1965. Of the 200 eligible students, 178 were rated and 153 records were sufficiently complete to be included in the analyses. There were significant differences in the proportion of records returned by ethnic group (92% returns for Other Ss as compared with 61% returns for Negro Ss), but not by sex. Nonreturns were due primarily to insufficient teacher time and to the fact that 11 pupils had left the school system between the time of selection and rating.

MEASURES

The teachers were asked to rate the students' adjustment on the following scale which was developed by Ullman (1952) and modified by Glidewell, Domkee, and Kantor (1963). The first two categories of Glidewell et al.'s scale were revised to emphasize social rather than academic accomplishment as the criterion of adjustment.

1. Well adjusted. A happy child who is well adjusted in his relationships with others and in his activities.

2. No significant problems. A child who gets along reasonably well and has little or no difficulty adjusting to others or to classroom activities.

3. Subclinically disturbed. A child who is not so happy as he might be; has moderate difficulties getting on; and to whom growing up represents something of a struggle.

4. Clinically disturbed. A child who has, or at his present rate is likely to have, serious problems of adjustment, and needs clinical help because of such problems.

It will be noted that with this instrument the teachers were not asked to identify students who presented problems in classroom management; attention was rather directed toward a more clinical definition of social and emotional adjustment.

The teachers were then asked to rate each of their students on the Classroom Behavior Inventory, (CBI), a recently developed 320-item questionnaire (Schaefer, Aaronson, & Burgoon, 1966). The questionnaire items were intended to describe behavior and to reduce as much as possible inferences about motives and feelings. Sample items included: "Often disagrees with what others suggest," "Brags how he is able to outwit others," "Begins work at once, as soon as something is assigned," "Seldom talks to other children before or after class," "Sticks to old ways of doing things; hates to make changes."

The teacher was asked to describe the behavior of each child for each item, with the following response options: 1. Not at all like the child, 2. Very little like the child, 3. Somewhat like the child, and 4. Very much like the child. The specific instructions were:

Please give a response to every item and base your response upon your personal observation and experience with the pupil. In the case of items relating to behavior which you have not observed, respond as you would expect this child to behave as a general rule.

There are 64 five-item scales. Scale reliabilities for the sample of 153 Ss as estimated by Kuder-Richardson formula 20 ranged from .73 to .96. The median internal consistency scale reliability was .86. A principal components analysis, Varimax rotation, yielded three factors. Scales describing perseverance, conscientiousness, concentration, achievement orientation, academic seriousness, and methodicalness had loadings of .76–.86 on Factor I, "Positive task orientation." Irritability, argumentativeness, attention seeking, boastfulness, quarrelsomeness, and dominance had loadings of .86–.93 on Factor II, "Verbal aggression." Active helpfulness, cheerfulness, and gregariousness had high negative loadings and social withdrawal, depression, and emotional passivity had high positive loadings on Factor III, "Introversion-extroversion." Adjustment ratings correlated .43, .43, and − .48, respectively, with the three factors. The average scores of each S were computed for the six scales with the highest loadings on each of the three factors. (Due to computer limitations, true factor scores could not be computed. The average scores would be expected, however, to correlate highly with the true factor scores.)

Scholastic aptitude was estimated by the California Mental Maturity Test, Short Form, (CMMT), which had been administered in the last part of the sixth grade. CMMT IQ equivalents were used in the analyses as measures of scholastic aptitude. Also reported are grade-equivalent scores for the Iowa Silent Reading Test, which was administered at the beginning of the seventh grade.

Results

The distribution of adjustment ratings by sex and ethnic group is shown in Table 1. Only 4% of all Ss were described as clinical problems, 33% of the students were described as very well adjusted, 40% were described as presenting no problems and 23% were described as subclinical problems, a distribution similar to that reported by Ullman (1952) for ninth-grade white students. Clinically and subclinically maladjusted categories were pooled for the following 2×3 comparisons. Girls were significantly more likely than boys to be rated as well adjusted ($X^2 = 15.24$, $p < .01$), whether the students were Other ($X^2 = 6.43$, $p < .05$) or Negro ($X^2 = 12.64$, $p < .01$). Other students were more likely than Negro students to be rated as well adjusted if the students were girls ($X^2 = 8.40$, $p < .05$), but not if the students were boys ($X^2 = 2.30$, $p < 50$).

Among Other students there was no significant relation between IQ and adjustment ($r = - .05$, $p > .10$), whether the students were girls ($r = - .16$, $p > .10$) or boys ($r = .06$, $p > .10$). There was no relation between scholastic aptitude and adjustment for Negro girls

TABLE 1

Percentages of Other and Negro, Male and Female Seventh-Grade Students Rated as Adjusted and Maladjusted by Their Teachers

RACE AND SEX	N	VERY WELL	NO PROBLEMS	SUBCLINICAL	CLINICAL
			TEACHER RATINGS OF ADJUSTMENT		
Other					
Male	42	31%	33%	33%	3%
Female	47	53%	32%	13%	2%
Negro					
Male	31	16%	35%	35%	13%
Female	29	24%	66%	10%	0%
Total	149	33%	40%	23%	4%

($r = -.01$, $p > .10$) but the less able Negro boys were more likely than were the brighter Negro boys to be described as subclinically or clinically disturbed ($r = -.48$, $p < .01$). Scholastic aptitude is thus shown to be a significant associate of teachers' ratings of adjustment only with Negro boys.

ANALYSES BY ETHNIC GROUP AND SEX FOR THE WHOLE SAMPLE

A two-way unweighted means analysis of variance (Winer, 1962) was computed for ethnic group and sex for each of the 64 scales. On 48 of the 64 scales, the effect of sex was significant at the .05 level. On 46 scales, the effect of ethnic group was significant at the .05 level. On only one scale, "Work fluctuation," there was a significant Ethnic Group × Sex interaction. The mean IQ for girls, 101.4, did not differ significantly from the mean IQ for boys, 100.2; the mean IQ for Negro Ss, 87.5, was significantly lower than the mean IQ, 113.0, for Other Ss. While scholastic aptitude would not seem to account for the differential desscription of boys and girls, the characteristics attributed to Negro Ss as compared to Other Ss might be associated with lower scholastic ability rather than with ethnic group per se.

There are considerable methodological difficulties in isolating the variance due to ethnic group and sex from that due to scholastic aptitude because of the low overlap in the CMMT distributions and the asymmetry of IQ/adjustment and IQ/CBI scale correlations. As an example, "submissive" correlated $-.30$ with CMMT IQ for Other girls and $+.40$ for Negro boys; "methodical" correlated .51 and .40 with IQ for Negro girls and Negro boys, but for Other boys, $r = .01$. Analysis of covariance was not appropriate since, except for Negro Ss, there was no reliable evidence of a linear relation between the dependent variables and scholastic aptitude as measured by the CMMT. Despite restrictions on generalizations to the upper end of the Other IQ distribution, the most defensible approach seemed to be a three-way analysis of variance for ethnic group, sex, and IQ.

ANALYSES BY SEX, ETHNIC GROUP AND SCHOLASTIC APTITUDE FOR IQ EQUIVALENT SUBSAMPLES

The overlap between Other and Negro CMMT distributions ranged from IQ 68 to 114. Other students with IQs above 115 ($N = 37$) were dropped from these analyses in order to facilitate matching IQ groups; all Ss with IQs below 68 ($N = 6$) were also dropped. "Higher" Ss were

TABLE 2

Means and Ns of Teacher Ratings on Factor Scores: I, Task Orientation (TO); II, Verbal Aggression (VA); Extroversion (E) and Introversion (I) by Scholastic Aptitude, Ethnic Group and Sex for Seventh-Grade Students

GROUP[a]	N	MEAN CMMT IQ	MEAN READING ACHIEVEMENT	TO	VA	E	I
Males—Negro							
Low IQ	15	81.5	3.9	9.8	12.1	11.6	12.7
High IQ	11	105.2	4.9	11.7	9.9	13.8	12.1
Other							
Low IQ	8	78.9	4.5	13.5	10.1	14.2	11.3
High IQ	11	109.4	6.6	11.8	11.7	13.4	10.8
VH IQ	20	122.9	9.5	13.2	9.5	13.8	12.6
Females—Negro							
Low IQ	18	86.7	5.4	11.7	9.1	13.8	10.5
High IQ	7	104.1	6.9	14.7	6.3	13.5	9.3
Other							
Low IQ	11	87.9	5.7	15.2	6.8	14.4	10.3
High IQ	17	108.2	7.6	15.7	7.1	15.5	8.9
VH IQ	17	123.5	9.6	15.0	8.1	15.5	9.1

FACTOR SCORE MEANS

[a] CMMT IQ (very high, 115–140; high, 99–114; low, 68–98).

defined by IQs between 99 and 114; "lower" Ss were defined by IQs between 68 and 98. Two-way unweighted means analyses of variance (ethnic group and scholastic ability) were computed for each of the 64 scales for the IQ-selected samples of boys and girls. Of the 128 Fs, 14 were significant for ethnic group at .10 level, 21 were significant for scholastic aptitude, and 27 of the interactions were statistically reliable. For expository simplicity we will describe the results primarily in terms of the $2 \times 2 \times 2$ unweighted means analysis of variance completed for average scores. To facilitate interpretation of the introversion-extroversion scores, the scales which measured introversion and extroversion were considered separately. The means for the eight cells for each of the four average scores are shown in Table 2.

Sex. As Table 3 indicates, on three of the four average scores, sex accounted for a significant portion of the variance: girls tend to be rated higher than boys in task orientation and were less likely than boys to be

TABLE 3
F Ratios for Unweighted Means Analyses of Variance by Scholastic Aptitude, Ethnic Group, and Sex Computed for Average Scores[a] Derived from Teachers' Ratings of the Classroom Behavior of Seventh-Grade Students

SOURCE	TO	VA	E	I
	F RATIOS FOR FACTOR SCORES			
A Scholastic aptitude	1.77	1.13	0.81	2.48
B Ethnic group	8.91[d]	0.31	3.81[b]	1.98
C Sex	14.27[e]	24.77[e]	2.92[b]	11.33[d]
A × B	4.82[c]	5.61[c]	0.42	.00
A × C	1.42	0.43	.00	.41
B × C	0.83	0.20	.00	.80
A × B × C	1.44	0.07	3.20[b]	.03

[a] I, Task Orientation (TO); II, Verbal Aggression (VA); III, Extroversion-Introversion (E-I); and Extroversion (E) and Introversion (I).
[b] $p < .10$.
[c] $p < .05$.
[d] $p < .01$.
[e] $p < .001$.

described as either verbally aggressive or as high in introversion; boys, regardless of ethnic group, were more likely than girls to be described as withdrawn, asocial, and emotionally passive. To see if the effect of sex was linear, analyses of variance were computed on factor scores for the Other students only by IQ (highest, higher, and lower) and sex: again, regardless of IQ, boys were described as more withdrawn, asocial, and emotionally passive than were girls. For the Other students only, with the highest IQ Ss included, girls were significantly more often described as cheerful, gregarious, and actively helpful. Sex did not interact with ethnic group or scholastic aptitude on any factor except extroversion (at the .10 level).

Scholastic aptitude. Scholastic aptitude did not account for a significant portion of the variance on any factor.

Ethnic group. Ethnic group accounted for a significant portion of the variance on task orientation and extroversion. Negro students were more likely than were Other students to be described as low in task orientation and, at the .10 level, were less likely to be described as helpful, cheerful, and gregarious. For two factors, task orientation and verbal aggression, the interaction of ethnic group with scholastic aptitude was significant. On task orientation, the difference between Negro and Other students was greater among lower-IQ than among higher-IQ Ss, regardless of sex. On verbal aggression, the effect of ethnic group depended on scholastic aptitude: among brighter students, Negro Ss were described as less verbally aggressive than were Other Ss, while among low-IQ students, Negro Ss were described as more verbally aggressive than were Other Ss. The interaction of sex, ethnic group, and scholastic aptitude were significant at the .10 level for extroversion; the difference between boys and girls, and Other and Negro students depended mainly on the low average rating of 11.6 received by low-IQ Negro boys and the high ratings of 15.5 and 15.5 received by high- and very high-IQ Other girls.

The results of these analyses and of analyses of the 64 individual scales for the IQ equivalent subsamples are summarized in the following section.

1. Among Negro students, low-IQ Ss were more frequently described as low in adjustment, low in task-orientation, verbally aggressive, rebellious, asocial, and unruly. They were seen neither as well behaved nor as studious. Higher-IQ Negro Ss were likely to be described as task oriented, methodical, persevering, sociable, trustful, submissive, and as low in rebelliousness and verbal aggression. They were seen as well behaved, hardworking, studious pupils.

2. Among Other students, low-IQ Ss were more frequently described as task oriented, low in verbal aggression, compliant, cooperative, and considerate. The CMMT and reading achievement scores suggest that they are not achieving despite the high level of academic and social effort described: not unpredictably, low-IQ Other Ss were also seen as lower in self-esteem, and as more tense and fatigued than were the other three subgroups. The higher IQ Other Ss were likely to be described as task oriented, verbally aggressive, inquisitive, enthusiastic, and as leaders.

In the IQ equivalent subsample, then, ethnic group is associated with descriptions of classroom behavior, but the direction of the association tends to be contingent on the scholastic aptitude of S and is due primarily to the unfavorable descriptions of Negro as contrasted to Other low-IQ students, particularly Negro boys. The classroom behaviors described by the teachers suggest that the low-IQ Other student and the higher IQ Negro student tend to cope with the demands of school by working hard and carefully and by offering few problems in classroom management. The low-IQ Negro student appears to have resigned from the educational process and is seen as poorly adjusted, unruly, and uninvolved, behaving in ways generally considered to be associated with educational failure and classroom management difficulty. The data suggest that the Other, higher IQ student may be freer to adopt a mode of response characterized by exploration, dominance, independence, and academic interest.

3. Regardless of ethnic group or scholastic aptitude, boys were more likely to be described as hyperactive, asocial, verbally and physically aggressive, and tense and were less likely to be described as friendly, methodical, persevering, task oriented, and well adjusted than were girls. They were not likely, however, to be described as lower in such traits as enthusiasm, inquisitiveness, leadership, verbal expressiveness, academic ability, nor as higher in conformance.

Discussion

One important finding of this study is that the unfavorable description of the Negro student is associated primarily with Ss of lower scholastic aptitude. At least two questions may be raised concerning the interpretation of this finding, in addition to the limitations imposed by the restricted range of scholastic aptitude and by the small Ns: (a) is it an artifact of social class and (b) are teachers' descriptions observations of actual behavior or perceptions that would be considered biased or limited in comparison to what other observers might report?

1. We do not know whether the interaction among scholastic aptitude and ethnic group is associated with Negroes in particular, with minority groups, or more generally with social class. The description of the low-IQ Other student suggests some effort by the child to conform to the demands of middle-class parents for good grades and good behavior in school while the description of the low-IQ Negro student does not and seems more consistent with behavior generally attributed to children from low-income families.

Schmuck and Luszki (1966) have reported that in a small, midwestern community, there were no differences in achievement, self-ratings, and teachers' classroom behavior ratings when socioeconomic status was carefully matched for Negro and white students. They conclude that relations among race, self-esteem, and achievement are confounded in other studies with social class. Only 63 pairs of students, ranging in age from 8 to 16 years, were involved in the study; a larger sample may be needed at each age and grade level to test the social-class interpretation rigorously and the nature of the community might itself be a relevant variable (cf. Davidson & Lang, 1960). In our sample, it is possible that despite the somewhat homogeneous neighborhoods, Other and higher-aptitude Negro students came from less-deprived homes than did lower-aptitude Negro Ss.

2. We have referred to teachers' descriptions rather than to either teachers' perceptions or students' behavior. The teachers had access to intelligence test and reading scores and knew the students' ethnic group and sex. Whether in this instance the frequently postulated interaction between expectations and observations is weighted more heavily with expectations or was formed by observation relatively independent of teachers' a priori values, is moot.

Considering the "observation" interpretation, results similar to ours have been noted for younger children whose teachers had volunteered for the assignment. Such teachers might be expected to be somewhat more favorably disposed toward the children than public school teachers assigned to schools in low-income Negro neighborhoods. Lamb, Ziller, and Maloney (1965) found, for example, that white girls gained most from Headstart experiences and that the Negro boy was both least favorably described by his teacher and least likely to benefit from the preschool program. The description of the brighter Negro students as more "compliant" is congruent with the report that in comparison to white liberal-arts college students, Negro liberal-arts students scored higher on deference and lower on exhibitionism, autonomy, and dominance on the self-descriptive Edwards Personal Preference Schedule (Pettigrew, 1964).

Considering the "opinion" interpretation, Rosenthal (1966) and Flowers (1966) have shown that students' IQs and classroom performance tend to increase when teachers are led to believe the child's intellectual potential is high relative to an equally bright control S whom the teacher believes has lower intellectual potential. Their effects have been demonstrated, however, more reliably in younger than older children. Rotter's (1967) studies also suggest that ". . . preconceptions influence one's perceptions and evaluations and that these might lead to differential treatment." Groups of white teachers read vignettes reporting a child's behavior. Analyses are reported for vignettes which differed in the sex ascribed to the child and classroom behavior: e.g., orderly/disorderly, "Ann carried a classmate's books"; "Billy carried a classmate's books." Sex and the interaction of sex with classroom orderliness were significant associates of teacher's rating on many of 80 bipolar scales, including a rating of boys as "dirtier." Race (white and Negro) and social class (middle and low) were also variables in the study and the technique should be of considerable value in separating "opinion" and "observations" in the descriptions of minority children by majority teachers.

Davidson and Lang's comments (1960, p. 114) on the antecedents of scholastic difficulty may be relevant here:

> It is likely, therefore, that a lower class child, especially if he is not doing well in school, will have a negative perception of his teachers' feelings toward him. These negative perceptions will in turn tend to lower his efforts to achieve in school and/or increase the probability that he will misbehave. His poor school achievement will aggravate the negative attitudes of his teachers toward him, which will in turn affect his self-confidence, and so on. This vicious entanglement must be interrupted at some point. The point of attack may well be the teacher whose capacity to reflect feelings conducive to the child's growth should be of concern to educators.

To this we would add that both the relatively high correlation between IQ and adjustment for Negro males and the analysis of variance results suggest that the low-IQ Negro is alienated from the school situation, that is, is not task oriented and is verbally aggressive and withdrawn. This finding supports the need for programs designed to raise the level of intellectual performance before the vicious cycle of low achievement, teacher rejection, and child alienation begins.

A second major finding in this study is that boys were described as less task oriented, more verbally aggressive, and more introverted than girls. The latter result is unexpected as girls have been generally described as less outgoing and more introverted than boys. Our initial interpretation of an introversion-extroversion analysis was that helpful classroom behavior, "extroversion," might be accounting for most of the variance: clearer sex differences were found, however, for the "introversion" than for the "extroversion" factor scores.

Interpretations of the sex differences in personality and attainment have ranged from biological forces to a greater disparity for boys than for girls between the classroom demands of female teachers and socially defined behavior appropriate to the student's sex. Maccoby (1966), reviewing this literature, has noted that peer group pressures on boys are often directed to nonacademic pursuits;

> that boys are more frequently engaged in efforts to achieve autonomy, especially in relation to their mothers, with the result that they are less willing to accede to the demands of their predominantly female teachers; and that even in high school, boys are more likely to do poorly in subjects that bore them [p. 32].

The observed higher "introversion" ratings for boys may thus indicate apathy in a traditionally academically oriented classroom situation rather than a more general trait.

References

Beilin, H. Teachers' and clinicians' attitudes toward the behavior problems of children: A reappraisal. *Child Development*, 1959, *30*, 9–25.

Charters, W. W., Jr. The social background of teaching. In N. L. Gage (Ed.), *Handbook of research on teaching*. Chicago: Rand McNally, 1963. Pp. 715–813.

Clark, K. Educational stimulation of racially disadvantaged children. In A. H. Passow (Ed.), *Education in depressed areas*. New York: Teachers College Press, 1963. Pp. 142–162.

Coleman, J. S., and others. Equality of educational opportunity. Report No. OD-38001, 1966, United States Office of Education, Washington, D.C.

Davidson, H., and Lang, G. Children's perceptions of their teachers' feelings toward them related to self-perception, school achievement and behavior. *Journal of Experimental Education*, 1960, *29*, 107–118.

de Groat, A. J., and Thompson, G. G. A study of the distribution of. teacher approval and disapproval among sixth grade pupils. *Journal of Experimental Education*, 1949, *18*, 57–75.

Deutsch, M. *Minority group and class status as related to social and personality factors in scholastic achievement*. Monograph No. 2. Ithaca: The Society for Applied Anthropology, 1960.

Flowers, C. E. Effects of an arbitrary accelerated group placement on the tested academic achievement of educationally disadvantaged students. Paper presented at the meeting of the American Psychological Association, New York, September 1966.

Fox, R. S., Lippitt, R. O., and Schmuck, R. A. Pupil-teacher adjustment and mutual adaptation in creating classroom learning environments. Intercenter Program of Studies on Children, Youth and Family Life. Document Series 16, Cooperative Research Project No. 1167, Institute for Social Research, University of Michigan, 1964.

Glidewell, J. C., Domke, H. R., and Kantor, M. Screening in schools for behavior disorders: Use of mothers' report of symptoms. *Journal of Educational Research*, 1963, *56*, 508–515.

Goldblatt, H., & Tyson, C. An ethnic study: Pupil evaluations. Research Library Report No. 12, 1962, Commission on Human Rights, New York.

Goldstein, K. M., and Chorost, S. B. Preschool and background factors in the school adjustment of culturally disadvantaged children. Paper read at the meeting of the American Psychological Association, New York, September 1966.

Katz, I. Review of evidence relating to effects of desegregation on the intellectual performance of Negroes. *American Psychologist,* 1964, *19,* 381–399.

Katz, I. Some motivational determinants of racial differences in intellectual achievement. *International Journal of Psychology,* 1967, *2,* 1–78.

Lamb, H. E., Ziller, R. C., and Maloney, A. W. The development of self-other relationships during Project Headstart. Project No. OEO-511, 1965, University of Delaware. (Mimeo)

Long, B., and Henderson, E. H. Self-social concepts of disadvantaged school beginners. Paper read at the meeting of the American Psychological Association, New York, September 1966.

Maccoby, E. E. Sex differences in intellectual functioning. In E. E. Maccoby (Ed.), *The development of sex differences.* Stanford, Calif.: Stanford University Press, 1966. Pp. 25–55.

Pettigrew, T. *A profile of the Negro American.* New Jersey: Van Nostrand, 1964.

Riessman, F. *The culturally deprived child.* New York: Harper & Row, 1962.

Rosenthal, R. Teachers' expectancies: Determinants of changing children's IQ by changing teachers' expectations. Paper read at the meeting of the American Psychological Association, New York, September 1966.

Rotter, G. S. The effect of sex identification in teacher evaluation of pupils. Paper read at the meeting of the Eastern Psychological Association, Boston, April 1967.

Schaeffer, E. S., Aaronson, M., and Burgoon, B. Classroom Behavior Inventory (Form for Grades 3 through 12). National Institute of Mental Health, 1966 (Mimeo).

Schmuck, R., and Luszki, M. A comparison of Negro and white students in several small midwest communities. Paper read at the meeting of the American Psychological Association, New York, September 1966.

Sexton, P. *Education and income: Inequalities in our public schools.* New York: Viking, 1961.

Ullman, C. A. *Identification of maladjusted children.* Public Health Monographs, No. 7, 1952.

Vroegh, K. and Handrich, M. Sex role typing in the preschool years: An overview. Research Report No. 13, Vol. 3. Chicago: Institute for Juvenile Research. 1966.

Winer, B. J. *Statistical principles in experimental design.* New York: McGraw-Hill, 1962.

VI. ON A TECHNOLOGY FOR MODIFYING THE BEHAVIOR OF ADOLESCENTS

Introduction

Certainly part of the reason for compiling this section on behavior modification techniques and principles is to answer the call that special problems require special solutions. We are forced to find ways of dealing with the adolescent whose behavior defies commonplace methods of interacting. Various investigators have explored a set of very effective techniques for dealing with problem behaviors in adolescents or problem adolescents, and people who intend to work with adolescents should be familiar with these techniques.

However, we feel compelled to articulate from the start that to confine one's thinking about the techniques discussed in this section to problem behaviors would be to impose an unintended limitation on their boundless applicability. Very simply stated, the behavior modification principles that work so well with problem children also offer fruitful applications to other children under normal conditions. The student who makes a serious effort to understand clearly the principles developed in this section may expect to find the creative application of these principles both helpful and rewarding.

After such a build-up, we should hasten to add that behavior modification techniques alone do not provide a panacea for solving behavior problems in the classroom. For example, in the absence of a relevant, interesting curriculum and sensibly arranged physical surroundings, no interactional or socializing techniques are going to shift students' undesirable activities to those that are conducive to learning.

Homme's paper on contingency management is intended to introduce the idea and nature of human behavior modification. His distinction between the omniscient operant conditioner and the contingency manager as an ordinary person who serves the routine needs of people is a valuable one. Homme also bridges the unnecessarily disturbing gap between the M & M mentality and more reasonable reinforcers by informing us of the Premack principle's almost limitless array of common and sensible behavioral reinforcers. Further, he provides a series of straightforward examples which show the efficacy of being a contingency manager in real-life situations.

The Schwitzgebel and Kolb paper initiates a series of four articles in which behavior modification techniques are successfully applied with adolescents. In their successful venture to induce changes in the behavior of adolescent delinquents, Schwitzgebel and Kolb report many valuable insights into the use of behavior modification with adolescent boys. For example, they helpfully point out that the rewarding features of a reinforcer do not necessarily inhere in the rewarding object but have some dependence on the manner in which it is presented. Thus, they would rather "share a single orange with a boy than give him a dozen of them." In addition to shaping specific behaviors, such as promptness in arriving for an appointment, these investigators also discuss the long-term effects of their therapeutic procedures.

Tyler and Brown bring us a little closer to the classroom in their concern with the academic performance of institutionalized delinquent boys. Their task was to test whether academic performance with contingent reinforcement (reinforcement that is contingent on a behavior) is superior to academic performance with noncontingent reinforcement. Their hypothesis was clearly supported through a design that precludes attributing success to a Hawthorne effect—an accusation all too often leveled at studies with positive results. This paper also presents the possibility of using extrinsic motivators to propagate desirable behaviors to the point where it becomes feasible to render them intrinsically motivated.

The next two empirical studies successfully apply behavior modification principles to improving the reading abilities of a single culturally deprived juvenile delinquent and of a group of potential urban school dropouts. Staats and Butterfield give a brief analysis of the onset of behavioral deficits and the role of negative reinforcement in the development of undesirable behaviors. They proceed to describe the impressive improvements in reading achievement their token reinforcement technique accomplished. One is easily convinced of the sound economics of their endeavor as they relate that their subject only required $20.31 in tokens during 4½ months of training, which involved 40 hours of reading training; for this negligible amount of money, the subject emitted 64,307 single-word reading responses for a trainer using procedures that were very specific and very simple. All of this denotes the potential employment of persons not highly trained in education in the use of these techniques.

Clark and Walberg carry the section a step further by an example of the use of positive reinforcement with a group of adolescents in the classroom. Their goal, also, was to improve reading ability. Repeating Staats and Butterfield's observation, these authors also refer to the negative reinforcement effect of school work on the students they worked with in this study. Their object was to replace the negative reinforcement quality of the classroom with a positive reinforcement quality. Their results bespeak a clear-cut success in accomplishing their objective.

A slight digression is in order at

this point. There is probably a variety of commonsense or intuitive understandings of what is meant by the terms positive and negative reinforcement. In the interest of decreasing confusion, let us agree on what we shall mean by these terms in this book. Reinforcement is construed as increasing the likelihood that a given response will occur; punishment decreases the likelihood that a given response will occur. Positive reinforcement occurs when a rewarding or pleasant stimulus is administered following a given behavior; negative reinforcement occurs when an aversive stimulus is removed following a given behavior. This distinction prompts us to distinguish negative reinforcement from punishment: (positive) punishment is the application of an aversive stimulus when a given behavior occurs. By extension, one can also classify the removal of a pleasant stimulus when a given behavior occurs as (negative) punishment.

The last paper in this section,

by Homme and others, serves to clarify the main components to be mastered by a person who would use behavior modification principles—that is, a "behavior engineer." The authors tell us that a behavior engineer has the task of identifying (a) the behavior he wants to see, (b) the stimuli to control it, and (c) the available reinforcers. They discuss these components separately and elaborate on them through examples. The paper closes with a restatement of what coverants (covert operants) are and a discourse on the uses of behavioral engineering ideas to increase joy, love, and a favorable self-concept. The authors also warn that a basic prerequisite to becoming a successful behavioral engineer is a commitment to apply reinforcers diligently.

Students interested in acquiring supplemental and background information on the readings in this section might profit from studying B. F. Skinner's *Walden Two* and *The Technology of Teaching*.

1. CONTINGENCY MANAGEMENT *

Lloyd Homme

It takes several years of graduate study to make an operant conditioner. Among other things, the student must learn about operant conditioning apparatus, about stimulus control, about dozens of reinforcement sched-

* *Newsletter* (of the Section on Clinical Child Psychology, Division of Clinical Psychology, American Psychological Association), 1966, 5(4). Reprinted with permission of the author and the *Newsletter*.

ules, and combinations of schedules (Ferster & Skinner, 1957), and about how operant conditioners are slightly superior to everyone else.[1] This all takes time, but many people think the time well spent. There is one other class of behaviors the operant conditioner is supposed to learn: how to discover new variables and relationships between variables of which behavior is a function. In other words, he is supposed to learn how to be a scientist.

Most of this behavioral repertoire is not needed by a contingency manager. The realization of this has made it possible repeatedly to show (Allen, Buell, Harris & Wolf, 1964; Ayllon & Michael, 1959; Davison, 1965; and Sulzer, 1962) that a contingency manager (sometimes called a behavioral engineer) can be trained in a very short time—sometimes in a matter of days, or even hours.

That is to say, operant conditioning and contingency management are not the same thing. Contingency management is a crucial bit of technology derived from operant conditioning, not operant conditioning itself. The reason this distinction is important is that there are people in our society—parents, teachers, and so on—who have to deal with tremendous amounts of behavior. They have neither the time nor the inclination to learn operant conditioning, but they welcome a small bit of technology which gives them some control over what is going to happen next in the world of behavior.

Teaching Contingency Management

The central theme in teaching contingency management is a simple and obvious one: The likelihood that behavior will recur depends on its consequences. To teach someone to become a skilled contingency manager, one simply has to teach him to take this fact of life seriously enough to observe that it holds for *all* behaviors, for *all* organisms, at all times, and that it is important even in the case of seemingly trivial bits of behavior, on the grounds that larger, more important response classes are built from them. As a matter of fact, it seems to be turning out that the difference between an excellent contingency manager and a not-so-excellent one is a willingness to reinforce approximations early in the game. From the examples of contingency management given below, it is quite clear that things would not have gone so smoothly without the reinforcement of successive approximations to the final behavior the contingency manager wanted.

---

[1] Lloyd Homme, personal communication, 1966.

Finding Reinforcers

The picture most psychologists conjure up when they think of an operant conditioner working with a child is that of an M&M candy dispenser dressed in a white lab coat. Happily, this stereotype, if it ever had any validity, is now quite old-fashioned, quite out of date.

The reason for this turn of events may be traced to the impetus given this area by the work of David Premack. This is not the place to review Premack's work; suffice it to say that he and others are finding considerable laboratory support for the elegantly simple notion (Premack, 1965, p. 132): "For any pair of responses, the more probable one will reinforce the less probable one." If the contingency manager takes this principle seriously—that is to say, literally—he will have thousands of reinforcers at his disposal where he may have had one or two before.

In the practical application of the Premack principle, one usually doesn't have the time or facilities to define behavior probabilities in terms of relative frequency of occurrence. Thus, the term *probability* is used in the everyday, nonrigorous sense. Children will often announce, without urging, what their high probability behaviors are at the moment. For example, when a child says, "Let's go for a walk," or "Let's play this game," or when he points to a drawing of a particular event on a menu of reinforcing events (Addison & Homme, 1966), he is informing the contingency manager of what will reinforce at that particular moment. To strengthen a low probability behavior, the contingency manager simply calls for an approximation of it, and then permits a short time for interacting with the reinforcing event.

Some Instances of Application
of Contingency Management with Children

In practice, the contingency manager specifies a series of micro-contracts which substantively take the form: "Execute some *amount* of low probability behavior; then you may immediately engage in some high probability behavior for a specified *time*."

The differential probability hypothesis is notable not only for what it says, but for what it does not say. It does not say: "Of any two responses, the more probable one will reinforce the less probable one in middle-class or upper-class children"; it does not say: ". . . in white children"; it does not say: ". . . in emotionally nondisturbed children"; it does not say: ". . . as long as the S has not come from a different culture."[2] What is being said is that, as long as the S is an organism, the differential probability rule will hold. Happily, as the following examples are intended to illustrate, we seem to be finding this to be the case.

THREE NORMAL MIDDLE-CLASS THREE-YEAR-OLDS

Our initial attempt in using the Premack principle proved remarkably effective with three exuberant three-year-olds (Homme, C. deBaca, Devine, Steinhorst, & Rickert, 1963). The high probability behaviors used as reinforcers were of the sort generally suppressed by the environment, e.g. running and screaming. The contracts specified by the contingency manager were of the sort, "Sit quietly and watch what I do at the blackboard; then you may run and scream until the timer goes 'Ding.'" Although, as it should, the technology employed in this initial attempt now looks crude, there can be little doubt that it was effective.

TWO CHILDREN OF POVERTY

There is no dearth of authorities to explain how and why children of the poor are different. To find out if they obeyed a different set of behavioral laws, staff members of this department sought out two Negro boys, five and six, of poor families. It may be argued that these were not "real" slum kids, since our town does not have slums, but they were at least poor.

What was most striking to us in this pilot project was the speed with which these children from a different culture learned middle-class behaviors. They learned instantly, for example, to knock on a door and inquire, "May I come in?" when entering the reinforcing event area was contingent on this behavior. They cheerfully fulfilled small contracts of the usual sort: "Execute some low probability behavior (Find another letter that looks like this one.), and then you can execute some high probability behavior." We were prepared to find that different high probability behaviors would have to be used to reinforce these children, but this was not the case. The usual program of water colors, crayons (after they were shown how to use them), pushing a castor-equipped chair, and so forth, served to reinforce behaviors very nicely.

TWENTY-THREE ADOLESCENTS

Guidance counselors were used to recruit Ss for a study (Homme, 1964) of adolescents who were high school dropouts or judged to be potential

---

[2] Obviously, the omission of such qualifiers has direct relevance to Masling's incisive comments about training of clinical child psychologists (*Newsletter*, 1966, V, 2).

dropouts. These adolescents had the behaviors usually associated with "street kids." They spoke a hip jargon, some of them were discovered to be carrying knives, some of them wore their sun glasses at all times, and so on. The low probability behavior for these Ss was getting themselves through programed instructional material in subjects like arithmetic and reading. Most of the high probability behaviors used to reinforce these were of the conventional sort: time for a break, coffee, smoke, coke, and so on. However, there were some surprises. For some of these Ss, going through a program in Russian proved to be a reliable high probability behavior. When this was discovered, their contracts would take a form like the following: "Do 20 frames of arithmetic; then you can work on Russian for 10 minutes." This does serve to illustrate that one need not know why a high probability behavior exists in order to use it as a reinforcer. My own speculation about why street kids' high probability behavior is learning Russian is that perhaps fuzz cannot read messages written in Russian.

The success of the project was mainly in terms of the excellent motivation exhibited by these Ss. After the first week, there were zero dropouts, and attendance was virtually perfect. Absences which did occur were all accounted for, and one hundred per cent of them were made up by working extra time. And there were no fights. A generally pleasant emotional atmosphere prevailed, in spite of the fact that these adolescents were of the "hard-to-handle" variety prior to the project.

FOUR PRESCHOOL INDIAN CHILDREN

Indian culture of the southwestern United States has been the subject of intensive and prolonged study. The study has been so intensive and so prolonged that the Indians themselves frequently say that a typical Indian family consists of the mother, the father, four children, and an anthropologist.

The ways in which American Indian culture differs from non-Indian American culture are real and interesting enough to be studied in their own right. But cultural differences are often used for scapegoat purposes; they are frequently used to explain the failure of conventional teaching methods.

To test the feasibility of a contingency management system (Homme, 1965a), staff members went to an Indian reservation [3] and set up a one-room school with two areas: one area for the execution of low probabil-

---

[3] An account of this project is also given in the film, "Teaching English Vocabulary to Preschool Indian Children at the San Felipe Indian Reservation."

ity behaviors; the other for high probability behaviors. The Ss the Governor of the Reservation had picked out for us to work with were the four children judged by him to be the least likely to succeed in school. They had brothers and sisters who had failed or were failing in school, and they were the shiest of all the children on the reservation. The low probability behaviors the contingency managers wanted to strengthen were English vocabulary items (Point to the horse, and say "horse."), and again the high probability behaviors used to reinforce these were quite conventional ones.

In summary, these preschool Indian children acted as though they were organisms. Further, by the time the six-week project was over, they were as noisy and nonshy as children ought to get. They were seen again about a month after conventional school had begun; their behavior was about what it was when we first saw them. Not all changes are lasting ones.

A FIVE-YEAR-OLD NONTALKING RETARDATE

Five-year-old Diana (IQ about 43) is about the size of a normal three-year-old. When she was first brought to the laboratory, she had a vocabulary of half a dozen words. Among them was the phrase, "What's that?" This phrase served quite reliably to get action from adults, particularly strangers. Unsuspecting staff secretaries, for example, were often heard giving quite complete, technical descriptions of their electric typewriters. The fact that Diana had comprehended nothing of the explanation, of course, did not stop her from repeating the question while pointing her finger in another direction.

Basically, the same contingency management system which worked with bright three-year-olds was quite satisfactory to Diana. The differences were that she was taught to use the menu by getting her to point at some object, having the object immediately appear. For example, if she pointed to a piece of candy, a piece of candy was immediately given to her; if she pointed at a ball, a ball was immediately rolled to her, and so on. Those familiar with laboratory procedures (Homme & Klaus, 1962) will recognize this as an instance of magazine training.

The low probability behavior we set out to strengthen was imitation of speech. Starting out with the requirement that one sound be approximated before a reinforcing event occurred, the requirement was gradually shifted upwards until the imitation of ten or so words could be demanded before a minute of reinforcing activity was permitted. With this kind of management, her vocabulary increased to around 200 words. But our chief interest in this project was not to see how much behavior we could install; it was rather to see whether contingency management would be effective in the case of a defective organism. It was.[4]

A BLIND SIXTEEN-YEAR-OLD INMATE
OF A STATE MENTAL HOSPITAL

On first coming into contact with contingency management and the Premack principle, students of behavior usually ask, "How do you find high probability behaviors?" The answer is, "Let the S tell you." The more experience we get in this area, the more we are inclined to think that S will always do this. He may not do it verbally, but he will find a way. The following contingency management interaction is illustrative.

When the contingency manager first saw the S, she was sitting quietly on a ward of a state mental hospital. Her chair was against one of the walls, and she was staring straight ahead through sightless eyes, just as she had been doing most of her waking hours for the eight years she had been hospitalized. What were her high probability behaviors? There appeared to be none. But when the contingency manager walked over to her and spoke, she indicated what at least one of them was. She seized his hand and smelled the back of it. To condition verbal behavior, the contingency manager simply withheld his hand until some approximation to an acceptable response to the command, "Say X," was executed (where X was some word or phrase). Immediately after the patient verbalized, the contingency manager would give her his hand to smell for a few seconds.

With this kind of management, within an hour, the contingency manager had reinforced sufficiently so that the verbal rate had increased considerably. The hospital's clinical psychologist interne remarked that the patient had never talked so much at one time since she had known her.

Psychotherapy: The Teaching
of Self-Management of Contingencies

The Premack principle makes no mention of who should manage the contingencies between high and low probability behaviors. This leaves the way open for the possibility of the S's managing his own contingencies. Of course, it is assumed that variables which maintain the controlling response (Skinner, 1953) are to be found in the external environment. Another assumption of this kind of psychotherapy is that covert

---

[4] This project is described in more detail in the film, "Teaching Verbalization by Contingency Management."

operants, which I have called coverants ("kuh-verants"), obey the same laws as overt operants (Homme, 1965b; Homme, 1966). Pertinent to the present topic is the pioneering work of Bandura and associates (e.g., Bandura & Kupers, 1964) on self-monitoring and self-reinforcement. How much of this kind of technology can be taught to children is simply unknown at the present time, but the possibility exists that some exciting new developments are in store for those who are willing to experiment.

References

Addison, R. M., and Homme, L. E. The reinforcing event (RE) menu. *NSPI Journal*, 1966, 5(1), 8–9.

Allen, K. E., Hart, B. M., Buell, J. S., Harris, F. R., and Wolf, M. M. Effects of social reinforcement on isolate behavior of a nursery school child. *Child Development*, 1964, 35, 511–518.

Ayllon, T., and Michael, J. The psychiatric nurse as a behavioral engineer. *Journal of the Experimental Analysis of Behavior*, 1959, 2, 323–334.

Bandura, A., and Kupers, C. J. Transmission of patterns of self-reinforcement through modeling. *Journal of Abnormal and Social Psychology*, 1964, 69, 1–9.

Davison, G. C. The training of undergraduates as social reinforcers for autistic children. In Ullman, L. P., & Krasner, L. (Eds.), *Case studies in behavior modification*. New York: Holt, Rinehart and Winston, 1965. Pp. 146–148.

Ferster, C. B., and Skinner, B. F. *Schedules of reinforcement*. New York: Appleton-Century-Crofts, 1957.

Homme, L. E. A demonstration of the use of self-instructional and other teaching techniques for remedial instruction of low-achieving adolescents in reading and mathematics. U.S. Office of Educ., Contract No. OE-4-16-033, 1964.

Homme, L. E. Final report, a system for teaching English literacy to preschool Indian children. Submitted to U.S. Department of Interior, Contract No. 14-20-065001506, October, 1965.

Homme, L. E. Perspectives in psychology—XXIV control of coverants, the operants of the mind. *Psychological Record*, 1965, 15, 501–511.

Homme, L. E. Coverant control therapy: a special case of contingency management. Paper read at the 1966 Convention of the Rocky Mountain Psychological Association, Albuquerque, May, 1966.

Homme, L. E., and Klaus, D. J. *Laboratory studies in the analysis of behavior*. Albuquerque, N.M.: TMI, 1962.

Homme, L. E., C. deBaca, P., Devine, J. V., Steinhorst, R., and Rickert, E. J. Use of the Premack principle in controlling the behavior of nursery school children. *Journal of the Experimental Analysis of Behavior,* 1963, *6,* 544.

Premack, D. Reinforcement theory. In Levine, D. (Ed.), *Nebraska symposium on motivation.* Lincoln: University of Nebraska Press, 1965.

Skinner, B. F. *Science and human behavior.* New York: Macmillan, 1953.

Sulzer, E. S. Behavior modification in adult psychiatric patients. *Journal of Counseling Psychology,* 1962, *9,* 271–276.

2. INDUCING BEHAVIOUR CHANGE IN ADOLESCENT DELINQUENTS *

R. Schwitzgebel and D. A. Kolb

There is no more powerful therapeutic factor than the performance of activities which were formerly neurotically impaired or inhibited. No insight, no emotional discharge, no recollection can be as reassuring as accomplishment in the actual life situation in which the individual failed.

ALEXANDER AND FRENCH
Psychoanalytic Therapy

Reviews by Krasner (1958) and by Bandura (1961) show that the majority of studies of operant conditioning with humans have successfully altered specific response variables (e.g. plural nouns, self-references, lever pulling) by the use of common generalized reinforcers (e.g. head nod, "good", "mm-hmm"). The subjects have typically been college students and hospitalized psychiatric patients.

The use of delinquents or criminal offenders in conditioning experiments has been reported much less frequently. Kadlub (1956) found that "criminal normals" and "criminal psychopaths" learned serial nonsense syllables with equal efficiency when cigarettes and verbal praise were used as reinforcers. Lykken (1957), however, reported that institutionalized "primary sociopaths" showed less anxiety than normals as measured by GSR and showed less conditioning to electric shock. Cairns

* R. Schwitzgebel and D. A. Kolb, "Inducing Behaviour Change in Adolescent Delinquents," *Behavior Research and Therapy,* 1964, *1,* 297–304. Reprinted with permission of the authors and the publisher, Pergamon Press.

(1960) suggested that "dependency-anxiety" among delinquents was positively related to the effectiveness of social reinforcers. Johns and Quay (1962) found that psychopaths showed significantly less increase in reinforced pronoun response categories than did neurotics. None of these studies used operant conditioning as a therapeutic procedure, and all Ss were incarcerated at the time of the investigation.

In 1958, a juvenile court programme was established in Cincinnati, Ohio, with a definite therapeutic orientation (Hahn, 1960). Young offenders were employed to participate in "milieu therapy" which included counselling and on-the-job work training. On a somewhat similar but more informal referral basis, a research project in Cambridge, Massachusetts, hired seven delinquents to take psychological tests and talk into a tape recorder as a means of introducing them to "intensive office treatment" (Slack, 1960). A mutual acquaintance of the delinquent and the therapist was used as a referral "contact". How to initiate co-operative attendance without the use of referrals remained a problem (Sidman, 1962). Even if it could be shown that most offenders would engage in counselling or other treatment by being paid, how could this be introduced where contacts were not available? And once participation was achieved, would what appeared to be successful treatment generalize to situations outside the office? The present study reports a procedure which was adopted whereby prospective employees were contacted directly on street corners, in pool halls, or at similar locations where delinquents spend much of their time. A storefront at the intersection of two busy city streets, donated by a local business firm, served as the first "Street Corner Research" laboratory.

Subjects

INITIAL CONTACT

The initial contact with a prospective experimental subject was informal but direct. The experimenter would usually joke with prospective Ss, side with their defences, readily admit his ignorance, and listen attentively to explanations. All this was done in the context of a legitimate job offer. The S was told that the purpose of the job was to find out how teenagers feel about things, how they come to have certain opinions, and how they change. The employee's task would be to talk into a tape recorder about anything he wanted. For this job he would be paid a dollar an hour or sometimes more.

It did not seem necessary to engage in devious means or to make exaggerated promises. In simple terms, the E wanted to hire a research subject, and the delinquent wanted to "make a fast buck". Neither party was required to sacrifice his social role of "research psychologist" or "delinquent", although the arrangement was admittedly somewhat unorthodox for both. (Perhaps one of the difficulties in getting delinquents into almost any intense relationship with a more law-abiding person is that the delinquent is usually required to sacrifice, in advance, what little identification or integrity he may feel he has. For the delinquent, it is often better to be "bad" than to be "nothing".)

The prospective S was reassured that he did not have to talk about anything he did not want to, and that he could quit whenever he wished. He was also warned that some of the previous employees had changed their opinions about many things, but that this was not a condition of the job. The E would then offer to take the prospective S and several of his friends to a nearby restaurant of their choice and buy them refreshments. It was explained that one of the "qualifications" for the job and for going to the restaurant was that the person had a court record and had spent time in a reformatory or prison.

Although prospective Ss were often suspicious that the E was a policeman, detective, homosexual, gangster, or even an escaped mental patient, they would usually go to the restaurant. Since it was a public place and they outnumbered the E, it appeared that there was nothing to lose. Informal conversation in the restaurant about topics of the boys' interest would be followed by an offer to visit the laboratory just to look the place over and see if they might want a part-time job. A common response was, "Well, I guess we don't have anything better to do". Once at the laboratory, the prospective S and one or two of his friends played with the tape recorder, asked numerous questions about the equipment and the secretaries, and participated as a group in an unstructured recorded interview. At the conclusion of this initial interview, the S was given an unexpected "bonus" of a dollar, and a time was set for an interview the next day. A S was permitted to bring friends along for the first few interviews until he felt comfortable in the laboratory and with the E.

GROUP CHARACTERISTICS

The first twenty Ss employed by the project formed the experimental group. These twenty Ss were found to have the following characteristics. Their age range was 15–21 with a mean age of 17·8. The average age of the first arrest was 13·5; the average number of arrests was 8·2. The group averaged 15·1 total months of incarceration in reformatory and prison. Eleven of the Ss had histories of active refusal to participate in treatment programs. Only four Ss had held a full-time job longer than six months, and only one S had completed secondary school. The majority of the Ss came from a lower-lower socio-economic background; the predominant religious preference was Roman Catholic.

After the characteristics of the experimental group had been established and verified, a control group was formed by matching each experimental S with another offender chosen from the records of state correctional agencies. None of the control Ss were interviewed by the Es. The pairs were matched on age of first offence, type of offence, nationality, religious preference, place of residence, and total number of months of incarceration. It was not possible to match the pairs on other variables such as the amount of school completed or the socio-economic class since this information is seldom available from correctional records.

Procedure

SHAPING ATTENDANCE

Anna Freud (1958) has described adolescents as being difficult to get into treatment because they tend not to co-operate, to miss appointments, and are seldom punctual. She suggests that their rapidly changing emotional patterns leave little energy to be invested in the analyst. It may be that characteristics such as these, often ascribed to adolescents, are not necessarily descriptive of the age but artifacts of the treatment procedure. Our approach has been to shape dependable attendance and other behaviours by the use of strategies similar to those suggested by Skinner (1953).

Whenever a S arrived at the laboratory for his second interview, regardless of the time, he was warmly welcomed and a Coke and some food was shared with him. If he did not arrive, the E would go back to their original meeting place at a later date. In a few cases, it was necessary to meet Ss at locations successively closer to the laboratory.

For example, S_{11} was initially contacted in a pool hall. He failed to arrive for his second interview. The E returned to the pool hall a couple days later and found the S. The S was somewhat bored and seemed glad to see the E. The E accompanied the S to the laboratory via the subway. The third meeting was arranged outside the subway station nearest the pool hall, before the toll gate. The S was reinforced by the Es paying the fares, offering the S a cigarette, and by showing interest in some topic of conversation begun by the S. The fourth meeting was arranged inside the subway station after the toll gate. In this case, part of the previous day's wage which the S had earned was in the form of two subway tokens. (It was assumed that the S would spend most of the cash he was given and therefore not be able to purchase a twenty cent token the next day.) This time the S was reimbursed for the fare and the E bought a candy bar for each of them. The next meeting was scheduled outside the subway station at the exit nearest the laboratory. Finally, the boy was met at the laboratory.

Several principles guided the Es in trying to shape attendance behaviour: [1]

(1) Reinforcers should be modest and natural. It would be better, the Es felt, to share a single orange with a S than to give him a dozen of them. "Charity" would probably offend the boy's pride.

(2) Punishment should be avoided. Ss were not reprimanded for missing a meeting or coming late. At most, they might lose some pay by not having a full hour to work.

(3) Reinforcers should be given on a variable ratio schedule. Initially, Ss were reinforced every time they arrived for a meeting, but the amount and type of reinforcement varied (e.g. cigarettes, food, small change). After attendance became dependable, a variable-ratio, variable-interval schedule was used. The reinforcements for attendance became irregularly less frequent, and attention was focused on some other aspect of the S's behaviour. For example, a S might arrive an hour late for tenth meeting. The E would welcome him, mention that this was much better than the previous day when he was an hour and a half late. For the "good effort" the boy was given a twenty-five cent cash bonus. The next day the boy might arrive within fifteen minutes of the appointed time—hoping perhaps for a dollar bonus. The E might mention nothing about his arrival, but the boy would be likely to call attention to the fact and ask about his bonus. It would then be explained that the employee can always expect to receive the basic wage but that bonuses depend entirely on the amount of money the E happens to have and on his feelings at the time. The boy might be disappointed until, later in the hour, he receives a fifty cent bonus for, say, showing curiosity about the meaning of a recurring dream. He might then realize that he could never be sure what he might receive a bonus for or what the bonus would be, but in general the whole thing seemed to be an interesting game. At the following meeting, the E might take the S to a restaurant for a sandwich if he arrived still more promptly.

Using the procedures we have outlined, it was possible to shape arrival to within a few minutes of the scheduled time for most Ss. The writers noticed on one occasion a boy waiting just outside the laboratory door for the chimes of a nearby church to ring in order that he might be

---

[1] The research reported in this paper was exploratory in nature. Investigations are presently under way to gather more complete and systematic data regarding the effectiveness of various employment procedures and reinforcement schedules.

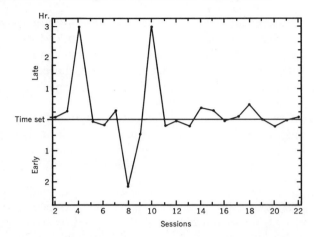

FIGURE 1   Arrival times of experimental subject S_2 for initial twenty-two meetings.

exactly on time. Such extreme punctuality was not expected nor required. Figure 1 shows the arrival times of a typical subject, S_2, for the first twenty-two meetings. For about ninety per cent of the Ss, attendance became dependable within fifteen appointments and prompt within twenty-five appointments.

INTERVIEWING

The tape recorded interviews were scheduled for one hour on an average of two or three times a week. Interviews were more frequent at the beginning of employment and less frequent toward the end. After a few hours of relating stories of their adventures and exploits, Ss often found that what appeared to be a "soft touch" (i.e. getting paid for just talking) was actually a rather difficult task. In some cases, the E's usual policy of attentive listening was modified to keep from arousing the S's anxiety. The E might suggest general topics to talk about, share with the S some personal experiences, or shorten the length of the interview. While some anxiety in the interview situation was assumed to be unavoidable, the E tried to avoid making the interview itself a punitive experience.

   The direction and tone of the interviews were gradually shaped by giving small cash bonuses, unexpected privileges, or verbal praise for "good work". The professional orientation of the various Es (e.g. a clinical psychologist, a social worker, a Jesuit priest) was clearly reflected in the content of later interviews. The principal investigators believed that the process of exploration into one's own feelings was itself of value, and they tended to give bonuses for interviews where the S talked about his own experiences in detail and with affect. Advice-giving was avoided, even when requested by the employee. It was believed that advice-giving generally prevents an individual from developing independent judgment—if the E's advice should prove wrong, the employee escaped some personal responsibility; if the E's should prove correct, the employee was robbed of a personal accomplishment.

After about two months of employment, Ss typically began to value the relationship with the project and the E as much or more than their small salary. A sixteen-year-old S reported the following conversation with a friend who wanted a job with the project (Schwitzgebel, 1960).

> I tell him to take the job. But there's no words for it. I tell him it starts out like a soft touch, but it isn't. I say "Things'll happen to you." But "things" isn't saying anything. He says, "yea", and he thinks to himself you're nuts. But he'll come around looking for the money.

In response to the common request to spend more than the scheduled hour at the laboratory, taped interviews were supplemented by activities such as preparing for driver's licence tests, building simple electronic equipment, answering correspondence. The pay for this supplementary work was very small.

Termination of employment came gradually. Ss would typically take part-time jobs in addition to the work at the laboratory. If the outside work went well, the frequency of the interviews decreased. If the outside work went poorly and the boy became discouraged, the E would take the initiative to schedule more interviews. After nine or ten months of employment with the project (assuming they had not been incarcerated in the meantime), Ss left for full-time jobs, trade school, or armed services. Separation from the project seemed a natural event in view of the difference in ages, interests, and backgrounds of the Es and Ss.

Results

Three years after termination of employment of the experimental group, an extensive follow-up of these twenty Ss showed a statistically significant reduction in the number of arrests and the number of months of incarceration as compared to the control group. Experimental Ss accumulated an average of 2.4 arrests during the follow-up period; the control group averaged 4.7 ($t = 33.0$; $p < 0.025$). The mean number of months of incarceration for experimental Ss was 3.5; the mean number of months for control Ss was 6.9 ($t = 2.79$; $p < 0.05$).

Experimental and control groups did not, however, show a significant difference ($p > 0.05$) in the number of persons from each group returned to reformatory or prison. The recidivism rate for the experimental group was 35 per cent; the recidivism rate for the control group was 45 per cent.

It appears that the research procedure was effective in reducing, but not eliminating, delinquent behaviours. While some Ss of both groups continued committing illegal acts for which they were apprehended, the experimental Ss seemed to do so less frequently (reduced number of arrests) and the type of offence seemed less severe (reduced months of incarceration). For example, one experimental S and a friend got into an argument with a cab driver regarding the fare they had been charged. They gave the driver ten dollars, pushed him out, and took the cab "for change". The boys were easily apprehended while randomly giving free rides to people in a neighbouring city.

Discussion

The evidence of the present study suggests that principles of operant conditioning may be effectively utilized in changing certain characteristic behaviours of adolescent delinquents. The frequency and severity of known crime was not reduced, in our opinion, by "direct attack". The tone of the project was clearly not one of "fighting" delinquency or delinquents but rather one of sympathy, firmness, and sharing. The Es attempted to establish conditions in which Ss could become secure enough to share experiences, to express honest opinions, and to explore new ways of feeling and living—in short, to become good employees. The fact that the job was both legitimate and difficult meant that good employees became quite involved and challenged by a non-criminal activity. In effect, delinquent behaviour was counterconditioned by the reinforcing of competing behaviours. Seldom were any reinforcers given for simply staying out of trouble.

The strong personal relationship which developed in most cases between the S and the E seemed to gradually generalize to other persons whom the S saw as being older, better educated, authorities, or employers. Once these and similar classes of people became less threatening to the S, he found the usual social situations in which adolescents are involved (e.g. commercial employment, training programs, armed services) relatively attractive. He could earn considerably more money than the research project offered, and at the same time he felt that he would be capable of making new friends. At this point the S usually initiated his own voluntary termination from the project.

To the best of our knowledge, many of the undesirable side-effects often assumed to accompany conditioning of humans were not present.

Generally, the concern is that conditioning (assuming it were effective) will somehow diminish man's freedom, initiative, privacy, creativity, spontaneity, and so forth. We shall mention briefly three values which we believe were sustained and supported in the course of the present behaviour-change process.

(1) *Recognition of individuality.* Each S was offered a job at a wage assumed to be appropriate for his age and needs. Each S was free to reject, accept, or bargain for his wages. Topics of the interviews were selected by the individual Ss. The failure of the E to arbitrarily assign topics was, in fact, often a source of discomfort for the Ss.

The type as well as the amount of rewards and bonuses varied for each S. Generalized reinforcers (e.g. food or money) were found to be effective initially, but gradually specific reinforcers (e.g. a particular brand of cigarettes which the S liked but could seldom afford) were used more frequently simply because they proved to be more effective. Reinforcers had to be empirically and operationally defined for each person. To the extent that individuals have different histories, the discovery of effective reinforcers always requires conditions which allow the S honest freedom of expression and which permit the E to exercise honest concern and attentiveness. We believe that the existential movement in psychology is of considerable value in reminding therapists of the unique history of each individual, the importance of free expression, and the value of relationships in which the therapist is "not being merely a shadowy mirror but an alive human being who is, at that hour, not concerned with his own problems but with understanding and experiencing, as far as possible, the existence (including the problems) of the patient" (May, 1959).

(2) *"Self-direction".* While the Es in the present study attempted to refrain from imposing many of their own idiosyncratic values on the Ss, they did overtly reinforce attempts of the Ss to explore feelings and solutions and to expand their capacity for self-direction. These values served as criteria for giving interview bonuses. "Self-direction" was defined as the ability of a person, through planning, to control his own reinforcers.

In general, we preferred Ss who were dominant, not submissive, in the process of their own behaviour change. It is at this point that the traditional medical "treatment" paradigm may be the most inadequate in describing the conditioning procedure. Technically, operant conditioning requires an active organism; medical treatment may require a more passive or immobilized organism. In conditioning the E pays the S for something of positive value; in treatment, the patient pays the physician to ameliorate a wrong (possibly caused by some failure to act). Furthermore, conditioning, as practiced in this research, did not require examinations, make formal diagnoses, promise cures, or assume legal responsibility for a S's behaviour or condition.

(3) *Personal freedom.* All Ss of the present study were non-incarcerated volunteers. Referrals were not required and infrequently used. As mentioned previously in this paper, prospective Ss were warned that they might change their ideas and feelings about many things. They were told that this was their own affair and that they were always free to quit the job whenever they wished. Literature about the project was available for the Ss to read or purposely shown to them in advance.

Continuation of employment was not contingent on becoming non-delinquent. But if a S became incarcerated, it was obvious that he would not be able to come to work at the laboratory. Ss did not report feelings of coercion or constriction. Most Ss looked on their experience favourably and recommended the project to their friends—with the warning: "Things'll happen".

One might try to measure "freedom" objectively in terms of the potential range of an individual's behavior. Prior to employment by the project, for example, only four Ss had held full-time jobs longer than six months. Following the project, most Ss were legally self-supporting for about three years. It is assumed that Ss were still capable of irregular employment and criminal acts but that they generally preferred to do something else.

We shall side-step any theoretical discussion of determinism versus (?) freedom. (Part of the complexity of this issue may be due to the diverse perspectives from which people may make predictions—in particular, whether a person making a prediction is himself part of the system about which the prediction is being made.)

As measured by results so far, the explicit use of a few elementary principles of operant conditioning to induce behavior change among adolescent delinquents has proved quite reinforcing for the experimenters. And, concomitantly, certain apprehensions on the part of the Es regarding the "inhumanity" of the procedure have been strongly disconfirmed. Perhaps the most discouraging aspect of almost any research is the number of variables left uncontrolled or unmeasured. The extent to which the results of this particular study may be generalized to other experimenters, to other work situations, or to other subject populations would be largely speculation at this time.

References

Bandura, A. Psychotherapy as a learning process. *Psychological Bulletin,* 1960, 58, 143–159.

Cairns, R. The influence of dependency—anxiety on the effectiveness of social reinforcers. Unpublished doctoral dissertation, Stanford University, 1960.

Freud, Anna. Adolescence. In *The psychoanalytic study of the child,* Vol. XIII. Pp. 255–277. New York: International Universities, 1958.

Hahn, P. H. Annual Report of the Work Therapy Dept. of the Court of Common Pleas, Juvenile Division, Cincinnati, Ohio, 1960.

Johns, J. H., and Quay, H. C. The effect of social reward on verbal conditioning in psychopathic and neurotic military offenders. *Journal of Consulting Psychology,* 1962, *26,* 213–220.

Kadlub, K. The effects of two types of reinforcement on the performance of psychopathic and normal criminals. Unpublished doctoral thesis, University of Illinois, 1956.

Krasner, L. Studies of the conditioning of verbal behavior. *Psychological Bulletin,* 1958, *55,* 148–170.

Lykken, D. T. A study of anxiety in the sociopathic personality. *Journal of Abnormal and Social Psychology,* 1957, *55,* 6–10.

May, R. The existential approach. In S. Areti (Ed.), *American Handbook of Psychiatry.* New York: Basic Books, 1959.

Schwitzgebel, R. A new approach to understanding delinquency. *Federal Probation,* 1960, pp. 5–9.

Sidman, M. Operant techniques. In A. J. Bachrach (Ed.), *Experimental foundations of clinical psychology.* New York: Basic Books, 1962. Pp. 170–210.

Skinner, B. F. *Science and Human Behavior.* New York: Macmillan, 1953.

Slack, C. W. Experimenter-subject psychotherapy: a new method of introducing intensive office treatment for unreachable cases. *Mental Hygiene, New York,* 1960, *44,* 238–256.

3. TOKEN REINFORCEMENT OF ACADEMIC PERFORMANCE WITH INSTITUTIONALIZED DELINQUENT BOYS *

Vernon O. Tyler, Jr. and G. Duane Brown

Many educators prefer to motivate academic performance with "intrinsic" rather than "extrinsic" reinforcers; if used at all, they say, extrinsic reinforcers should be employed with caution (Marx, 1960). At the same

* From: Vernon O. Tyler, Jr. and G. Duane Brown, "Token Reinforcement of Academic Performance with Institutionalized Delinquent Boys," *Journal of Educational*

time it is recognized that delinquent youngsters often have academic difficulty in the usual school situation (e.g., Bloch & Flynn, 1956; Briggs, Johnson, & Wirt, 1962). Since the IQs of delinquent youngsters may average well within the normal range (e.g., Tyler & Kelly, 1962), low motivation appears to be responsible for their poor school performance.

Various approaches have been suggested for motivating these "underachievers." As Birnbrauer, Wolf, Kidder, and Tague (1965) have indicated, these include (a) the use of "intrinsically reinforcing" materials which "are 'interesting,' 'meaningful'," etc., (b) "using materials and procedures which combine interest value and high probabilities of success," and finally, (c) "presenting social and/or symbolic reinforcers, e.g., teacher approval, grades, and stars." But as Birnbrauer et al., point out, none of these methods may be adequate for the retarded, school dropouts, and behavior problems. They suggest token reinforcement systems may be more effective. In such systems the tokens which are exchangeable for tangible reinforcers become generalized reinforcers (Skinner, 1953). A few examples of token reinforcement systems which have strengthened academic performance include studies with youngsters having reading difficulties (Staats, Staats, Schutz, & Wolf, 1962), retardates (Birnbrauer, Wolf, Kidder, & Tague, 1965), nursery school youngsters (Heid, 1964), and elementary school children (Michael[1]). However, work with delinquent youths appears to be quite rare. Cohen (Cohen, Flipczak, & Bis, 1965) has described a promising program for institutionalized delinquents. Of course, Slack (1960) and Schwitzgebel (e.g., Schwitzgebel & Kolb, 1964) have used operant techniques with

Psychology, 59, 1968, 164–168. Copyright 1968 by the American Psychological Association, and reproduced by permission.

This study was conducted at Fort Worden Treatment Center (Washington State Department of Institutions, Division of Juvenile Rehabilitation), Port Townsend, Washington. Grateful appreciation is due Superintendent Gus Lindquist and Assistant Superintendent Robert H. Koschnick and Principal John Kanarr for their support and encouragement of this study; teachers Sam Rust, Jr., and William Harrison for their original thinking, which made this study possible, and for preparing and administering the tests; Cottage supervisor Allen Hodge and his staff Edith Smith and Lew Streit for administering the "token economy"; John D. Burchard and Don R. Shupe for their invaluable consultative services; Don Blood and B. L. Kintz for their comments on statistical procedures; and Patricia Soapes, Sara Burchard, Doreen Beazley, and Mary Wagner for collecting and compiling data.

A version of this paper was read at the Western Psychological Association, San Francisco, California, May, 1967.

The authors are also at the Oregon State School for the Blind, Salem.

---

[1] J. Michael, personal communication, June 16, 1965.

delinquents, but not directly in the area of academic performance so far as is known.

For the present study it was assumed that many delinquent youngsters lack reinforced practice in the skills that result in teacher ratings of satisfactory performance. Apparently, the typical school situation does not provide the type of reinforcements necessary to strengthen these skills. The purpose of this study was to develop procedures for improving the academic functioning of a group of delinquent boys. This essentially involved setting up a "token economy" based on academic performance. More specifically, it was hypothesized that academic performance with contingent reinforcement will be superior to performance with noncontingent reinforcement in both between- and within-group comparisons.

Method

The subjects (Ss) in this study were 15 court-committed boys, 13–15 years of age, who resided in a one-cottage living unit of a state training school. They attended school in their own self-contained classroom supervised by two team teachers. At 6 PM every evening, Monday through Friday, the television set in the cottage day room was turned on to the Huntley-Brinkley news broadcast. Youngsters were permitted, but not required, to watch the program; the only requirement was that all youngsters in the vicinity of the television set remain quiet so that those who wished to watch could do so. The following morning in school, Ss were administered a 10-item true-false test on the news program. The teachers wrote the questions the night before while watching the program. They wrote a new question every time there was a change of subject and two or three items to cover special subjects presented at the end of the program. The items were simple statements concerning the current events presented in the broadcast. Of course, this method meant the items were not standardized for difficulty. Immediately after administration, the tests were graded and the scores entered on a grade sheet which each student carried with him. Upon returning to the cottage, in the afternoon, those Ss on contingent reinforcement were paid in tokens according to the scores they had earned on the test; Ss on noncontingent reinforcement were paid a "straight salary." The tokens were redeemable for canteen items (candy, gum, etc.) and privileges in the cottage.

The Ss were paid the tokens according to a schedule designed by the experimenters (Es). The Es looked at each S's scores on the true-false test for the 20 school days prior to the beginning of the experiment. Considering these data and S's presumed level of motivation, a judgment was made as to what his schedule should be to maximize test performance; for example, if an S had been averaging 6 items correct, and had been earning approximately 20 ¢ a day in tokens, he would be given about 15¢ for 6 items correct, 20 ¢ for 7, 25¢ for 8, 27¢ for 9 and 30¢ for 10 correct. The goal was to let each S earn his previous average "income" with a slight improvement in performance and even more with greater improvements. The Es' judgments were influenced by a subjective assessment of S's level of aspiration, tolerance for frustration, and limitations on the research budget for reinforcers.

Twenty Ss were randomly assigned to groups in the design outlined in Table 1. However, because of the rapid turnover of population in a crowded institution, some Ss left the institution prior to completion of the study resulting in unequal Ns in the two groups.

In Phase I, Ss in Group 1 were placed on contingent reinforcement and Ss in Group 2 on noncontingent reinforcement (paid 21¢ a day regardless of how well they did on the test). In Phase II, Group 1 was placed on noncontingent reinforcement and Group 2 on contingent reinforcement. A counterbalanced design was necessary to compensate for uncontrolled variability in the difficulty of the tests from day to day.

Although Group 1 (mean age 15.6) averaged a year older than Group 2 (mean age 14.6), both groups were functioning in the low average IQ range (mean IQs 94 and 98, respectively).

In addition, problems in data collection should be mentioned. On some occasions Ss were absent from school and could not take the tests. Because the tests were not equated for difficulty from day to day, the problem of missing data was a serious one. Only data for the days on which scores from at least 12 of the 15 boys were available were included for analysis. Missing scores for each S were replaced with the S's mean score for the phase. From Phase I, data are reported from 17 of

TABLE 1
Design for Administration of Current Events Test Reinforcement [a]

SUBJECTS	PHASE I (DAYS 1–17)	PHASE II (DAYS 18–29)
Group 1	Contingent reinforcement	Noncontingent reinforcement
Group 2	Noncontingent reinforcement	Contingent reinforcement

[a] For Group 1, $N = 9$; for Group 2, $N = 6$.

the 27 days on which tests were administered; from Phase II, data are reported from 12 out of 29 days. As is apparent, it was necessary to eliminate large quantities of data in order to make comparisons in which most of the Ss of both groups were represented.

Results

Mean daily test scores for both groups for Phases I and II over the 29 days reported are presented in Figure 1. Means for each phase are also included. The data show a clear pattern: during Phase I, Group 1 surpassed Group 2 on 15 out of 17 days; during Phase II, Group 2 surpassed Group 1 on 9 out of 12 days. Reversals when they did occur were quite small in contrast to the predicted differences between groups. The irregular, spiked form of the curves suggests that the tests varied a good deal in difficulty level from day to day as was expected. The nearly parallel form of the two curves indicates the groups responded to these variations in difficulty in a highly consistent, reliable fashion.

The S means for each phase were treated with a Lindquist (1953) Type I design analysis of variance. The summary of this analysis in Table 2 indicates there was no difference between Groups 1 and 2 (B comparison), but that the difference between Phases I and II (A comparison) and the interaction between Groups × Phases (AB compari-

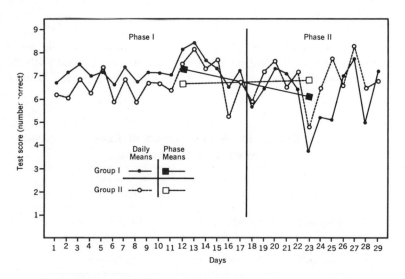

FIGURE 1   The effect of contingent and noncontingent token reinforcement on true-false test performance.

TABLE 2
Analysis of Variance of Subject
Mean[a] Test Scores under Contingent
and Noncontingent Reinforcement

SOURCE	df	MS	F
Between Ss			
B (Groups)	1	.02	
Error (b)	13	.43	
Within Ss			
A (Phases)	1	2.60	7.43[b]
AB	1	2.49	7.11[c]
Error (w)	13	.35	

[a] Analysis based on two values from each subject: the mean of his 17 daily scores from Phase I and the mean of his 12 scores from Phase II.
[b] $p < .025$; two-tailed
[c] $p < .0125$; one-tailed.

son) were both significant ($p < .025$ and $p < .0125$, respectively). No difference was expected in the B comparison because of counterbalancing of treatments. The difference between phases may be attributed to uncontrolled day-to-day variability in the difficulty level of the tests. The interaction effect indicates that under contingent reinforcement, performance was at a significantly higher level than under noncontingent reinforcement. Since the direction of the interaction effect was predicted, the probability value was halved (one-tailed test).

While the within-S variances against which the interaction effect was tested were not significantly heterogeneous, some question could be raised about the normality of distributions of within-S difference scores. To avoid the assumptions of homogeneity of variance and normality of distributions and to study individual S performance, the data were subjected to nonparametric treatment. Mean scores for each S for each phase (same data as for analysis of variance) were classified as to whether the trend in the data supports ($+$) or does not support ($-$) the prediction that each S will perform at a higher level when token reinforcement is contingent on his test score than when it is not. Twelve of the 15 Ss did better under contingent reinforcement; only two Ss did worse. The Wilcoxon matched-pairs signed-ranks test (Siegel, 1956) was applied to these data yielding a highly significant T of 11 ($p < .005$; one-tailed test).

The between-groups effects were also tested for each phase separately, using the Mann-Whitney U test for independent measures (Siegel, 1956).

As predicted, using one-tailed tests, during Phase I, Group 1 surpassed Group 2 ($U = 13$, approaches significance at the .05 level); during Phase II, Group 2 surpassed Group 1 ($U = 12$, $p < .05$).

Discussion

Both between-groups and within-groups data clearly indicate that contingent reinforcement was associated with higher test performance than when reinforcement was noncontingent. This pattern emerged in spite of the use of quickly prepared unstandardized test items which varied considerably in difficulty from day to day and in spite of unstable conditions such as the shifting institutional population.

Moreover, this pattern appeared and was maintained with consistency over a 12-week interval. This would suggest more than a transitory effect, more than delinquents "playing games" with the program or a novelty that wore off.

While the effect of the contingent reinforcement is statistically significant, the practical educational significance appears limited at this point. The Ss on contingent reinforcement averaged less than one test item better performance than when they were on noncontingent reinforcement. On the other hand, it should be noted that Ss were attending small classes (10 students per teacher) led by teachers who in Es' judgment were about the most competent they had ever seen. These teachers had a knack with obstreperous youngsters; they knew how to discipline them and yet they were quite skilled and ingenious at devising methods of exciting the interests of even the most apathetic youngster. Thus the token reinforcement was tried against the severe competition of undoubtedly powerful social reinforcements supplied by these teachers.

That the reinforcement showed an effect in addition to what was generally regarded as an effective instructional program is further evidence of the importance of tangible reinforcers with delinquent and disadvantaged youngsters. It is doubtful that the tokens would have been this effective in a prosperous urban junior high school in which the youngsters were satiated with tangibles, enjoyed school, and were achieving "success" in the middle-class culture.

Replication of this study with more precise controls would more clearly demonstrate the effectiveness of this procedure. These controls should include an unreinforced control group and test items constructed to be more nearly equal in difficulty. Previous efforts by the investigators to produce improved academic performance with token reinforcement showed no results, presumably because of inadequate controls, particularly with regard to the measurement of the criterion.

Ultimately, of course, efforts must be made to "wean" youngsters from token reinforcers and link academic performance to the more traditional reinforcers such as social approval and perhaps even the "intrinsic" reinforcement of work "for the joy of the working [Kipling, 1896]." However, the results of the present study are encouraging and suggest that many youngsters who are uninterested and antagonistic toward school work can learn that school work can "pay off."

References

Birnbrauer, J. S., Wolf, M. M., Kidder, J. D., and Tague, C. E. Classroom behavior of retarded pupils with token reinforcement, *Journal of Experimental Child Psychology*. 1965, *2*, 219–235.

Bloch, H. A., and Flynn, F. T. *Delinquency, the juvenile offender in America today*. New York: Random House, 1956.

Briggs, P. F., Johnson, R., and Wirt, R. D. Achievement among delinquency-prone adolescents. *Journal of Clinical Psychology*, 1962, *18*, 305–309.

Cohen, H. L., Flipczak, J. A., and Bis, J. S. *CASE Project: Contingencies Applicable for Special Education, Brief Progress Report*. Silver Spring, Md.: Institute of Behavioral Research, 1965.

Heid, W. H. Nonverbal conceptual behavior of young children with programmed material. Unpublished doctoral dissertation. University of Washington, 1964.

Kipling, R. *The seven seas*. New York: Appleton-Century-Crofts, 1896.

Lindquist, E. F. *Design and analysis of experiments in psychology and education*. Boston: Houghton Mifflin, 1953.

Marx, M. H. Motivation. In Marie R. Liba (Ed.), *Encyclopedia of educational research*. New York: Macmillan, 1960. Pp. 888–901.

Schwitzgebel, R., and Kolb, D. A. Inducing behaviour change in adolescent delinquents. *Behaviour Research and Therapy*, 1964, *1*, 297–304.

Siegel, S. *Nonparametric statistics for the behavioral sciences*. New York: McGraw-Hill, 1956.

Skinner, B. F. *Science and human behavior*. New York: Macmillan, 1953.

Slack, C. W. Experimenter-subject psychotherapy: A new method of introducing intensive office treatment for unreachable cases. *Mental Hygiene*, 1960, *44*, 238–256.

Staats, A. W., Staats, C. K., Schultz, R. E., and Wolf, M. M. The conditioning of textual responses using "extrinsic" reinforcers. *Journal of Experimental Analysis of Behavior*, 1962, *5*, 33–40.

Tyler, V. O., Jr., and Kelly, R. F. Cattell's HSPQ as a predictor of the behavior of institutionalized delinquents. *Psychology Research Report*

No. 2. Port Townsend, Wash.: Fort Worden Diagnostic & Treatment Center, 1962.

Wingo, G. M. Methods of teaching. In Marie R. Liba (Ed.), *Encyclopedia of educational research.* New York: Macmillan, 1960. Pp. 848–861.

4. TREATMENT OF NONREADING IN A CULTURALLY DEPRIVED JUVENILE DELINQUENT: AN APPLICATION OF REINFORCEMENT PRINCIPLES *

Arthur W. Staats and William H. Butterfield

Staats (1964c; Staats & Staats, 1963) has previously discussed behavior problems and their treatment in terms of learning principles. In doing so it was indicated that problem behaviors can arise in part (1) because behavior that is necessary for adjustment in our society is absent from the individual's repertoire, (2) because behaviors considered undesirable by the society are present in the individual's repertoire, or (3) because the individual's motivational (reinforcement) system was inappropriate in some respect.

Although a complete account is not relevant here, several points pertinent to the above conceptions will be made in introducing the present study. The notion that many behavior problems consist of deficits in behavior is important in the study of child development. Behaviorally speaking, a child is considered to be a problem when he does not acquire behaviors as other children do. It is conceivable that a deficit in behavior could arise because the child simply cannot acquire the behavior involved, even though the conditions of learning have been entirely adequate.

* *Child Development*, 1965, *36*, 925–942. Copyright 1965, by the Society for Research in Child Development, Inc. The present methods of reading training were formulated, and the present paper written, by the first author as part of a long-term project applying learning principles and procedures to the study of language-learning and reading. The methods were applied by the second author in his position as an officer of the Maricopa County Juvenile Probation Department. The second author also collected and tabulated the data and aided in its graphic presentation. Appreciation is expressed to Chief Probation Officer John H. Walker for lending cooperation in the conduct of the study. In addition, Mary J. Butterfield made important contributions in the preparation of the reading materials used in the study, Brenda Shields typed the materials, and Janet Munir typed the present manuscript.

It would be expected, however, that behavioral deficits would also arise in cases where the conditions of learning have been defective. Learning conditions can be defective in different ways. For example, the child may never have received training in the behavior he must later exhibit. Or the training may be poor, even though the "trainers," parents or teachers, and so on, have the best intentions.

In addition, however, a child may be exposed to learning conditions that are appropriate for most children but, due to the particular child's past history of learning, are not appropriate for him. It is especially in these cases that people are most likely to conclude erroneously that since other children learn in the same circumstances, the child's deficit must be because of some personal defect. For example, in cases where the training is long term, adequate reinforcement must be available to maintain the attentional and work behaviors necessary for learning. As Staats has indicated (1964c; Staats & Staats, 1963; Staats, Staats, Schutz, & Wolf, 1962), the reinforcers present in the traditional schoolroom are inadequate for many children. Their attentional behaviors are not maintained, and they do not learn. Thus, a deficit in an individual's behavioral repertoire may arise although he has been presented with the "same" training circumstances from which other children profit. Learning does not take place because the child's previous experience has not provided, in this example, the necessary reinforcer (motivational) system to maintain good "learning" behaviors. It would seem that in such a circumstance the assumption that the child has a personal defect would be unwarranted and ineffective.

However, after a few years of school attendance where the conditions of learning are not appropriate for the child, he will not have acquired the behavioral repertoires acquired by more fortunate members of the class—whose previous experiences have established an adequate motivational system. Then, lack of skilled behavior is likely to be treated aversively. That is, in the present case, the child with a reading deficit (or other evidence of underachievement) is likely to be gibed at and teased when he is still young and ignored, avoided, and looked down upon when he is older. Although the individuals doing this may not intend to be aversive, such actions constitute the presentation of aversive stimuli. Furthermore, this presentation of aversive stimuli by other "successful" children, and perhaps by a teacher, would be expected to result in further learning, but learning of an undesirable nature. These successful children, teachers, academic materials, and the total school situation can in this way become learned negative reinforcers, which may be translated (see Staats, 1964b) to say the child acquires negative attitudes toward school.

At this point, the child is likely to begin to "escape" the school situation in various ways (daydreaming, poor attendance, and so on) and to behave aversively in turn to the school and its inhabitants (vandalism, fighting, baiting teachers and students, and the like). Thus, a deficit in behavior, resulting from an inappropriate motivational system, can lead to the further development of inappropriate reinforcers and inappropriate behaviors.

The foregoing is by no means intended as a complete analysis of delinquency, dropouts, and the like. However, it does indicate some of the problems of learning that may occur in school. In addition, it does suggest that an analysis in terms of laboratory-established learning principles, when applied to problems such as in classroom learning of the above type, can yield new research and applied hypotheses. It was with this general strategy that the study of reading acquisition employing learning principles and reinforcement procedures were commenced (Staats, 1964a; Staats et al., 1962; Staats, Finley, Minke, & Wolf, 1964a; Staats, Minke, Finley, Wolf, & Brooks, 1964b). The present study is a replication and an extension of these various findings to the development of a program for training nonreaders to read. The program, which adapts standard reading materials, is based upon the principle of the reinforcer system employed in the previous studies with the younger children, thus testing the principles of reinforcement in the context of remedial reading training, as well as the feasibility of using the type of reinforcement system with a new type of S. As such, the study has implications for the study of nonreading children of pre-adolescent, adolescent, and young adult ages. In the present case, S was also a culturally deprived delinquent child—and the study thus involves additional information and implications for the special problems associated with education in this population of children.

Methods

SUBJECT

The S was a 14-year-and-3-month-old boy of Mexican-American ancestry. He was the fifth child in a family of 11 children and the mother and father. The parental techniques for controlling their children's behavior consisted of physical and verbal abuse. Both parents described their own childhood conditions as primitive. The father was taken out of school after completing the fifth grade to help with his father's work. Each of S's four older brothers had been referred to the juvenile court for misbehavior. The parents appeared to be at loss as to how to provide effective control for family members.

The S had a history of various miscreant behaviors, having been referred to the juvenile department nine times for such things as running away, burglary, incorrigibility, and truancy. During the course of the Study S was again referred on a complaint (with three other boys) of malicious mischief for shooting light bulbs and windows in a school building with a BB gun. He associated with a group of boys who had been in marked difficulty with the law. The S smoked, and on occasion he drank excessively.

The study commenced when S was residing with his family. However, after the complaint on malicious mischief S was sent to a juvenile detention home. During his stay there he was allowed to attend school in the daytime. The study was finally concluded when S was committed to an industrial school for juvenile-delinquent boys. This occurred because S baited the attendants at the detention home and caused disturbances which, although not serious, were very unpleasant and disruptive.

On the Wechsler Bellevue Form I, given when S was 13-10, he received Verbal and Performance IQ's of 77 and 106, respectively, for a Full Scale IQ of 90. The examiner concluded that S was probably within the normal range for this test. On the basis of this test and HTP Projective Drawings, S was characterized as having a poor attention span and poorly integrated thought processes and as lacking intellectual ambitiousness. He was also described as seeking satisfaction in fantasy and as having good conventional judgment.

The S had continually received failing grades in all subjects in school. He was described as having "been incorrigible since he came here in the second grade. He has no respect for teachers, steals and lies habitually and uses extremely foul language." The S had been promoted throughout his school career simply to move him on or to "get rid of him." He was disliked by the teachers and administrators in grade school because of his troublesome behavior and was described by the principal as mentally retarded even though one of the tests taken there indicated a score within the normal range. Another test taken there gave him an IQ of 75. During the study S was attending a local high school and taking classes for low-level students.

REINFORCER SYSTEM

In previous studies (Staats, in press; Staats et al., 1964a; 1964b), a reinforcer system was demonstrated that was capable of maintaining attention and work behaviors for long-term experimental studies. This system worked well with preschool children of ages 2 to 6 and with educable and trainable retardates of ages 8 to 11. The principle of the system was based upon token reinforcers. The tokens were presented contingent upon correct responses and could be exchanged for items the child could keep. In the previous studies toys of various values could be obtained when a sufficient number of tokens had been accrued in visible containers.

This system was adapted for use with the adolescent S of the present study. In the adaptation there were three types of token, distinguished by color. The tokens were of different value in terms of the items for which the tokens could be exchanged. A blue token was valued at $\frac{1}{10}$ of one cent. A white token was valued at $\frac{1}{5}$ of a cent. A red token was worth $\frac{1}{2}$ of a cent.

The child's acquisition of tokens was plotted so that visual evidence of the reinforcers was available. The tokens could be used to purchase a variety of items. These items, chosen by the subject, could range in value from pennies to whatever the subject wished to work for. Records were kept of the tokens earned by S and of the manner in which the tokens were used.

READING MATERIALS

The reading material used was taken from the Science Research Associates (SRA) reading-kit materials. The SRA kits consist of stories developed for and grouped into grade levels. Each story includes a series of questions which can be used to assess the reader's comprehension of the story. The reading training program was adapted from the SRA materials as follows:

Vocabulary words.—A running list was made of the new words that appeared in the series of stories. The list finally included each different word that appeared in the stories that were presented. From this list, the new vocabulary for each story was selected, and each word was typed on a separate 3 × 5 card.

Oral reading materials.—Each paragraph in the SRA stories was typed on a 5 × 8 card. Each story could thus be presented to S paragraph by paragraph.

Silent-reading and comprehensive-question materials.—Each SRA story, with its comprehensive questions, was typed on an 8½ × 13 sheet of white paper.

PROCEDURE

Vocabulary presentation. The procedure for each story in the series commenced with the presentation of the new words introduced in that story. The words were presented individually on the cards, and S was asked to pronounce them. A correct response to a word-stimulus card was reinforced with a midvalue token. After a correct response to a word, the card was dropped from the group of cards yet to be presented. The S was instructed to indicate words that he did not know the meaning of, and this information was provided in such cases.

When an incorrect response to a word stimulus occurred, or when S gave no response, E gave the correct response. The S then repeated the word while looking at the stimulus word. However, the word card involved was returned to the group of cards still to be presented. A card was not dropped from the group until it was read correctly without prompting. After an error on a word stimulus, only a low-value token was given on the next trial when the word was read correctly without prompting. The vocabulary-presentation phase of the training was continued until each word was read correctly without prompting.

Oral reading. Upon completion of the vocabulary materials, each paragraph was individually presented to S in the order in which the paragraph occurred in the story. When correct reading responses were made to each word in the paragraph, a high-value token was given upon completion of the paragraph. When a paragraph contained errors, S was corrected, and he repeated the word correctly while looking at the word. The paragraph was put aside, and when the other paragraphs had been completed, the paragraph containing errors was again presented. The paragraph was repeated until it was done correctly in its entirety —at which time a midvalue token was presented. When all paragraphs in a story had been completed correctly, the next phase of the training was begun.

Silent reading and comprehensive questions. Following the oral reading S was given the sheet containing the story and questions. He was instructed to read the story silently and to answer the questions beneath the story. He was also instructed that it was important to read to understand the story so that he could answer the questions.

Reinforcement was given on a variable interval schedule for attentive behavior during the silent-reading phase. That is, as long as S appropriately scanned the material he was given a low-value reinforcer an average of every 15 seconds. The exact time for reinforcement was determined by a table of random numbers varying from 1 to 30 seconds. Whenever he did anything else than peruse the material, no reinforcement was given. The next interval was then timed from the moment S returned to the silent reading, with the stipulation that no reinforcement be given sooner than 5 seconds after S returned to the reading. If the interval was less than 5 seconds, a token was not given until the next interval had also occurred. Timing was done by a continuously running stopwatch. The S was also given an extra midvalue token at the end of the silently read story on those occasions where he read without moving his lips.

Upon completion of the story, S wrote his answers to the questions typed below the story and gave his answers to E. For each correct answer, S received a high-value token. For an answer with a spelling error, S was reinforced with a midvalue token when he had corrected the answer. For incorrect answers S had to reread the appropriate paragraph, correct his answer, and he then received a midvalue token.

Vocabulary review. Some of the vocabulary words presented to S in the first phase of training were words he already could read. Many others, however, were words that the procedure was set up to teach. The oral-reading-phase performance indicated the level of S's retention of the words he had learned—and also provided further training trials on the words not already learned. A further assessment of S's retention of the words that he did not know in the vocabulary training was made after each 20 stories of the SRA materials had been read. This test of individually presented words, for each story, was started about 3 days after completion of the 20 stories and constituted fairly long-term retention.

This test was also used as a review for S, and further training on the words was given. This was first done by reinforcing S with a low-value token for every word he read correctly. However, S's attention was not well maintained by this reinforcement, and the procedure was changed to provide a midvalue token for correctly read words. When S could not read a word, or missed one, he was prompted and had to correctly repeat the name of the word while looking at the word. This word card was then put aside and presented later, at which time S was reinforced with a low-value token if he read it correctly. If not, the procedure was repeated until a correct unprompted trial occurred.

Achievement tests. Prior to the commencement of the training, S was tested to assess his reading performance, and during the period of experimental training he was given two additional reading-achievement tests. The first one given was the Developmental Reading Test. (At this time the S's vision and hearing were also tested and found to be normal.) After 45 training sessions another reading test was given S, this time the California Reading Test, Form BB, for grades 1, 2, 3, and L-4. Twenty-five sessions later, just before the termination of the study, S was given the California Reading Test, Form BB, for grades 4, 5, and 6. The S's performance on the three reading tests constituted one of the measures of his progress. The tests were given at the Arizona State University Reading Center.

Training sessions. The training sessions would ordinarily last for 1 hour or less, although a few sessions were as short as 30 minutes or as long as 2 hours. Not all of this time was spent in reading, however. A good deal of time was spent in arranging the materials, recording S's performance, keeping count of the reinforcers, plotting the reinforcers accrued, and so on. The time spent actually reading was tabulated. During the 4½-month experimental period, 70 training sessions were conducted, with an average of about 35 minutes spent per session for a total of 40 hours of reading training.

Results and Conclusions

During the period of training S made many reading responses. Figure 1 shows the number of single-word reading responses S made as a function of the hours of time spent in training. An estimate of the number of single-word reading responses was obtained from tabulating each presentation of a word card, the number of words in the stories, and the reading-comprehension questions at the end of each story, as well as the words presented to S in the later single-word retention test. Actually, the number of words in the stories was an estimate obtained from the mean number of words in two out of each five stories. Thus, rather than giving the true absolute number of reading responses made, the figure gives an estimate. However, the most important aspect of the figure is to indicate the rate of this single-word reading-response measure as a func-

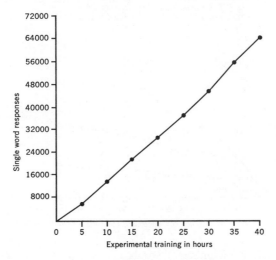

FIGURE 1 Number of single-word reading responses as a function of the time in experimental reading training.

tion of time in experimental training. As can be seen, as the training progressed S covered the reading material at a slightly more rapid rate, as is shown by the slight positive acceleration in the curve. The importance of this result is to indicate that the child's behavior of attending to the task and making the appropriate reading responses did not diminish throughout the period of training. Thus, the reinforcement system employed was capable of maintaining the behavior for a long period of time. During this time the attentional and cooperative behaviors instigated resulted in many, many learning trials—a *sine qua non* for the acquisition of achievement in any skill.

Before reading each story S was presented with individual cards for all the words included in that story which had not been presented in a previous story. When these words were presented, S would read a certain proportion correctly on first presentation, the other words being missed on the first presentation. The ones missed were considered to be new words for S, words that he had not previously learned. These words were separately tabulated. The cumulative number of these new words as a function of every 5 SRA stories read is shown by the top curve of Figure 2. (The data for the first 10 stories are not presented since they were not available for all three curves.) As this curve indicates, 761 new words were presented to S during the training.

Thus, S missed 761 words when they were first presented to him. However, he was given training trials on these words, and then he then

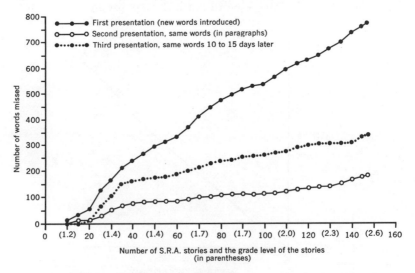

FIGURE 2   Number of words missed on first, second, and third presentations for the 150 SRA stories.

read them again in the oral reading of the paragraph. The number of these words that he missed in this oral-reading phase is plotted in the bottom curve of Figure 2. This curve then indicates the number of errors made on the second reading test of the words that had been previously learned. Thus, only 176 words out of the 761 (about 23 per cent) were missed in the oral-reading phase—showing retention for 585 words. The results indicate that the criterion of one correct unprompted reading trial in the original vocabulary-learning phase produced considerable learning when the words were read in context.

The middle curve in Figure 2 involves a measure of long-term retention of the words that had been learned. This measure was obtained by testing S on the words, presented singly, that had been learned in the preceding 20 stories. This test was given 10 to 15 days after the training occurred. The training thus included the previous single-word presentations of the words, as well as those same words read orally and silently. In addition, however, S had also learned a considerable number of other words by the time of this test. As the middle curve shows, when tested 10–15 days later, S read 430 of the 761 words correctly, or, conversely, 331 words (about 43 per cent) were missed. Thus, the procedures produced retention when the words were later presented out of context after a considerable intervening period.

The results appearing in Figure 2 indicate that the child covered a considerable amount of reading material, that he learned to read a number of new words when presented individually or in context, and that he retained a good proportion of what he had learned. The results also indicate that the child improved during the training in his retention. That is, his rate of getting new words in the first-presentation phase continues at a high rate throughout the study. (This supports the results shown in Fig. 1 indicating that the child's behavior did not weaken during the training.) However, his "rate" of missing the new words on the second and third presentations decreased, that is, he retained more of the words he had learned. Thus, tabulation indicated that for the first 35 stories only about 33 per cent of the words learned were retained 10–15 days later, whereas S's subsequent retention increased to about 55 per cent. It should be noted that this improvement occurred even though the difficulty of the words (as shown in Fig. 2 by the numbers in parentheses) became progressively greater during the training, moving from the 1.2-grade level of difficulty to the 2.6-grade level.

These results receive support from the data presented in Figure 3. As already indicated, on the first presentation of the vocabulary of a story, some words were missed out of the total presented—and S was then presented with training on these words. Figure 3 shows the number of the words presented and missed in ratio to the total number presented,

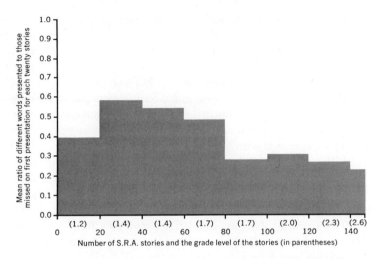

FIGURE 3   Ratio of words presented to those missed on
first presentation for the 150 SRA stories.

as this ratio is related to the number and difficulty of the stories presented. A smaller ratio indicates that S missed fewer of the total vocabulary words when they were presented for the first time. As can be seen
in Figure 3, as the child read more stories in his training (even though
they become more difficult), he missed fewer and fewer words that were
presented to him. It should be stressed that he was thus improving in
the extent to which he correctly responded to new words on *first* presentation. This improvement appeared to be correlated with other observations that indicated that S was also beginning to learn to sound out
words as a function of the training. For example, he remarked when in
the judge's office that he thought a sign said "information," because he
could read the "in" and the "for" and the "mation." In addition, S reported a number of times that the training was helping him in school,
that reading was getting easier for him in school, that he liked the reading training better as he went along, and so on. It would be expected
(as will be supported by other data) that as the reading training improved his reading in school, the things he learned in school would also
improve his performance in the reading training. It is this effect that
may also be reflected in his increasing ability to read the new words
presented to him.

In addition to this direct evidence of the child's progress in reading
training, and the foregoing indirect evidence that the reading training
was having general effects upon the child's behavior, the study was formulated to obtain other sources of information concerning the child's

progress. One means of doing this was to give the child reading-achievement tests before beginning the reading training as well as during the
training. The results of these tests are shown in Figure 4. The first point
on the curve is a measurement obtained by use of the Development
Reading Test giving a total score of reading achievement showing that S
was performing at the grade-2 level. After 45 reading-training sessions,
S's performance on the California Reading Test showed a gain to the
3.8-grade level. By the end of the training, after 25 more training sessions, S had advanced to the 4.3-grade level on the California Reading
Test.

Another indication of the general effect of the reading training came
from the child's performance in school, both in school achievement and
deportment. The period of reading training coincided with a school
term. The boy received passing grades in all subjects: A C in physical
education, a D in general shop, a D in English, and a D in mathematics.
It should be emphasized that these grades represent the first courses
that this child had ever passed, and thus his finest academic performance.

Furthermore, S began to behave better while in school. The boy had
always been a behavior problem in school, and this continued into the
period during which S received reading training. As Figure 5 shows,
during the first month of the training S committed 10 misbehaviors that
resulted in the receipt of demerits. The behaviors were as follows: disturbance in class (2 times), disobedience in class (5 times), loitering

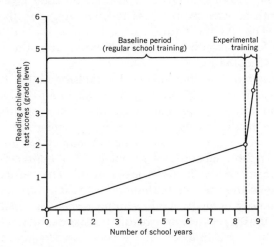

FIGURE 4   Reading-achievement test scores as a function of
8½ years of school training and 4½ months of experimental
training.

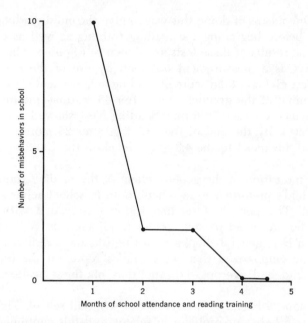

FIGURE 5 Number of official misbehaviors in school as a
function of time in the experimental training.

(2 times), and tardiness. In the second month he was given demerits for
scuffling on the school grounds and also for creating a disturbance. In
the third month he was given demerits for cutting a math class and for
profanity in class. As the figure shows, however, no misbehaviors occurred in the fourth month or in the half month after this until the conclusion of the school term.

The S requested that the tokens be exchanged for items that he
wanted in sessions 12, 17, 25, 31, 35, 43, 49, 55, and in the last session he
was given the value of the remaining tokens in cash. Items included
were a pair of "beatle" shoes, hair pomade, a phonograph record, an ice
cream sundae, a ticket to a school function, money for his brother who
was going to reform school, and so on. Further information regarding
the reinforcement system is given in Figure 6. The vertical axis of the
graph represents the ratio of the number of tokens obtained by S relative to the number of single-word reading responses which he emitted.
Lesser ratios thus indicate more reading responses per reinforcer. This
ratio was plotted as a function of the progress S made in the training
program, as given by the number of SRA stories he had completed. As
the training progressed S gradually made an increasingly greater number of reading responses per reinforcer. This effect was not accom-

plished by changing the rules by which the reinforcers were administered. The effect, which was planned in the training program, resulted from the fact that the SRA stories became longer as the grade level was raised. Since, for example, paragraph reading was reinforced by the paragraph, the longer the paragraph, the greater the number of reading responses that had to be emitted before reinforcement was obtained. At the end of training, thus, S was getting about half as much reinforcement per response as at the beginning of training. It should also be indicated that the stories were more difficult as the training progressed, so the effort involved in reading was increasing—although reinforcement for the reading was decreasing.

During the 4½ months of training, which involved 40 hours of reading training and the emission of an estimated 64,307 single-word reading responses, S received $20.31.

Discussion

In this section the various aspects of the reading-training procedures will first be discussed. Then the implications of the results and analysis will be outlined both for further studies of remedial reading training as well as for a learning conception of certain aspects of cultural deprivation and delinquency.

The method of reading training used in the present study was derived

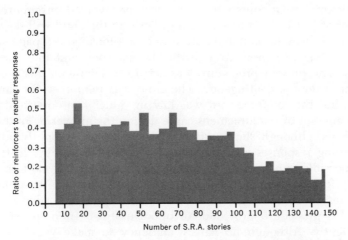

FIGURE 6   Ratio of the number of tokens received divided by the number of reading responses made as a function of the number of SRA stories read.

from previous study (Staats, 1964a, in press; Staats et al., 1962) with preschool children in which words were first presented singly, then in sentences, and finally in short stories. The present study indicated that SRA materials can be adapted for a similar type of presentation in conjunction with the type of reinforcer system previously developed (Staats et al., 1964a; 1964b). From the SRA materials it was possible to present single-word training trials and oral-reading training and to develop a silent-reading training procedure, all involving reinforcement.

When the training of reading, at least in part, is considered as operant discrimination learning, the learning task consists of having S emit the correct speech response while looking at the verbal stimulus—this process being followed by reinforcement. This basic procedure was elaborated in the present study to include two levels of reinforcement. An unprompted reading response on the first trial was reinforced more heavily than one that had been previously missed. This procedure appeared to produce learning that was retained very well when the child later read the words orally in a paragraph, with considerable retention also occurring when the child was tested on the individual words 10–15 days later.

It may seem incongruous at first to attempt to reinforce silent reading, since this behavior is not observable. However, it should be remembered that the subject actually has two types of behavior in the silent-reading act. He looks at the verbal stimuli—that is, attends—and he makes "reading" verbal responses to the verbal stimuli. While the reading responses cannot be monitored when they are covert, the attending behavior can be. Of course, there is a danger involved in reinforcing the behavior of just looking at something. Perhaps the child will do nothing else. If he is heavily reinforced for sitting and looking at a page, and the actual reading responses are effortful, he may not emit the reading responses. The present procedure was set up to eliminate this possibility by using a double contingency. The child was reinforced for simple attention, but the reinforcement was low in value. The opportunity for a greater amount of reinforcement came during the answering of the questions. Thus, although simple attention was reinforced lightly, attention and reading responses were reinforced much more heavily. In this way it was possible to use reinforcement in a procedure designed to maintain reading for "understanding," in addition to simple "word-naming." (These results could be generalized to other types of learning.) Furthermore, this procedure provided an opportunity to train the subject to read silently. Although he had a tendency to make vocal or lip responses while reading, it was possible to strengthen reading without these other responses through differentially reinforcing the correct silent reading.

Thus, it may be concluded that the reading program increased the child's reading vocabulary as shown by the various measures of retention used in the study, the tests of reading achievement, as well as the child's improved school performance and his verbal description of improved attitude toward and performance in reading in school. There were also suggestions that the child was acquiring a "unit-reading repertoire," that is, the general ability to sound out words through making the correct response to single letters and syllables. Thus, for example, the child made errors on fewer and fewer of the new words presented as the training progressed, even though the words were of greater difficulty. In addition, he retained a greater proportion of the words he learned as he went on. Further research of the present type must be conducted to test the possibilities for using a more phonic system of remedial reading training with the present type of subject.

A final point should be made concerning the training procedures used in the present study. The procedures are very specific and relatively simple. Thus, it was not necessary to have a person highly trained in education to administer the training. In the present case the trainer-experimenter was a probation officer. It might also be suggested that anyone with a high-school education and the ability to read could have administered the training. This has implications for the practical application of the present methods, since one of the questions that arises in this context concerns the economy of the procedures. Although the procedures as described involved a one-trainer-to-one-student ratio, as many remedial teaching procedures do, in the present case the simplicity of the procedures suggests the possibility that savings may be effected because the trainer need not be so highly trained. Thus, the procedures could be widely applied or adapted by various professionals, for example, social workers, prison officials, remedial teachers, tutors, and so on. In an even more economical application, helpers of professionals could be used to actually administer the procedures; for example, selected delinquents (or prisoners) could administer the procedures to other delinquents. Thus, the procedures could be utilized in various situations, such as settlement houses, homes for juvenile delinquents, prison training programs, parts of adult education, and so on. All that is needed is a suitable system of reinforcers to back up the tokens. These conclusions are supported by another study by A. W. Staats now being prepared for publication in which analogous methods developed for work with preschool children were applied by a graduate student who was untrained in teaching; the results suggest possibilities for economic innovations in education generally.

In the same context, it may be worthwhile pointing out that the results indicated that the child advanced as many years in reading achievement, as measured by the tests, during the experimental training as he had in his previous school history. A comparison of the relative costs—in the present case, about 70 hours of time of a person not necessarily trained in teaching and $20.31 for the reinforcers versus 8½ years of trained teachers' time, albeit in a group situation—suggests that the procedure introduced in the present study may not be uneconomical, even without improvements in the method. And, as will be further described, the child's failure in school may in many cases be considered as a contributor to the child's delinquency—which also carries a high cost to society. The present results, in suggesting that the training procedures may also effect general improvements in behavior, including misbehaviors in school, thus have further implications concerning the economy of the procedures.

The present study, among other things, tests the feasibility of using the type of reinforcing system, previously applied successfully to younger children, to the study of learning in older children—in this case a 14-year-old juvenile delinquent. The reinforcer system worked very well with the present S, maintaining his attention and working behaviors in good strength for a long period of time. And there was every reason to expect that the study could have been continued for a much longer period, probably as long as it would have taken to train the child to read normally.

It should be noted that although the amount of reinforcement given decreases during the training, as shown in Figure 6, the reading behavior is maintained in good strength throughout the study, as shown in Figures 1 and 2; thus, less and less reinforcement is needed to maintain the behavior even though the material increases in difficulty. As already described, this occurred because a progressively greater number of reading responses was necessary per reinforcer. This is analogous to gradually raising the ratio of responses to the reinforcers as considered in terms of ratio schedules of reinforcement. Staats has suggested that this type of gradual increase must occur to produce good work behaviors in humans (Staats & Staats, 1963).

This result in the present study is in part an answer to the question whether the use of extrinsic reinforcers in training will produce a child who is dependent upon these reinforcers. It is not possible to discuss this topic fully now. However, it may be said that the extrinsic reinforcement can be gradually decreased until, as was happening with the present child, reading becomes reinforcing itself, or other sources of reinforcement maintain the behavior.

A word should be said concerning the relevance of reinforcement variables in the treatment of nonlearning in culturally deprived children. Typically, as in the present case, such children do not, as a result of their home experiences, acquire "reinforcer systems" appropriate for maintaining learning in the traditional classroom. Rosen (1956) has shown that, in the present terminology, lower-class children do not have experiences that make school achievement and learning itself positively reinforcing. This deficit, among others that affect the reinforcer system, can be expected to lead to poor school learning and other behavioral deficits. In such cases, there are increased opportunities for other poor social attitudes and undesirable behaviors to develop, as suggested in the introduction and exemplified in the present case.

The present study suggests that these conditions can be reversed through the application of learning principles and reinforcement variables to the task of repairing the child's behavioral-achievement deficit. There were indications that this treatment resulted in improvement in the reinforcement value of (attitudes toward) school for this child and consequently in the decrease in incidence of misbehaviors in school. The results thus suggest that under appropriate conditions the deficit in behavior stemming from the child's inadequate reinforcing system may be, at least in part, repaired by a properly administered, effective reinforcement system, resulting in a decrease in undesirable behaviors.

A comment should be made about the possibility of a Hawthorne effect, that is, that the social reinforcement by the E and possible extraexperimental reinforcement contributed to the results in the present study. It would be expected that such reinforcers could contribute to the overall effect—and in the present case the expenditure for the material reinforcers was small. In general, it can be expected that individuals will vary in the extent to which social reinforcers will be effective. For example, in preschool children social reinforcement is ineffective for long-term training (Staats, 1964c; Staats et al., 1962), and the same would be expected for many individuals with behavior problems. Ordinarily, it might be expected that the weaker other sources of reinforcement are for the individual, the stronger must be the reinforcer system of the treatment procedure.

In conclusion, the present study helps support and replicate the previous findings and extends the general procedures and principles to the study of an adolescent child who is culturally deprived and is also a juvenile delinquent. The various sources of data used suggest that the present procedures and principles are applicable to this population also. Based upon these suggestions, further studies will be conducted on culturally deprived children, delinquent and nondelinquent, as well as studies of other types of nonachieving or underachieving readers.

It should also be indicated that the present study indicates the possibility for developing procedures for the objective application and test of laboratory-derived learning principles within the context of an actual problem of behavior. As previously indicated (Staats, 1964a), verification of learning principles in the context of a problem of human behavior constitutes one way to further the generality of the principles themselves. It may thus be suggested that such studies have two types of implication: they have implications for people interested in dealing with the problems of human behavior, as well as for those interested in the extension and verification of the basic science.

It is relevant to add here that the type of token reinforcer system employed in the present study was developed by the first author in 1959 in the context of an exploratory study of remedial reading. Token reinforcer systems have since been applied widely in a number of other studies of various behavior problems producing results which support the preceding conclusions. Furthermore, additional studies have been conducted in the present project to further substantiate the general efficacy of the reinforcer system and the reading procedures, with various types of subjects. Thus, the present training procedures have been employed successfully in a study involving eighteen additional children (including 7 educable retardates as well as several emotionally disturbed children) of junior high school age. The instructional-technicians were nine average high school students and nine adult volunteers (Staats, Minke, Goodwin, and Landeen, 1967). In a later study with Karl A. Minke now being prepared for publication, thirty-two Negro ghetto children with behavior problems were given the treatment. The instructional-technicians were literate Negro high school children from ghetto schools in Milwaukee and two formerly unemployed Negro adults who were employed on the project in full-time positions. The treatment was conducted for a semester and the results were again successful. Increases were shown in achievement tests, grades, attendance, and deportment, in comparison to a control group of thirty-two children. In addition, Staats (1968) has conducted a long-term project with young children in the study and treatment of cognitive deficits in such areas as first reading acquisition, number skill learning, and writing acquisition. The present methods and principles receive strong support as being generally applicable from these various studies.

References

Rosen, B. C. The achievement syndrome: A psychocultural dimension of social stratification. *American Sociological Review*, 1956, *21*, 203–211.

Staats, A. W. A case in and a strategy for the extension of learning principles to problems of human behavior. In A. W. Staats (Ed.), *Human learning*. New York: Holt, Rinehart and Winston, 1964. (a)

Staats, A. W. Conditioned stimuli, conditioned reinforcers, and word meaning. In Staats, A. W. (Ed.), *Human learning*. New York: Holt, Rinehart and Winston, 1964. (b)

Staats, A. W. (Ed.) *Human learning*. New York: Holt, Rinehart and Winston, 1964. (c)

Staats, A. W. An integrated-functional learning approach to complex human behavior. In B. Kleinmuntz (Ed.), *Problem solving: research, method and theory.* New York: Wiley, in press.

Staats, A. W., Finley, J. R., Minke, K. A., and Wolf, M. Reinforcement variables in the control of unit reading responses. *Journal of the Experimental Analysis of Behavior,* 1964, 7, 139–149. (a)

Staats, A. W., Minke, K. A., Finley, J. R., Wolf, M., and Brooks, L. O. A reinforcer system and experimental procedure for the laboratory study of reading acquisition. *Child Development,* 1964, 35, 209–231. (b)

Staats, A. W., and Staats, C. K. *Complex human behavior.* New York: Holt, Rinehart and Winston, 1963.

Staats, A. W., Staats, C. K., Schutz, R. E., and Wolf, M. The conditioning of textual responses utilizing "extrinsic" reinforcers. *Journal of the Experimental Analysis of Behavior,* 1962, 5, 33–40.

5. THE INFLUENCE OF MASSIVE REWARDS ON READING ACHIEVEMENT IN POTENTIAL URBAN SCHOOL DROPOUTS *

Carl A. Clark and Herbert J. Walberg

Most theories of learning emphasize reinforcement as an important determinant of behavior, and yet no randomized, controlled experiments have been done in school classrooms (Parton and Ross, 1965). This study reports an investigation of this problem in an after-school reading program for children in the Chicago Public Schools.[1] The experiment took place in the south side of the innercity, an area populated by rural, Negro migrants from Alabama, Georgia, and Mississippi and their first and second generations. The neighborhood is characterized by low

* *American Educational Research Journal,* 1968, 5(3), 305–310. Reprinted with permission of the authors and the American Educational Research Association.

[1] This research was supported by a Ford Foundation grant to the Chicago Public Schools under the Great Cities School Improvement Program.

standards of living and high rates of social pathology: unemployment, crime, and school attrition. Nationally standardized achievement tests of children in this part of the city show that they are from one to four years behind typical levels of children in the same age and grade. One can imagine—and confirm by observation—that for these children, school work is frustrating and negatively reinforcing. The object of this study was to make the reinforcement positive with massive verbal rewards given by the teacher and tallied by each child, and to observe its effect on reading achievement.

There were three problems faced in conducting this experiment. The first had to do with the random assignment of pupils to experimental and control conditions necessary for statistical tests. If there is random assignment within classrooms, there is the problem of interaction between experimental and control subjects. If intact classes are assigned to experimental and control conditions, there is the problem of non-chance differences, and there are usually not enough classes available for an adequate "groups within treatments" or "random replications" design (Lindquist, 1953). Fortunately, for our experiment, the administrators and teachers cooperated insofar as to enable random assignment of pupils to class as well as classes to experimental and control conditions.[2]

The second problem was the control and measurement of rewards. For the present study we used individual cards given daily to each pupil, each card containing numbered squares the pupil could circle when rewarded and told to do so by the teacher. The basic reason for the use of the cards was not to introduce a special reward system, but to have a means of quantifying the number of rewards received by each pupil. Other systems are possible, one being to have observers record the rewards; but this system involves an intrusion into the normal classroom situation, and could have its own effect, hard to assess. Another way is to have the teacher record the rewards given to each pupil, but this method takes a good deal of the teacher's time and attention from his work.

With the card system used, the cards could be collected at the end of the period and the number of rewards for each pupil tallied. Of course this system is not foolproof either. A pupil could mark his card when he is not receiving rewards. In order to help control for this possibility, the pupils were given special blue pencils with blue-colored "leads" that they were to pick up and use only when, after being praised, they were told to circle a number. Numbers circled with their ordinary pencils would not count, and it would be fairly obvious if a pupil picked up

---

[2] The writers wish to thank Louise Dougherty and Alfred Rudd for administrative support, the cooperating teachers for their participation, and Ina Turner for clerical assistance.

and used the special blue pencil—obvious to the teacher and to the other pupils.

A special problem with the use of the blue pencil and card reward recording system was the possible "gadget effect." So far as this effect in itself contributed a reward there was not much of a problem since we were more concerned with the fact of reward than the type of reward. We did two things, however, to lessen and to control for a "gadget effect" and for the so-called "Hawthorne effect." One was to have both the experimental and control groups use the cards for tallying rewards, and the other was to have both groups go through a control period of several sessions, during which time the novelty effect could wear off.

Finally, there was the problem of measuring the effect of rewards on the dependent variable, which was reading achievement in this experiment. When pre and post test scores are used over a comparatively short time interval, several problems are introduced into the analysis: there are the effects of regression toward the mean, item memory practice, and others which obscure the results. It was decided, therefore, that the main analysis would be based on a single reading test given at the end of the experiment. Some control over initial individual differences would be attained by using IQ as a control variable in an analysis of covariance procedure.

Method

SUBJECTS

The 110 children in the experiment were from 10 to 13 years of age and from one to four years behind in their school work. For these reasons they were considered potential dropouts and were assigned on a random basis to nine classes in an after-school remedial reading program with from 10 to 15 children in each class.

PROCEDURE

At the beginning of the experiment all the teachers and children were asked to follow the same instructions. Each child received the especially prepared tally card which we have described, and the teachers were asked to distribute the praise rewards so that each child, even the very slow ones, would get at least several each day. After the teacher made a rewarding remark, she directed the rewarded child to make a tally mark on his card on a list of numbers, from 1 to 50. The child made the marks sequentially, beginning with number one. At the end of the class session he wrote down the total number of tally marks (therefore of rewards) he had received for the day. The teachers checked the card markings for accuracy, and sent the cards to the experimenters after each class.

After six sessions the reward rates per child and per teacher appeared to stabilize, and the five teachers (randomly determined) of the experimental groups were confidentially asked to double or triple the number of rewards while the four teachers of the control groups were asked to "keep up the good work." After these requests were made, large increments appeared in the number of tally marks on cards for the experimental group while the numbers for the control group remained at approximately the same levels.

At the end of the second three week period, the 62 children in the experimental groups and the 48 in the control groups took the Science Research Associates Reading Test, Intermediate Form. The total raw scores only were used in the analyses.

Results

The mean for the experimental groups was 31.62, with a standard deviation of 7.43, and the mean for the control groups was 26.86, with a standard deviation of 8.60. The analysis of variance for the unadjusted raw scores produced in F-ratio of 9.52 (p less than 1 percent; see Table 1). In the covariance analysis with Kuhlman-Anderson IQs as the control variable, the F-ratio was 7.90 (p less than 1 percent). This F-ratio is smaller than the one for unadjusted scores, even though the error mean square is smaller, because the between treatments mean square for adjusted scores was only slightly lower. The mean IQ for the experimental group, 92.05, was slightly but not significantly higher than the control group mean, 90.73.

Discussion

The hypothesis was strongly supported: children who were massively rewarded scored significantly higher on a standardized reading test. Although the idea that reinforcement enhances learning has long been known in the field of psychology, it seemed revolutionary to the teachers and children in this experiment. It is not enough apparently, simply to instruct student teachers or regular teachers to use rewards to control behavior. The use of a reward tally card which focused the attention of the teacher and the child on the rewards seemed much more convincing. The request to distribute the rewards to insure that each child got at least a few each time also had a beneficial effect.

TABLE 1
Analyses of Variance and Covariance for
SRA Reading and K-A Intelligence Test Scores

SCORES	SUM OF SQUARES	df	MEAN SQUARES	F-RATIO
SRA Reading				
Between	616.82	1	616.82	9.52 [a]
Within	6994.45	108	64.76	
Total	7611.27	109		
K-A Intelligence				
Between	176.55	1	176.55	1.84
Within	10,337.41	108	95.72	
Total	10,513.96	109		
Adjusted SRA [b]				
Between	488.40	1	488.40	7.90 [a]
Within	6614.43	107	61.82	
Total	7102.83	108		

[a] Significant at the 1 percent level.
[b] The correlation between the SRA and the KA was .26.

Some logical steps follow from this study. One would examine the effects of distinct reward schedules (ratio and interval); the ones used in this study were mixed. Another would determine the long-term efficacy of massive rewards. One interesting hypothesis is that it is the increase differential across time that increases learning rather than continuous high rates which may lead to satiation. A third possible avenue of research would be to investigate the validity of these findings across children grouped by age, socio-economic class, sex, school class and other relevant factors.

Parton and Ross (1965) in a review of research on social reinforcement of children's motor behavior have criticized the methods of previous studies in this area particularly with regard to the common omission of the control group. Methodologically, we have shown here that it is possible to randomly assign children to experimental and control groups in school classrooms, to randomly administer (with the class as the unit) an experimental treatment (massive verbal rewards) in measured amounts (tallied on cards by the pupils themselves), and to demonstrate significant differences between groups on a measure of achievement (a standardized reading test). Theoretically, we have confirmed

the hypothesis from reinforcement theories of learning that verbal rewards have efficacy in the control of operant behavior in human subjects. And lastly, from a practical point of view, we have shown in an
actual educational setting, that the teacher's increased use of verbal
praise has a positive effect on the scholastic learning of children who
are potential dropouts from inner-city schools.

References

Lindquist, E. F. Design and analysis of experiments in psychology and
    education. Boston: Houghton Mifflin, 1953.
Parton, David A., and Ross, Allan O. Social reinforcement of children's
    motor behavior: A review. Psychological Bulletin, 1965, 64, 65–73.

6.   WHAT BEHAVIORAL ENGINEERING IS *

Lloyd Homme, Polo C'de Baca, Lon Cottingham, and Angela Homme

It is asserted that behavioral engineering is not simply a matter of contingency management, but a combination of two technologies: the technology of
contingency management and the technology of stimulus control. Contingency
management involves mainly an emotional commitment or willingness to pay
off for the behavior wanted; the technology of stimulus control involves techniques for arranging circumstances so that the response is made while S is observing the appropriate properties of the stimulus which is to control the response.

Recognizing that a technology for installing behaviors does exist, it is
suggested that research in behavioral engineering take the direction of installing in S's repertoire behaviors relatively neglected by behaviorists, such as the
early education of the child, and responses such as the favorable self-concept,
love, and joy.

The phrase "behavioral engineering" has been around a long time and
all of us understand it. The only trouble is—we haven't told anyone, including ourselves, what it means. It probably is true that everyone

* The Psychological Record, 1968, 18, 425–434. Reprinted with permission of the
authors and The Psychological Record. We thank Rebecca Robinson and Gary Keys
for their creative and energetic technical assistance and Thomas Topich, departmen-
tal secretary and librarian, for coming to work almost every day.

would agree that behavioral engineering is "arranging the environment so that one gets the behavior one wants," [1] or, more generally, that behavioral engineering is the application of laws of behavior to practical problems. Nevertheless, the topic of what behavioral engineering is could stand some elaboration. This becomes most apparent when one sets out to shape up a behavioral engineer. Then it quickly develops that behavioral engineering is a blend of two technologies: the technology of contingency management and the technology of stimulus control. Needless to say, no special degrees or certificates are required to put the technologies to use. The laws of nature do not care about such matters; they go on working in any case.

In analyzing a behavioral engineering task, the engineer must determine: (a) exactly what behavior he wants to occur, (b) what stimuli are to control it, and (c) what reinforcers are available.

The technology of contingency management deals with managing reinforcers (c), and the technology of stimulus control with arranging stimuli so that they come to control (b). Society at large generally decides on what behaviors should occur (a), but the time may have arrived when behavioral engineering itself may have something to say. The relationships between the technology of contingency management and the technology of stimulus control and behavioral engineering may be summarized by relating them to the familiar three-term contingency:

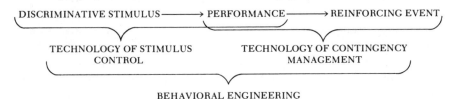

FIGURE 1   Relationships between the three-term contingency and behavioral engineering.

Clearly it is possible to be a contingency manager and understand little about stimulus control, but the reverse certainly is not true. In order to bring a behavior under stimulus control, contingencies have to be properly managed.

The Technology of Contingency Management

Contingency management is the management of what events are contingent upon what behavior. It is clear that contingency management is

---

[1] R. E. Ulrich, personal communication, 1967.

merely the taking seriously (literally) that great law of life: When reinforcing events are contingent upon a given behavior, the behavior will increase in strength; when they are not, the behavior will decrease in strength. The power and generality of contingency management is by now becoming clearer and clearer (Ferster & Perrott, 1968; Homme, 1967; Krasner & Ullman, 1965; Ullman & Krasner, 1966).

The great law of life is simple, but this fact ought not be allowed to obscure another fact: The law is powerful.

Also, the simplicity of the overriding consideration of contingency management (that behavior depends on its consequences) should not lead one to believe it is always simple to teach; some trainees grasp the principle and are able to put it to work instantly; others, in our experience, never. The critical ingredient appears to be an emotional commitment or willingness to *pay off* for desirable behavior. With this commitment, things proceed apace; without it, nothing good happens.

One can make a pretty good case that, basically, there are only two things that a good contingency manager has to know and do: (*a*) to reinforce the behavior he wants, and (*b*) to recognize and reinforce *approximations* to this behavior.

The Relationship between Operant Conditioning and Contingency Management

Everybody strengthens, weakens, or suppresses operants, and everybody, in this sense, is an operant conditioner. And, since everybody at some time or other arranges consequences for behavior, everyone is a contingency manager. Assuming that we all agree that these usages are too broad to be useful, let us get on to narrowing them down.

Let us reserve the phrase "operant conditioning" to designate the basic laboratory science from which behavioral engineering is derived. This means, then, that an operant conditioner is an operant conditioner only as long as he remains in his laboratory. When he leaves the laboratory and systematically applies the *principles* of behavior to problems like getting his offspring to pass a progress check on his homework before he gets points which can be used to buy reinforcers, the operant conditioner becomes a behavioral engineer. We are calling him a behavioral engineer rather than a contingency manager, because we are assuming he knows the rules underlying the technology of stimulus control as well as those underlying contingency management. From this standpoint then, the nurses whom Ayllon and Michael (1959) called behavioral engineers should more properly be called contingency managers; Ayllon and Michael were the behavioral engineers. Similarly, in the Gelfands and Dobson study (1967) of who reinforces what in a mental hospital, the patients, nurses, and nurses' assistants were contingency managers (albeit poor ones), not behavioral engineers. In the same view, when Ogden Lindsley (1960) did his pioneering work on psychotics pulling plungers in an experimental enclosure, he was an operant conditioner, but now that he is teaching teachers and parents to teach (Lindsley, 1966), he is engaged in behavioral engineering. Both Lindsley and Homme were once operant conditioners, but they quit.

It may be worthwhile to mention some differences between the operant conditioning laboratory model and contingency management, which employs the *principles* of operant conditioning but not the *intact model* of the operant conditioning laboratory. To elaborate: In the animal operant conditioning laboratory, one usually is working with a deprived organism; the deprivation operations serve to insure that one class of events will be a reinforcer—the presentation of the event of which the beast was deprived. The reinforcing event, e.g. presentation of food, is thus stable and highly effective as a reinforcer both within and between experimental sessions. With non-deprived humans, the model is often unsatisfactory; reinforcers often wear out and lose their reinforcing properties quickly. Because of this, we have found Premack's differential probability hypothesis, which states that *any* response can reinforce *any other* response of lower probability, of immense usefulness (Homme, 1966; Premack, 1959). We find that the differential probability hypothesis combined with the use of a reinforcing event menu, on which many reinforcers are listed or pictured (Addison & Homme, 1966), highly useful in generating tens or hundreds of reinforcers where we had one or two before. By having S select his reinforcer from a menu, one determines precisely what is the most effective reinforcer here and now for this S.

The Technology of Stimulus Control

A behavioral engineer's definition of stimulus control is a simple one: Stimulus control exists to the extent that the presence or absence of a stimulus controls the probability of a response. It is interesting to compare this with the basic researcher's definition: "Stimulus control refers to the extent to which the value of an antecedent stimulus determines the probability of occurrence of a conditioned response" (Terrace, 1966, p. 271). The key difference in these two definitions lies in the words, *extent* and *values*. It is clear that the behavioral engineer is really interested in approximations to only two probability values, 1.0 and 0.0; the basic researcher, on the other hand, has to worry about values between these two values—the slope and shape of generalization gradient.

FAULTY STIMULUS CONTROL

"He won't mind!" "He's stubborn!" "He knows how to do it, but he doesn't feel like it." "I meant to do it, but I forgot." In all these cases, one is speaking of faulty stimulus control. As a matter of fact, one could make an excellent case for the fact that *most* behavioral engineering problems are problems of faulty stimulus control; that is, the S has the response in his repertoire, all right, but it is not made when the stimulus is presented.

CORRECTING FAULTY STIMULUS CONTROL

The fundamental rule for correcting faulty stimulus control is the same as that for establishing stimulus control in the first place. Get the behavior (or some approximation to it) made while the S is attending to the stimulus which is to control it. This means, among other things, that the engineer must be able to reinstate the control stimulus whenever he wants to.

USING THE BEHAVIOR OF THE SUBJECT
TO REINSTATE THE DISCRIMINATIVE STIMULUS

Over 30 years ago, Guthrie (1935, p. 18) published the following story about stimulus control. It may be time to take it seriously.

> The mother of a ten-year-old girl complained to a psychologist that for two years her daughter had annoyed her by a habit of tossing coat and hat on the floor as she entered the house. On a hundred occasions the mother had insisted that the girl pick up the clothing and hang it in its place. These wild ways were changed only after the mother, on advice, began to insist not that the girl pick up the fallen garments from the floor but that she put them on, return to the street, and reenter the house, this time removing the coat and hanging it properly.

With the usual perspicacity of mommies, the lady for two years had been getting the response out in the presence of the wrong stimuli. The stimuli which were supposed to control the response were those prevailing immediately after the child entered the house; instead, the response was repeatedly evoked in the presence of some stimulus such as, "Please pick up your coat."

To show that the laws of behavior don't change every 30 years or so, it is worth examining one more example. Evans relates that, during a visit, his four-year-old niece was exhibiting a minor, but irritating, behavior disorder.[2] The child, who was nicely toilet trained, never seemed able to remember to flush the toilet at the appropriate time. Instead, she would leave the bathroom and have to be ordered back to do that job.

This problem, it turned out, had persisted for at least a couple of years until finally Uncle Jim intervened. Instead of ordering the child back to flush the toilet, he instructed her to make believe that she was just finishing going to the toilet; she was to make believe to the extent that she was to take down her pants, climb up on the toilet, imagine she was just finishing, get off the toilet, pull up her pants, then flush the toilet and rejoin the adults. This exercise worked; the child gives every sign that she will grow up to a happily married lady who flushes the toilet a lot.

The Effectiveness of Guthrie's Technique

There are at least two considerations which account for the effectiveness of Guthrie's technique of getting the S to go back and run off some of the behavior chain which leads up to the point of difficulty. The first is that the effect of a stimulus persists for some time after the stimulus is terminated. The second is that an important portion of the stimuli which are going to control is response-produced.

Both of these factors can be seen at work in the case of Guthrie's example. The effects of the "outdoor stimuli" obviously do not terminate the instant the child crosses the threshold. If it is a brisk day, for example, she may still be feeling the effects of the cold, she may be panting from running, and the little tyke may even be saying sentences to herself such as, "Christ, it's cold today."

It is worth noticing in the same example that all of the stimulus changes under discussion were produced by the behavior of the organism: The visual and other changes brought about when the S opened the door; the changes in stimulation caused by the removal of the coat and dropping it on the floor; the other changes in visual stimuli caused by the child's moving her head or her eyes. Note that a description of proprioceptive stimuli, as important as they may be, was not required in this discussion of response-produced stimuli. This is worth noting because sometimes proprioceptive stimuli and response-produced stimuli tend to get equated when, of course, they should not be.

In summary, then, the technique of requiring the S to run off the part of the behavioral chain just preceding the response which is giving difficulty is as successful as it is, because it is a way of insuring that the stimulus which is to control the response is, in fact, reinstated. It is im-

---

[2] J. L. Evans, personal communication, 1965.

portant to notice that this is true whether or not the behavioral engineer can specify all of the portions of the stimulus complex which are likely to be present when the response is to be executed; running off the immediately preceding chain members automatically guarantees the presence of the control stimuli.

An Example
of Behavioral Engineering:
Teaching Phonic Reading

There are children who cannot read, but whose parents and/or teachers insist that they "know phonics." It may be true that they know phonics in the sense that, shown any letter, they can give its sound. Thus, to the printed word stimulus "cat" the student can respond, "cuh-aa-tuh." It is from here on that trouble arises. To the self-generated stimulus, "cuh-aa-tuh," he may respond "supersonic transport," or whatever else happens to be at high strength at the moment. Analysis of phonic reading, then, yields the kinds of chains shown in Fig. 2.

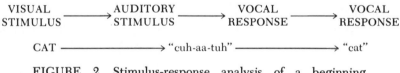

| VISUAL STIMULUS | → | AUDITORY STIMULUS | → | VOCAL RESPONSE | → | VOCAL RESPONSE |

CAT ⟶ "cuh-aa-tuh" ⟶ "cat"

FIGURE 2   Stimulus-response analysis of a beginning phonic reading sequence.

In the S just described, it is obvious that he simply had not learned the last member of the chain—the translation of "cuh-aa-tuh" to "cat." In the laboratory, the last member of the chain is the first one taught (Homme & Klaus, 1967); so we adopted the same strategy in teaching reading. The first thing taught to the child is the "sound-the-word game." This simply consists in making reinforcing events contingent upon the child's translating phoneticized words. For example, the contingency manager may say to the child, "Tell me what I'm saying, 'chuh-air'." The child who knows the game will answer, "Chair." The contingency manager then says, "Good. Choose what you'd like to play with from the menu." It has been our experience that very shortly the child will begin to make up phoneticized words with which to puzzle the contingency manager.

Once the end of the chain (the translation skill) has been established, it is a simple matter to move up the chain, step by step.

With these kinds of procedures, it has been possible to keep preschool children responding eight hours a day and to teach phonic reading in a matter of days, rather than semesters or years.

Behavioral Engineering Research

The behavioral engineering field is about at the same stage of development as Goddard's rocket program was in 1935 (Lehman, 1963). At this time, those who know about such matters say that not only had the basic research been done, but plenty of technology was available to put an object into space. (Goddard had already blasted a rocket up a thousand feet.) What was required, and what took our society 20 or so years to realize, was a real effort at implementation.

Just as space scientists and engineers didn't have to wait until the "gravitational process" was better understood before the law of gravity could be exploited, so behavioral engineering need not wait until the "learning process" is better understood before we can get on with some important jobs. For openers, we can develop a technology for routinely producing superior human beings. We may have sufficient technology —here and now—(Homme, 1967) to be able to guarantee that, given a physiologically normal human being, and given control of his reinforcement contingencies and stimulus conditions, we can shape him into a superior organism. He will be superior not only intellectually, he will be superior emotionally. He will be happier than most, have a better self-concept—he will have a better repertoire in all the ways we can think of to make it better.

Another way of saying this is that we have the technology for installing any behavior we want. The problem now is, what behaviors do we want installed. We submit that some leading candidates are a preschool academic repertoire, a favorable self-concept, love, and joy.

THE INTELLECTUAL REPERTOIRE
OF THE PRESCHOOL CHILD

No one knows how much a preschool child can learn. This is so despite the thousands of developmental studies on how much children *usually* learn by a given age. There is no research which has, in a systematic manner, explored the limits of a child's capacity to learn when contingencies were intelligently managed, and stimulus control criteria were met.

Since behavioral engineering views reading as discriminative responding, the ridiculous problem of "When is the child ready to read?" never arises. From a behavioral engineering standpoint, a child is reading objects as soon as he can discriminatively respond to them (e.g., name them). Once a child has begun to read, no one knows, really, how fast his education may proceed. With the opportunity to read coupled with unsystematic contingency management, one scholar who learned to read at age three read at the fifth-grade level by the time she was five.[3] (Her brother, the control group, learned to read exactly when educational researchers said he should—at 6.5 years of age.) Once having learned to read, even at a primitive level, the child can begin going through existing programed instructional materials—say, in arithmetic. With contingency management, the excuse that existing programs are boring, dull, or no good, is not valid. One does not hear the rat in the Skinnerbox or the human at the slot machine complain about the dullness of his task. He eagerly does his job, although he may have done the same thing hundreds of times before. And programed instruction, even though bad, does offer more variety than slot machines; it is the payoffs which have to be arranged.

And even if stimulus control in the program is faulty—as is often the case—this can be corrected by means of progress checks. Progress checks are short tests on material just covered in the program—criterion items which should have been, but were not, built into the program. The sequence of events shown in Fig. 3 thus results.

N FRAMES OF PROGRAM ———→ PROGRESS CHECK ———→ REINFORCER

FIGURE 3   Sequence of events which maintains behavior and insures appropriate stimulus control.

With a schedule of events of this sort, no one knows how fast a child's intellectual development might proceed. We do have enough preliminary data to know that there is no danger in "pushing" a child too fast with such a system. Three-year-olds have been kept working eight hours a day with no signs of the "I don't want to do this any more" response. On the contrary, having found a place where someone was willing to pay off for desired behavior rather than punish for unwanted behavior, they wanted *more* of the same at the end of the day—to the despair of the worn-out contingency managers.

JOY

Psychologists have been assiduous in studying the unpleasant aspects of life. Pain, depression and anxiety have received considerable attention,

---

[3] J. L. Evans, personal communication, 1967.

but the same cannot be said for joy and happiness. No "Manifest Joy Scale" exists. The point is, the serious study of joy is overdue.

Skinner (1953, p. 127) has observed that the emotion called joy involves the whole repertoire of the organism. ". . . our [joyful] subject speaks to everyone, reacts in an exaggerated fashion, walks faster and seemingly more lightly, and so on. This is particularly obvious in the behavior of young children—for example, on the eve of a holiday or festival."

It may be that the overwhelming nature of this fact—that joy involves the whole repertoire—is what has impeded the study of joy. Behavioral engineering certainly has no tools for dealing directly with a whole repertoire at once. But if we take seriously what Keller and Schoenfeld (1950) and Skinner (1953) have said about what joy is, we can reduce the joy problem to manageable size. They say that joy is the anticipation of reinforcing events. This simple, but profound, observation is clearly borne out by the amount of laughter and smiling which occurs when children's contingencies are planfully managed. Reinforcements are frequent, and there is little doubt that the child quickly learns to anticipate reinforcing events and to plan what he will next select from a reinforcing event menu.

In order for the behavioral engineer to strengthen the joy response, then, he calls for it immediately preceding a reinforcing event. E.g., to a child, "Tell me something good that's going to happen to you; then go to the menu and choose what you'd like to do."

In less formal situations the same rules hold: Make the S pay for reinforcing events by verbalizing the anticipation of other reinforcing events. "Tell me something good that you're going to do, and then we'll go to the store."

Of course, since everyone is an organism, one can try this out on oneself. One can increase the frequency with which one coverants joy events (Homme, 1967) and observe the effect. (The word "coverants" is a contraction of covert operant, and is pronounced "kuhverant"; when used as a verb, it means "think about," "imagine.") A convenient property of self-management research is that one always has a S close at hand.

LOVE

Joy is difficult to define, but perhaps even more difficult is love. Many famous writers, for example, have written a great many words to persuade the reader that the love *he* is talking about is indescribable. That may be so, but the behavioral engineer, assuming that love in the repertoire is desirable, must get on with the job of trying to install it.

If one examines the behavior of a human who is said to exhibit love, one can quickly detect one very public behavior. This is verbal behavior with the verb "love" in it. Assuming that this is a genuine signal of love, or an approximation to it, it is a straightforward matter to install this kind of verbal behavior. E.g., the following class of verbal behaviors can be easily and quickly installed in a S's repertoire.

"Why do you love Becky (the contingency manager)"?

"I love Becky because . . ."

If one also accepts the proposition that love is manifested by a tendency to reinforce, then another approximation would be to evoke and strengthen reinforcing verbal behavior in the S. "Go whisper to Becky that you love her because . . ." Observations suggest that verbal behavior such as this from a preschool S can turn an adult on. This state of affairs makes it almost unnecessary to instruct the contingency manager to reinforce. We have the impression that she couldn't refrain if she tried.

A FAVORABLE SELF-CONCEPT

This also is a complex phenomenon, we are told. How can you teach someone to think favorably of himself? Put this way, the question may indeed seem formidable. However, analysis leads to the same conclusion as that to which Ellis (1958) has come. When we speak of a self-concept, we may simply be talking about the aggregate of sentences the S says *to* himself (and others) *about* himself. Viewed in this light, it becomes a simple matter to install a favorable self-concept: One simply strengthens a class of verbal behavior. E.g., after a good performance, "That was a fine job. Go whisper to your teacher, 'I am a fast learner'." At this point, the teacher reinforces verbally and by making the menu available. It has been our experience that after a very few trials of this sort, the "I am a fast learner" conception of himself competes quite successfully with the child's "I sure am dumb" concept.

A similar technology can be brought to bear in psychotherapy. For example, the "poor, helpless me" self-concept is replaced by the self-mastery statement, "I'm in charge of my own behavior," by having S program himself so that this coverant occurs with high frequency.

There are many, many fascinating engineering research areas which have not been touched upon, of course. For example, Bandura's (1964) modeling concepts, if taken seriously, suggest that, before a great child can become a great adult, he has to know a great adult. We may have to face up to the fact that the Fred Skinners of the world are not spread thin enough.

References

Addison, R. M., and Homme, L. The reinforcing event (RE) menu. *NSPI Journal*, 1966, 5(1), 8–9.

Ayllon, T., and Michael, J. The psychiatric nurse as a behavioral engineer. *Journal of the Experimental Analysis of Behavior*, 1959, 2, 323–334.

Bandura, A., and Kupers, C. J. Transmission of patterns of self-reinforcement through modeling. *Journal of Abnormal and Social Psychology*, 1964, 69(1), 1–9.

Ellis, A. Rational psychotherapy. *Journal of General Psychology*, 1958, 59, 35–49.

Ferster, C. B., and Perrott, M. C. *Behavior principles.* New York: Appleton-Century-Crofts, 1968.

Gelfand, D. M., Gelfand, S., and Dobson, W. R. Unprogrammed reinforcement of patients' behavior in a mental hospital. *Behavioral Research and Therapy*, 1967, 5(3), 201–207.

Guthrie, E. R. *The psychology of learning.* New York: Harper & Row, 1935.

Homme, L. Contingency management. *Newsletter*, Section on Clinical Child Psychology, Division of Clinical Psychology, APA, 1966, 5 (4).

Homme, L. A behavior technology exists—here and now. A version of this paper was given at the Aerospace Education Foundation's "Education for the 1970s" Seminar, Washington, D. C., 1967.

Homme, L., and Klaus, D. J. *Laboratory studies in the analysis of behavior.* (3rd ed.) Albuquerque, N.M.: Westinghouse Learning Corporation, 1967.

Keller, F. S., and Schoenfeld, W. N. *The principles of psychology.* New York: Appleton-Century-Crofts, 1950.

Krasner, L., and Ullman, L. P. *Research in behavior modification.* New York: Holt, Rinehart and Winston, 1965.

Lehman, M. *This high man: The life of Robert H. Goddard.* New York: Farrar, Straus, 1963.

Lindsley, O. R. Characteristics of the behavior of chronic psychotics as revealed by free-operant conditioning methods, *Diseases of the Nervous System* (Monograph Supplement), 1960, 21(2).

Lindsley, O. R. An experiment with parents handling behavior at home. *Johnstone Bulletin*, 9, 27–36.

Premack, D. Toward empirical behavior laws: I. Positive reinforcement. *Psychological Review*, 1959, 66, 219–233.

Skinner, B. F. *Science and human behavior.* New York: Macmillan, 1953.

Terrace, H. S. Stimulus control. In W. K. Honig (Ed.), *Operant behavior: Areas of research and application.* New York: Appleton-Century-Crofts, 1966. Pp. 271–344.

Ullman, L. P., and Krasner, L. (Eds.) *Case studies in behavior modification.* New York: Holt, Rinehart and Winston, 1966.

VII. ON THE OCCUPATIONAL PREPARATION OF HIGH SCHOOL YOUTH

Introduction

The papers in this last section focus on the realities of occupational preparation of the great majority of American high school students—our noncollege youth. We live in a society that places a higher premium on acquiring a college degree than on entering the work market after high school. The ultimate dream of most American parents is to have their children attend and complete a four-year college. In many instances, this dream is incompatible with the realities of their son's or daughter's circumstances and desires. Nonetheless, our stereotypes unfairly favor college-bound youth and degrade work-bound youth; our high schools perpetuate and reflect these stereotypes. These feelings are cogently expressed in the dialogue with six high school juniors presented in the first section of this book.

What the consequences of these false priorities will be is not altogether certain yet. One result that seems clear, though, is that many students who ordinarily would be satisfied to pursue a noncollege occupation are deprived of this satisfaction. These students follow the lure of a college degree with a great deal of uncertainty, only to get pushed out of college as failures or to struggle on in mediocrity. At best, some manage to reassert their original desires and wind up losing a few years by returning to the route they should have taken after high school. Many do not grasp the lure and continue through life with a feeling of second-class citizenship. Everyone has had contact with one of these persons; they regret not having gotten a "college education" and very often overcompensate by trying to make up for their self-inflicted deficit. Some rebel and completely disregard or consciously flaunt the system that requires them to choose to prepare for college or for work by making no choice. A few manage to know what they want and are content to adhere to their choice. One finding that may surprise some is that most students who attend separate vocational high schools are in this last category and are youth who at least know what they want and feel secure in their noncollege strivings.

This last section, then, is meant to offset our society's unwholesomely blind priorities for college-bound youth. It takes a look at what it's like to be a noncollege or work-bound youth in America. It is a nudge on the pendulum to swing back to where educators, parents, and especially students can feel that wanting to prepare for the world of work is as laudable a pursuit as wanting to go to college.

The first four papers serve to re-orient us toward noncollege aspirations by looking at what has been learned about the outcomes of various types of students who fall into this work-bound category: any student who is not in an academic program or not preparing to go to college. The fifth paper in this section has some jarring observations to contribute about the relationship of measured interest to abilities and on advising students on the basis of aptitude and interest information obtained from paper and pencil tests.

The first paper, Little's longitudinal study of the occupations of noncollege youth, introduces this group by telling us that 75 to 80 percent of American youth are not completing college degrees. Many of Little's comparisons involve a measure of occupational attainment among three groups of graduates: (a) those who went no further than high school, (b) those who went to a vocational school, and (c) those who went to college. One interesting fact he uncovers is that, although occupational attainment is related to educational level, differences in high school performance had very little effect on level of occupation attained in any of these three groups.

The Combs and Cooley paper brings the data of the vast Project TALENT study to bear on high school dropouts in a large-scale, longitudinal study of boys and girls who dropped out of school sometime after the ninth grade (in 1960). The comparison or control group in this follow-up study was a random subsample of high school graduates who were also ninth graders in 1960 but who did not enter a four-year college or a junior college. The authors appropriately point out that this control group is more meaningful than one composed of high school students in general. Perhaps the highlight of this study is that the investigators failed to find that noncollege high school graduates were much better off than high school dropouts as far as future earnings and employment were concerned. Male dropouts not only earned more than controls but had earned it longer; they were also as frequently employed in the same types of jobs as the controls. Combs and Cooley note that their 1964 study is a one-year follow-up study for the control group and that it is likely that the long-range benefits of a high school diploma will eventually appear.

The next two papers analyze the perceived conditions of students in vocational and comprehensive high schools and the experiences of graduates of these two kinds of schools. Purnell and Lesser examine the two major stereotypes that unfortunately relegate separate vocational high schools to an unacceptable position for many students: (1) the notion that they are "dumping grounds" and (2) the belief that compared to comprehensive high schools they offer inferior educational experiences to work-bound youth. Analyses are based on comparisons among vocational school students and academic, commercial, and general comprehensive school students. The two global stereotypes are discredited; if anything, vocational school students are found to fare better than work-bound youth in comprehensive schools in that they are not degraded by fellow students and have a sense of worthwhile accomplishment and pursuit of occupation.

The Kaufman and others study arrives at the same conclusions about vocational school students as Purnell and Lesser, but their findings are based on the responses of graduates, teachers, employers, and union leaders. Furthermore, Kaufman and his colleagues examine the adequacy of vocational training and the role of vocational education for minority groups and students from disadvantaged homes.

Ewens' concentrated paper investigates the relationship of interest to aptitude by profiles and by interest areas. His results demonstrate the distressingly low connection between interests and aptitudes as measured by pencil and paper tests, when scores are correlated by areas. For some students, however, it is meaningful to examine their interest-aptitude profiles. One is simply not justified in naively expecting high interests to "naturally" reflect high aptitudes and vice versa as measured by standard pencil and paper tests.

1. THE OCCUPATIONS OF NON-COLLEGE YOUTH *

J. Kenneth Little

The world of work is placing increasing premium upon advanced levels of education and specialized types of training. Yet, 75–80 percent of American youth are not completing college degrees. What is the occupational destiny of youth with differing levels of education? For what part of the occupational world is attainment dependent upon education beyond high school? What are the characteristics of youth who reach differing levels of occupational attainment?

* American Educational Research Journal, 1967, 4(2), 147–154. Reprinted with permission of the author and the American Educational Research Association. This study was a project of the Cooperative Research Program of the U. S. Office of Education. A complete report is available at The Center For Studies in Vocational-Technical Education, B171 Social Science Building, University of Wisconsin, Madison.

In the spring of 1957, a state-wide inquiry gathered information from over 35,000 graduating seniors of Wisconsin's public and private high schools. About 95 percent of all graduates from about 95 percent of Wisconsin's high schools participated. This information included statements about educational plans beyond high school, statements of occupational aspirations, and much background data about the graduates, their parents, and their school experiences (Little, 1958).

During the calendar years 1964 and early 1965, follow-up inquiries were directed to the parents of a probability sample of about one-third of the male youth of this 1957 crop of graduates. Usable returns were received from 85 percent of the sample.

Of the 4,186 graduates about whom information was received, 378 were attending a vocational school or college; 447 were in military service; and 58 were unemployed. The total number for whom occupational attainment scores were available was then 3,378.

Relation between Plans and Action

The plans of the youth as stated by them at their high school graduation considerably underestimated the number who would continue their schooling. Of 511 boys who did not plan further education, 303 actually attended a vocational or trade school, and 208 attended a four-year degree granting college. On the other hand, 365 boys who had planned some further education failed to continue their schooling. The net result was that 40 percent of the total group had no further schooling; 16 percent attended a vocational or trade school; and 43 percent attended college (Table 1). Of those who attended college, however, more than a third (35 percent) did not complete baccalaureate degrees.

The relative stability of the stated plans varied considerably among

TABLE 1
Educational Plans and Their Fulfillment

	PLAN	ACTION	DIFFERENCE
To Attend College	1584 (37.8%)	1792 (42.9%)	+208
To Attend Vocational School	363 (8.7%)	666 (15.9%)	+303
To Get No Further Schooling	2239 (53.5%)	1728 (41.2%)	−511
Total	N = 4186 (100.0%)	4186 (100.0%)	0

the three groups of youth. For example, 82 percent of those planning to attend college did enroll in college; 67 percent of those who planned no further schooling did not enroll in a post-high school institution; and 39 percent of those who intended to enroll in a vocational or trade school did so enroll.

Thus, while forces prompting youth to acquire education beyond high school are clearly visible, the formal education of almost 60 percent of the graduates ended with high school graduation, and for almost three-fourths of them (73 percent) education stopped short of completing a baccalaureate degree.

Occupational Attainment

Attention now turns to the occupations attained by the three groups of graduates. On the scale used in this study (Hatt, 1947), occupations that require professional, scientific, or technical training, or high level executive or managerial abilities, typically have prestige scores above 75. Occupations that require little or no specialized training, including service workers, operatives and laborers, have prestige scores below 55. The large body of middle level occupations that include clerical and sales-workers, craftsmen, foremen, sub-professional technicians, farmers and farm managers, and many others, have prestige scores that range from 55 to 75. For convenience, these three groups of occupations are called high prestige, low prestige, and middle-level occupations.

About a fourth of the graduates attained high prestige occupations; another fourth were in low prestige occupations; and one-half in middle-level occupations (Table 2).

As expected, the prestige level of occupations increased with the type and level of education attained, but the differences in occupational attainment within each group were as noteworthy as the differences between the groups. For example, more than half of the youth who attended college did not attain high prestige occupations, and only two out of five graduates who had no further education were in low prestige occupations. About half of each of the three groups were in middle-level occupations.

The major difference among the three groups was the extent to which their members were able to reach high prestige occupations or to escape low prestige occupations. In this respect the non-college going group were clearly at a disadvantage. The vocational school group was an approximate cross-section of the total group and attained occupations in all prestige levels somewhat proportionately.

TABLE 2
Occupational Prestige Scores by Level of Education

OCCUPATIONAL PRESTIGE SCORES	NONE (N = 1529)	VOCATIONAL (N = 576)	COLLEGE (N = 1156)	ALL GRADUATES (N = 3261)
90–99	—	—	4	4
80–89	14	17	266	297
70–79	293	200	558	1051
60–69	442	211	205	858
50–59	636	132	107	875
40–49	132	14	16	162
30–39	8	1	—	9
20–29	4	1	—	5
10–19	—	—	—	—
0–9	—	—	—	—
75th percentile	68.3	73.7	79.6	75.0
50th percentile	59.8	66.7	74.3	64.4
25th percentile	53.8	59.7	67.3	57.7

To summarize, occupations at any of the prestige levels were attained by persons with any of the three levels of schooling. The overlapping was particularly large in the middle-level occupations where college degrees are not a stated prerequisite. However, the occupational advantage of most persons who had attended college is definite; the occupational handicap of most persons who had no education or training beyond high school is serious. This is not to imply, however, that the differences in occupational attainment were attributable to differences in educational opportunity. Variations in human aptitude and aspiration growing out of a complex of psycho-cultural factors were definitely at work.

Background Factors in Occupational Attainment

The attainment of high prestige occupations was found to be associated with the following background factors: attendance at college, above average scholastic aptitude and achievement; family in upper-third in socio-economic status; father in a white-collar occupation, and attended

TABLE 3
Characteristics of Graduates in High and Low Prestige Occupations[a]

	HIGH PRESTIGE			LOW PRESTIGE		
Characteristics	(1) %	(2) %	(3) diff.	(1) %	(2) %	(3) diff.
1. Size of Community						
Counties with cities:						
Not over 10,000	38	30	−8	38	48	+10
10,000–24,999	7	7	0	7	8	+1
25,000–49,999	22	22	0	22	22	None
Metropolitan areas	33	41	+8	33	22	−11
2. Socio-economic Status						
Low 1/3	33	20	−13	33	40	+7
Middle 1/3	34	33	+1	34	40	+6
High 1/3	33	47	+14	33	20	−13
3. Father's Occupation						
Farming	22	15	−7	22	35	+13
Unskilled	39	35	−4	39	42	+3
Skilled	10	10	None	10	9	−1
White collar	20	25	+5	20	11	−9
Professional	9	15	+6	9	3	−6
4. Father's Education						
No high school	46	34	−12	46	58	+12
Some high school	16	13	−3	16	17	+1
High school graduate	26	32	+6	26	19	−7
Some college	12	21	+9	12	6	−6
5. Scholastic Aptitude						
Low 1/2	52	32	−20	52	67	+15
High 1/2	48	68	+20	48	33	−15
6. High School Achievement						
Low 1/2	62	41	−21	62	77	+15
High 1/2	38	59	+21	38	23	−15
7. Level of Education						
High school only	43	18	−25	43	76	+33
Vocational school	16	14	−2	16	13	−3
Some college	41	68	+27	41	11	−30

[a]Columns (1) Percent of all graduates in sample; Columns (2) Percent of all graduates who attained high or low prestige occupations; Columns (3) Difference and direction of difference

college; attended high school in a metropolitan community (Table 3).

Background characteristics associated with low prestige occupations were: no education or training beyond high school; below average scholastic aptitude and achievement; father in a farming or unskilled occupation, and had not attended high school; attended high school in a rural community; and family in lower third in socio-economic status (Table 3).

Background characteristics associated with middle level occupations showed no major difference from the background characteristics of the total group of graduates, except that slightly higher proportions were above average in scholastic ability and high school achievement, and had attended college. More than two-thirds of the middle level occupations were held by persons who did not attend colleges; one third, by college-going students. This two to one ratio is practically the same as the ratio of non-college-going to college-going youth in the total group.

The plight of those in the low prestige occupations is sad. Meager economic and cultural circumstances plus lack of much success in school combine to depress both aspiration and achievement, whether educational or occupational. Such circumstances are especially prevalent although not limited to small, rural communities. In metropolitan areas, however, the handicap seems to be less frequent, probably because of a greater number and variety of occupational possibilities.

Occupational Aspiration

At the time of their high school graduation, the seniors had stated the occupations which they hoped eventually to enter. The prestige scores of these occupations were compared with those eventually attained. Two observations resulted from this comparison.

First, the occupational aspirations of the graduates were consistent with their educational plans. Non-college youth aspired to lower level occupations than did either the vocational school or college-bound youth. The aspirations of the vocational school group were predominantly in the middle range.

Second, the occupational attainments of non-college going youth were close to their expectations. In fact, the correspondence between the occupational aspiration and occupational attainment scores of all three groups suggests that the graduates had sorted and sized themselves with considerable accuracy and realism. Individual instances of unrealistic optimism and unnecessary pessimism occur among all three groups. College-going students were the only group that had not attained occupations equal to their aspirations. Many of the college group, however, aspired to occupations which require prolonged professional or advanced training; and some have been at work a comparatively short time. Others did not complete degrees and may have changed their occupational goals.

It is an interesting sidelight that college-going youth who did not complete degrees had definitely lower occupational aspirations than those who obtained degrees. Over half (53 percent) of the college-drop-outs had not planned to attend college.

Relation of Occupational Attainment to High School Achievement

To test the relationship of scholastic performance in high school to level of occupational attainment, the graduates were ranked by deciles in total high school achievement and median occupational prestige scores were calculated for the graduates in each decile. The interesting fact emerged that although difference in level of education produced important differences in level of occupations, differences in high school perfor-

TABLE 4
High School Achievement and Occupational Attainment[a]

HIGH SCHOOL PERCENTILE RANK	MEDIAN OCCUPATIONAL PRESTIGE SCORES		
	(1)	(2)	(3)
90-99	59	67	79
80-89	66	71	72
70-79	62	71	73
60-69	57	66	75
50-59	64	67	73
40-49	62	66	72
30-39	59	67	73
20-29	59	67	73
10-19	56	65	74
0-9	58	65	73

[a] Column (1) No further schooling; Column (2) Attended vocational school; Column (3) Attended College

mance had very little effect on the level of occupations attained in any of the three groups (Table 4).

The median percentile rank of graduates who were in occupations that had prestige scores below 70 was the rank of the average male graduate—38th percentile. Graduates in occupations with a prestige score above 70, however, had a much higher median level of scholastic performance, ranking at the 55th percentile. Because girls receive a much larger proportion of the better marks in high school, a boy ranking at the 55th percentile in his total class would excel 80–85 percent of his male classmates.

These facts are consonant with the knowledge that high prestige occupations typically are open only to those who complete college degrees, and that those who complete college degrees are typically drawn from graduates who rank in the top fourth of their high school classes. High-achieving students who did not continue their schooling not only failed to attain occupations at a level equal to high-achieving students who did continue; they failed to attain occupations that were substantially better than the occupations of their lower-ranking classmates. Even more remarkable, is the fact that low-achieving students who attended college attained occupations equivalent to their much higher-ranking college classmates. Only the college-going students in the top decile showed a sizable difference in occupational attainment from college-going students in other deciles.[1]

It is possible that within occupations, or within occupational levels, differences in occupational attainment may be associated with differences in scholastic achievement. The findings of this study, however, agree with the common sense observation that rank in high school class is a statistic seldom used outside educational institutions, except possibly for initial job entry of a new high school graduate. The profile of human characteristics most valued by the occupational world is not identical with the profile of characteristics most rewarded by the educational system.

Today's high school youth are subjected to a barrage of publicity by newspapers, magazines, television, and radio telling him that the road to occupational success is through advanced education. It is interesting that a very large part of youth either do not hear or do not heed this counsel.

The fact that only 16 percent of the graduates enrolled in vocational

---

[1] The correlation coefficient between rank in graduating class and prestige score on a trained occupation was found to be .08 by Brian Heath in a doctor's thesis, University of Wisconsin, 1965.

and trade schools does not match either the increasing need for technicians and sub-professional workers, or the number of high school graduates who have aptitudes for such occupations. In fact, it might be expected that the largest part of the graduates would be preparing for middle-level occupations. Since more than a third of the graduates who attended college did not graduate a question occurs whether it would have been better for them to attend a two-year vocational or technical program and succeed than to begin a four-year college degree program, then drop out. Certainly also a sizeable part of the youth who did not continue their schooling had the abilities needed to complete a two-year program of vocational-technical training.

But the educational system and the society which supports it have much to do if they are to meet their responsibilities for non-college youth. Given the wide range of human aptitudes and aspirations, it is natural and right for youth to leave the educational system at different ages and stages. The tragedy is not leave-taking from school. The tragedy occurs when they leave school for the wrong reasons, whether because of economic barriers, racial discrimination, artificial or illusory incentive or unsuitable school programs. Our society must find work for the kinds of youth we have. And our schools must prepare youth for effective performance in the kinds of work that need to be done.

The purpose of the educational system, of course, is not merely to match people to jobs. This study emphasizes occupational objectives, however, because man's occupation is one of his chief characteristics. His occupation, and his achievements in it, lie close to the center of both his self-respect and the nature of his contribution to society.

An important item of unfinished educational business, then, is conceiving and developing realistic and practical programs of 'middle education'—the level between mid-high school and mid-college—during which three-fourths of American youth end their formal schooling. These are the youth who as adult workers occupy the great range of middle-level occupations and who as citizens are the bedrock of a democratic society.

Reference

Little, J. Kenneth. *A state-wide inquiry into decisions of youth about education beyond high school.* School of Education, University of Wisconsin, September 1958.

2. DROPOUTS: IN HIGH SCHOOL AND AFTER SCHOOL*

Janet Combs and William W. Cooley

In 1960 Project TALENT tested approximately 440,000 students attending over 1,300 public and private high schools in all parts of the country. The second phase of this large-scale longitudinal study of American youth was the collection of follow-up data from the same young people tested in 1960. Using data collected from one of the grades participating in the original testing, the ninth grade, Project TALENT has identified students who did not complete high school. These boys and girls who dropped out of school after grade nine are the topic of this study.

Although numerous studies of dropouts have already been reported in the education literature, the particular combination of characteristics of this study make it somewhat unique in comparison with other efforts. First of all, it is longitudinal in nature; the initial measurements were made when the subjects were in ninth grade in 1960, with a follow-up in 1964. Secondly, the sample of subjects is a probability sample of the entire national ninth-grade population. Therefore, it is possible to estimate parameters of the dropout population which could not be estimated previously. Also, the TALENT test battery covers a broad spectrum of attributes. Thus, not only "IQ," but differential aptitudes and abilities, interests, self-perceptions, socioeconomic environment, school curriculum, career plans, and a variety of post-high-school activities can be considered. Another important aspect of this study is that the sample consists of both males and females. Too often only male dropouts are considered, even though females drop out just as frequently as males. Finally, comparisons can be made between dropouts and their former classmates who remained in school until graduation.

In most of the analyses reported in this article, all of the known drop-

* *American Educational Research Journal*, 1968, 5(3), 343–364. Reprinted with permission of the authors and the American Educational Research Association. Both authors were associated with Project TALENT from 1964 to 1967, Janet Combs as Research Associate and William Cooley as Director.

outs in the original TALENT ninth-grade sample are contrasted with random subsamples of high-school graduates from the same grade sample who did not enter a four-year or junior college. These subsamples, designated the "controls," consist of 25 percent of the male and 20 percent of the female graduates on the TALENT data file who did not continue their education beyond high school. Comparing dropouts with these control groups seemed more meaningful than comparing them with high-school graduates in general. The number of subjects constituting each of the four samples used in this study is as follows:

Dropout Males	1,864
Control Males	1,757
Dropout Females	1,817
Control Females	2,056

(Missing data reduced these N's for some of the analyses. As indicated in the several tables which follow, the losses were only slight.)

Information about the post-high-school activities of dropouts and controls was obtained through a follow-up survey conducted in 1964. For most of the members of the ninth-grade class of 1960, this was one year after high-school graduation. For the dropouts, it could have been as many as four years after leaving high school. The first phase of the follow-up survey consisted of four waves of mailed questionnaires. Thirty-seven percent of the sample responded to one of these four mailings. To correct the nonrespondent bias, field surveys of a stratified sample of approximately four percent of the nonrespondents were conducted. Then, by combining and weighting data from these two groups, respondents and the sample of nonrespondents, unbiased estimates of national subpopulations such as dropouts after grade nine, can be made. Analyses using these weighted data are so indicated. (See Flanagan and Cooley, 1966, for a description of the Project TALENT followup surveys.)

Although dropouts tended not to respond to the mailed questionnaires, a comparison of dropout respondents with those dropouts found in the nonrespondent follow-up revealed that the dropout respondents do not differ significantly from the dropout nonrespondents. It was also found that the nonrespondents located in field surveys do not differ significantly on traits previously measured in high school from those nonrespondents who were not located. Therefore, even though all possible dropouts were not located, the evidence indicates that the descriptions of the dropouts reported here are not significantly biased by incomplete data. The bias is that our sample of dropouts is smaller than would be expected, but this, of course, is adjusted by the weighting system.

The Boys Who Dropped Out

ABILITIES

The first measure which will be discussed is the General Academic Ability Composite in the TALENT battery. (See Flanagen *et al.*, 1962 and 1964 for descriptions of the Project TALENT tests.) The percentages of dropouts and controls in each of four ability levels are shown in Table 1.

These levels represent quarters in the 1960 grade nine population. Quartiles are estimated from the total national Project TALENT norms, which include individuals who enter college. (Flanagan *et al.*, 1964.)

As this table indicates, more than one-half of the dropouts were in the bottom quarter (1), compared to 28 percent of the controls. In the middle levels (2 and 3) were 40 percent of the dropouts and 61 percent of the graduates. Only five percent of the dropouts ranked in the highest level, compared to 11 percent of the controls.

As Table 1 reveals, not all dropouts are below average in ability, as many people think. Other studies are in line with this finding. A report by Warner (1964) presented the results of three statewide studies, one U.S. Department of Labor study involving seven communities, and five studies conducted by city schools. There were 21,497 dropouts involved. Approximately 19 percent of this sample were reported to have I.Q.'s between 90 and 109 and 11 percent with 110 or above I.Q.'s. French (1965) summarizes additional studies revealing that not all dropouts are below average in ability.

TABLE 1
Academic Ability of Dropouts, Graduates, and All Grade 9 Males
(Percentages Based on Weighted Frequencies)

LEVEL	DROPOUTS ($N = 1,686$)	CONTROLS ($N = 1,655$)	ALL GRADE 9 MALES ($N = 48,734$)
1 (Bottom Quarter)	55	28	25
2	25	39	25
3	15	22	25
4 (Top Quarter)	5	11	25
	100	100	100

TABLE 2
Mean Scores of Male Dropouts and Controls
on TALENT Ability Tests

	DROPOUT MEAN $(N = 1,494)$	CONTROL MEAN $(N = 1,533)$	POOLED STANDARD DEVIATION	F RATIO[a]
English Total	63.9	71.5	13.5	255
Information I Total	100.7	117.8	32.1	232
Information II Total	49.4	57.8	17.6	181
Reading Comprehension	19.0	23.5	9.9	167
Introductory High- School Math	7.0	8.5	3.4	156
Arithmetic Reasoning	5.9	7.0	3.0	114
Arithmetic Computation	9.0	19.8	28.9	110
Abstract Reasoning	6.8	8.0	3.1	109
Word Functions in Sentences	5.8	7.0	3.3	105
Table Reading	1.9	5.5	12.3	67
Disguised Words	9.8	11.4	5.6	63
Memory for Words	8.1	9.3	4.2	62
Creativity	6.4	7.3	3.5	52
Memory for Sentences	7.9	8.7	3.1	51
Clerical Checking	8.8	14.7	23.2	50
Visualization in Three Dimensions	7.4	8.1	3.2	47
Mechanical Reasoning	10.2	11.1	4.0	39
Visualization in Two Dimensions	11.4	12.6	5.6	37
Object Inspection	17.5	18.7	9.0	13

[a] All are significant at the .01 level (nfd's are 1 and 3025).

Table 2 shows the mean scores of dropouts and controls on 19 Project TALENT ability tests. Controls scored significantly higher than dropouts on all these tests. The variables are ordered according to their F ratios, indicating the extent of the differences between the two groups. As can be seen in this list, the groups tended to exhibit smaller differences on the nonverbal tests than on the verbal ones.

INTERESTS

In the TALENT Interest Inventory the student was given a list of 205 occupational titles and names of vocationally-related activities and instructed to state his degree of liking for each. Seventeen scales were derived from this inventory. Table 3 reports the mean scores of dropouts and controls on each of the scales showing significant differences. The variables are organized according to the degree and nature of the observed differences.

Dropouts and controls differed significantly (.01 level) on only five of the seventeen scales. Dropouts had significantly higher scores on the Labor, Skilled Trades, and Musical scales. Although the musical interest result is puzzling, it is clear that the dropouts tended to be more willing to engage in manual labor. It is also interesting to note that boys expressing an interest in sports were less likely to drop out.

SELF-PERCEPTIONS

To give the participants an opportunity to describe their concepts of themselves, the TALENT battery included a Student Activities Inventory. This inventory presented 150 statements, such as "I am sensitive," "I am usually at ease," and "I'd rather be with a group of friends than at home by myself." One set of distractors applied to all of the statements:

Regarding the things I do and the way I do them, this statement describes me:
  A. extremely well
  B. quite well
  C. fairly well
  D. slightly
  E. not very well

TABLE 3
Mean Scores of Male Dropouts and Controls
on TALENT Interest Inventory Scales

	DROPOUT MEAN ($N=1,494$)	CONTROL MEAN ($N=1,533$)	POOLED STANDARD DEVIATION	F RATIO[a]
Controls Higher than Dropouts				
Sports	24.0	26.0	9.7	31
Physical Science, Engineering, Math	18.1	19.4	8.3	16
Dropouts Higher than Controls				
Labor	14.4	12.7	6.8	43
Skilled Trades	15.2	14.0	7.2	18
Musical	12.9	11.6	10.0	13

[a]Significant at the .01 level.

TABLE 4
Mean Scores of Male Dropouts and Controls
on TALENT Student Activities Inventory Scales

	DROPOUT MEAN ($N = 1{,}494$)	CONTROL MEAN ($N = 1{,}533$)	POOLED STANDARD DEVIATION	F RATIO
Controls Higher than Dropouts				
Tidiness	4.0	4.5	2.5	25
Calmness	3.0	3.3	2.1	20
Vigor	3.0	3.3	1.9	20
Self-Confidence	4.2	4.5	2.1	15
Culture	3.8	4.1	2.1	14
Mature Personality	8.6	9.2	4.5	12
Sociability	5.3	5.6	2.7	7
Dropouts Higher than Controls				
Impulsiveness	2.0	1.7	1.6	18
Leadership	1.1	1.0	1.2	7

Each scored item contributed to the scaling of one of the ten scales.

The mean scores of dropouts and controls on each of these scales are presented in Table 4. Controls scored significantly higher than dropouts on seven of the scales: Tidiness, Calmness, Vigor, Self-Confidence, Culture, Mature Personality, and Sociability. Dropouts had higher mean scores on only two: Leadership and Impulsiveness. Lichter (1962) has also indicated that dropouts have difficulty in controlling their impulses. And the results of a study by Kelly, Veldman, and McGuire (1964) showed that an impulsivity measure significantly separated dropouts, delinquents, and normals.

HIGH-SCHOOL ACTIVITIES

Part of the Student Information Blank consists of items on student activities. Lohnes (1966) generated 11 scales based upon selected SIB items:

1. Memberships: 10 items on participation in school clubs.
2. Leadership: 3 items on frequency of elected office in various school activities.
3. Hobbies: 20 items indicating extent of participation in hobbies or extra-curricular activities.
4. Work: 17 items summarizing extent of paid work experience.

5. Social: 5 items on nature and extent of dating.

6. Reading: 9 items on extent of spare time reading.

7. Studying: 26 items based on study habits.

8. Curriculum: 1 item indicating difficulty level of school program in which student is enrolled.

9. Courses: 4 items on amount of college-preparatory work taken.

10. Grades: 7 items indicating school grades.

11. Guidance: 16 items on frequency with which school and work plans were discussed with counselors and other school personnel.

The differences between dropouts and controls on these 11 activities scales are summarized in Table 5. The two largest differences were the greater frequency of dating among the dropouts (Social scale) and their reporting much more difficulty in studying and concentrating on their classwork than the graduates (Studying scale).

A very interesting difference is that the dropouts reported (as ninth-graders) having had many more guidance contacts with counselors and other school personnel than did the controls.

SOCIOECONOMIC ENVIRONMENT

A socioeconomic index was computed for each student on the basis of nine 1960 Student Information Blank questions. This index gives a mea-

TABLE 5
Mean Scores of Male Dropouts and Controls
on TALENT Student Information Blank Scales

	DROPOUT MEAN ($N = 1,494$)	CONTROL MEAN ($N = 1,553$)	POOLED STANDARD DEVIATION	F RATIO
Controls Higher than Dropouts				
Studying	49.8	56.2	17.1	108
Curriculum	2.5	2.8	1.7	23
Grades	11.5	12.5	7.3	14
Dropouts Higher than Controls				
Social	11.7	9.7	5.3	112
Work	21.8	19.2	8.6	68
Courses	3.8	3.0	3.2	58
Guidance	22.0	18.7	14.1	42
Memberships	11.5	9.6	9.7	28
Reading	14.7	13.4	9.3	15

sure of the general socioeconomic level of the family environment. The items in the index are summarized as follows:

1. If your family has bought (or is buying) your home, what is its present value?

2. Please make the best estimate you can of your family's total income for last year (1959). Include money earned by both parents or anyone else in the household who worked.

3. How many books are in your home?

4. How many of the following articles are in your home: automatic washer, automatic clothes dryer, electric dishwasher, electric or gas refrigerator, vacuum cleaner, home food freezer (separate from refrigerator)?

5. How many of the following articles are in your home: telephone, television set, radio, phonograph?

6. How many of the following articles are in your home: a room of my own, my own study desk, a typewriter?

7. Which of the following comes closest to describing the work of your father (or the male head of your household)?

8. Mark the one answer indicating the highest level of education your father reached.

9. Mark the one answer indicating the highest level of education your mother reached.

Table 6 presents the percentages of dropouts and controls in each of the four socioeconomic levels, the levels being determined by national norm quartiles. The percentages of dropouts and controls in each level were quite similar. Fifty-one percent of the dropouts and 48 percent of the graduates were in the lowest level. In the middle levels (2 and 3) ranked 43 percent of the dropouts and 49 percent of the controls. Six

TABLE 6
Socioeconomic Level of Dropouts, Controls, and All Grade 9 Males
(Percentages Based on Weighted Frequencies)

LEVEL	DROPOUTS ($N=1,715$)	CONTROLS ($N=1,660$)	ALL GRADE 9 MALES ($N=48,734$)
1 (Bottom quarter)	51	48	25
2	27	30	25
3	16	19	25
4 (Top quarter)	6	3	25
	100	100	100

percent of the dropouts were in the highest level, compared to three percent of the young men who completed high school.

It is important to note that there was *no* significant difference between the dropouts and controls on this socioeconomic environment variable, indicating that the economic conditions of the home do not appear to be forcing students out of school.

REASONS FOR LEAVING

Before talking about what dropouts did after high school, their stated reasons for leaving school should be mentioned. Although the young men reported many reasons for dropping out (for example, needed at home, didn't like school, failing, got married, felt too old to stay in school), it is unwise to say that so many dropped out because of reason 1, so many because of reason 2, etc. A dropout may say that he left school because he was failing. The reason for his failure, however, may have been that he was working every night to help support his family. Another reason given was "felt too old to stay in school." The cause of his being older than his classmates was probably an early failure, which may have been due to physical or emotional problems or lack of ability. Therefore, this reason, "felt too old," really tells us little, as do most of the other reported explanations.

Other investigators share this feeling. For example, after reviewing data collected from 12,608 dropouts in Ohio in 1962–63, Nachman, Getson, and Odgers (1962) concluded that the reason for leaving school given by the dropout was usually not supported by his school record or the opinion of his counselor. In a survey of dropouts in Maryland (Huffington, 1962), "lack of interest" was found to be above a dozen other reasons for leaving school, such as cost, marriage, pregnancy, institutionalization, and military service. In second place was "lack of scholastic success." But "lack of interest" or "lack of scholastic success" are only symptoms, not the problems.

As far as being sorry about their decision to leave school, 57 percent of the young men reported that they regretted dropping out.

POST-HIGH-SCHOOL ACTIVITIES

In 1964, the employment rates of dropouts and controls were quite similar. Ninety percent of the dropouts who did not continue their education after leaving high school were employed, 87 percent full-time, three percent part-time. Of the controls with no further training, 89 percent had full-time jobs and two percent part-time. The greatest percentages of dropouts were unskilled workers (driver, laborer, miner, etc.), skilled workers (electrician, machinist, mechanic, etc.), or service workers (waiter, hairdresser, barber, etc.). The greatest percentages of controls were unskilled, skilled, or clerical and sales workers.

Although the difference between the percentages on active military duty was not striking (30 percent, dropouts; 33 percent, controls), there was a difference between the percentages serving in each branch. The greatest numbers of dropouts were in the Army or Navy, while the controls were most likely to serve in the Navy or the Air Force.

For the dropouts who were employed, the mean yearly salary was $3650; for controls, it was $3500. The probable reason for this difference is that dropouts had been working longer than controls, in some cases four years longer.

In the analysis of employment rates and salaries reported above, dropouts and controls *who had had some additional training after high school* were excluded, i.e., 36 percent of the dropouts and 38 percent of the controls. The greatest percentages from both of these groups who furthered their education attended an Armed Forces enlisted man's school. Seven percent of the dropouts and four percent of the controls went to trade schools. And technical schools were attended by five percent of the controls, compared to only .7 percent of the dropouts.

Another comparison between male dropouts and controls concerns marriage. In 1964, 37 percent of the dropouts were married, compared to only 15 percent of the controls.

COMPARISONS BETWEEN 1960 AND 1964 DATA

Because the 1960 Project TALENT testing and the one-year follow-up survey did not, in general, gather the same kinds of information, it is not possible to make many comparisons between dropouts and controls in 1960 and in 1964. However, two comparisons can be made. The first concerns high-school curriculum; the second, career plans.

High-School Curriculum. The percentages of dropouts and controls who, in ninth grade, were either enrolled in or expecting to follow one of six curricula are shown in the left-hand columns of Table 7. The percentages who answered on the one-year follow-up questionnaire that they *had* taken one of six curricula are shown in the right-hand columns of the same table. As indicated, the percentages in all curricula, except *general*, decreased from grade 9 to grade 12. For dropouts, the percentage in the general curriculum rose from 25 to 73 percent; for controls, from 34 to 59 percent. A question arises here—Did enrollment in this general curriculum, which generally offers neither the intellectual stimulation of the academic curriculum nor the practical instruction of the vocational courses, influence the dropouts' decision to leave school? An an-

TABLE 7
High-School Curriculum of Male Dropouts and Controls
(Percentages Based on Weighted Frequencies)

	CURRICULUM EXPECTED AT GRADE 9		CURRICULUM MEMBERSHIP AT TIME OF LEAVING HIGH SCHOOL	
	DROPOUTS ($N=1,655$)	CONTROLS ($N=1,590$)	DROPOUTS ($N=1,801$)	CONTROLS ($N=1,734$)
General	25.2	33.8	73.2	59.3
College Prep	21.9	22.8	5.0	14.9
Commercial-Business	15.8	9.2	2.3	7.8
Vocational	18.1	15.9	6.8	6.7
Agricultural	9.8	8.9	5.5	2.6
Other	9.2	9.4	7.2	8.7
	100.0	100.0	100.0	100.0

swer cannot be given here, but educators should give some thought to the matter.

Career Plans. The second comparison which can be made from 1960 to 1964 concerns career plans. In ninth grade (1960), 36 percent of both dropouts and controls planned careers requiring a college degree. The greatest percentages of dropouts wanted careers as engineers (15 percent), farmers (10 percent) or skilled workers (six percent). As ninth-graders, controls were most likely to plan careers in engineering (15 percent), the Armed Forces (10 percent), or farming (eight percent).

In 1964 only two percent of the young men who dropped out and seven percent of the controls planned careers for which a college education was required. The greatest percentages of dropouts wanted to be structural (13 percent) or skilled workers (12 percent). The most common choices of the controls were skilled worker (12 percent), structural worker (seven percent), and engineering or scientific aide (seven percent).

The Girls Who Dropped Out

ABILITIES

In Table 8 are the percentages of female dropouts and controls who ranked in each of four General Academic Ability Composite levels. These levels represent quarters in the 1960 grade 9 female population.

TABLE 8
Ability Levels of Dropouts, Controls, and All Grade 9 Females
(Percentages Based on Weighted Frequencies)

LEVEL	DROPOUTS ($N = 1,670$)	CONTROLS ($N = 1,954$)	ALL GRADE 9 FEMALES ($N = 50,442$)
1 (Bottom quarter)	40	17	25
2	34	36	25
3	19	32	25
4 (Top quarter)	7	15	25
	100	100	100

TABLE 9
Mean Scores of Female Dropouts and
Controls on TALENT Ability Tests

	DROPOUT MEAN ($N = 1,537$)	CONTROL MEAN ($N = 1,847$)	POOLED STANDARD DEVIATION	F RATIO[a]
Information I Total	92.8	107.4	27.3	260
Information II Total	49.8	58.3	16.0	257
Introductory High-School Math	7.3	9.1	3.5	241
English Total	72.9	79.3	12.9	220
Reading Comprehension	21.5	25.8	9.6	176
Arithmetic Computation	18.2	27.6	23.2	144
Abstract Reasoning	6.8	8.0	3.1	143
Word Functions in Sentences	7.0	8.7	4.4	136
Arithmetic Reasoning	5.7	6.9	3.0	134
Disguised Words	11.0	13.3	6.2	111
Memory for Words	9.4	10.9	4.7	84
Creativity	6.2	7.2	3.3	82
Table Reading	6.0	8.3	8.8	60
Mechanical Reasoning	7.0	7.8	3.2	57
Memory for Sentences	8.6	9.4	3.0	55
Clerical Checking	18.6	22.8	20.4	34
Visualization in Two Dimensions	9.8	10.9	5.3	34
Visualization in Three Dimensions	6.7	7.2	2.7	27
Object Inspection	18.9	20.0	8.0	17

[a]All significant at .01 level.

As this table indicates, 40 percent of the dropouts were in the bottom quarter, compared to only 17 percent of the controls. Fifty-three percent of the dropouts and 68 percent of the controls ranked in the middle quarters. In the top ability quarter were seven percent of the girls who left high school and 15 percent of the controls.

Table 9 reports the mean scores of dropouts and controls on the TALENT ability tests. As in the males' analysis the graduates had significantly higher scores than the controls on all the tests. Also, the ordering of the variables by discriminating power (F ratios) is very similar to the male order in Table 2.

INTERESTS

Table 10 presents the mean scores of dropouts and controls on the significant Interest Inventory scales. Notice that the female dropouts tended to have higher scores on the more masculine interest scales, while the two most important scales on which the controls were higher were social service and biomedical interests. Interests seem to be more

TABLE 10
Mean Scores of Female Dropouts and Controls
on TALENT Interest Inventory Scales

	DROPOUT MEAN ($N=1,537$)	CONTROL MEAN ($N=1,847$)	POOLED STANDARD DEVIATION	F RATIO[a]
Controls Higher than Dropouts				
Social Service	22.3	23.4	7.3	17
Biological Science-Medicine	13.2	14.5	9.8	16
Computation	14.6	15.5	7.6	13
Sports	17.4	18.5	9.5	10
Physical Science, Engineering, Math	10.3	11.0	7.1	8
Public Service	10.0	10.9	10.6	6
Dropouts Higher than Controls				
Labor	8.9	7.9	6.3	21
Skilled Trades	9.0	8.2	5.4	20
Mechanical-Technical	7.8	7.2	6.3	8
Hunting-Fishing	13.8	12.8	11.6	6

[a] All significant at .01 level.

highly related to dropping out for the females than for the males, where only five scales produced significant differences (Table 3).

SELF-PERCEPTIONS

The mean scores of dropouts and controls on the Student Activities Inventory are shown in Table 11. Controls were significantly higher than dropouts on eight of the scales: Tidiness, Mature Personality, Vigor, Culture, Calmness, Sociability, Social Sensitivity, and Self-Confidence. There was no significant difference between the groups on Impulsiveness or Leadership as was the case for the male dropouts (Table 4).

SOCIOECONOMIC LEVEL

In Table 12 are the percentages of dropouts and controls in each of four socioeconomic levels. These levels represent quarters in the 1960 grade nine population. Sixty-one percent of the dropouts were in the lowest level, compared to only 41 percent of the controls. In the middle levels ranked 36 percent of the dropouts and 51 percent of the controls, and in the top socioeconomic quarter were three percent of the girls who dropped out and eight percent of the controls. Socioeconomic factors appear to be more related to dropping out among the females than among the males (compare Table 12 with Table 6).

TABLE 11
Mean Scores of Female Dropouts and Controls
on TALENT Student Activities Inventory Scales

	DROPOUT MEAN $(N=1,537)$	CONTROL MEAN $(N=1,847)$	POOLED STANDARD DEVIATION	F RATIO[a]
Controls Higher than Dropouts				
Tidiness	5.2	5.8	2.7	45
Mature Personality	9.1	10.2	4.8	44
Vigor	3.1	3.4	2.1	29
Culture	4.8	5.2	2.2	23
Calmness	3.5	3.8	2.3	22
Sociability	6.4	6.9	2.9	21
Social Sensitivity	4.4	4.7	2.3	15
Self-Confidence	4.5	4.8	2.3	10

[a] All significant at the .01 level.

TABLE 12
Socioeconomic Levels of Dropouts, Controls, and All Grade
9 Females (Percentages Based on Weighted Frequencies)

LEVEL	DROPOUTS ($N = 1,711$)	CONTROLS ($N = 1,958$)	ALL GRADE 9 FEMALES ($N = 50,442$)
1 (Bottom quarter)	61	41	25
2	22	28	25
3	14	23	25
4 (Top quarter)	3	8	25
	100	100	100

REASON FOR LEAVING

Approximately three-quarters of the girl dropouts reported, "Got married," as their reason for leaving high school. Of all the female dropouts, 56 percent reported that they were sorry they did not graduate.

POST-HIGH-SCHOOL ACTIVITIES

Although the employment rates were quite similar for male dropouts and controls, they were quite different for girls from these two groups, primarily because of the higher percentage of early marriages among the dropouts. About 26 percent of the female dropouts had full-time jobs in 1964, 18 percent of those who were married, and 58 percent of those still single. Of the girls who graduated from high school, but who did not go on to college, 53 percent were employed full-time. Two percent of the dropouts had part-time jobs, compared to six percent of the girl graduates. Three percent of the dropouts and five percent of the graduates reported that they held jobs, but did not indicate whether these jobs were full-time or part-time.

There were differences, too, in the kinds of jobs held. Dropouts were most likely to work as miscellaneous service workers (food preparation, catering, and other food services; masseuse and other personal services; domestic, boardinghouse keeper) or laborers (miscellaneous skilled occupations, machine operator, etc.). Female controls, on the other hand, worked mainly as stenographers, secretaries, or clerical workers.

As previously reported, male dropouts earned more than controls. With the girls, however, this was not the case. The mean yearly salary for dropouts was $2,570; for graduates, $2,790. Remember here, too, that the dropouts had, in many cases, been working longer than the controls.

Another interesting comparison is schools attended after high school. Only 16 percent of the girls who dropped out had some further training, compared to 38 percent of the controls. Of the dropouts, the greatest percentages went to trade or business school. These two schools were also the most common choices of the girl controls, although the percentages attending were higher than those for dropouts.

As would be expected, the percentage of girl dropouts married was quite a bit higher than that for boys. By August 1964, 81 percent of the female dropouts were married or had been married at one time. Of the controls, only 44 percent were married or had been.

COMPARISONS BETWEEN 1960 AND 1964 DATA

High-School Curriculum. Table 13 compares the expected curricula of future dropouts and controls at grade nine with their curriculum membership at the time they left high school. The percentages in each curriculum, except *general,* decreased between the time these young people were in ninth grade and the time they either dropped out or graduated. The percentage of dropouts in the general curriculum increased from 25 to 67 percent; the percentage of controls, from 22 to only 36 percent.

TABLE 13
High-School Curriculum of Male Dropouts and Controls
(Percentages Based on Weighted Frequencies)

	CURRICULUM EXPECTED AT GRADE 9		CURRICULUM MEMBERSHIP AT TIME OF LEAVING HIGH SCHOOL	
	FUTURE DROPOUTS ($N=1,642$)	FUTURE CONTROL ($N=1,885$)	DROPOUTS ($N=1,722$)	CONTROL ($N=2,036$)
General	25.3	22.1	66.9	35.5
College Prep	16.1	22.0	4.0	14.0
Commercial-Business	38.6	41.8	20.8	41.5
Vocational	12.1	5.4	2.9	1.2
Agricultural	.4	.4	—	—
Other	7.5	8.3	5.4	7.7
	100.0	100.0	100.0	100.0

Career Plans. Comparing the career plans of dropouts and controls in 1960 (grade nine) and in 1964 we find that in ninth grade, the greatest percentages of future dropouts chose careers as housewives (24 percent), office workers (21 percent), or nurses (12 percent). Of the graduates-to-be, 34 percent planned to be office workers; 14 percent, nurses, and 11 percent, housewives. In 1964 over one-half of the dropouts planned to be housewives. The percentage previously planning to be office workers decreased to four percent, the percentage planning nursing careers to two percent. In the same year, 34 percent of the controls reported that they expected to be housewives; 23 percent, office workers; seven percent, service workers.

Summary

Using data from the 1960 TALENT testing and the one-year follow-up study, comparisons were made between dropouts and high-school graduates not going to a four-year or junior college (the controls). In the 1960 testing, male controls scored significantly higher than dropouts on all the TALENT ability tests. The differences for verbal tests were greater than those for the nonverbal. The ability findings were similar for girls. On the Interest Inventory scales, male controls had significantly higher mean scores on Sports and Physical Science, Engineering, Math; dropouts, on Labor, Skilled Trades, and Music. The girl controls indicated greater interest than the dropouts in seven areas: Physical Science, Engineering, Math, Biological Science-Medicine; Public Service; Social Service; Sports; and Computation. Female dropouts scored higher than controls on Hunting-Fishing, Mechanical-Technical, Skilled Trades, and Labor. On the Student Activities Inventory scales, male controls perceived themselves to be more sociable, vigorous, calm, tidy, cultured, self-confident, and mature than did the boys who dropped out; dropouts had higher mean scores on two SAI scales: Leadership and Impulsiveness. As for the girls, controls scored significantly higher than dropouts on all the scales except Leadership and Impulsiveness, on which the two groups did not differ significantly. A comparison of the socioeconomic levels of dropouts and controls revealed that the female controls were more likely to rank in the upper socioeconomic levels than were dropouts. For boys, however, the differences were not significant.

Data from the one-year follow-up study also revealed differences between young people who graduated from high school and those who did not. The male dropouts reported many reasons for leaving school; for girls, the most common explanation was marriage. As far as employment was concerned, the percentages of male dropouts and controls with jobs in 1964 were similar. However, there was a slight tendency for controls to hold higher level jobs than dropouts. The difference between the percentages from the two groups on active military duty was not striking. A comparison of salaries revealed that the male dropouts earned slightly more than controls. The young men who completed high school were more likely to further their education after high school; they were less likely to be married by 1964.

As might be expected, female controls were much more likely than dropouts to be employed in 1964. Controls were also more likely to hold higher level jobs than dropouts and to earn more. Comparing the percentages continuing their education after high school reveals that more than twice as many controls as dropouts had some further training. The percentage married was also quite different for the two groups, the percentage of dropouts being almost twice that of the controls.

Two comparisons were made between 1960 and 1964 data. The first concerned high-school curriculum. For boys and girls, dropouts and controls, the percentage in each curriculum except *general*, decreased from 1960 to 1964. However, the percentages of dropouts, male and female, in the general curriculum at the time of leaving high school were higher than the percentage of controls in that curriculum. The second 1960–1964 comparison dealt with career plans. For all groups, male and female dropouts and controls, career plans were more realistic in 1964 than in 1960, with the percentages planning professional careers decreasing. For both males and females, there was a tendency for controls to plan higher level jobs than dropouts.

Of course, it is one thing to show a long list of significant differences between dropouts and controls and quite another to predict which ninth-graders will subsequently drop out of high school. Attempts to do the latter with multivariate prediction techniques are summarized in a Project TALENT monograph (Lohnes and Cooley, 1968).

One of the reasons for undertaking this dropout investigation was to try to develop data about dropouts for use in high-school guidance. It was hoped that the results would reveal that the non-college high-school graduate (the control) was much better off than the high school dropout as far as future employment and earnings are concerned. Large differences in this area might help to dissuade some students from leaving high school before graduation. Although there are other cultural advantages in continued education, such practical data would probably have a more direct impact on potential dropouts.

Unfortunately, the results were not consistent with these expectations. Not only were the male dropouts earning as much as the controls, but they had been earning it longer. Thus, economically, the dropout was certainly at an advantage over the student who stayed to graduate. Of course, it must be remembered that when the follow-up data were collected, the dropouts were only about 19 years old. Many of the consequences of leaving high school prior to graduation may not become apparent until later in life. Project TALENT is continuing to collect follow-up data on these people and perhaps subsequent criteria will show more precisely the disadvantages of dropping out of high school.

References

Flanagan, John C., Daily, John T., Shaycoft, Marion F., Orr, David B., Goldberg, Isadore F., and Neyman, Clinton A. *Design for a study of American youth.* Boston: Houghton Mifflin, 1962.

Flanagan, John C., Davis, Fred B., Daily, John T., Shaycoft, Marion F., Orr, David B., Goldberg, Isadore F., and Neyman, Clinton A. *The American high-school student.* Pittsburgh: Project TALENT Office, 1964.

Flanagan, John C., and Cooley, William W. *Project TALENT one-year follow-up studies.* Pittsburgh: Project TALENT Office, 1966.

French, John. High school dropouts of high ability. *Vocational Guidance Quarterly,* Winter 1965–1966, 123–127.

Huffington, P. W. *Pupil dropout study: Maryland public schools.* State Department of Education, 1962.

Kelly, Francis J., Veldman, Donald J., and McGuire, Carson. Multiple discriminant prediction of delinquency and school dropouts. *Educational and Psychological Measurement,* 24, 535–543, 1964.

Lichter, Solomon O., Rapien, Elsie B., Siebert, Frances, and Sklansky, M. A. *The dropouts.* New York: Free Press, 1962.

Lohnes, Paul R., and Cooley, William W. *Predicting development of young adults.* Palo Alto, Calif.: Project TALENT Office, American Institutes for Research, 1968.

Nachman, L. R., Getson, R. F., and Odgers, J. G. *Ohio study of high school dropouts 1962–1963.* State Department of Education, 1964.

Warner, O. R. The Scholastic Ability of School Dropouts. *Selected reports and statistics on school dropouts.* U.S. Office of Education, 1964.

3. EXAMINING STEREOTYPES ABOUT YOUTH IN VOCATIONAL AND COMPREHENSIVE HIGH SCHOOLS *

Richard F. Purnell and Gerald S. Lesser

For many years, several unchallenged stereotypes about vocational education have undermined the occupational preparation of countless students entering American high schools. Apparently, many students, parents, and educators are grossly misinformed about secondary vocational education in this country: to their minds, it is undesirable, degrading, and inferior education. In reality, a vocational high school education is probably exactly what a large number of adolescents want and need, but the existence of erroneous stereotypes keep them from realizing it.

This paper reports the findings of a study designed to (1) examine the experiences of work-bound youth in vocational high schools and (2) compare them with those of work-bound and college-bound youth in comprehensive high schools. The aim in this study is to examine data relevant to the stereotypes that exist about work-bound youth in vocational and comprehensive high schools, using the students' own perceptions of their ongoing experiences in these two types of schools.

Essentially, two related stereotypes account for the widespread misconception about vocational and comprehensive high schools. First, vocational schools are seen as a "dumping ground" for lazy students and slow learners. Second, comprehensive high school education is seen as superior to vocational high school education for work-bound youth. Although these stereotypes probably are a carry-over from the conditions of a generation or so ago, the dumping-ground image may have some current basis in reality in some vocational schools in huge urban areas. The second stereotype is more complex—more deeply entrenched in American society—and cannot be dismissed as easily as the first.

Two main parts of the stereotype that comprehensive high schools offer educational experiences superior to vocational high schools for work-bound youth are embodied in (a) Conant's (1959, 1967) argu-

* The research presented herein was performed persuant to grant number OE-5-85-017 from the U. S. Office of Education, Division of Adult and Vocational Research.

ments favoring comprehensive high schools for work-bound youth, and (b) the widespread belief that preparation for college is the "best" high school education. Conant's arguments surely have bolstered this stereotype. His position rests squarely on the assumption that the community is served best by placing diverse educational programs under one educational roof; future holders of different statuses and occupations supposedly benefit from the opportunity to interact with and get to understand one another.[1] The preference for a college education that permeates American society supports the stereotype in its turn by fostering a concomitant distaste for "lower" educational programs.

Various other beliefs are expressed about the comparative conditions and experiences of youth in comprehensive and vocational high schools:

> Vocational education does not provide for the education of the whole person.

> Placement in a vocational program tends to lower social expectations for these students, thereby limiting their aspirations unnecessarily.

> Vocational school populations are often too homogeneous in terms of experiences, capacities, and interests, as well as ethnic and socioeconomic background.

> Vocational high school provides far fewer opportunities for extracurricular interaction than does comprehensive high school.

> Vocational students have less drive to compete and achieve in high school.

However, these stereotypes really are subsumed under the two related, major stereotypes stated earlier; our analyses address these and other sub-stereotypes about work-bound youth in vocational and comprehensive high schools.

Students

Of the students in this study, 3060 (1981 boys; 1079 girls) attended six vocational high schools and 1827 (890 boys; 937 girls) attended three comprehensive high schools. The vocational high schools were selected from six different states to represent the distribution of separate voca-

---

[1] During our questionnaire pretesting, informal interviews with about fifty regular and vocational high school students revealed that among students in the various comprehensive high school programs barriers favoring the academic students are set up and solidified. Further, vocational students said they sought separate vocational high schools in an effort to escape the stigmas and ordeals encountered in comprehensive high school systems.

tional high schools in this country. The three comprehensive high schools were drawn from New England, the Mideast, and the South. Most of the schools had all, or predominantly, white students, so only whites were used in our analyses.[2] Most of the schools were four-year high schools. Agriculture and home economics were not included in the programs of the vocational schools in our sample. All vocational schools had trade and industrial students, while only some had technical, distributive, business, and health education programs.

Procedure

Self-administered questionnaires were distributed to the students in the high schools by the investigators and their staff. In most of the schools, the students responded to the questionnaires in their classrooms; in the large schools, questionnaires were administered to larger groups in auditoriums. The vocational school data were collected in March 1967, whereas the comprehensive high school students received their questionnaires in the spring of 1965. The students were promised anonymity in that their responses were to be reported as group statistics only; teachers were not present during the administration of the questionnaires. The questionnaires and items had been pretested several times in order to render them as meaningful and appropriate as possible for their respondents.

Results

The presentation of results is organized around the two global stereotypes introduced earlier: the dumping-ground stereotype and the superiority of the comprehensive high school stereotype. For the dumping-ground sterotype, we present findings on (a) the students' reasons for going to a vocational high school, (b) their valuations of vocational high schools, and (c) the distributions of occupations and education among vocational and comprehensive high school students' parents. The superiority of the comprehensive high school stereotype is examined in terms of (a) students' perceptions of school achievement and satisfaction with school, (b) student involvement in school activities, (c) student behaviors outside of school, and (d) student aspirations.

---

[2] One comprehensive school was one-fifth Negro, and Negroes differed significantly from the whites on many of the items of the questionnaire. For our present purpose, the Negro subjects were not included in the data analyses.

We have condensed the results of the original report here; for more detailed analyses and tables of the data, the reader is referred to the larger report.[3] All the results reported here are based on the students' perception of and feelings about their experiences and the conditions in their high schools as they related them on the questionnaires.

ON THE DUMPING-GROUND STEREOTYPE

Reasons for going to a vocational high school. Why do adolescents decide to go to a specialized vocational high school? What is the relative importance of their various reasons? We asked students to respond to eight different considerations—found in pretests to be commonly employed by students in deciding to attend a vocational high school—by checking that each was either very, somewhat, or not important.

The reason overwhelmingly chosen as very important by both boys (82 percent) and girls (81 percent) was "to learn a trade," reflecting the very practical bent of these students.

Although mentioned considerably less often than learning a trade as very important, the items next most frequently mentioned by students involve either informal knowledge of a vocational high school or the urgings of some older person. Thus, much weight is assigned to liking a school's reputation (boys, 28 percent; girls, 37 percent) and to knowing a graduate of a school (boys, 21 percent; girls, 26 percent). Parents are mentioned only somewhat more frequently (boys, 21 percent; girls, 24 percent) than teachers and guidance counselors (boys, 14 percent; girls, 19 percent) as adults influencing entrance into vocational high school.

Considerably weaker are reasons of "to be with friends" (boys, 7 percent; girls, 16 percent) and "studies are easier" (boys, 9 percent; girls, 9 percent). The fact that relatively few students report having given major importance to friends and easy studies in deciding on a vocational school education suggests that more pragmatic objectives were given greater weight in their decisions.

Students' valuations of vocational high school. Here we deal with two different, but related, aspects of the experiences of vocational high school students: (1) the valuations students place on their programs, their training, the help they receive from the school, and other related aspects of their school life; and (2) the scholastic performances and outlooks of vocational students from their own points of view. The finding that the large majority of students elected to go to a vocational school

---

[3] Purnell, R. F., and G. S. Lesser, *Work-bound and College-bound Youth: A Study in Stereotypes*, Cambridge: Laboratory of Human Development, Harvard Graduate School of Education, 1969.

for the very practical reason of wanting to learn a trade provides the background against which to assess the results of this section. We want to learn how the students feel about what is done to help them attain their goal of learning a trade. The fact that only a very small portion of students choose to enter a vocational high school in order to escape to easier studies leads one to expect positive orientations toward relevant scholastic endeavors and a serious appreciation for shop work from these students.

According to our results, the large majority of vocational students repeatedly express a good deal of satisfaction with their experiences in vocational high schools. More specifically, (a) most of the students (boys, 86 percent; girls, 80 percent) are taking the trades they want to learn; (b) most programs are viewed by the students as enjoying high statuses (boys, 87 percent; girls, 90 percent); (c) both male (90 percent) and female (93 percent) students are quite satisfied with the training they are receiving; (d) only a handful of students (boys, 6 percent; girls, 6 percent) find nothing to be satisfied with in their vocational schools; (e) most students report that they enjoy working hard in school (boys, 91 percent; girls, 95 percent); and (f) a great portion of the students (boys, 71 percent; girls, 75 percent) are pleased with the help with their future plans they receive from the school staff. It was also found that most of the students (boys, 66 percent; girls, 72 percent) and teachers (82 percent) favor vocational education in a separate school to vocational education in a regular high school. In spite of this widespread satisfaction with the vocational high school experiences from within, there is reason to believe that persons outside the vocational school do not hold it in high regard. Seventy percent of the vocational school teachers report not being satisfied with the reputation of vocational schools among regular high school teachers.

The results of questions pertaining directly and indirectly to scholastic performance produce a picture of the vocational student as someone who (1) wants to get good grades, (2) does his homework to get them, and (3) works well with his fellow shop students. Vocational students also profess that it is very important for them to be good at their trades and that they (boys and girls, 95 percent) wholly approve of others who want to be excellent students.

Our findings do not support the dumping-ground stereotype for this sample of specialized vocational high schools. Rather than being dumped and bored, the results suggest that specialized vocational high school students, for the most part, are serious, satisfied, and achievement-oriented. They prefer separate vocational high schools in which to learn their trades. They vie with one another to enter these schools, as evidenced by the relatively low student selection ratios (principals report it to be about one third) used in vocational schools. The dumping-ground stereotype may have some validity for certain vocational schools in our great urban centers. Looking at the results in a positive light, however, it appears that separate vocational high schools actually provide a satisfactory and desirable setting and education for most of their students.

Occupation and education among vocational and comprehensive students' parents. This section reports our findings on the distribution of occupations and education among the parents of vocational and the three major groups of comprehensive high school students (that is, academic, commercial, and general students). We studied these variables to learn if there are large differences in the percentage of students from the various social levels in the four programs. Finding large differences would demonstrate that statuses derived from parents, for whatever underlying reasons, tend to perpetuate across generations, a condition that is antithetical to an important reason for having comprehensive high schools. In a democracy, the schools are expected to serve the ideal of enabling the individual to cross social-class barriers. Thus, these results are yet another way of examining the claim that vocational high schools are dumping grounds—in this case, for students from the lower social classes.

Father's occupation is significantly related to the type of program that students enter. More boys and girls in the academic programs come from homes with fathers in clerical and sales, professional, and managerial fields; more commercial and general students have fathers in unskilled, semi-skilled, and skilled occupational categories. The distribution of father's occupations among vocational students closely resembles those of the two work-bound student programs (commercial and general) in comprehensive high schools.

Not unexpectedly, the distributions of father's and mother's education by student programs reflect the same patterns found for fathers' occupation. More work-bound students have parents with less education than college-bound (academic) students. Once again, the distributions were significantly different among students from the four programs and among the students in the comprehensive high school programs.

Thus, social-class differences exist between college-bound youth and work-bound students in both comprehensive and vocational high schools. The work-bound youth in both types of high school have similar social class distributions, as indicated by fathers' occupation and parents' education. More college-bound youth have parents with white-collar jobs and more years of education, while more work-bound youths' fathers hold blue-collar jobs and have less education. The findings reveal that if students are channeled into vocational high schools by social class, they are similarly channeled into work-bound programs in comprehensive high schools.

ON THE SUPERIORITY OF THE COMPREHENSIVE SCHOOL STEREOTYPE

This section examines students' perceptions related to the belief prevalent among the American public that work-bound students in comprehensive high schools are somehow better off than work-bound students in vocational high schools. To some extent, we already have addressed that belief indirectly: in our examination of the first stereotype, we showed that the great majority of vocational students in our sample prefer vocational programs in separate vocational high schools to vocational programs in comprehensive high schools. Here we compare the responses of vocational students in separate vocational schools and academic, commercial, and general students in comprehensive high schools regarding: (a) achievement and satisfaction in school, (b) involvement in school activities, (c) student behaviors outside of school, and (d) student aspirations. We hope to provide a more accurate view of what it means to be a work-bound youth either in a comprehensive or a vocational high school, comparing work-bound youth in each of the two conditions with college-bound youth. In addition to permitting comparisons between vocational and "academic" students, using four groups of students allows us to make comparisons among the three major student tracks of the comprehensive high school. The lack of such comparisons in other studies of high school youth, we feel, restricts the meaning of their findings.

School achievement and satisfaction. Our comparisons of students on indices of their school achievement and satisfaction with school suggest that vocational students in specialized vocational high schools and academic students in comprehensive high schools believe that they achieve more in school and are more satisfied with their schooling than commercial and general students in comprehensive high schools. Commercial students usually place third on achievement in and satisfaction with school, while general students are always last on these two counts. General students, usually accompanied by commercial students, are significantly less achievement-oriented in school than academic students. Vocational students in specialized vocational schools have many of the same achievement values and behaviors and satisfaction with school as the academic students. Thus, in terms of achievement and satisfaction, the two work-bound groups are quite different. We conclude from our results that the vocational students in separate high schools more often view their experiences as educationally valuable than do commercial and general students in comprehensive high schools. The stereotype that comprehensive schools provide superior educational experience to those of vocational schools, as indicated by achievement orientation and satisfaction with school, must be modified: academic students in a comprehensive school and vocational students in a specialized school more often view their experiences positively than do commercial and general students in comprehensive schools.

Involvement in school activities. In addition to being satisfied with school and interested in doing well at school, high school students generally give considerable attention to sports and extracurricular activities. The extent to which students report themselves participating in these school activities and the importance they place on them may be used to examine another facet of the claim that comprehensive high schools offer better experiences and opportunities to their students than vocational high schools.

The opportunities for participation in extracurricular activities and sports are not viewed as better for work-bound youth in comprehensive high schools than for work-bound youth in vocational high schools. Involvement in extracurricular activities and sports seems to be the same in these two types of schools for work-bound students, although this similarity probably exists for different reasons: comprehensive work-bound youth have to compete with academic students, whereas vocational students have jobs and other interests. Work-bound youth in comprehensive high schools report having fewer experiences or opportunities to engage in sports and extracurricular activities than academic students. Rather, students in academic programs, who place greater emphasis on sports and extracurricular activities as part of their social systems, predominate in these high school activities. In addition, academic students, more than commercial or general students, report belonging to leading crowds in their comprehensive high schools. Much lower leading-crowd memberships are reported among vocational high school students. Indeed, it is very likely that the nature of the leading crowd in a vocational school is quite different compared to one in a comprehensive high school. Vocational students, in interviews, have expressed their distaste for the leading-crowd conditions of neighboring comprehensive high schools and have cited these conditions as part of their reasons for preferring vocational high schools. These findings offer further evidence against the stereotype of superior experiences for work-bound youth in comprehensive high schools.

Behaviors outside of school. Differences in in-school experiences among students in the four educational tracks may be extended by examining behaviors and activities outside of school. Of course, what students do outside of school also partly reflects their socioeconomic statuses, but it is worth exploring these behaviors in order to compare the experience of work-bound youth from similar social classes under different high school conditions.

Differences among work-bound and college-bound youths' reported behaviors outside of school may be summarized by pointing out that college-bound youth appear to suppress involvements that are incompatible with their educational goals. They (a) go to the movies less often, (b) watch less television, (c) less often own cars, (d) spend more evenings at home, (e) have fewer jobs outside of school, and (f) "date" less than their work-bound counterparts. On serious reading not for school, however, they report spending more time than commercial and general students, although vocational boys read about as much as academic boys. Vocational students are similar to other work-bound students on these outside school behaviors, except that the boys own far more cars than comprehensive school students (which may be related simply to their greater opportunities in school to work on their cars as part of their training).

Student aspirations. A final avenue of insights into the conditions in vocational and comprehensive high schools is provided by looking at the aspirations of students in the different types of schools.

We found that among all students working hard is most often chosen as the best way to get ahead in life, this being a rather pervasive value in American society. In terms of what they prefer in a job, academic students (girls more than boys) stress a feeling of accomplishment, while they place less value than work-bound students on high income. Vocational and commercial boys are more interested in advancement than general boys; vocational boys show a greater concern for accomplishment than commercial and general boys. General students have the lowest expectation of finishing high school and going to college. Almost 80 percent of the academic students propose to go to college. About a third of the vocational and commercial students plan to go to college. After academic students, almost all of whom aspire and expect to be in professional jobs fifteen years after high school, vocational students show the next strongest aspiration for professional positions. The remaining work-bound students seem committed to skilled jobs. Commercial students, in both their aspirations and expectations, scatter equally over all occupational categories from unskilled to professional. General students expect unskilled jobs and report uncertainty about what they expect will become of them in fifteen years. Vocational students are least often uncertain about what they will be doing in fifteen years. These findings lead us to believe that, among work-bound adolescents, the aspirations produced in vocational high schools are at least as desirable as, if not more desirable than, the aspirations produced by comprehensive high schools.

These findings dealing with students' perceptions of their achievement and satisfaction with school, involvement in school activities, behaviors outside of school, and aspirations, are interpreted as contradicting the stereotype that comprehensive high school experiences are superior to vocational high school experiences for work-bound youth. What they seem to suggest is that work-bound students in comprehensive high schools, particularly general students, suffer perceived inferior status and experiences as a result of having to vie with college-bound youth.

Conclusions

In an attempt to examine two global and long unchallenged stereotypes about the experiences and conditions of work-bound youth in vocational and comprehensive high schools, we gathered the perceptions of 3060 vocational and 1827 comprehensive high school students. The two misleading stereotypes prevalent in the American public are (1) that vocational high schools are dumping grounds for lazy students and also slow learners and (2) that the experiences and education of comprehensive high schools are perceived as superior to those of vocational high schools for work-bound youth. For the first stereotype, we looked at (a) students' reasons for entering vocational high schools, (b) their valuations of vocational high schools, and (c) the occupational and educational distributions among vocational, academic, commercial, and general students' parents. The second stereotype was examined in terms of (a) the various students' perceptions of school achievement and satisfaction with school, (b) student involvement in school activities, (c) student behaviors outside of school, and (d) student aspirations.

Our findings are that students go to vocational schools for serious, practical reasons, that they are satisfied and strive to achieve their goals there, and that they are in social milieus much the same as those found among the work-bound youth in comprehensive high schools. In short, we found the dumping-ground stereotype to be unwarranted and inaccurate among the specialized vocational schools of our sample.

In comparison with the academic, commercial, and general students in comprehensive schools, vocational students have more positive perceptions; they do not lack opportunities at extracurricular school activities compared to their work-bound counterparts in comprehensive schools, who do have fewer and less than equal opportunities at these activities because they share them with college-bound youth; and the aspirations of vocational students are at least as desirable as, and probably more admirable than, those of work-bound youth in comprehensive high schools.

The two global stereotypes about youth in vocational and comprehensive high schools are no longer unchallenged. The stereotypes will be redressed only insofar as these results allay the misunderstandings that the stereotypes generate about separate vocational high schools. Furthermore, the results suggest that there are positive grounds for continuing and cultivating separate vocational high schools for work-bound youth who welcome and appreciate them.

References

Conant, J. B. *The American high school today.* New York: McGraw-Hill, 1959.

Conant, J. B. *The comprehensive high school.* New York: McGraw-Hill, 1967.

4. THE ROLE OF SECONDARY SCHOOLS IN THE PREPARATION OF YOUTH FOR EMPLOYMENT: SUMMARY, CONCLUSIONS, AND IMPLICATIONS *

Jacob J. Kaufman, Carl J. Schaefer,
Morgan V. Lewis, David W. Stevens, and
Elaine W. House

Section I: Introduction

THE ISSUES

In the coming years America will have entering its labor force a larger number of young people than at any time in its past. These young people will be entering a labor market where the need for the unskilled and

* University Park, Pa.: Institute for Research on Human Resources, The Pennsylvania State University, 1967. Summary and conclusions part of report, reprinted with permission of the author.

untrained is at its lowest point. At the same time technology is becoming increasingly complex and the need for skilled manpower has never been higher.

These trends have been evident, of course, to educators, government officials, economists, and others interested in the efficient allocation of human resources. One result of this awareness was the Vocational Education Act of 1963. Through it, the nation pledged itself to make a substantially greater effort to train its young people.

Despite this commitment at the highest levels, vocational education has been the subject of continuous, heated, and, at times, even bitter debate. This debate usually centers on issues such as the usefulness, or adequacy, of vocational education. Do graduates really use the training they receive in school? How effective is this training? Does it really prepare for the types of jobs young people obtain upon graduation? Should training be conducted in a comprehensive or separate vocational high school? Another issue often raised concerns the image of vocational education which is seen by some observers as only appropriate for those students who cannot succeed in the more "demanding" academic curriculum. The phrase "dumping ground" is often heard when this point is discussed. A third issue, probably the most sensitive of all, is the role of vocational education with regard to minority groups and others from disadvantaged backgrounds.

THE METHOD

This study gathered data on all these points so that this very necessary dialogue on vocational education could be conducted with reference to the appropriate facts.

This study was conducted by selecting nine communities which met criteria of size, labor force composition, type and quality of vocational programs, and geographic accessibility. Profiles of the economic and demographic characteristics of the cities were prepared.

When the cooperation of the school officials of the selected cities was obtained, those parties most vitally concerned with vocational education were contacted and their attitudes and experiences were examined. These parties were the schools, employers (including direct supervisors), and unions, and, of course, the graduates themselves.

The schools were examined through an on-site evaluation of their vocational programs. This evaluation was conducted in the nine selected cities by a group of educators each of whom was an authority on the vocational program he assessed. Included on this team were guidance experts and representatives from labor and management. During the school visitation, classes were observed and interviews were conducted with administrators, teachers and students. Questionnaires were distributed to the teachers to measure their attitudes towards vocational and college preparatory education. In all, programs in 25 schools were visited and evaluated, and 1,600 questionnaires were completed by teachers.

Employers and union officials were personally interviewed. The employers were questioned about the jobs for which they hired young people, and how well their current applicants were trained for these jobs. They were also asked about their contacts with the ideas about vocational education. After the interviews, they were given an attitude questionnaire and asked to complete it and return it by mail. Of the 658 employers interviewed, slightly over half (52 per cent) returned the questionnaire.

Many of the questions directed to the 90 union officials were identical to those asked of the employers. These were the questions on contact with and ideas about vocational education. The questions that were asked only of union people concerned their sources of new members, their attitudes towards young people as union members, and the role of their union in the training of young people.

The direct supervisors of the graduate respondents were asked to complete a rating scale on the preparation and job performance of these graduates. Usable ratings were received from 2,826 supervisors. These represented 55 per cent of the graduates interviewed.

A total of 5,181 usable graduate interviews were obtained. The total was composed of almost equal numbers of vocational (2,111) and general curriculum (2,023) graduates with the remainder (1,047) being academic (college preparatory) graduates. All of these respondents had entered the labor force upon graduation. Graduates who entered college directly from high school were eliminated from consideration before the interview sample was drawn.

The graduates were questioned at some length about each job they had held since leaving high school. These questions included: type of job, how obtained, and length of time held; type of company; pay, both starting and leaving (or current); ratings of school preparation and job satisfaction; and their reasons for leaving each job they had left. They also completed a standardized measure of job satisfaction, and were asked about their school experiences and family background.

As a check on the data obtained from these interviews, another 3,342 respondents completed and returned mail questionnaires. The results from these questionnaires were compared to those obtained from the personal interviews. The actual significant differences as a proportion of the total possible responses were only slightly higher than would be expected by chance.

All of these data were analyzed with reference to the issues in vocational education mentioned above. Each of the chapters of the main report focuses on one or more of these issues. This summary, however, does not discuss these chapters separately. The last section of each chapter contains a summary and conclusion. Instead an attempt will be made to interrelate the major issues with the various sources of data bearing on each issue.

The first major issue discussed is the question of adequacy. Data from all the sources bore on this point. The second major issue is the image of vocational education. The interviews with employers and union officials, the attitude questionnaires, and the impressions of the labor and management representatives on the visiting team provided the material for this area. The third major issue presented is concerned with vocational education and groups with special problems. The interviews of the graduates, about 20 per cent of whom were nonwhite, were the primary source for this data. One group with special problems some might be surprised to find included in this section—females. The results indicate females are in many ways being ignored by vocational education.

Section II: The Adequacy of Vocational Education

ADEQUACY AS EVALUATED BY THE VISITING TEAM

An examination of the economic and demographic profiles prepared for each community revealed little relationship between the proportions of enrollment in the various vocational programs and the occupational distributions in the communities. The proportions of graduates placed in related occupations as reported by the schools were relatively high. But even if these are accepted, the small enrollments negate any significant impact on manpower needs. The relationships between training and employment found by the follow-up interviews were, for many of the vocational programs, much lower than those reported by the schools. Apparently, the schools were using a more liberal definition of related employment than that used in this study.

The low enrollments existed despite the generally high quality of the programs being offered. The visiting teams consistently rated quality of instruction, physical facilities, equipment, etc., as adequate or better for all programs. The weaknesses that were noted usually referred to such things as the limited number of offerings, the lack or inadequate use of advisory committees, and poor guidance, placement, and follow-up.

The school officials in charge of the vocational programs had limited opportunity to expand their offerings or provide auxiliary services. Most of the vocational directors did not have easy access to their superintendents and hence were not able to assure that adequate attention and re-sources were directed to vocational offerings.

In the small communities better communications existed and resulted in an understanding of the goals of vocational education across all levels of administration. Consequently, these communities were judged to have the best overall vocational curriculum both in quality and in the propor-tion of students enrolled.

The medium-sized communities had sympathetic administrations which provided good facilities and adequate materials. Despite this sup-port, the programs offered were frequently narrowly conceived and stu-dents were not attracted in sufficient numbers to fill all available work stations.

The strength of the vocational offerings in the large cities lay in their greater breadth and in their potential to meet the needs of all students. In these cities, however, the goals of vocational education were found to have had the least influence on total educational policy, and, in propor-tion to enrollment, the vocational expenditures were lowest.

In general, the results of the program evaluations present a picture of sins of omission rather than sins of commission. What the schools were doing, they were doing adequately. Their weaknesses reflect those things they should have been doing but they were not. Most prominent among these omissions was the failure to develop programs for those students who could not profit from present offerings. The proportion of students enrolled in the vocational curriculum compared to the proportion of those who obtained jobs upon leaving school attests to the need for new approaches. Other significant weaknesses were the poor guidance pro-grams and the insufficient use of advisory committees. Each of these areas is discussed further below.

ADEQUACY AS EVALUATED FROM FOLLOW-UP INTERVIEWS

If, as indicated by the progam evaluations, the schools were training their vocational students adequately, this training should be reflected in the actual work experiences of these graduates. Comparisons were made on various measures of the job experiences of graduates of all three curricula—vocational, academic, and general. Few advantages were found in these measures for any of the curricula.

There were some differences in the occupational distributions of the graduates from the three curricula. Graduates of the vocational curricu-lum obtained more manufacturing jobs while graduates of the academic and general curricula obtained more white collar, primarily clerical, jobs. Despite these differences, graduates from all three curricula tended to earn about the same amount of money, to remain on jobs for about the same length of time, to leave jobs for much the same reasons, and to have about the same levels of job satisfaction. The differences that were associated with curricula referred to evaluations of training. The vocational graduates clearly thought that they had been better prepared for their jobs than did the academic or general graduates. These attitudes of the respondents, however, were not confirmed by their direct supervisors who rated the preparation of students provided by all three curricula about the same.

Another major difference in occupational experiences among the curricula was the method used to obtain a first job. The primary method used by all graduates was by direct application or other personal methods, revealing the tendency to find jobs in a rather disorganized fashion. Although vocational graduates, both male and female, were much more likely than graduates of the other curricula to have been placed by their school, the extent of school participation was generally quite low.

From these findings a clear case cannot be made that vocational education has a direct payoff in the occupational experiences of its graduates. These graduates do believe they are better prepared, and their schools do find jobs for a greater proportion of them, as compared with the other curricula. Besides these measures, there are few objective indices that show a definite advantage to the vocational graduates.

Despite the lack of clear differences, it cannot be concluded that one curriculum provides as good a preparation for employment as another. There were many differences in the characteristics of students in the three curricula. Attempts were made to control for the more obvious of these, but it was impossible to control for all of them. For many characteristics, such as personality, interest, and motivation, no measures were available, and these variables may have had just as much influence as IQ or curriculum on the vocational experiences of graduates. It could reasonably be argued that the personal qualities that enable a boy to complete the typical general curriculum will also enable him to do well in the labor market. It might also be contended that without the appeal that the vocational curriculum has to many students, these young people might never have completed high school. Although these are legitimate questions for further research, it might be suggested that the physical environment of vocational education—the large shops, some degree of individualized instruction, the attempt to relate academic to vocational subjects, etc.—might be the "holding" factor for many students.

THE ADEQUACY OF GUIDANCE IN VOCATIONAL EDUCATION

When considered in light of need, it is the vocational and not the academic or general curriculum graduate who needs guidance the most.

The decision to follow the vocational track is a more limiting one, in terms of post-high school options, than the choice of either of the other curricula. This is not to say that a decision made in the ninth or tenth grade must be followed throughout the individual's career. Quite the reverse is usually true. For example, in this study the percentage of trade and industrial graduates who obtained jobs that were directly related to their training was less than one-third. This figure is confirmed by other studies.

When choices that do not follow from previous decisions are made, the individual must accept the costs involved. In the case of the vocational graduate, one of the inevitable costs of such a change is the loss of the investment, both personal and social, made in obtaining skills that are not used.

The uninitiated observer, upon considering these facts, would expect the major counseling effort in the schools to be directed towards helping the vocationally-oriented student to choose among the possible occupational clusters that interest him. Anyone familiar with the operation of American high schools knows that the prevailing situation is just the opposite.

Data from this study revealed that the vocational students were the least likely to have discussed either their course choices or their occupational plans with a guidance counselor. Among the vocational graduates about one-half recalled discussing their course choices, and about one-fifth recalled discussing their job plans. Among the academic graduates about three-fourths reported discussing their course choices and about one-third reported discussing job plans. Neither of these sets of figures is reassuring, but the direction of the difference should cause the most concern.

The conclusions reached from the analysis of the follow-up interviews were fully confirmed by the evaluation of the guidance programs in the schools. The primary reason for the inadequate counseling was the high, unrealistic student-counselor ratio. On the average in the senior high schools this ran about 440 students to one counselor. At best, this ratio would make it extremely difficult to see each student, if for only one hour during the total school year. The handicap of this ratio is coupled with the fact that typically counselors spend most of their time with college-bound students. When these two facts are considered, it is easy to understand why the follow-up interviews, all of which were with graduates who did not go on to college, revealed few contacts with counselors.

Many other specific weaknesses of guidance programs were noted in the evaluation. These referred to such things as inadequate physical facilities, lack of counselor-employer contact, incomplete pupil records, etc. By any criterion, guidance, as currently carried on, was one of the major weaknesses found in this study of vocational education.

THE PROPER SETTING FOR VOCATIONAL EDUCATION:
THE COMPREHENSIVE OR SEPARATE VOCATIONAL HIGH SCHOOL

Another issue often raised in connection with the adequacy of vocational education is whether it should be conducted in a comprehensive or in a separate vocational high school. Those who argue for the separate school claim such schools can offer better training. Their claims are made on the basis of greater student interest, broader offerings, modern equipment, coordinated courses, etc. The advocates of the comprehensive school will concede some of these advantages for the separate vocational school, but counter with the democratic virtues of the comprehensive high school. In these schools, it is claimed, students from all segments of society study together and acquire increased familiarity and understanding of one another. What these advocates tend to ignore is that "form" is not a substitute for "substance." The advantages of a comprehensive school accrue from activities and programs in such a school which lead to an integration of the academic and vocational students.

The interviews of graduates from the two types of schools did not support the claims of either of the advocates. There was no evidence that graduates of separate vocational schools were better prepared or more successful in their first jobs. Neither was there any evidence that comprehensive schools were leading to greater acceptance among students from different curricula. On the contrary, male vocational graduates from comprehensive schools were much more likely than graduates of separate schools to report they felt "looked down on" because of the courses they took. Other questions on friendship groups and participation in school activities yielded similar patterns of responses.

The case, therefore, was not made for either school. In a negative sense, though, the evidence was more favorable to the separate school. While it did not appear that graduates of the separate schools were better trained, neither did these graduates perceive attitudes of condescension in their school. If a decision as to type of school were to be based on probable attitudes of its students, the evidence would favor the separate vocational school.

Section III: The Image of Vocational Education

In any discussion of vocational education the phrase "image problem" is almost sure to be heard. The implications of this phrase are that while vocational education is commonly seen as a second-class education, it is in reality as successful as any other type. The follow-up interviews indicated that vocational graduates performed just as well in their jobs, and, in fact, considered themselves better prepared for them. Still vocational education is considered by many as in some way "inferior" and the term "dumping ground" is often applied to it.

THE IMAGE IN THE SCHOOLS

Negative attitudes toward vocational education were even detected among teachers. The 1,600 attitude questionnaires returned by the teachers were analyzed both by subjects taught and by the type of school in which the teachers worked. Type of school was found to be more closely associated with attitudes towards vocational education. Teachers from exclusively vocational high schools were the most favorable. Teachers of academic subjects in these schools were as favorable as vocational teachers from comprehensive high schools.

It was the academic teachers from comprehensive high schools who ranked lowest in support of vocational education. Tallies of their responses to the separate scale items revealed that they agreed with the idea of vocational education, but were skeptical of the effectiveness of its actual operation. It was these teachers who tended to reject any suggestion to expand vocational education. They believed more "basic" education was necessary. They also thought vocational students had inferior ability. This last attitude apparently was communicated to their students for it was vocational students from comprehensive schools who were most likely to feel "looked-down on."

THE IMAGE IN THE COMMUNITY

The labor and management representatives, on the school evaluation team, detected similar attitudes in their conversations with employers, labor officials, and other community representatives. Many employers, especially large ones, were pessimistic about vocational education. These employers thought they could give better training themselves. Union officials in the skilled trades were reluctant to give credit for training received in the school programs.

These findings of the labor and management representatives were, of necessity, impressionistic, because they spoke with only a few people in each community. The large scale interviewing of samples of employers and union officials largely confirmed these impressions. Few employers expressed a strong preference for vocationally trained graduates. Personal characteristics, such as initiative and conscientiousness, were the traits most desired in prospective employees. Most employers were, however, satisfied with the preparation their young employees were receiving. Few union officials knew what curriculum their young members had taken in high schools. They reported that their major source of new members was from sons or relatives of current members.

When employers said they could train their employees, they were usually referring to on-the-job training. Most of this training is specific to the particular job and has little transfer value. In general, neither employers nor unions had really thought about the problem of where young people acquire the training necessary to take a productive place in society. When asked about current and projected future skill needs, the majority of both groups either could not answer or replied in vague generalities. They were concerned with the need for training only as it affected their day-to-day operations. One of the major reasons for this lack of interest may have been their limited contact with vocational education. This is discussed further under the topic of advisory committees.

THE IMAGE AND ADVISORY COMMITTEES

The weaknesses cited most frequently in the evaluations of all the vocational programs were their inadequate use of advisory committees. Many programs were being conducted without any advisory committees; other programs had committees in name only or had so few meetings that the committees could not function effectively. Where they were in existence, large employers and union officials were either absent or poorly represented. The evaluation team, both the program experts and the labor and management representatives, concluded that the schools were not utilizing the full resources of the community.

The interviews of employers and union officials led to an identical conclusion. These interviews revealed that the respondents had had limited contact of any type with the vocational programs in their communities. A comparison of the degree of support of vocational education, as measured by the attitude questionnaire, and the type of contact with it, showed that employers who had had the more active types of contact were most favorable. Those employers who had only been visited by representatives of the schools were no more favorable than those employers who had no contact.

Advisory committees would appear to be a natural way of solving both problems—the limited use of advisory committees and the limited contact of the community with the schools. The responsibility is, of course, with school officials to stimulate increased participation. The key seems to be the degree of activity. A few meetings of an advisory committee each year is not sufficient. Continuous cooperation in such efforts as work-study and apprenticeship programs, career days, adult education and retraining, the planning of new programs to meet community needs, etc., offers more promise.

There is reason to believe that any technique that increases community participation in some phase of vocational education will be associated with more positive attitudes. This is the reverse of the usual approach of attempting through educational programs to change attitudes which, it is hoped, will lead to changes in behavior. Bringing about a change in behavior is, of course, more difficult than just disseminating information. One way to bring about behavioral changes may be for school officials to approach employers, union officials, and others with specific requests for participation in specific projects. The probable pay-offs of such attempts to all phases of vocational education warrant their increased use.

Section IV: Vocational Education and Groups with Special Problems

VOCATIONAL EDUCATION AND MINORITIES

The role of vocational training in the education of the urban disadvantaged, primarily Negro, groups has been the topic of considerable discussion. To some observers, vocational training appears to be the quickest, most direct way to convert an alienated or unskilled youth into a productive member of society. Critics of this approach claim that it is the old "hewers of wood" argument in a new form—the justification of the inferior position of Negroes in terms of their alleged "natural inferiority." Vocational educators, for their part, point out that traditionally vocational education is not designed for the individual of limited abilities. The skills usually taught require average or better ability. They further state that many of the problems that have plagued vocational education have resulted from the "dumping" of poorer students into its programs. In addition, some vocational administrators believe it is necessary to advise qualified Negroes not to take vocational training because of what the administrators see as barriers to their employment.

In light of this debate, what is the evidence concerning the experiences of Negroes who completed the vocational curriculum? It must be kept in mind that these findings are based on interviews with Negro graduates. Because they are graduates, they may not be typical of severely disadvantaged, alienated Negroes. The socio-economic background of these Negro graduates did differ from that of whites in predictable ways: family income was lower, fathers were more often absent or employed in service or non-specific skill jobs, and more mothers were employed full-time. In addition, the measured IQs of these graduates were definitely skewed towards the lower scores in comparison to the IQs of the white respondents. Thus, in many ways, these graduates reflect the characteristics of the severely disadvantaged, but there are probably differences in degree.

Given the differences between the white and Negro respondents and the employment problems Negroes face, one would expect quite different school and labor market experiences and quite different attitudes concerning these experiences. There were differences, but they were not as sizable or as frequent as might be expected, especially for the vocationally trained graduates.

Negroes from each of the three curricula tended to react to their school experiences in much the same way as whites from the same curricula. Both Negro and white vocational graduates thought they were better prepared for employment than academic and general curricula graduates. With regard to feelings of acceptance by classmates and school officials, Negroes were just as positive as whites. This last finding is qualified by the fact that most of the Negroes attended segregated schools. They evaluated their acceptance with reference to classmates of the same color.

Two questions on school experiences did reveal some differences. Male Negro graduates of the general curriculum were over twice as likely as any other group to report that they chose that curriculum on the advice of school officials. There was some evidence from the school evaluations that some Negro males who expressed a preference for training in one of the skilled trades were persuaded not to take that training. The school officials explained that this advice was given because it was impossible to place Negroes in trades requiring apprenticeships. This may well explain the disproportionate number of Negro males who took the general curriculum at the suggestion of school officials. The other question on school experience will be discussed after the work experience data are presented.

The most obvious difference in the employment experiences of the Negro and white respondents was in the distribution of the types of jobs they obtained. Negro males and females were both more heavily represented in the manufacturing and service sectors than were whites. Negroes also received less pay than whites for all comparable sex-curriculum classes. Negro males from a vocational curriculum, however, received the best pay relative to the difference in the other Negro-white comparisons.

Despite these differences in occupational distribution and wage levels, there were few differences associated with color in individual perception of job satisfaction. The exceptions were male Negroes from the academic curriculum. These respondents were less satisfied than their white counterparts with their work, pay, and promotion opportunities.

The Negro male who graduated from a vocational curriculum showed up as relatively "better off" than the Negro graduates of the other curricula. The indices of his work experience were not as favorable as the white graduates', but it seemed that the vocational curriculum had the greatest yield for the Negro—at least for the Negro male. When the respondents, however, were asked if they would recommend their curriculum to a young person, there were no differences consistently associated with sex or race. This was about the only evaluation of school experience where the vocational curriculum did not yield an advantage for Negro males.

These findings, of course, do not answer all the charges with regard to vocational education and minorities. They do, however, suggest that Negroes can benefit from the vocational curriculum and, given present conditions in society, probably benefit more than from the other curricula. If these conditions—employer and union discrimination, guidance, and family environment—were to change, the relative outcomes of the various curricula might not be significantly different.

VOCATIONAL EDUCATION AND GIRLS

Some observers could argue, after reviewing the results of the study of vocational education and females, that there is little justification for including these data under the section "Groups with Special Problems." They could point to the high percentage of girls from the vocational and general curricula who obtain jobs that are directly related to their training. They could cite the measures of job satisfaction and the ratings of the female graduates and their direct supervisors as to the adequacy of the graduates' school preparation. On all of these measures the female graduates were rated as high as the males, and there were no differences of any real significance among the curricula.

On most of the questions regarding school experiences the results for the female graduates are more favorable than the results for the males. Among the vocational graduates, females were less likely than males to report feelings of condescension and exclusion from school activities. Girls from each of the curricula were more likely than males from the same curricula to have received guidance in their course choices and job plans.

The only question on which females responded in a way that might be considered less favorable than the way males responded concerned reasons for their course choices. Girls were twice as likely as males to say they chose courses to prepare for a job, and they were less likely to say they chose courses on the basis of interest. These results were unexpected for it is males who are supposed to be concerned about jobs and careers. Females, it was revealed by other questions in the interview, regarded post-high school employment as an interlude before they assumed their real roles as wives and mothers.

These apparently contradictory results are explained by the limited number of vocational offerings available to females. Office occupations accounted for about half of all the students, male and female, enrolled in the vocational curriculum. It was the only vocational program open to girls which could accommodate any significant number. Girls who wanted to obtain vocational preparation had very few options open to them. They chose their high school courses, therefore, not out of interest, but to prepare for a job.

The girls did not react negatively to the limitations on the choices available to them. They have learned their cultural lessons well; there are few occupations appropriate for girls; girls should only plan on working until they get married; girls should not prepare themselves for important jobs because they will marry and waste their training. All of these cultural stereotypes restrict the schools in the programs they offer to girls, and, even more, they restrict the vocational self concepts of young girls so that they are satisfied with these limited offerings.

The result of these limitations is that many girls of high natural ability never prepare themselves for the occupations they are capable of filling. Their skills are lost to society throughout their vocational lives. And many women, contrary to the stereotype, do have extensive occupational experience. Girls, however, are not made aware of their probable vocational careers, and they are not trained to plan and to prepare for them. It would seem the schools should take the lead in expanding the vocational self-concepts of young girls. Through expanded offerings and skillful guidance, young girls can be led to prepare themselves for the variety of occupations where their skills are needed.

The school, itself, cannot change the attitudes of the girls regarding their occupational goals. It must be recognized that the family environment and the social milieu in which the girls are raised contribute significantly to the development of their attitudes. The school, however, can play a role in changing these conditioning factors which can lead to a fuller utilization of the natural capabilities of women.

5. RELATIONSHIP OF INTEREST TO APTITUDE BY PROFILES AND BY INTEREST AREAS *

William P. Ewens

The relationship of interest to aptitude has been extensively studied but the findings are consistently contrary to what might be anticipated in recognition of the psychological literature in the area of motivation. It appears that an individual should measure high in those interest areas where there is relatively high aptitude and that low interest would accompany relatively low aptitude. These relationships might be expected due to the tendency for one to achieve somewhat greater success in those experiences where there is a correspondingly greater aptitude. It might be argued that greater interest should accompany success, that there would be a high relationship between interest and aptitude. Research has not supported this view.

In a recent review of the research relating interest to aptitude Miller [4] reported a generally low interest-aptitude relationship. In discussing the research Miller [4, p. 356] stated that "somehow it seems there ought to be such a relationship but if we mean tested ability and inventoried interests, the accumulated evidence is so overwhelming in the negative that there is little to be gained by laboring the point." This conclusion is similar to those presented earlier by Carter [1] and by Super [8]. Nugent [6] related interest to aptitude for three areas of the Kuder Preference Record and the Differential Aptitude Tests for the purpose of determining high and low interest-aptitude discrepancies. This study gives no data on the extent of the relationship of interest to aptitude.

There has appeared periodically in the literature the suggestion that the methods of studying the interest-aptitude relationship have been inappropriate. Researchers have generally selected an area of interest measured by the Kuder Preference Record or the Strong Vocational Interest Blank for Men and have determined Pearson coefficients relating interest to aptitude by interest areas. The criticism of this research method seems particularly relevant if a forced-choice instrument is

* Personnel and Guidance Journal, December 1963, 359-363. Copyright 1963, by the American Personnel and Guidance Association, Inc.

being used to determine interest. Hypothetical interest and aptitude profiles (FIGURE 1) will facilitate the discussion of this point.

The interest profile for John Doe is similar to many from preference measures in that there are areas of both strong and limited interests. The aptitude profile was drawn to represent a student of generally low aptitude but having a profile pattern similar to interests. A high, average, or variable aptitude profile would have served the same purpose.

If one conducts a study of the relationship of interest to aptitude by areas of interest and John Doe is a subject in the study, raw scores for area zero would contribute to a low correlation since the scores would plot high interest and low aptitude on a scatter-gram. Within the sample for the study there would surely be subjects with generally high aptitude. Some of these generally high aptitude subjects would likely have low area zero interest and their raw scores would also contribute to low interest and aptitude relationship. For John Doe, raw scores for areas three, five, and nine would contribute to high interest-aptitude relationships. Areas one, two, four, six and eight would suggest low relationship between interest and aptitude.

From this illustration one might argue that the generalizations in the literature relative to the relationship between interest and aptitude reflect the method of study and are entirely inappropriate as basis for generalizing the relationship between these variables. A more defensible approach to this problem would seem to be an examination of similarity of aptitude and interest profiles.

The technique for the study of profile relationship of achievement and interest used by Frandsen and Sessions [3] appears to be appropriate to

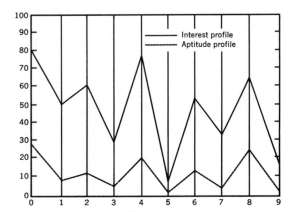

FIGURE 1 Hypothetical interest and aptitude profiles for John Doe.

apply to the present study of interest and aptitude. Carter [1] and Remmers [7] encouraged the study of interest and aptitude relationships by profiles or interest patterns.

Problem

This is a study of the relationship of interest to aptitude (1) by interest areas and (2) by profile patterns. Data on interests were obtained by using both the Kuder Preference Record (preferred interest), and the Activity Experience Inventory (manifest interest). These inventories and selected tests for measuring aptitudes were administered to all of the ninth and twelfth grade students in a relatively small urban high school. A few students did not complete all tests and were therefore not included in this study. The Activity Experience Inventory was developed by the writer and is described in Ewens [2].

The following tests were selected for measuring the various aptitudes after careful consideration of available instruments.

Mechanical	Mechanical—Aptitude Tests for Occupations
Computational	Computational—Aptitude Tests for Occupations
Scientific	Scientific—Aptitude Tests for Occupations
Persuasive	General Sales—Aptitude Tests for Occupations
Artistic	Lewrenz Test in Fundamental Abilities of Visual Art, Test 1 and Test 2
Literary	Verbal Score from School and College Ability Test
Musical	Seashore Measures of Musical Talents
Social Service	Personal—Social—Aptitude Tests for Occupations
Clerical	Clerical Routine—Aptitude Tests for Occupations

Some authorities may question the choice of instruments, and this may be viewed by the reader as a limitation of the study. There is a limited number of tests from which one can choose in developing an aptitude profile.

Method of Study

In examining these data it became evident that the mean interest and aptitude scores for several of the areas showed significant sex differences and between grade differences. These data were, therefore, treated as four distinct groups. The groups are identified as (1) ninth grade boys, (2) ninth grade girls, (3) twelfth grade boys, and (4) twelfth grade girls.

The relationship of interest to aptitude by interest areas was determined by calculating Pearson coefficients from raw scores. This relationship was studied for both preferred and manifest interest. In this paper the interest-aptitude relationship by areas is referred to as the "cross-sectional" relationship.[1]

To examine profile relationships all raw scores were converted to standard scores with the means and standard deviations for the areas of groups serving as base for the conversions. The rank order of standard scores was used for calculating rho coefficients in determining interest and aptitude profile relationships. Both preferred and manifest interests were compared with aptitude profiles.

Findings

Coefficients reflecting the relationship of Kuder Preference Record interest area scores to aptitude scores are given in TABLE 1. These coefficients vary from −0.53 for the persuasive area for twelfth grade boys to 0.57 for the literary area for twelfth grade girls. Only six of the 36 coefficients can be considered significantly different from zero. These were computational for ninth grade boys, mechanical for ninth grade girls, musical and persuasive for twelfth grade boys, and artistic and literary for twelfth grade girls. These data are similar to the interest-aptitude relationship reported from other studies [4, pp. 356–357].

The cross-sectional study of manifest interest from the Activity Experience Inventory scores and aptitude scores gives coefficients of similar magnitude as noted in TABLE 2. The coefficients vary from −0.31 in social service for ninth grade boys to 0.86 in artistic for twelfth grade girls. Only seven of the coefficients show a significant relationship between

---

[1] "It is believed that patterns of ability may bear significant relationships to patterns of interest. Cross-sectional studies showing the interrelationships among ability measures and interest scores at any one time are not regarded as adequate" [1, p. 9].

TABLE 1
The Relationship of Kuder Preference Record Interest
Scores to Aptitude Scores in Corresponding Areas

	9TH GRADE		12TH GRADE			
	M $N=26$	F $N=19$	M $N=22$	F $N=16$		RANGE
Mechanical	0.27	0.54[a]	0.09	0.22	0.09	-0.54[a]
Computational	0.45[b]	0.30	0.22	-0.17	-0.17	-0.45[b]
Scientific	0.24	0.28	0.14	0.05	0.05	-0.28
Persuasive	-0.25	0.15	-0.53[b]	-0.18	-0.53[b]	-0.15
Artistic	0.32	0.29	0.32	0.55[a]	0.29	-0.55[a]
Literary	0.25	0.05	0.25	0.57[a]	0.05	-0.57[a]
Musical	0.36	0.29	0.56[b]	0.31	0.29	-0.56[b]
Social Service	-0.27	0.20	-0.40	-0.28	-0.40	-0.20
Clerical	0.23	0.10	0.15	-0.20	-0.20	-0.23

[a] Significant at the 0.05 level.
[b] Significant at the 0.01 level.

manifest interest and aptitude. These were musical for ninth grade boys, musical and clerical for ninth grade girls, and mechanical, artistic, literary, and musical for twelfth grade girls.

The range of coefficients, both preferred and manifest interest with

TABLE 2
The Relationship of Activity Experience Inventory
Scores to Aptitude Scores in Corresponding Areas

	9TH GRADE		12TH GRADE			
	M $N=26$	F $N=19$	M $N=22$	F $N=16$		RANGE
Mechanical	0.37	0.36	0.36	0.52[a]	0.36	-0.52[a]
Computational	0.23	0.14	0.39	0.45	0.14	-0.45
Scientific	0.34	0.43	0.13	0.49	0.13	-0.49
Persuasive	0.13	0.24	0.04	0.10	0.04	-0.24
Artistic	0.38	0.32	0.50	0.86[b]	0.32	-0.86[b]
Literary	0.06	0.19	0.41	0.67[b]	0.06	-0.67[b]
Musical	0.46[a]	0.62[b]	0.22	0.67[b]	0.22	-0.67[b]
Social Service	-0.31	-0.16	-0.08	0.01	-0.31	-0.01
Clerical	-0.02	0.48[a]	0.31	0.05	-0.02	-0.48[a]

[a] Significant to the 0.05 level.
[b] Significant to the 0.01 level.

aptitude, present a pattern of inconsistency. The data would seem to justify the generalization that little if any relationship exists between these variables, when studied cross-sectionally.

In a further study of TABLES 1 and 2 one notes that the largest coefficients were obtained from the mechanical, computational, artistic, literary, and musical areas. The scientific and clerical areas from TABLE 2 also included some relatively large coefficients although no consistency is being suggested. It may be important to note that aptitude tests in these areas have been extensively used, have been studied for validity and reliability, and are fairly acceptable on both criteria.

The relationship between interest and aptitude for the persuasive and social service areas was consistently low. The aptitude tests selected for these two areas seemed less defensible. The low relationship between interest and aptitude in these areas may be due, to a degree, to the weakness in the measuring instruments.

To examine the relationship between interest and aptitude patterns, the rho coefficient for the subjects of this study are summarized in TABLE 3. Median rho coefficients relating profiles of preferred interest to aptitude varied from 0.11 to 0.27, and for manifest interest to aptitude a variation from 0.08 to 0.33 was noted. The range of coefficients indicates that for many students in this study there was no relationship between interest and aptitude patterns.

For the purpose of further analysis of these data, the 25th and 75th percentile positions are indicated on TABLE 3. A study of this column indicates that approximately 25 per cent of the students had from a fair to

TABLE 3
Median and Range of Rank Order Relationship of Interest and Aptitude Profiles

	MDN	RANGE	25^{P}75
9th Grade Male, N = 26			
Preference and Aptitude	0.13	−0.60 to 0.77	0.03 to 0.32
Manifest and Aptitude	0.33	−0.40 to 0.75	0.08 to 0.48
9th Grade Female, N = 19			
Preference and Aptitude	0.27	−0.18 to 0.72	−0.04 to 0.42
Manifest and Aptitude	0.25	−0.65 to 0.92	0.14 to 0.55
12th Grade Male, N = 22			
Preference and Aptitude	0.11	−0.64 to 0.47	−0.08 to 0.25
Manifest and Aptitude	0.08	−0.46 to 0.52	−0.10 to 0.38
12th Grade Female, N = 16			
Preference and Aptitude	0.14	−0.32 to 0.68	−0.10 to 0.37
Manifest and Aptitude	0.25	−0.33 to 0.82	0.08 to 0.48

a high relationship between the interest and aptitude profiles. For this group the coefficients relating preferred interest and aptitude varied from 0.32 to 0.77 for ninth grade boys, from 0.42 to 0.72 for ninth grade girls, from 0.25 to 0.47 for twelfth grade boys, and from 0.37 to 0.68 for twelfth grade girls.

Twenty-five per cent of the students on manifest interest and aptitude profiles varied from 0.48 to 0.75 for ninth grade boys, from 0.55 to 0.92 for ninth grade girls, from 0.38 to 0.52 for twelfth grade boys and from 0.48 to 0.82 for twelfth grade girls. There seems to be a higher relationship between the profiles of manifest interest and aptitude than between preferred interest and aptitude.

These data would suggest that for many students there is a fairly high relationship between patterns of interest and aptitude; for others the relationship is low or negative. The relationship between interest and aptitude, therefore, does not seem to be a general factor but must be determined for each individual.

Summary

1. Based on this study it would appear that the relationship between aptitude and interest may not be a general condition and a relationship revealed by studying a single interest-aptitude area.

2. The determination of interest-aptitude relationship seems to be more appropriately studied by examining profiles of interest and aptitude.

3. Similarity or dissimilarity of interest and aptitude profiles seems to be a characteristic of an individual rather than a factor associated with people generally. This might raise the question of relationship of self-concept to aptitude and interest profile congruency.

4. The data for this study further raises several questions that have *research* implications.

    a. How realistic is the self-concept of students with dissimilar interests and aptitude profiles in contrast to students with similar profiles?

    b. Does similarity or dissimilarity of profiles relate to personality characteristics (Nugent, 6, 7), school grades, attitudes toward work experiences, motivation, etc.?

    c. Is counseling effective in producing greater similarity in interest and aptitude profiles, and does this in turn relate to change in self-concept and adjustment?

References

1. Carter, H. D. *Vocational interests and job orientation.* Stanford, Calif.: Stanford University Press, and London: Humphrey Milford, Oxford University Press, 1944.
2. Ewens, W. P. The development and standardization of a preliminary form of an activity experience inventory; a measure of manifest interest. *Journal of Applied Psychology,* 1953, *40,* 169–174.
3. Frandsen, Arden N., and Sessions, Alwyn D. Interests and school achievement. *Educational and Psychological Measurement,* 1953, *13,* 94–101.
4. Miller, Carroll H. *Foundations of guidance.* New York: Harper & Row, 1961.
5. Nugent, Frank A. Interest-aptitude congruency: a theoretical synthesis and a suggested method of investigation. *Personnel and Guidance Journal,* 1962, *40,* 523–530.
6. Nugent, Frank A. The relationship of discrepancies between interest and aptitude scores to other selected personality variables. *Personnel and Guidance Journal,* 1961, *39,* 388–395.
7. Remmers, H. H., and Gage, N. L. *Educational measurements and evaluation.* Revised Edition. New York: Harper and Row, 1955.
8. Super, Donald E. *Appraising vocational fitness.* New York: Harper & Row, 1949.

AUTHOR INDEX

SUBJECT INDEX